DEA1

Christopher Mitchell is the author of the ε
in Edinburgh before living for several yeaı
taught English. He returned to study class
with his wife and their four children.

By Christopher Mitchell

The Magelands Origins

Retreat of the Kell
The Trials of Daphne Holdfast
From the Ashes

The Magelands Epic

The Queen's Executioner
The Severed City
Needs of the Empire
Sacrifice
Fragile Empire
Storm Mage
Soulwitch Rises
Renegade Gods

The Magelands Eternal Siege

The Mortal Blade
The Dragon's Blade
The Prince's Blade
Falls of Iron
Paths of Fire
Gates of Ruin
City of Salve
Red City

City Ascendant
Dragon Eyre Badblood
Dragon Eyre Ashfall
Dragon Eyre Blackrose
Dreams of Kell
God Restrainer
Holdfast Imperium
World's End

The Magelands Dominion

Serpent Dominion
Demon Witch
Death Seer
Blood Burden

Brigdomin Books Ltd
First Edition, August 2023
ISBN 978-1-915978-18-9

To Deirdre

ACKNOWLEDGEMENTS

I would like to thank the following for all their support during the writing of the Magelands Dominion - my wife, Lisa Mitchell, who read every chapter as soon as it was drafted and kept me going in the right direction; my parents for their unstinting support; Marilyn Hopwood for reading the books in their early stages; James Aitken for his encouragement; and Grant and Gordon of the Film Club for their support.

Thanks also to my Advance Reader team, for all your help during the last few weeks before publication.

NOTE ON THE DOMINION CALENDAR

Due to a larger moon, Athumia's rotation is slower than that of the Earth, adding almost five minutes to each day; while the duration of Athumia's orbit around its Sun remains the same as the Earth's. This has brought the Lunar and Solar Calendars into alignment, allowing for Thirteen Months, each containing 28 days – creating a Solar Year of 364 days (with no Leap Day required). In response to this astronomical correspondence, High King Gahad devised the Dominion Calendar by shortening the existing months in the Divine Calendar to 28 days, and adding an extra month at the end of the year in his honour.

Each month (or 'inch') is named after one of the Twelve Ascendants (the old Gods); but over long millennia, the names have drifted from their originals.

In the Dominion Calendar, each year begins on the 1st day of Beldinch.

- Beldinch (January) – after Belinda, the Third Ascendant
- Summinch (February) – after Simon, the Tenth Ascendant
- Arginch (March) – after Arete, the Seventh Ascendant
- Nethinch (April) – after Nathaniel, the Fourth Ascendant
- Duninch (May) – after Edmond, the Second Ascendant
- Tradinch (June) – after Theodora, the First Ascendant
- Abrinch (July) – after Albrada, the Eleventh Ascendant
- Lexinch (August) – after Leksandr, the Sixth Ascendant
- Tuminch (September) – after Tamid, the Eighth Ascendant
- Luddinch (October) – after Lloyd, the Twelfth Ascendant
- Kolinch (November) – after Kolai, the Fifth Ascendant
- Essinch (December) – after Esher, the Ninth Ascendant
- Ghadinch (Extra Month) – after King Gahad, Praise be His Name

THE TWO EMPIRES OF ATHUMIA

The Two Empires of Athumia (in 1589, when *Death Seer* takes place)

Two Empires dominate the continents of Athumia:

The Dragon Dominion – The Dominion originated in **Inopei** – a continent in the Eastern half of Athumia, with the arrival of the Dragon King. The calendar used in the Serpent Isle dates from the formation of the Dominion. The rule of the Dragons then spread south to encompass **Aucteran** and **Jalan**, and then the Dominion conquered the lands of the Bullan (**Klediomira Haga**). Upon completion of the conquests of Inopei, Aucteran and Jalan, the entire native population was exterminated by Dominion forces. There is no Dominion military presence on Klediomira Haga, as the Bullan are allied, rather than occupied. As tribute, the Bullan send soldiers each year to serve in the Dominion armed forces.

Much later (c.1300), when the Dominion began to cross the ocean to the Western half of Athumia, their forces also conquered **Elso** and **Irlan**. Dominion forces now occupy the **Serpent Isle**, Irlan and Elso, ruling over the native inhabitants. It is the stated aim and belief of the rulers of the Dragon Dominion that all of Athumia should be united under their sovereign authority.

The Gunstian Empire – Centred around the city of **Great Gunst**, the Gunstian Empire covers the northern portion of the western continent of **Kinheria**. Their Empire also includes the tributary state of **Tannum**, a heavily-forested region. Shielded by mountains and the Tvali Desert to the south, and protected by oceans on its other three flanks, the Gunstian Empire is the only inhabited place left on Athumia that has never been ruled by the Dragon Dominion. The Dominion have unsuccessfully invaded Gunst three times – in c.1050, c.1350, and 1488. All three invasions were defeated by the Gunstians, and the Dominion were forced to withdraw.

Social Hierarchy of Zamata (The Serpent Isle)

The Rulers	Dragons	Immortal Dragons	3	Igatz
		Mortal Dragons	2	
Aucterian Colonists	Upper	Aristocracy, Landowners, Bankers, Senior Officers etc	500	Mainly in Igatz
	Middle	Merchants, Smallholders, Junior Officers	4500	
	Lower	Farmers, Shopkeepers, Crafts	15000	
Foreign Soldiers	Military / Police	Bullan Soldiers	5000	Across Island
Northern Fleet		Dominion Navy (Aucterian)	5000	Handshore Naval Base
Native Police		Militia (Zamatan)	1000	Across Island
Native Zamatan Islanders	Upper	Farmers, Builders, Merchants, Militia Officers, Teachers	10000	Mainly in Kaugatz and Surrounding Villages
	Lower	Villagers, Crofters, Labourers, Servants	30000	
Descendants of former Colonists	Gunstians	Labourers etc	10000	Kaugatz
Sailors from Irlan	Irlanians	Sailors	3000	Igatz
Bottom of the Heap	Mixed Heritage	Zamatan/Aucterian	4400	Kaugatz
	Bullan Heritage	Zamatan/Bullan	600	

Dragon Royal Family

King Gahad & His Three Consorts

Snowdrift

- ♂ Tegru, 1541
- ♂ Naghad, 1497
- ♀ Macsin, 1456
- ♂ Malum, 1381
- ♀ Famula, 1319
- ♂ Saphben, 1266

Opal Min Tarsu

- ♂ Opelan, 493
- ♂ Rylan, 476
- ♀ Lykot, 401
- ♀ Natali, 352
- ♀ Marda, 331
- ♂ Tarsun, 278

Nightsheen

- ♀ Lykona, 1100
- ♀ Lenta, 1091
- ♂ Irvan, 1062
- ♀ Gilt, 1055
- ♀ Abda, 991
- ♂ Girvine, 928
- ♀ Shana, 899
- ♂ Konran, 834
- ♀ Tirna, 747

The numbers represent age in 1588

DRAMATIS PERSONAE

Zamatans

Lahnos Laimos, Horned Part-Bullan

Leona, Gifted Rebel Leader

Reyn, Part-Bullan Rebel

Karl Laimos, Lahnos's Brother

Bauchlie, Zamatan Rebel Leader

Jancke, Villager from Fidalaimos

Smithy, Villager from Fidalaimos

Saewa, Half-Aucterian Agent

Kamasta, Quarter-Gunstian Housekeeper

Abilo, Bauchlie's Mother

Aucterians

Cisca, ex-Dragon Corps Captain

Lyla, ex-Dragon Corps Major

Jair, Army Captain

Bullan

Efizel, Renegade Bullan Warrior

Gunstians

Farakai, Rebel Agent

Arrosa, Gifted Child

Luka, Arrosa's Uncle

Dragons (in order of seniority)

Abda Min Gahad, Daughter of Gahad

Rylan Mon Gahad, Younger Son of Gahad

Natali Min Gahad, Sister of Rylan

Ecsin Mon Macsin, Grandson of Gahad

Labran Mon Abda, Grandson of Gahad

Givra Mon Girvine, Grandson of Gahad

Gradham Mon Gradag, Great Grandson of Gahad

Sigum Mon Sigel, Mortal Dragon

Sengilla Min Inglis, Mortal Dragon

Gallus Mon Galla, Mortal Dragon

Brotan Mon Brota, Mortal Dragon

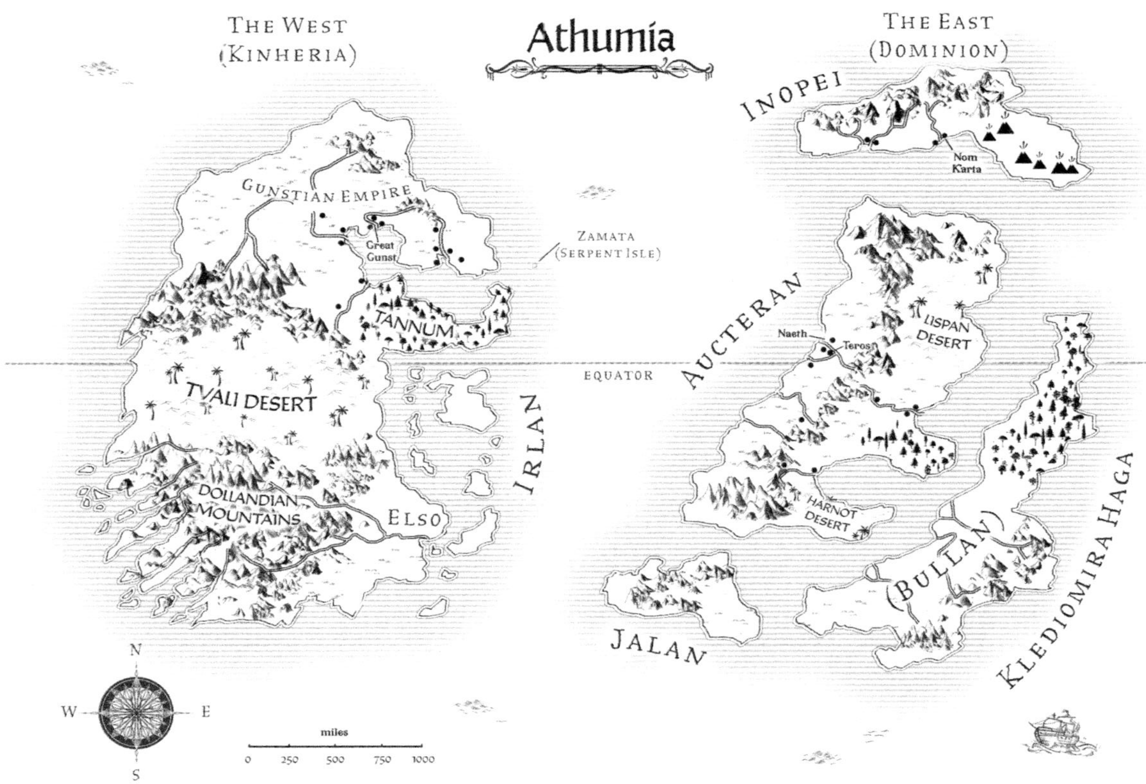
Athumia
The West
(Kinheria)
The East
(Dominion)
Gunstian Empire
Great Gunst
Zamata
(Serpent Isle)
Tannum
Tvali Desert
Irlan
Equator
Dollandian Mountains
Elso
Inopei
Nom Karta
Aucteran
Naeth
Teros
Lispan Desert
Harnot Desert
(Bullan)
Klediomira Haga
Jalan
N
W
E
S
miles
0
250
500
750
1000

Zamata – The Serpent Isle

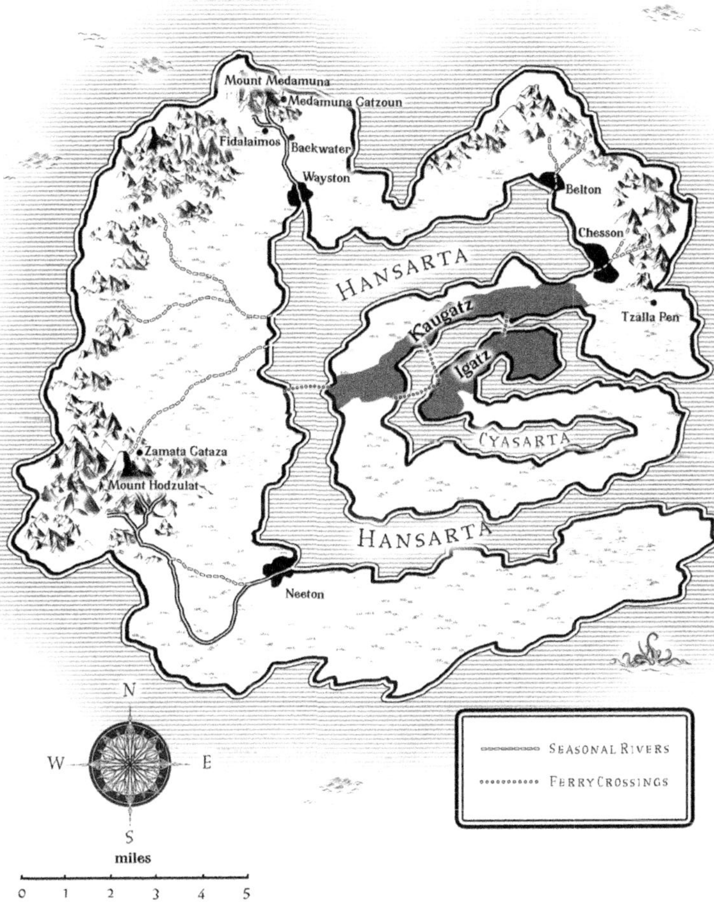

The Serpent Isle – Close-up of Kaugatz and Igatz

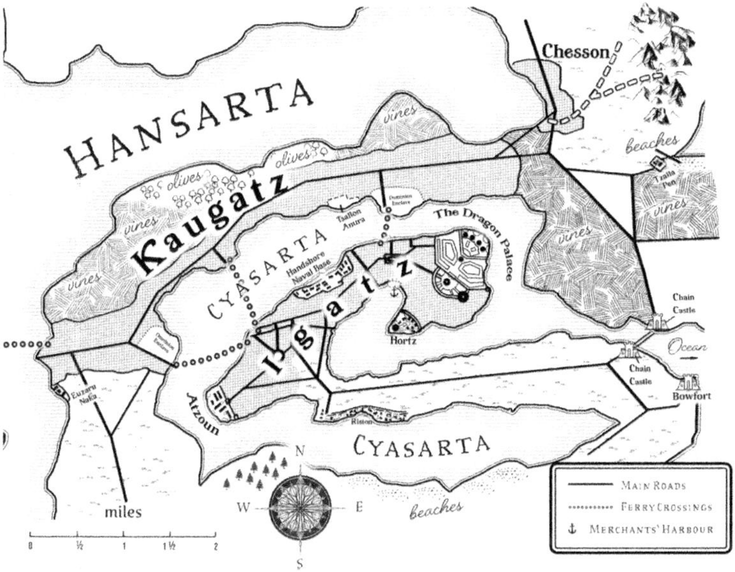

CHAPTER 1
A COLD WELCOME

North of the Serpent Isle – 14th Tuminch 1588

The towering peak of Mount Medamuna loomed up out of the ocean, its bare, grey summit reflecting the mid-afternoon sunlight. Every Zamatan on the flight deck of Lord Sigum's dragon carrier had been staring at it since it had become visible that morning, as though the mere sight of the island was enough to cure their every ill.

'I wonder if Reyn is up there,' said Lahnos, 'hiding somewhere in the ruins of Medamuna Gatzoun.'

Karl rolled his eyes. 'Do you think you could go five minutes without mentioning that damn girl, brother?'

Smithy laughed. 'The lad's in love, Karl.'

'How do you think the women have been coping without us?' said Jancke.

'Just fine,' said Smithy; 'if I know my wife.'

Jancke frowned. 'Nah. We'll be lucky if Fidalaimos is still standing. The women will have been sitting around, doing nothing but weeping; while we've been... well, you know what we've been doing. None of them will understand what we've been through.'

'I think they'll have a pretty good idea,' said Smithy.

'Will they?' said Karl. 'They've been safe and comfortable; and...'

'Safe?' said Lahnos. 'How could they be safe when there are thousands of Bullan and Aucterian soldiers on the island?'

'They've still been safer than us,' said Karl.

'It's not a damn competition,' said Smithy. 'They've missed us, and we've missed them; let's leave it at that.'

'The Dominion won't be happy that so many of us are coming home,' said Lahnos; 'they expected us all to die in Gunst. They might not let us get off the ships – we should be ready if that happens.'

'Do you think they know what happened to the invasion force?' said Jancke.

'I doubt the rulers of the Dominion know,' said Lahnos, 'but the dragons and soldiers on the island will. Lord Sigum told me that several dragons fled Toraq – some of them might have reached Zamata by now.'

'If that's true,' said Karl, 'then wait until they realise that the Imperial Gunstian Fleet has been chasing us for the last twenty days; they'll be clamouring to get on board those empty dragon carriers.'

At that moment, two dark specks appeared over the northern coast of Zamata. The squad from Fidalaimos quietened as they each stared up into the cloudless sky. The two black specks circled and wheeled over the hills between Wayston and Belton, but neither approached the small fleet.

'At least they know we're here,' said Smithy.

'Then why aren't they coming any closer?' said Jancke.

'They are ashamed,' said Lahnos. 'They abandoned us in Gunst, and probably presumed that none of us would ever get back to Zamata. I wouldn't be surprised if they've already told everyone that there were no survivors.'

'I hope they don't attack us,' said Jancke.

'They won't,' said Lahnos. 'Karl was right – they won't want to sink their only hope of returning to the East. They'll let the carriers enter the Cyasarta; it's what they'll do to us afterwards that worries me.'

A broad soldier with horns and a tail approached, his shadow falling over the men sitting on the wooden flight deck.

'Corporal Laimos,' he said, 'Lord Sigum wishes to speak to you.'

Lahnos glanced up at Efizel. 'What does he want?'

'He did not specify, but I am sure that you can work it out for yourself. We shall be reaching the Cyasarta within a couple of hours.'

Lahnos pulled on his boots and got to his feet. He and Efizel threaded their way through the large groups of Zamatans on the wide deck and approached the rear lift. The large silvery-green dragon was waiting there, surrounded by Bullan soldiers. Several Zamatans nodded to Lahnos as he passed, and he could see the nervous anticipation in their eyes as they tried to come to terms with the fact that they were so close to home. Trailing the huge ship were the other five dragon carriers that had fled from Toraq, and the nine supply vessels were clustered around their enormous hulls. On either side of the carriers, the surviving destroyers and frigates were flanking the small fleet, and the decks of each were full of sailors and soldiers gazing at the coastline of Zamata.

'You've been spending a lot of time with the other Bullan these past few days,' Lahnos said, as they walked. 'Have they accepted you back into their ranks?'

'No,' said Efizel, 'and most of them never will. I shamed my regiment, and the only ones who have spoken to me belong to the group you saved in the camp outside Great Gunst. The others look through me as though I did not exist. I am dead to them.'

'Sorry about that.'

'I made my choice, Lahnos; and I do not regret it.'

The Bullan guarding Lord Sigum parted to allow Lahnos and Efizel through, but none glanced in their direction. The dragon was sitting on the rear section of the flight deck, his wounded wing held close to his side. He watched as Lahnos approached, then lowered his head a fraction.

'Greetings, Laimos,' the dragon said. 'Did you see my kindred flying over the hills to the south?'

'I did,' said Lahnos. 'Did you recognise them?'

'Yes. Both are fugitives from the invasion of Gunst – Lord Givra Mon

Girvine, a grandson of the mighty King Gahad; and Lady Sengilla Min Inglis. I flew with both during the destruction of Toraq City.'

'I thought as much,' said Lahnos. 'Your return has shamed them.'

'I wish that were not the case,' said Sigum, 'but you may be correct.'

'How's the wing?'

'It has almost fully recovered, my friend,' said the dragon. He stretched it out a little. 'I will be able to fly in perhaps another ten days or so. You are aware, I am sure, that I will no longer be in command once we arrive in the Serpent Isle. Other dragons there will outrank me, and I will lose the authority I possessed during our long voyage from Gunst. In other words, I will be powerless to intervene in any decisions that are made regarding the future of the Zamatan regiments. The fate of the Aucterians and Bullan on board these ships is fixed: they will continue to serve the Dominion; but I cannot foresee what will be done with the Zamatans.'

'We should be demobilised and allowed to return to our homes and families,' said Lahnos. 'That would be fair.'

'It would be naïve of you to expect that outcome,' said the dragon. 'We are still at war and the Imperial Gunstian Fleet remains in pursuit. The Dominion will have need of soldiers.'

'Then we should be deployed to defend Zamata,' said Lahnos; 'and we should be trained and given proper equipment.'

One of the Bullan guards narrowed his eyes. 'You are speaking to a noble lord of the Dominion, boy,' he said. 'Show more respect.'

'Or what?' said Lahnos. 'None of you would be here if I hadn't discovered the location of the Gunstian fleet.'

The Bullan soldier raised his crossbow, and Efizel stepped in front of Lahnos.

'Lower your weapon,' said the dragon. 'You may not like Lahnos Laimos, but he has earned my respect. Leave us to speak alone.'

The Bullan soldier frowned. 'Yes, my lord.' He gestured to the other guards, and they pulled back from the silvery-green dragon.

Lord Sigum brought his head down to Lahnos's eye-level.

'I will do what I can for you and the Zamatans,' the dragon said, 'but you must be prepared for anything. Lord Malum and Lady Macsin were left in charge of the Serpent Isle, and both were stalwart supporters of King Naghad. In fact, Lord Malum will be next in line to the throne; while I am still unable to fly. You may be nearing your home, but I doubt I shall be seeing mine for a long time to come.'

'I will have no problem helping Malum, if he decides to defend the island from the Gunstians,' said Lahnos; 'but if he orders us all to retreat to Aucteran, then I will resist.'

The dragon smiled. 'You have an arrogance about you that ill suits your stature, human. Malum could destroy you with a glance.' He looked up at the coastline. 'I owe you my life. Were it not for you, my head would be rotting upon a wooden stake in Gunst, and the bones of the soldiers and sailors of this little fleet would be lying upon foreign shores. Temper your passion, Lahnos, and become the leader you have already proved yourself to be. Make no hasty decisions, for the other Zamatans look to you. If you mutiny against the Dominion, then many will follow you down that path. You saved seven thousand of your kinsmen from disaster in Gunst; did you do this only so that they could be massacred upon their homecoming?''

'I never asked to be their leader.'

'The best leaders never seek power; it falls to them according to their abilities. Will you listen to my advice?'

'I will.'

'Adopt a conciliatory stance when we arrive, Lahnos. Take time to judge the situation before you act. We do not know what has transpired upon the Serpent Isle in our absence, and this we must learn before committing ourselves to any decision.'

Lahnos eyed the huge dragon. 'If I rebel, will you strike me down?'

'I will not harm the one who saved every life aboard this fleet. But nor will I be able to protect you. Remain by my side for the rest of the voyage, along with the officers from the Bullan, army and navy. You shall speak for the Zamatans when we arrive.'

Lahnos nodded, then he turned to gaze at the coast of the island. The two dark specks in the sky had vanished.

Demon Witch, he said in his mind; *if you can hear me, now would be a good time to make an appearance.*

Silence. Lahnos lowered his eyes. What had he expected? The Demon Witch had said nothing to him since that terrible night outside the walls of Great Gunst. Perhaps she had finally taken his words to heart, and had deserted him forever.

The fleet rounded the north-eastern coast of Zamata, and Lahnos watched as the hills blocking the view of Chesson fell away. The flat land to the south of the hills was covered in groves and vineyards, and a few white-washed cottages and farmsteads were visible in the light of the sun as it lowered towards the west. In the distance, the two peaks of Hodzulat and Medamuna rose up above the rest of the island like sentinels, while the rest of the island was obscured by a late-summer heat haze. The sailors on board Lord Sigum's dragon carrier guided the fleet south, and then the ships slowed as they reached the opening to the Cyasarta. The fleet turned west, and funnelled up the inlet towards the narrows. The two Chain Castles were intact, and Dominion banners were fluttering in the ocean breeze from their keeps. The Zamatans crowded on the flight deck of the lead ship fell into silence, as they approached the massive chains blocking the entrance to the Cyasarta. Most had never seen the island from that angle before, and the high cliffs on either side of the inlet seemed forbidding and unwelcoming.

The admiral on board approached Lord Sigum and bowed.

'Should we anchor here, my lord?' he said. 'The chains have been raised against us.'

'We have no choice but to do so,' said the dragon. 'Bring the fleet to a halt, and then send out a launch to request that the chains be lowered.'

'Yes, my lord,' said the admiral.

'Why would they raise the chains against us?' said an army major.

'That is what we shall discover,' said Sigum. 'It is possible that the island garrison believes that the entire invasion force was obliterated.

Perhaps they fear that we are Gunstians, come to deceive our way into the island's interior.

'What should I instruct the officers on the launch to say, my lord?' said the admiral.

'The truth,' said Sigum. 'We have nothing to hide.'

The admiral bowed again, then began to issue orders to his junior officers.

'Should I go with them?' said Lahnos.

'No,' said Sigum. 'You shall remain on board. Leave this to the Aucterians, Lahnos.'

The ship's launch was lowered over the side of the carrier, and Lahnos watched as several naval officers walked down a gangway and boarded the small vessel. It was rowed away from the carrier's flank, and then the crew raised a solitary sail, and it sped off in the direction of the northern Chain Castle. The launch had a shallow keel, and it skimmed over the raised chains at their centre point, where they were submerged a few feet under the surface of the water. Once it had passed the chains, the launch docked at the small jetty that poked out into the Cyasarta, and its passengers disappeared behind the rocks in the cliff face.

Lahnos heard a commotion behind him, and he turned to see Karl being pushed back by the Bullan soldiers surrounding Lord Sigum.

'Get your hands off him,' Lahnos cried, as he strode forwards. 'He's my brother.'

The Bullan glanced up at the dragon, who tilted his head a fraction; then they allowed Karl to pass. Efizel escorted him to Lord Sigum's side.

'Greetings, brother of Lahnos Laimos,' said the dragon. 'How may I help you?'

Karl stared up at Sigum's scales and fangs, his mouth opening.

'He's never been this close to a dragon before,' said Lahnos.

'I, uh...' Karl stammered; 'I wanted to speak to Lahnos. The squad were worried that something had happened to him.'

'He is perfectly safe,' said Sigum. 'Where are your horns?'

'I... I don't have any,' said Karl. 'I mean, my lord.'

'But you were birthed from the same mother, and fathered by the same man?'

'Eh, yes.'

'Then you, too, have Bullan blood in your veins,' said the dragon.

Karl's face flushed.

'That's true,' said Lahnos; 'but only I was lucky enough to grow horns. Poor old Karl didn't get any.'

His brother shot him a look.

Efizel pointed in the direction of Igatz. 'My lord, dragons are approaching.'

Sigum turned his long neck as three winged figures in the sky soared towards them.

'It is Lord Givra and Lady Sengilla again,' the dragon said, 'accompanied by Lord Gallus Mon Galla, another fugitive from the invasion of Gunst. That is strange. I had expected the Governor of the island to investigate, or perhaps one of the others left upon the Serpent Isle.' He glanced at the Bullan soldiers. 'Clear a space on the flight deck for our guests.'

The soldiers began shepherding the crowds of Zamatans to either side, until a wide area was sitting empty. The three dragons flew closer then one, a purple-scaled male with black wings, began to descend. He alighted onto the flight deck, his talons scoring deep gouges across the wooden boards, then he turned, his eyes glancing at the humans around him.

'Lord Givra,' said Sigum, 'I see you made it safely to the Serpent Isle.'

The purple dragon moved his head round until he was staring at Sigum. Sparks flew across his open jaws, and his white eyes shone with contempt.

'Are you besmirching my honour, Lord Sigum?' he said. 'What are you accusing me of?'

'I am accusing you of nothing, my lord' said Sigum. 'I am glad that you survived the catastrophe in Gunst.'

Givra advanced a few paces, then his eyes went to Sigum's left wing, and he laughed.

'Still unable to fly?' he said. 'Did you require all of these humans to escort you here?'

'I felt that it was my duty to lead them home,' said Sigum.

'Are you saying that I am a coward?' cried Givra. 'Are you saying that I abandoned them?'

'Those are your words, Lord Givra, not mine,' said the silvery-green dragon. 'I feel no shame about my actions.'

'But you expect me to feel shame about my own? I am a grandson of the mighty King Gahad!'

Sigum tilted his head. 'You are, my lord. Tell me; where is Lord Malum? I expected to see him surveying the ships I have brought from Toraq.'

'The blessed Lord Malum is dead,' said Givra, 'and so are Lady Macsin and Lady Lenta. They were slain by the Demon Witch while we were in Gunst.'

'This news greatly grieves me,' said Sigum.

'I do not believe you, Sigum,' said Givra. 'You feared and loathed Lord Malum, and you were even more scared of Lady Macsin. Her son is here.'

'Lord Ecsin Mon Macsin has also returned from Gunst?'

'He has, and his wrath is beyond any words I could speak.'

'Is Lord Ecsin now the Governor of this isle?'

'No,' said Givra, 'for two Children of Gahad are present. Lady Natali Min Gahad returned here with me, but her elder brother Lord Rylan Mon Gahad was already on the Serpent Isle when we arrived. He is the sole survivor from the dragons left here by King Naghad. Lord Rylan is the new Governor.'

'Then where is he, my lord?'

'He was wounded and, like you, he is unable to fly. Our shame deepens, for no dragon who cannot take to the skies should be in a position of authority.'

Sigum's blue eyes gleamed. 'Does Lord Rylan know how you speak of him?'

Givra ignored the question, his eyes roving over the other ships in the fleet. 'Are those dragon carriers all fit to sail to Inopei?'

'They are in need of some repairs, my lord,' said Sigum, 'but they are capable of making the voyage. You should be aware that the Imperial Gunstian Fleet has been pursuing us since we passed through the Great Bay of Gunst. We have observed their vessels in the distance from time to time, monitoring our progress. I estimate that they will arrive within the next few days.'

'All the more reason to ensure the dragon carriers can depart before then,' said Givra.

'Are we not staying to defend the Serpent Isle?' said Sigum.

Givra narrowed his eyes. 'You were struck with the Gift of Pain in Gunst, were you not?'

'I was, yes, my lord.'

'Was it that, or was it your fall into a cliffside that addled your brains, Sigum? We have no king, and that vile traitor Tegru will be laughing at us. We must return to Inopei to prevent him from seizing the throne. This island was only useful as a stepping stone to invade Gunst. Let our enemies take it. All that matters is that the dragons of royal lineage are evacuated before the Gunstians arrive.'

'But...'

'Silence, Sigum. Remember your place. You shall order the ships into the Cyasarta, and anchor off Handshore, but no one shall be allowed to disembark the fleet unless given express orders. Is that understood?'

Sigum's eyes hardened. 'Where is the Demon Witch?'

'No one knows,' said Givra. 'Answer my question.'

Sigum tilted his head. 'Yes, my lord. I understand.'

'If you try to shame me again, Sigum, I shall have you left here on the island when we depart,' Givra said. 'I will tell your noble father that you died a coward in Gunst.'

The purple and black dragon extended his wings and soared up into the sky. He circled once over the fleet, then joined the other two dragons and they flew back towards Igatz.

'Thank you, Lahnos,' said Sigum.

'For what?' he said.

'For not speaking during Lord Givra's visit. I could sense your great anger, but an outburst from you would have only made things worse.'

'Am I free to speak now?'

'You are.'

Lahnos clenched his fists. 'What a stupid, ignorant, ungrateful bastard that Givra is. You bring him ships and warn him about the Gunstians, and he had the nerve to speak to you like that? He's a damned coward – they all are.'

'Lord Rylan is not a coward,' said Sigum. 'He did not abandon his post.'

'All right; not him,' said Lahnos. 'But the others are. They flee from Gunst and...'

'My appearance here has shamed them deeply,' said Sigum. 'Each will know in their hearts that they betrayed the humans they were supposed to protect. I expected this welcome. They will hate me, but I can live with that. Can you?'

Lahnos glanced away, his rage simmering. 'I will try.'

'Do not give the dragons who fled Gunst any excuse to take out their wrath upon the Bullan, Aucterians and Zamatans on board this little fleet. To ensure their survival, we might have to swallow our pride for a while.'

'Was he right, my lord,' said Karl; 'about Lord Malum and Lady Macsin?'

'I am sure Lord Givra would not lie about their deaths, Karl,' said the dragon.

'I didn't mean that, my lord. I meant about how he said that you hated them.'

'Hate is too strong an emotion to describe my feelings regarding the late Malum and Macsin,' said Sigum. 'But yes, I feared them.'

'Can I ask another question, my lord?' said Karl.

'You are Lahnos's brother,' said Sigum. 'You can ask me anything.'

'Is the Demon Witch real?'

Lord Sigum raised his head, his gaze on the coastline of the island. 'I cannot say with any certainty, as I was not in Nom Karta when King Gahad was slain. But, if Lord Givra says it was she who slew Lord Malum and Ladies Macsin and Lenta, then logic dictates that this information must have come from the mouth of Lord Rylan. I am intrigued to discover how the new Governor was the sole survivor of the Demon Witch's attack.'

'My lord!' cried a naval officer. 'The chains are being lowered.'

'Send signals to the rest of the fleet,' said Sigum, 'and proceed into the Cyasarta. Issue a command that no one is permitted to leave any of the ships. We shall anchor off the breakwaters of Handshore.'

Efizel tugged at Lahnos's sleeve as the dragon busied himself with more orders to the naval officers.

'May I have a quick word?' he whispered.

'Stay here, Karl,' said Lahnos, then he walked away with the Bullan renegade. They went to a quieter part of the flight deck, and watched as the chains slipped below the waves in front of the great ship.

'It seems your friend the Demon Witch has been hard at work,' Efizel whispered. 'Three dragons? You are putting me into an impossible position, for how can I serve you, if you serve someone who has destroyed three Children of Gahad?'

'How am I supposed to answer that?' said Lahnos. 'She must have had her reasons.'

'You are turning me into a rebel.'

'But I am not a rebel.'

'You threatened to mutiny not fifteen minutes ago.'

'The Dominion has a duty to defend Zamata,' said Lahnos. 'If the dragons choose to abandon us, then I will abandon them.'

Efizel rubbed his face.

'You saved my life many times in Gunst,' Lahnos went on. 'If you want to go your own way, then I won't stop you.'

'Do not cheapen the oath I made to you. I will serve you unto death, Lahnos; but I cannot serve the Demon Witch.'

'Perhaps she's gone. Perhaps this was her parting gift. It's been twenty-three days since she last spoke to me, and I think she only did that to help me get out of Gunst. Maybe she's done with me.'

'And if you are wrong?'

Lahnos smiled, but said nothing. What did Efizel want from him? Lahnos had never been able to predict what the Demon Witch would do or say; did the Bullan imagine that he exerted any control over her actions? Part of him missed hearing the voice in his head, but life would be a lot simpler if she had gone for good. They watched as the lead carrier slipped into the narrows of the Cyasarta inlet. The launch was lifted back onto the rear of the flight deck, while two destroyers flanked Sigum's vessel as it passed the Chain Castles. The town of Igatz came into sight, and the white marble façade of the Dragon Palace was gleaming in the light as the sun neared the hills on the western coast. The fleet turned for the north-west, and then sailed along the channel between Igatz and Kaugatz. Many of the Zamatans on the flight deck began shouting down at the civilians watching them from the shore, and a large crowd started to assemble as the women, children and old folk of Kaugatz gathered to see who had arrived. Waves of jubilation and relief washed over the watching crowds, as the news filtered down to them that thousands of Zamatan men were on board. One soldier jumped from the side of the carrier and dived into the clear waters of the Cyasarta. Moments later, he bobbed back up to the surface and began swimming towards the shore of Kaugatz. Bullan soldiers moved into the roiling crowds of Zamatans on the flight deck, shoving them back from the railings.

'No one is to disembark!' one cried. 'The next Zamatan to try gets a crossbow bolt in the back.'

The civilians on the shore of Kaugatz were massing in their thousands, and several launched small vessels to get closer to the passing ships.

'Order the destroyers to flank us on the northern side,' said Sigum. 'Allow no civilian to board any ships under my command.'

The sailors on the flight deck rushed off to relay the dragon's orders, while the Zamatans were crying out in frustration. They were shoving and pushing the thin line of Bullan by the starboard railings, and the soldiers were responding by pointing their bows into the crowd.

'Patience!' Sigum called out, his low voice booming over the flight deck. 'We are servants of the Dominion, and we shall obey the orders given to us. Have patience, my loyal Zamatans; you will see your kin soon.' He glanced at Lahnos. 'Tell them, Laimos; they will listen to you.'

Lahnos suppressed a groan.

'I am asking you to do this as my friend,' the dragon said; 'otherwise we shall have chaos on our hands.'

Lahnos raised his arms in the air and strode towards the crowd of Zamatan men on deck.

'Shut up, all of you!' he cried. 'We are so close; don't throw it all away now. Let's give them one night. We'll stay on board until morning, and pack up our things and get ready to go ashore. We've been away for months; you can last one more night!'

The crowd quietened.

'One more night!' Lahnos repeated. 'Settle down and step back from the Bullan. We fought by their side in Gunst; they are not our enemies.'

To Lahnos's surprise, the Zamatans obeyed him. Many still looked angry, but they pulled back from the railings and moved to the centre of the flight deck.

'Thank you, my friend,' said Sigum.

Lahnos eyed the enormous dragon. 'I meant what I said. One more night on board, and then I won't be able to hold them back.'

The dragon tilted his head. 'Then let us pray that one night will suffice.'

CHAPTER 2
BENEATH THE RUINS

Medamuna Gatzoun – 14th Tuminch 1588

'Well done, Major,' said Cisca, as she placed the mug of water back on to the side table. 'Now, let's try some soup.'

Major Lyla stared into space as she lay upon the bed, a blanket covering her thin body. The young woman had lost weight in the days since they had fled the monastery of Zamata Gataza, and her complexion was wan and starting to become gaunt. Cisca picked up the bowl of warm soup, then dipped in a spoon.

'It has some fish and vegetables in it,' she said. 'Try some; you'll like it.' She raised the filled spoon and held it in front of Lyla's mouth. 'Open wide.'

Lyla didn't respond.

Cisca frowned. On some days, it seemed clear to her that the major understood at least some of what Cisca said, but on other days it was like talking to a boulder.

'Open your mouth,' she said. 'You need to eat something, Major.'

'Why do you still call her that?'

Cisca bit back an angry response, then she turned her head and glanced at Leona; who was standing by the doorway to the small chamber.

'I call her *major*, because that is her rank,' Cisca said. 'I sometimes also call her *ma'am*. Is that all right with you?'

Leona's features remained impassive. 'Major Lyla is dead.'

'Oh? Then who am I attempting to feed, Lady Takri?'

'Lady Takri is also dead,' said Leona. 'The woman lying on the bed is the Demon Witch.'

'Really?' said Cisca. 'Is that so? Do you have any proof of this claim? No, I thought not. Now, was there a reason for this visit? As you can see, I am a little busy.'

'I was wondering if there had been any improvement.'

Cisca put down the bowl of soup. 'Well, she hasn't tried to bite me today; and there have been no fits of weeping and screaming. Would you count that as an improvement?'

Leona narrowed her eyes. 'Why are you adopting this tone with me?'

'Would you prefer to hear every reason, or just the most important ones?' said Cisca. 'Let's see – you blackmailed me; you lied your way into Lord Malum's confidence; you stood by and watched as Lady Macsin slaughtered thousands of Gunstian civilians; you threatened to have the dragons execute me; you...'

'I did what I had to do,' said Leona; 'and you are not the only one to have suffered.'

'Yes, but my suffering was caused by you.'

'Your suffering was caused by your feelings towards Bauchlie. Tell me; how is that going? I watched you both at breakfast; you could barely look each other in the eye. Is the reality of Bauchlie a little different from your fantasy of him?'

Cisca turned away from Leona, her anger bubbling close to the surface. She picked up the bowl again, and tried to manoeuvre the spoon into Lyla's mouth. The woman clamped her lips shut as the spoon approached, and most of its contents dribbled down her chin and onto the blanket.

'Would you like some help?' said Leona.

'Not from you, thank you,' said Cisca. 'You have done quite enough to interfere in my life.'

She reached down and picked up a cloth, then she dabbed Lyla's chin with it.

'Open your mouth, Major,' she said.

Lyla kept it closed.

Cisca suppressed a curse, then she turned to say something rude to Leona; but the Zamatan woman had gone. Cisca placed the bowl onto the side table and rested her head in her hands. She regretted some of the things she had said to Leona, but not all. Perhaps she should have resisted the temptation to say anything. Should she be alienating one of the few people who spoke to her in the caverns beneath the ruins of Medamuna Gatzoun? The tunnels and caves were filled with Zamatan rebels who mistrusted her; they all knew she was an officer in the Dominion armed forces, and she had heard many whispered threats and insults as she had passed people in the busy caverns. Had it not been for Bauchlie's express order that she was not to be harmed, then she doubted she would still be alive. She glanced at Lyla's face in the flickering light of the oil lamp. Caring for the major had become her sole occupation; it gave her a purpose and a reason to get up in the morning. Part of her had assumed that she and Bauchlie would be spending every moment together, but that had been nothing but a foolish dream. The scarred rebel commander had no time for anything but his doomed rebellion. He would train his small band of fighters, and then lead them out on operations; and if he wasn't doing that, he would be meeting with other rebels from across the island, organising supplies of weapons, or interrogating captured Aucterian soldiers. He had no time or inclination for any kind of romantic entanglement – he loved his island, and nothing else.

Lyla opened her lips. Cisca hurried to pick up the spoon, and shovelled a portion of soup into Lyla's mouth.

'That's it, ma'am,' said Cisca, and she fed her a second spoonful. 'You know, you are actually getting a little better; I can see it day by day.

It's almost as though you were waking up after a long sleep, only instead of taking a few moments, you are taking a few weeks.'

Lyla's eyes narrowed a fraction.

'Are you listening to me?' said Cisca. 'Can you hear my words?'

Lyla seemed to nod, but perhaps Cisca was mistaken. She spooned in the last of the soup, then placed the bowl back down.

'I wish I knew more about your family and background,' Cisca said; 'then I could talk to you about things you might remember; but you were always a little discreet with your personal details. I know you were in the army for many years, and I know that you are twenty-six – so I'm guessing that you joined the military as a cadet officer. I also know that you are from Teros City, and that your family is rich. Well, I'm assuming that part because of your accent. I wish I had managed to cultivate my accent – it would have saved me a lot of trouble.

'So, let's see – you joined the army at sixteen, graduated as a junior lieutenant at eighteen, and then I remember that you told me you had campaigned in the Dollandian Mountains, and that you had been to Irlan and Elso several times. I have never been to any of those places. I don't think that you are married – I'm sure you might have mentioned it to me if you were; although I wouldn't say that we were close friends. But, right now, you are the only friend I have.'

Lyla narrowed her eyes again, then she opened her mouth but nothing came out.

'Try to blink your eyes, ma'am,' Cisca said. 'No? Never mind. Perhaps you should get some rest. Sleep, water and food – that's all I can offer you, but you'll need all three if you are going to get better.'

She reached over and extinguished the oil lamp, then she got to her feet.

'I'll be back in an hour or so,' she said from the open doorway.

She closed the door behind her, then she turned and followed the gloomy tunnel to where it opened out into a large stairwell. A shaft had been dug through the rock to allow in fresh air and sunlight, and she took the stairs that led up a level. She needed to get outside, she realised; the stuffy, oppressive atmosphere underground was making her feel claustrophobic; but there were strict rules about straying beyond the caverns, and each entrance was guarded. She reached a long, low cavern, where over a dozen rebel women were sorting through crates of purloined Dominion weapons and armour. They stopped talking when they saw Cisca approach, and she ignored them in return. She ascended more rough-cut steps in the darkness, and came into another cavern, which was lit by several large lamps hanging from chains attached to the rock ceiling. Bauchlie was sitting next to a low table, with a few of his officers gathered close by, only one of whom was a man.

Bauchlie glanced up at her. 'Sit.'

Cisca eyed him. 'Why?'

'You were in the Dragon Corps, weren't you?' he said. 'I have been brought some information and you might be useful in expanding upon it.'

Cisca smothered her feelings, and took a seat on the bench on the other side of the table from Bauchlie.

'One of our agents has returned from Igatz,' Bauchlie said. 'He has given me a list of the dragons currently living in the Dragon Palace. I will read out their names, and you will tell me what you know about them.'

Cisca nodded.

'Two dragons arrived from Gunst on the twenty-seventh of Lexinch,' Bauchlie went on, his eyes on a scrap of paper in his hands; 'a Lord Gallus Mon Galla and a Lady Sengilla Min Inglis.'

'I have never heard of either,' said Cisca; 'though both are clearly mortal dragons, unrelated to the Royal Family.'

Bauchlie nodded. 'Then, on the second of Tuminch, Lady Natali Min Gahad arrived with Lord Givra Mon Girvine.'

'I am aware of them,' said Cisca. 'Lady Natali is Lord Rylan's younger sister, and Lord Givra is one of King Gahad's grandsons. Both are royalty, though neither are higher in rank than Lord Rylan. Lord Givra is descended from King Gahad's second mate, while Rylan and Natali are the children of the former King's third mate. This will mean that Givra will probably not be happy about taking orders from Rylan.'

Bauchlie nodded again. 'Finally, on the sixth of Tuminch, a Lord Ecsin Mon Macsin arrived alone.'

Cisca frowned. 'Lady Macsin's son. I have met him a few times. He is not a pleasant character. Like Givra, he will be dissatisfied at having to obey Lord Rylan. Is that all of them? Do we now have six dragons upon the Serpent Isle?'

'It's called Zamata,' said Bauchlie, keeping his eyes on the scrap of paper. 'Yes; there are six of the bastards – four royals and two mortals.'

'Strictly speaking,' said Cisca, 'the grandchildren of Gahad are probably also mortals. Several have died of natural causes over the years, while only a few have lived longer than a normal mortal life span. No one knows for certain how many of King Gahad's grandchildren are true immortals.'

'What will their orders be?' said Bauchlie.

Cisca shrugged. 'Are the rumours definitely true? Is King Naghad dead?'

'It seems so. It also seems clear that the five newcomers fled Gunst in some panic. My agent has informed us that they have been spreading stories that there were no survivors from the invasion force.'

'That might be true,' said Cisca.

Bauchlie gave her one of his rare smiles, then he got to his feet. 'Come with me, Cisca. There's something you might want to see.'

'I very much doubt that.'

'It's outside,' he went on. 'In the fresh air. The sun is out.'

Cisca got to her feet. 'Lead the way.'

Bauchlie escorted her through a few more tunnels, and then up another flight of stairs. They came to a narrow opening that faced a cliff overgrown with bushes and passed the two rebel fighters on duty. They squeezed through the bushes, then Cisca gasped in relief as a cool ocean breeze struck her face. She closed her eyes and savoured it, then felt Bauchlie's hand on the small of her back as he turned her a little.

'What do you see?' he said.

She opened her eyes, and her mouth fell open. She was looking out to the north, where the vast ocean spread across her line of vision. The steep slopes of Mount Medamuna fell away in tiers to where the waves were crashing against the ragged shore, but Cisca's gaze was on the mass of ships that was sailing east. She counted.

'Six dragon carriers?' she cried. 'But...'

'Keep your voice low,' Bauchlie said. 'Give me your interpretation.'

'They must have come from Gunst,' she said. 'Survivors. But, I can't see any dragons. Each ship is lying low in the water, so I'm guessing that they are full of Dominion soldiers and sailors, rescued from the invasion force. But where are the dragons?'

'There is one on the lead dragon carrier,' Bauchlie said. 'You can't see him from here any more, but I was standing in this spot twenty minutes ago, and had a better view. The dragons who have been arriving in Igatz have not been entirely honest.'

'Was King Naghad on the lead ship?'

'No. This dragon was silver and green, and for some reason he wasn't flying. There's more, Cisca. The decks of several ships were filled with men; Zamatan men.'

'How do you know they were Zamatan?'

'Because they were dressed in irregular uniforms and were unarmed. The Aucterian sailors and soldiers, and the Bullan, are all wearing their own uniforms, while many of these men were dressed as farmers. Do you realise that this is exactly what the Demon Witch told Leona? That means Lahnos is probably down there somewhere.'

'Have you told Reyn?'

'I'm about to. I haven't told Leona yet, either. You tell her, while I find Reyn.'

Cisca frowned.

'Do you have a problem with that?' said Bauchlie.

'No.'

'Good.' He turned for the cavern entrance.

'Bauchlie,' she said, 'will we ever... I mean, will...? We never have any time.'

'Time for what?' he said.

She glanced away. 'Nothing.'

They re-entered the cavern, and Cisca's spirits fell as she breathed in the warm stale air. The ruins of Medamuna Gatzoun spread out across the entire flank of the mountain, and the rock was riddled with tunnels. Cisca had been told that over six hundred monks had once lived in the ancient monastery, and many had preferred to dwell on their own in small cave-like hermit cells dotted over the landscape. The Bullan had climbed the mountain more than once during Cisca's stay, but they had never come in numbers large enough to conduct a thorough search, and had always left without discovering the rebels' hideout. Bauchlie and Cisca went their separate ways once they reached a large cavern, and Cisca descended some dark steps to where Leona had a small cavern to herself. Despite being Colonel Friel's most trusted advisor, Bauchlie didn't seem to know what to do with the young woman, and Leona was rarely seen at any of the large rebel meetings.

Cisca reached Leona's cavern, but it was dark and quiet. Where was she? Cisca retraced her steps, and then went through several large chambers. Over two hundred people lived under the ruins, and they tended to gather in a half dozen different locations. Cisca visited them all, but saw no sign of Leona. News about the return of the six dragon carriers had reached the rebels, however, and many were discussing what it could mean. Cisca resisted the temptation to ask some of them for help in finding Leona. The underground network of tunnels was extensive, and she feared getting lost, so she went down a few more flights of stairs until she reached Lyla's chamber. It was time to check on her, and she decided that Leona could wait.

She reached the stairwell with the ventilation shaft, and saw a dim illumination coming from Lyla's room. Had the woman managed to light the oil lamp? Cisca quickened her steps, then frowned as she peered through the open doorway. Leona was sitting by the bed, talking to Lyla.

'Can you remember your real name?' Leona was saying. 'It's not

Major Lyla, as Cisca keeps telling you, and I only know you as the Demon Witch. You must have a real name. Try to think.'

Lyla said nothing. Her eyes were open, but there was no emotion passing over her drawn features.

Cisca coughed, and Leona turned.

'What are you doing here?' said Cisca.

'What does it look like?'

'You are filling the major's head full of nonsense.'

'That's your opinion,' said Leona. 'Believe it or not, I am trying to help.'

'How? By confusing her?'

'I know you mean well, Cisca, but has it occurred to you that you might be wrong?'

Cisca's temper snapped. 'How dare you? Who has been sitting by Major Lyla's side day after day, feeding her, cleaning her, and trying to help her rest? Who has been changing her bed sheets and her clothes? Which of us has been bitten and scratched over a dozen times? Who has had soup spat in their face? You? Don't make me laugh.'

'I offered to help today.'

'Do you expect congratulations? Leave her alone.'

Leona narrowed her eyes. 'This woman is not your possession, Cisca.'

'Is she yours?'

'Of course not.'

'Then get out!'

Leona got to her feet and stared at Cisca. 'I want to help. Will you let me help?'

'No!' Cisca cried, then Lyla let out a low moan and began to weep.

'Do you see what you've done?' said Cisca.

'It wasn't me who raised their voice, Cisca. But, I will respect your wishes and leave.'

'That's right; leave me when she starts crying.'

Leona turned by the doorway. 'Can I stay? I would like to help.'

'Just go,' said Cisca. She sat by the bedside and took Lyla's hand.

'There, there. It's all right. Everything's all right.' Lyla closed her eyes and fell silent, and Cisca turned back to Leona. 'Six dragon carriers have passed Mount Medamuna,' she said. 'They're heading towards the Cyasarta. I think they've come from Gunst – the survivors of the invasion force.'

Leona's eyes widened. 'What?'

'You heard me. I've been looking for you for half an hour.'

Leona raced out of the chamber and disappeared into the gloom. Cisca gazed at Lyla, but the woman was at peace again. Had her shouting brought on the tears? She sighed, extinguished the lamp, and followed Leona.

The main chambers were hives of activity when Cisca walked through them. Dozens of fighters had been outside to gaze down at the passing fleet, and the talk was filled with the possibility that at least some of the Zamatan men were on board. Cisca found Leona in a quiet corner of one of the chambers, talking with Bauchlie and Reyn.

'Reyn,' said Bauchlie, 'take three trusted fighters who are good at blending in and head straight for Kaugatz. I need to know how many Zamatans are on the fleet. Once you have made a few enquiries, send one of the fighters back up here to let me know what you have discovered.' He narrowed his eyes at her. 'Don't get your hopes up. I know what you are thinking, and I hope you are right, but try to lower your expectations.'

'There's no chance of that, boss,' said Reyn. 'If Lahnos is there, I'll find him.'

'I want to go, too,' said Leona.

'I don't think that's a good idea,' said Bauchlie. 'Too many people in Kaugatz know your face.'

'That's bullshit,' said Leona. 'Besides, Reyn lived in Kaugatz for years; people there know her face, and she has horns.'

'She'll be wearing a head scarf, and she lived in one small part of Kaugatz,' said Bauchlie. 'You, on the other hand, used to consort with the high and mighty. It's not worth the risk. If you are captured by Aucterian soldiers, then you will lead them here.'

Leona's anger was obvious on her face. 'So could Reyn.'

'Reyn has been trained for this. She's a rebel fighter, whereas you are...'

'Yes? Go on. I'm what?'

Bauchlie said nothing.

'Colonel Friel trained me for years, Bauchlie,' Leona said. 'And before that I managed to live on my own on the streets.'

'No,' he said. 'You're not going. I have made my decision.'

'Should I leave now, boss?' said Reyn.

'Yes,' said Bauchlie. 'Good luck.'

Reyn saluted, then she rushed off, leaving the cavern by one of its many entrances.

'This makes no sense and you know it,' said Leona. 'I could blend into Kaugatz as well as Reyn.'

'Shut up,' said Bauchlie. 'You know far too much about every aspect of the resistance movement, Leona. I could hardly say so in front of Reyn, but you're too valuable to lose.'

'Am I a prisoner here?'

'No.'

Leona shook her head. 'Are you forgetting that I'm Gifted, you stupid asshole?' She noticed Cisca, and her frown deepened. 'You two are made for each other.'

Cisca said nothing as Leona stormed off.

Bauchlie chewed his lip. 'I could have handled that better.'

Cisca smiled. 'Yes.'

'I'm used to dealing with men who never questioned my orders,' he said. 'Leona questions everything.'

'Then perhaps you should let her leave.'

'She'll leave of her own accord, unless I post guards to follow her about.'

'Then let her,' said Cisca. 'Let her slip out. Allow her to think that she has outwitted you.'

'And if she gets caught by the Aucterians?'

'The Aucterians already know you're here, Bauchlie. If she's caught and interrogated, then it will hardly come as a surprise to the authorities to learn that you have been hiding under Medamuna Gatzoun. The whole island knows you're here. Let Leona go, then block up whichever entrance she uses to escape.'

Bauchlie sat down on a stone bench and leaned back against the wall of the cavern. 'You don't like her, do you?'

'No. Do you?'

'I respect her. What she did as Lady Takri took a lot of guts. She risked her life every day she worked for Malum.'

'She risked my life, too. Had you forgotten that part?'

'No.'

Cisca sat down next to him. 'Leona is probably the most intelligent person I have ever met. And I agree that she has plenty of courage; but what do you need her here for? I haven't once seen you use her skills. She's better at undercover work. Let her be Leona. Let her do what she's good at doing.'

'And you'll be free of her at the same time?'

'Yes. I admit it. I still hold a grudge after everything she put me through.'

'But you don't hold a grudge against me for what I put you through?'

'That was different.'

A slight trace of a smile flickered over his lips.

'You were an honest criminal,' she went on. 'I knew exactly what you wanted, and where you stood. Leona... well, she's sly.'

'She's not sly. She's cunning; I'll grant you that, but not sly.'

'All right; she's cunning. The difference is that one never knows how she will react to a situation, whereas you are more transparent.'

'Did you mean that to sound like an insult?'

Cisca glanced away.

'You mentioned something before,' he went on. 'You said we don't have time. Time for what?'

Cisca took a breath. 'Forget I said that.'

'No.'

'I… I am alone here,' she said. 'I am the only Aucterian amid two hundred rebel Zamatans, most of whom are women.'

'What does that have to do with anything?'

'Well, I see the way that some of them look at you. Not all; but some.'

'How do they look at me?'

She peered at him. Was he really oblivious to the attentions of so many young women in the caverns? A few rebels had almost thrown themselves at him; hadn't he noticed?

'Never mind,' she said. 'This whole conversation is a mistake.'

Bauchlie narrowed his eyes and stood. He walked away, then turned. 'It's at times like these that I wish I had the Gift of Truth,' he said, 'then I might have a chance of understanding what you're talking about. See you around, Cisca.'

Cisca watched him leave, then she exhaled. Lyla would be needing more water soon, so she got to her feet, and began to make her way back to the lower caverns.

CHAPTER 3
CARTED OFF

Medamuna Gatzoun – 15th Tuminch 1588

The sun was rising over the lowlands of the island as the little cart made its way down the mountain track. Leona kept her hands on the reins, guiding the two dappled grey ponies through the olive groves that flanked the village of Fidalaimos.

It had been easy to slip out of the caverns under Medamuna Gatzoun. So easy, in fact, that Leona knew that Bauchlie must have allowed it. He was letting her go, while remaining officially opposed to her departure. How else could she explain the series of unguarded tunnels, or the ease with which she had been able to steal the cart? Her pride had almost demanded that she go back into the ruins of the monastery to tell Bauchlie that she knew what he was doing, and to ask him if he thought she was stupid; but her common sense had won out and, instead, she had done something that she knew would annoy and upset Cisca.

The cart reached the edge of the terraced olive groves, and a spectacular view of the island opened out in front of her. Leona glanced over Zamata, her eyes drawn to the collection of ships anchored in the glistening waters of the Cyasarta. Six dragon carriers. The Demon Witch had been right. No, she thought – there was more to it than that.

The Demon Witch hadn't merely been right; she had saved the ships, and every man that was on board. The effort it had taken had exhausted her, leaving her weakened, and allowing Lord Malum to draw her down into the body of Major Lyla. It seemed obvious to Leona; so why had Cisca doubted it? The Dragon Corps captain had been present at the time – she had witnessed what had happened in Zamata Gataza with her own eyes, and yet she struggled to believe the truth.

The track entered a thick grove of orange trees, and she lost sight of the fleet anchored off Handshore Naval Base. She passed another track to her right that led to Friel's mountain cottage, and her thoughts went to the colonel's last words. If Lahnos had survived, then she would need to watch him carefully for any signs that he possessed more Gifts. She wondered how it could be possible to be Gifted and not realise it. Her own Gift had appeared in her youth, and it hadn't taken her very long to associate the tingles in her head with their cause. It occurred to her that not all Gifts were like that. If Lahnos hadn't touched his grandmother's hand, then he would probably still be unaware that he had the Gift of Death Reading. The implications of that simple idea rolled around her mind. How many others were out there, living in complete ignorance of their Gifts? How many potential death-readers spent their entire lives without ever touching a corpse? The Gunstians did things differently, she knew. They sought out the Gifted within their territories, using those with Kenning to search for others with Gifts, so that they could become both servants and rulers of the Gunstian Empire. It was not the same in Zamata. The Dominion had no means to discover who was Gifted; but the colonel had known. He would have sensed every individual on the island with a Gift – so why had he never shared this information with her? Why had he waited until he was dying before telling her the truth about Lahnos?

The cart turned towards the south, and she glimpsed a view of the devastated wheat fields that stretched all the way to the blackened ruins of Neeton. She hoped that many thousands of the men from Zamata had survived the invasion of Gunst but, at the same time, their arrival would put even more pressure on the island's dwindling food supplies. She had been right to help Lord Malum root out the Gunstian agents responsible for the disaster; but what had happened as a consequence of that had haunted her dreams ever since. She had learned that not every Gunstian on the island had died; there were still a few families living on isolated homesteads, and several had managed to hide until the Bullan searches had been called off by Lord Rylan in the aftermath of Malum's death. She glanced up at the peak of Mount Hodzulat in the distance. The monastery of Zamata Gataza was just visible, clinging onto the steep mountainside. It was quiet again, after Lord Rylan had relocated his court back to the Dragon Palace in Igatz, keen to be as far as possible from the place where the Demon Witch had caused the deaths of three so-called immortal dragons. Leona wondered how the monks felt about their most sacred site being desecrated in such a manner.

She glanced over her shoulder, but the track behind her that led back to the ruins of Medamuna Gatzoun was clear. There would probably be a pursuit once Bauchlie and Cisca realised what she had taken with her, and Leona knew that she needed to be clear of Mount Medamuna before that happened. She urged the ponies on, driving them down the slope towards the coastal road that led to the ferry terminal.

Three hours later, Leona stepped down from the cart in a back street of Kaugatz. She glanced along the alleyway to check it was empty, then she crouched down and lifted a cracked cobble by the base of a wall that ran round an abandoned property. Under the cobble was a set of keys, placed there by Colonel Friel during the uprising. Leona picked them up, and walked to the wooden gates close to where the ponies were standing. She unlocked a padlock, pulled the chain free, and opened the gates. She paused for a moment, her eyes scanning the rear of the building as she listened. There were many empty properties in Kaugatz, and several had been occupied by squatters, but she could hear nothing coming from inside the building. She took the reins and led the ponies into the rear yard of the building, then she closed and locked the gates.

She fed and watered the ponies, then secured them within a small stable block set into the side of the yard. She had brought no luggage with her, but the house contained everything that she needed. She had last seen it used when Friel had been conducting one of his illicit affairs with an Aucterian aristocrat. On that occasion, she had been asked to wait outside, but she had been in the elegant two-storey townhouse more than once. She unlocked the back door and pushed it open. The hinges squealed and groaned, then she stepped inside. She went from room to room, checking that nothing had been disturbed, but stayed out of the colonel's bedroom. She would sleep elsewhere, she decided; perhaps the study could be converted, or maybe the small dining room. The kitchen was well-stocked, despite lacking any fresh food, and the water pump was still working. She would need to compile a list of what she required, but there was plenty of money hidden in a strongbox under Friel's old desk. She went upstairs and opened the shutters, letting the midday sunlight spill into the old house. Dust particles glistened in the air. She would have to spend a few hours cleaning, but before she could begin, she needed to return to the cart.

Leona went back outside to the rear yard, and climbed up onto the back of the cart. She knelt down by a large pile of blankets, and moved them to the side. Beneath, Lyla was still sleeping, and Leona felt a twinge of guilt for having poured a tincture of poppy essence into the woman's water before she had taken her from Medamuna Gatzoun. Cisca would know what she had done; she checked on Lyla every few hours, and had no doubt gone crying to Bauchlie to complain. Hurting Cisca's feelings was the least of Leona's worries. If the Demon Witch was buried somewhere inside Lyla, then it would be up to Leona to draw her out. She leaned over the woman's body and gripped her shoulders, then she hauled her along the back of the cart. She jumped down to the cobbles, then took hold of Lyla's shoulders again and pulled her down. Leona grunted with the effort, then she dragged Lyla to the rear door of the house and into the sitting room, placing her onto a long couch.

Leona sat on the edge of the couch and gazed down at the unconscious woman. What should she call her? Unlike Cisca, she believed that naming her Major Lyla would serve only to confuse her; but she didn't know the Demon Witch's real name. She moved a strand of brown hair from the woman's face, then stood up, her eyes going to the layers of dust coating every surface. She frowned, and got to work.

Leona was mopping the kitchen floor when the doorbell rang.

She froze. Had Bauchlie caught up with her already? She was almost certain that the rebel commander had been unaware of the address she had chosen. The colonel had owned several properties around the island, and Leona was convinced that only she knew about some of them. She leaned the mop against the kitchen wall, then untied the apron and placed it over the back of a chair. The doorbell rang again, and she walked through the house to the front door. She breathed, then smoothed down the front of her long dress, and slid the bolt free. She opened the door.

Standing outside were two men that she didn't recognise.

'Yes?' she said. 'Can I help you?'

One of the men glanced up and down the quiet street, then he glanced at her. 'Who are you?'

'I might ask you the same question,' she said. 'What do you want?'

'That depends on who you are, ma'am,' he said.

'Do you have any right to be here, miss?' said the other man. 'Do you know whose house this is?'

She smiled. 'It's my house.'

'And how did you acquire it, ma'am?' said the first man.

'It was an inheritance.'

The two men glanced at each other.

'Can we come in, miss?' said the second man.

'Are you armed?'

One of the men shifted his cloak, revealing a short-bladed knife attached to his belt.

'You could have lied,' she said.

'If you are who we think you are, ma'am, then there wouldn't have been any point.'

She narrowed her eyes. 'Say my name.'

'You are Leona, aren't you?'

She searched her memory. She knew that the colonel had agents on the island that she had never met, their identities kept from her in case she was ever questioned by the authorities.

'Tell me who you are and why you want to talk to me.'

'Very well, ma'am,' said the first man. 'We worked for the colonel, just as you did. We want to speak to you to discuss the way forward for Zamata. I believe we can help each other.'

Leona felt no twinge. She moved to the side, and gestured for them to enter.

'How did you know I was here?' she said, as they stood in the entrance hall.

The second man smiled. 'I live across the street, miss, and I saw you open the upstairs shutters.'

'That's when he came for me,' said the first man.

Leona closed the front door. 'Is that a Gunstian accent you are attempting to hide?'

The first man nodded. 'It is,' he said, 'though few are able to detect it. I generally pass for Zamatan these days, which was how I managed to evade being slaughtered along with the rest of the Gunstians on the island.'

'I see,' said Leona, as she lowered her gaze. 'You should flatten your vowels a little more, but other than that, it is quite convincing.'

'My true name is Adannu, ma'am,' the first man went on, 'but I go by Farakai now. The Gunstian community cast me out when I was a teenager.'

'Why?'

'Because I stopped believing in Chadura, ma'am. Can you guess who took me in and looked after me? You weren't the only person the colonel rescued from the streets.' He gestured to the other man. 'This is Saewa, your new neighbour.'

Leona led them into the colonel's little study, and they sat around the desk.

'I'm afraid I cannot offer you anything to eat or drink,' she said. 'I was in the middle of cleaning the house when you arrived, and I have yet to purchase any fresh supplies.'

Saewa smiled. 'There should be some brandy in the desk drawer, miss, along with glasses.'

Leona reached out and opened the drawer. She removed a full bottle of brandy, opened it, and poured out three measures.

Farakai raised his glass. 'To the colonel.'

They drank.

'Did you see him die, ma'am?'

She nodded. 'He was killed by Bullan soldiers while trying to escape from Zamata Gataza. What did he tell you about me?'

'Very little,' said Farakai. 'Two things come to mind – that you are Gifted; and that we should report to you if anything were to happen to him.'

'Report to me?' she said.

'Yes. We work for you now, ma'am. We have a network of a dozen other agents embedded into Kaugatz and Igatz.'

'And what are your roles?'

'I am the lead agent for Kaugatz, ma'am,' said Farakai. 'I organise the others.'

'He's my boss,' said Saewa. 'I deal with the part-Bullan. Intelligence gathering and suchlike. I watched out for Lahnos for several years on the colonel's behalf. I also keep an eye on this house, to make sure no one tries to rob or squat in it.'

'We two are the only agents who are aware of this particular property,' said Farakai, 'and we shall keep it that way. You are wanted by the Dominion, as I am sure you already know, so I would advise that you keep a low profile.' He smiled. 'I am sure that you are aware of that, too, ma'am.'

'It is still good advice,' she said. 'How long have you worked for the colonel?'

'Since I was in my teens,' said Farakai; 'more than three decades ago. Saewa has been an agent for a little over eight years. I recruited him myself.'

She nodded. 'What do you know about a certain Lady Takri?'

Farakai frowned. 'We have been looking for her. She appeared not long after you and the colonel were arrested by the Dominion. She advised the dragons on matters that are unknown to us, and she was present at the massacre of the Gunstian civilians that took place in Lexinch. We believe she was in Zamata Gataza, ma'am; did you see her there?'

Leona felt no tingle. 'No, but I was aware of her presence. She was killed in the same attack that destroyed Malum and Macsin.'

'Takri is dead?' said Farakai.

'Yes. I asked about her because I still wonder where she came from. I suspected that she might be Gifted, and, if so, there may be others like her working for the Dominion.'

'Perhaps she hailed from Irlan or Elso, miss,' said Saewa. 'There are rumours that the Dominion is actively seeking Gifted from those regions to employ as agents.'

'Let me know if you hear of any more like her,' said Leona.

'We shall,' said Farakai. 'Is there anything else we can do for you, ma'am?'

Leona pondered for a moment. 'I am in need of a discreet housekeeper,' she said. 'Someone who can be trusted to keep their mouths closed about what they see here.'

'I will find you someone,' said Farakai. 'Will they require any particular skills?'

'Patience,' she said. 'They will need to possess lots of patience; and be experienced in caring for someone who is ill.' She got to her feet. 'I need to show you something; or rather, someone.'

The two men got to their feet, and she led them out of the study. She walked to the sitting room door and paused.

'Complete secrecy is required for what I am about to reveal to you. Let me hear you say that you will tell no one.'

'I will tell no one,' said Farakai.

'Nor I,' said Saewa.

Leona felt no tingles, and she smiled. 'Apologies for that; I need to be careful.'

'We understand, ma'am,' said Farakai. 'It takes time to earn trust. Has anything Saewa or I told you been a lie?'

'No,' she said. 'You have both been honest.'

Leona opened the door, and the two men peered inside, their eyes going to the unconscious woman lying on the couch.

'Who is she, ma'am?' said Farakai.

'She used to be Major Lyla,' said Leona.

They walked into the sitting room, and Farakai knelt by the couch.

'Who, ma'am?' he said. 'I have never heard of a Major Lyla.'

'She was in the Dragon Corps,' she said. 'Lord Malum killed her in Zamata Gataza. He then revived her body, and placed the essence of the Demon Witch into it.'

'The Demon Witch?' said Farakai. 'The Demon Witch is inside her?'

'She is. My new housekeeper will be required to care for her – feed her, bathe her, and so on. If the Dominion discovers that the Demon Witch is living in this house, they will send dragons to burn it to the ground.'

'I don't understand,' said Saewa. 'How could Lord Malum place the Demon Witch into someone else's body?'

'The same way that the god Nathaniel placed Gahad into a dragon's body,' she said.

'Who else knows of this, ma'am?' said Farakai.

'Just a small handful of people,' she said. 'Commander Bauchlie, a Dragon Corps officer who has switched sides, and a part-Bullan rebel fighter; and now you two. The only reason I am telling you this is because I need my housekeeper to understand that... Major Lyla is liable to behave unpredictably. I need someone who will be able to deal with that.'

'I would advise against telling your new housekeeper that this woman contains the spirit of the Demon Witch, or that she used to be in the Dominion armed forces,' said Farakai. 'The woman I have in mind is a quarter-Gunstian, and she might take exception to caring for someone who was a member of the Dragon Corps.'

'I agree,' said Leona. 'We will continue to call her Lyla, but we shall drop the *major*, and we shall remain silent on the subject of the Demon Witch. You can omit the details about her background when you speak to the housekeeper.'

Farakai got back to his feet. 'Understood, ma'am. Is there a reason why... Lyla appears to be unconscious?'

'I drugged her before travelling here from Medamuna Gatzoun, to prevent her from crying out. She will awaken soon. Could I have the housekeeper here by nightfall?'

'That might be difficult, ma'am,' said Farakai. 'Most Zamatans are lining the shores of the Cyasarta to see if anyone will be allowed to disembark the vessels anchored off Handshore. There are rumours going around that several of the ships are packed full of Zamatan men.'

'The rumours are true,' said Leona. 'Why were neither of you rounded up and sent to Gunst?'

'I still have my old Gunstian identity card, ma'am,' said Farakai. 'We were exempt.'

'And I am the son of an Aucterian merchant,' said Saewa. 'That was enough to get me off the list.'

'You are half-Aucterian?'

'Yes, miss. My mother is Zamatan. I was born on this island.'

Leona nodded.

'We should leave now, ma'am,' said Farakai. 'I will track down and approach your new housekeeper, while Saewa will go to the market and buy fresh food for you and Lyla. If you need to contact me, walk across the street to Saewa's house. It has a red door. With any luck, I shall be back this evening; but I will use the rear entrance from now on. I have a key.'

'I also have keys,' said Saewa, as he dipped a hand into a pocket. He withdrew a set and held them out for Leona. 'These are for my house. If this location is compromised and you need somewhere to hide in a hurry, then my home will be available at any time.'

'Thank you,' said Leona.

'We shall see ourselves out, ma'am,' said Farakai. 'It was a pleasure to meet you at long last.'

Leona remained where she was as the two men strode from the sitting room. She waited until she had heard the front door open and close, then she went back to the study and retrieved her glass of brandy. When she returned to the sitting room, she took a seat in a comfortable armchair, her gaze on Lyla's body. It rankled that she had lied to her new employees regarding the identity of Lady Takri, but it would be far better if they believed that she had been slain in Zamata Gataza. Lady Takri was dead, and best forgotten about.

Lyla stirred on the couch, and her eyes opened. Leona stood, and helped the woman sit up on the couch, then she left the sitting room. She filled a clean jug with fresh water from the pump, and walked back to where Lyla was seated. The woman's gaze fell upon Leona, and her eyes widened a fraction.

'Would you like some water?' Leona said.

Lyla said nothing.

'Can you hear me?'

Lyla blinked.

Leona walked over and poured some water into a glass. She held it to Lyla's lips and the woman took a sip.

'Does a blink mean yes?' she said.

Lyla blinked again.

'Who taught you that? Was it Cisca?'

Another blink.

'What about *no*? How does that work?'

Lyla blinked twice.

Leona sat down next to her. 'Can you speak?'

Lyla opened her mouth, but nothing came out, and she started to cry.

'It's all right,' said Leona. 'I know that you are confused. This is your new home.'

Lyla blinked twice, and the tears continued, running down her cheeks as she sobbed. She reached out with a hand, and struck the glass held by Leona. Its contents splashed out over the rug, then Lyla gripped Leona's wrist and squeezed.

'Ow!' cried Leona. 'That hurts. You're strong.'

Lyla squeezed harder. Leona wrenched her wrist free and backed away a few paces.

'Why did you do that?' she said. 'I am trying to help you.'

Lyla blinked twice.

'What do you mean?' said Leona. 'Have I upset you?'

The woman blinked once.

'How?'

Lyla opened her mouth again, as if desperate to say something. She made a strange hissing sound.

'Yes?' said Leona.

'Sss... sss... sisss...'

Leona's expression fell. 'Cisca?'

Lyla blinked once as she wept.

'You want Cisca? Shit. I'm sorry, but I will be taking care of you from now on. Cisca believed things about you that weren't true; and she was confusing you. I know she was kind, and I promise that I will try to be as kind as she was.'

Lyla stared at her blankly, as though she hadn't understood most of what Leona had said.

'Are you the Demon Witch?' Leona said.

Nothing. Lyla's sobs quietened, and she sat still, as though terrified, her hands trembling.

'I won't hurt you,' Leona said. 'I will help you.'

Lyla screamed.

CHAPTER 4
THE PECKING ORDER

Cyasarta, Serpent Isle – 15th Tuminch 1588

Lahnos checked the position of the sun. Midday. He cursed. One more night – that was what he had told the Zamatans on the flight deck of Lord Sigum's dragon carrier, and the news had filtered down to every ship that had men of the island on board. One more night, and they had obeyed. Their angry protests had dissipated, and the night had passed in peace, while the gentle waters of the Cyasarta had lapped against the hulls of the small fleet.

'Stay back!' cried a Bullan soldier. 'The next man to jump overboard dies!'

Lahnos turned, as the noise from the crowd increased. Just as they had done the day before, the Zamatans were filling the long, wide flight deck, while a thin cordon of Bullan soldiers was preventing them from leaping down into the inlet. The fleet's two frigates were sailing back and forth along the north-western flank of the line of six dragon carriers, in a futile attempt to deter the Zamatans from trying to swim to the shore of Kaugatz. A swarm of small fishing vessels had assembled close to the town's central ferry terminal, ready to sail out to the fleet to bear the men away, but the frigates had loosed several warning shots from their forward ballistae.

'What shall we do, my lord?' a Bullan officer said.

Lord Sigum turned his gaze away from the shoreline of Kaugatz and regarded the ragged mob crowding the flight deck.

'Hold your positions,' said the silvery-green dragon, 'but do not loose into the Zamatans.'

'Yes, my lord,' said the officer. 'You should be aware that the disquiet is spreading to the Aucterians in the fleet. The sailors are remaining at their posts, but the soldiers are starting to join the protests. If it comes to a fight, the Bullan will be out-numbered ten-to-one.'

'I am expecting a reply to my message to arrive at any moment,' said the dragon; 'but I shall address the men.' He glanced at Lahnos. 'You shall accompany me.'

The silvery-green dragon strode forwards without another word, and Lahnos walked by his side.

'Men of the Dominion,' Lord Sigum called out, 'hear me.'

The crowds on the flight deck turned, and their cries fell away, as each listened.

'We have shared the trials that have come our way,' the dragon said. 'We fought and bled on the fields of Gunst; we witnessed our brothers and kin fall to the swords and Gifts of the enemy. We have all suffered. We departed this island in the hope that our victory would be swift and assured, and have returned chastened by defeat. The King of the Dominion is dead, and countless thousands of Aucterians, Bullan and Zamatans lie by his graveside, swallowed up by the ruins of Toraq and the mud of Great Gunst.' He paused, his eyes scanning the crowd. 'I share your frustration. I share your desire to disembark these ships and to feel the touch of solid ground beneath us. Many of you have families and loved ones upon the island – they are so close you can almost touch them, and yet the orders we received yesterday told us to remain on board. I have sent an urgent message to the Governor of the Serpent Isle, requesting the immediate disembarkation of all soldiers – the Aucterians to Igatz, and the Zamatans to Kaugatz.'

The crowd cheered, raising their fists in the air.

'Now we must wait for the reply,' said Sigum, and the cheers died away. 'I have guided you here from Toraq City,' the dragon went on. 'You placed your trust in me then; now trust me to deliver you to your homes.'

One of the Bullan pointed towards Igatz. 'Dragons, my lord!'

Every eye on the flight deck turned. Two dragons were approaching from the direction of the Dragon Palace, their great wings extended as they soared over the houses and streets of Igatz. When they reached the Cyasarta, one remained high, circling overhead, while the other began to descend.

'Clear the area!' shouted a Bullan sergeant. 'Allow the blessed dragon to land.'

The Zamatans on the flight deck scrambled back, until a large space in front of Lord Sigum was empty. The dragon descending was smaller than Lord Sigum, but her bulk remained substantial, and she barely squeezed into the space when her talons dug into the wooden boards of the flight deck. Her red eyes glanced at the crowds of men around her, then she tilted her head towards Lord Sigum.

'Lady Sengilla,' said Sigum, as he tilted his own head in greeting. 'Welcome aboard.'

'You have done well, Lord Sigum,' said the other dragon. 'Despite your injury, you have shepherded these ships and men all the way from Gunst. By doing so, you have provoked the ire of several of my kin, who feel you have shamed them.'

'It was not my intention to shame anyone,' said Sigum.

'I understand,' said Sengilla. 'I, too, fled the field of battle and took to the air when I discovered the fate of our beloved King Naghad. For six days I flew, avoiding the towns and cities of the Gunstians, and for six days I felt nothing but the bitter taste of cowardice. Tell me – would you have also fled had your wing not been injured?'

'I cannot answer that,' said Sigum. 'I am fortunate that I was not tested as you were. I am glad that you survived the catastrophe, and I shall never accuse any of the returning dragons of cowardice.'

'You don't need to say a word,' said Sengilla. 'The truth pains us all. The Dragon Palace of Igatz is in tumult – such is the effect of your arrival here. Anger and shame make for unfriendly conversations, and wild accusations have been hurled among our kin. Is it true that the Imperial Gunstian Fleet has been shadowing your voyage here?'

'I cannot state their exact location with any certainty, as I have been unable to fly and scout their position, but yes – they have been pursuing us since we traversed the Great Bay of Gunst. We were seen by the coastal garrisons as we entered the ocean.'

Lady Sengilla lowered her gaze. 'That is as I believed. However, I bring fresh orders from the Governor of this island, the noble Lord Rylan.'

The crowd of Zamatans hushed.

'Lord Rylan has decreed that all soldiers are to disembark as soon as possible,' she said, to a great roar of voices from the men on the flight deck. Lady Sengilla eyed the crowds. 'The Aucterian regiments,' she went on, 'are to report to the army headquarters in Handshore; the Bullan are to make their way to the garrison occupied by their kinsfolk at the Dragon Palace; and the Zamatans are to be temporarily demobilised, and allowed to return to their homes.'

Lahnos smiled as the roar grew in volume. Zamatans were hugging each other, and some were weeping with relief and joy.

'Hear me!' cried Sengilla, and the noise abated. 'All Zamatans enrolled in the army of the Dominion remain soldiers, and this release is conditional upon circumstances. You can go to your homes – yes; but if called upon, you will return to active duty. This is the decree of Lord Rylan.'

Lord Sigum turned to the naval officers. 'Order the frigates to dock in Handshore, and permit any small vessels to approach the fleet. Have rope ladders and nets draped over the flank of every ship containing Zamatans, and allow them to disembark.'

The officers saluted and dispersed.

Lady Sengilla stared at Sigum. 'I have orders for you, also, my old friend. Lord Rylan demands that you present yourself before his blessed presence, along with your senior officers. You may dock this vessel, along with the rest of your fleet, within the breakwaters of Handshore, but the other five dragon carriers are to remain anchored in the Cyasarta.' She narrowed her eyes. 'Are you able to fly?'

'Not yet,' said Sigum; 'but I shall have no difficulty disembarking once we have docked in Handshore. I shall walk from there to the Dragon Palace.'

Lady Sengilla tilted her head. 'Will you allow me to walk by your side?'

'I would be honoured, my lady,' said the silvery-green dragon. He turned to Lahnos. 'You shall have to wait a little longer before being reunited with your loved ones, my friend. Find a fresh, clean uniform, for you shall be accompanying us to the palace.'

Three hours later, the two dragons were striding out from the gates of Handshore Naval Base, a full company of Bullan soldiers flanking them as they walked along the wide streets of Igatz. Lahnos stayed close to the left-hand side of Lord Sigum, the only Zamatan among the party of Bullan and Aucterian officers selected to go to the Dragon Palace. They had left behind scenes of chaotic jubilation, as the Zamatans on board had scrambled down the nets and into the large array of fishing vessels and ferries that had come alongside the vessels anchored in the Cyasarta. Lahnos had helped the squad from Fidalaimos clamber onto a fishing boat. Efizel had gone with them, as he had been informed that he was not welcome to accompany the Bullan soldiers to their barracks in Igatz. Instead, Karl had promised that the villagers of Fidalaimos would look after him until Lahnos was free to rejoin them. Lahnos had embraced each of the squad in turn, and then had watched as the fishing boat had pulled away from the side of the carrier and sailed towards the crowded shoreline of Kaugatz.

A few hundred Aucterian civilians were lining the roads of Igatz as the two dragons passed, but the atmosphere was muted, and several buildings looked abandoned, their windows and doors boarded up. Repairs had been carried out following the fighting that had taken place during the brief Gunstian occupation of the town, but the roads were still rutted, after their cobbles had been ripped up to be used by catapults. The procession passed the main square, and they turned for the palace. The huge, elegant buildings of the Temple and Palace Districts were still standing, and the tower of the Temple of the Undying Serpent rose above the red-tiled rooftops. The Bullan on duty by the entrance to the palace gardens had opened the repaired gates, and they stood aside to allow Sigum and Sengilla to enter. Palace guards and staff were outside, their heads lowered as the dragons approached the gleaming white marble façade. The trees of the garden had been devastated in the Gunstian attack, and many had been replaced by young saplings, while long stretches of the lawn had also been replaced.

Lord Sigum tilted his head at the main entrance, and Lady Sengilla took the lead. She strode into the palace, and the others followed. They made their way down the vast corridors and came into the central audience chamber, where five other dragons were waiting for them. In the middle of the chamber, atop a great heap of cushions, sat a grey and yellow dragon, his wings scarred and folded in close to his body.

Lady Sengilla bowed low. 'My lord Governor,' she said, 'may I please introduce Lord Sigum Mon Sigil, the leader of the survivors from the Gunstian invasion?'

The grey and yellow dragon raised his head. 'I have met Lord Sigum before, Lady Sengilla, but I thank you for the introduction.' His eyes went to Sigum. 'My old friend, how good it is to see you again.'

'And you, Lord Rylan,' said Sigum.

Lahnos glanced at the other dragons. He recognised Lord Givra from his visit to the dragon carrier the previous day, and had been told the names of the others. Givra was glaring at Sigum, and so too was the massive black and tan male dragon to his left. On the other side of Rylan stood a female with the same colouring as the Governor, and then a much smaller male dragon stood by her side.

'Thank you, my lord,' Sigum went on, 'for allowing the Zamatan regiments to return to their homes. They fought bravely in Gunst, and served the Dominion with pride and honour.'

The black and tan dragon snorted, his eyes burning. 'That is quite the exaggeration, Lord Sigum,' he said.

Rylan glanced at him. 'Do you have anything to add, Lord Ecsin? Tell me – did you flee the field of battle before or after seeing the Zamatans fight?'

The chamber tensed, as Ecsin reared up, his jaws crackling with sparks.

'Let no one here question the bravery of Lord Sigum,' said Rylan, 'nor that of a single soldier or sailor that he has rescued from Gunst. At a stroke, Lord Sigum has brought us thousands of reinforcements, and we shall need all of them to defend this island from the approaching Gunstians.'

'Do we mean to stay here, my lord?' said Sigum.

'That is my decree,' said Rylan. 'Tell me, how many humans have you brought from the shores of Gunst?'

'The ships bore over three thousand Aucterian soldiers, my lord,' said Sigum, 'along with five and a half thousand Aucterian sailors. In addition to that, we also brought seven thousand Zamatan men back to the Serpent Isle, and a thousand Bullan.'

'Well done, my friend,' said Rylan; 'my gratitude for your courageous actions knows no bounds.' He glanced at the other dragons. 'Did you hear that? We now have an army of ten thousand to repel any invasion, and we also have a powerful fleet.'

'My noble brother,' said the dragon with the similar colouring to Rylan, 'perhaps we should reconsider our choices. Our blessed King is dead, and there may be turmoil in Inopei when the news reaches its shores. Should we remain here when the Dominion is at risk of a civil war? The coward Lord Tegru will be rallying his forces, and Nom Karta will be under threat.'

'Natali, my beloved sister,' said Rylan, 'is this island not also a part of the Dominion? Should we meekly surrender it to the Gunstians?'

Lady Natali bowed her head, saying nothing.

'This policy borders on treachery,' said Lord Ecsin. 'The throne lies empty, and yet you counsel that we remain here on this tiny outpost in the midst of the ocean? We are needed in Inopei, my lord, far more than we are needed here. Or is it your secret intention to allow the coward Lord Tegru to seize the throne?'

'Lady Famula Min Gahad was appointed regent by King Naghad,' said Rylan. 'She will govern the Dominion from its heart, while we defend its frontiers. The only treachery I discern belongs to those who fled Gunst.'

The chamber stilled as the dragons tensed again.

'I believe in second chances,' Rylan went on. 'If you wish to redeem yourselves, then look no further than the defence of this island, under my command. The Gunstian fleet will be coming soon and...'

'Yes,' cried Ecsin, 'because that fool Sigum has led them here!'

'Do not interrupt me!' roared Rylan. 'I am a Child of Gahad, and you will respect my orders!'

'There were three other Children of Gahad left here to rule the Serpent Isle,' said Ecsin; 'my blessed mother, Lord Malum, and Lady Lenta. Tell me, Governor – how was it that you were the sole survivor?'

'If I may, my lords and ladies?' said Lord Sigum. The others turned to him. 'I feel I should point out that the Imperial Gunstian Fleet intends to conquer this island, and that was their intention from the moment King Naghad fell. They pursued us, yes, but they would be coming here regardless. We have only a few days before they reach the Serpent Isle.'

'How did you evade the Gunstians in the Great Bay?' said Rylan.

'I had help, my lord,' said Sigum. He gestured with a forelimb towards Lahnos. 'This part-Bullan discovered the location of the enemy fleet, and we were able to avoid detection. We owe him our thanks.'

Lord Ecsin and Lord Givra started to laugh.

'You reveal your weakness,' said Ecsin. 'No dragon on Athumia owes the humans a thing, especially not a hybrid sub-created specimen such as this part-Bullan. How is your wing, Sigum? Are you unable to fly? Notice, my kin, how those too weak and injured to take to the skies naturally find solace in each other's company. You make a fine pair – an injured coward, and an injured Governor.'

'Shut up,' said Lahnos. 'Lord Sigum has more courage in a single talon than you possess in your entire body, you worthless lizard.'

Lord Ecsin roared in rage, and his claws flashed out. Sigum extended a forelimb, and pulled Lahnos closer to his body.

'I shall defend this human to my last breath, my noble Lord Ecsin,' said Sigum. 'Every man who arrived with me owes him his life.'

'Then you will surely perish,' cried Ecsin.

'There shall be no violence here,' said Lord Rylan, but the other dragons were no longer listening to him.

A squad of Bullan raced into the chamber.

'My lords and ladies!' their officer cried. 'Four more dragons are approaching Igatz.'

The dragons turned.

'Who?' said Lord Rylan.

'The dragon in the lead is the most noble Lady Abda Min Gahad, my lord,' the officer said.

Ecsin laughed, long and hard. 'Lady Abda? It seems that you are about to be out-ranked, Lord Rylan.'

Rylan said nothing. Instead, he stepped down from the great mound of cushions and stood next to his sister Lady Natali.

'Escort them into the palace,' Lord Ecsin said to the Bullan. 'Lady Abda shall be the new Governor of this blasted rock from the moment she alights upon its soil.' He turned to Rylan as the Bullan bowed and retreated from the chamber. 'Your brief reign as king of the Serpent Isle appears to be over,' he said. 'It is time for you to hide in obscurity again, where you belong.'

Lord Rylan remained silent, his eyes dimmed as he bowed his head.

A loud commotion came from the nearby passageways, followed by the sound of dragon claws on marble; then a huge teal dragon entered the chamber, flanked by three others.

'Lady Abda!' cried Lord Ecsin. 'My heart soars to see that you are still alive; I had lost hope that you would return safely from Gunst.'

Abda's giant head regarded each of the dragons within the chamber.

'I see that I am the senior dragon here,' she said. 'Where is Lord Malum?'

'He fell, my blessed lady,' said Ecsin, 'as did my noble mother, and Lady Lenta. Lord Rylan is all that remains of those left to govern this remote outpost.'

Abda's eyes darkened. 'They fell?' She turned to Rylan, and her eyes widened at the sight of his damaged wings. 'How did this happen, little half-brother?'

'The island was attacked by the Demon Witch, my lady,' said Rylan, keeping his gaze lowered. 'I barely survived.'

Abda let out a low strangled cry of despair. 'How I wish that it had been you who had been taken from us instead of the others! My sister Lenta, and the most noble and mighty Malum and Macsin... My heart rips within my breast. Did you catch and slay the foul Demon Witch? Tell me that you did so, for that will soothe some of my anguish.'

'He did not, my lady,' said Ecsin. 'He allowed the Witch to escape.'

Abda lowered her head. 'So, while we were suffering and dying in Gunst, young Rylan presided over another calamity? The fate of the Dominion hangs by a slender thread; but hope remains. My comrades and I were harried and delayed at every turn through our long journey from Gunst, but I was able to follow the ships led by Lord Sigum.' She turned to the silvery-green dragon. 'You did well, Sigum. You have delivered the means by which we shall be able to return with all haste to Inopei.'

Lord Sigum bowed his head. 'Thank you, my lady.'

'You should be aware, my lady,' said Ecsin, 'that Lord Rylan has ordered us to remain here to defend this island.'

Abda's eyes widened. 'Why?' She stared at Rylan. 'Why would you order such a foolish course of action? The way ahead is clear – the six dragon carriers brought here by Lord Sigum shall allow us to prevent the coward Lord Tegru from assuming power in Nom Karta.' She ascended the great mound of cushions. 'I am taking the reins of power into my own grasp with immediate effect. Here are my new orders – the fleet shall be made ready for departure at the earliest opportunity. The

Gunstians are mere days away, and it is imperative that we leave the Serpent Isle before they can attempt to blockade the Cyasarta. Every sea-worthy warship shall accompany us, along with every Bullan, and every able-bodied Aucterian soldier and sailor. We shall strip the island bare, and leave nothing behind for the Gunstians. With this taskforce, we shall sail to Nom Karta and go to Lady Famula's assistance. Is that clear?'

Every dragon bowed their head.

Lahnos slipped out from behind Sigum's forelimb and strode into the centre of the hall.

'Are you abandoning us?' he said.

The chamber fell into a complete silence.

Lady Abda glanced around, as if unsure where the dissenting voice had come from, then she lowered her gaze to Lahnos.

'A part-Bullan speaks?' she said. 'How amusing.'

'Over ten thousand Zamatans fought for the Dominion in Gunst,' Lahnos went on, 'and you are going to leave us to be slaughtered by the Gunstians? You filthy cowards – you disgust me. Go on then – run away, just like you deserted us in Gunst. Fleeing seems to be the only thing you know how to do.'

Abda laughed. 'The Gunstians would no doubt make a sport of killing you, my boy, and all others like you.' She glanced at Sigum. 'One of yours?'

'This soldier helped rescue the ships and survivors from Gunst, my lady,' Sigum said. 'Please disregard his outburst, I beg you.'

'That I cannot do,' said Abda. 'He has insulted the honour of the Royal Family, and will pay for his insolence. Bullan, place him under arrest, and hang his gutted corpse from the tower of the Temple of the Undying Serpent. Make sure the citizens can see the body.'

Several Bullan moved forward, and Sigum raised his claws.

'Are you defending this creature?' said Abda.

'His name is Lahnos Laimos,' said Sigum, 'and he is the leader of the Zamatan regiments. If you execute him, the Zamatans will rebel.'

'Do you think I care what the Zamatans do?' said Abda. 'In a few days, we shall be leaving this island, and the Gunstians can do whatever they please with it. It is of no more use to us, as we shall not be attempting to invade Gunst in the foreseeable future. Lower your claws, Sigum, and for the sake of what you did to bring the fleet here, I will forgive this lapse in judgement.'

Lahnos glanced up at Sigum's face, and saw that the dragon had resigned himself to his fate.

'There is no need,' Lahnos said. 'I surrender myself to the Bullan.'

He raised his empty hands and walked towards the soldiers, who pulled his hands down and bound them behind his back.

Abda shook her head at Sigum. 'For this folly, Lord Sigum, I command you to remain here when the fleet departs. Since you seem to love the natives of this island more than your own kin, I am sure you will derive some satisfaction from dying for them.' She turned to Rylan. 'And you, my weak little half-brother – you shall also remain here. Let two feeble flightless dragons defend this worthless rock. You can be Governor once again, and Lord Sigum shall assist you.'

Rylan said nothing, his head lowered.

The Bullan officer standing by Lahnos bowed. 'Shall we execute the prisoner, my lady?'

Abda turned back to them, and her eyes narrowed. 'Not yet. Keep him securely confined until the fleet is about to leave. There is no need to allow disorder to hinder our departure. Let it be known that he will be tortured to death if any Zamatan attempts to oppose our will; and then, just as the fleet sets sail, eviscerate him, and throw his body into the Cyasarta.'

'Yes, my lady,' said the Bullan officer. He signalled to his men, and they surrounded Lahnos and marched him out of the chamber.

'You stupid boy,' one of the Bullan muttered under his breath, as they descended a flight of stairs to the prison cells. 'This morning you were a hero, and now you're just another damned Zamatan rebel.'

Lahnos smiled. 'One day you Bullan will wake up, and realise that the dragons don't give a shit about any of you. I just hope I'm there to see it.'

CHAPTER 5
FLOTSAM DRIFTING

Medamuna Gatzoun, Serpent Isle – 19th Tuminch 1588

Cisca stared into the empty chamber. Four days had passed since Leona had abducted Lyla from the caverns under the ruins of the ancient monastery, and Cisca still struggled to believe that it had happened. What did Leona know about caring for someone as fragile and vulnerable as Major Lyla? Cisca clenched her fists with anger. How dare she? Hadn't they allowed Leona to think that she had fooled them by letting her escape? She cursed Leona's name. Sly was too polite a word to describe her – she was a devious little bitch.

Even worse, in some ways, had been Bauchlie's reaction. He had told Cisca that he didn't care what Leona had done, and that he had no interest in either tracking her down, or in attempting to rescue Lyla from the woman's clutches. Like Cisca, he harboured serious doubts about the story Leona had repeated over and over again to them – that Lyla's body was hosting the spirit of the Demon Witch; and Major Lyla meant nothing to him. As far as he was concerned, she was just another Dominion officer, and what Leona did with her was Leona's business.

Cisca sat down on the bed in the semi-darkness, and rested her head in her hands. What would her parents think of her if they could see what she had become? She had betrayed the Dominion, and for what? Her name had appeared on a list of wanted rebels and criminals, along with a reward for her capture. It was substantially less than the sum being offered for the capture of Bauchlie, but that was irrelevant. If word reached Neath, then Cisca would never be able to return home.

'I thought I might find you here.'

Cisca raised her eyes and frowned at the sight of Bauchlie standing in the doorway.

'Can you ride a horse?' he said.

'Why?'

'Don't answer my question with another question,' he said. 'Can you ride a horse?'

'Of course I can ride a damn horse.'

'Then come with me.'

He turned and disappeared into the shadows of the stairwell. Cisca thought about remaining where she was to spite him, but his words implied that she would be allowed to venture out of the caverns into the fresh air, and she longed to feel the sun on her skin. She would go, she told herself. She wouldn't speak to Bauchlie, but she would go.

She got to her feet and walked out of the room. There was no sign of Bauchlie, so she ascended the steps in the darkness, her hands on the rough rock to guide her way. She reached a higher level, and saw Bauchlie waiting for her.

'Are you still angry with me?' he said.

'Take a guess.'

'It was your idea to allow Leona to leave.'

'Is that the part you think I'm angry about?' she said. 'I'm glad Leona has gone; I couldn't stand the sight of her. But she took my friend with her – a friend that can't speak, that can't even feed herself. And you don't give a shit, do you? Admit it.'

'All right. I don't give a shit about Major Lyla. Now, do you want to know where we're going?'

'If it isn't to rescue my friend, then no, not really.'

'Have you ever been to Tzalla Pen?'

Cisca folded her arms across her chest. 'No.'

'It's another old monastery,' he said.

'I know what it is.'

'It lies on the coast, about two miles south-east of Chesson.'

'I also know where it is. Why are we going there?'

'To watch,' he said. 'Follow me.'

He led her down a dark tunnel, and they passed through several chambers filled with stores and equipment. He selected a tunnel that Cisca had never ventured down, and they came to a small room carved out of the rock, where sunlight was coming in through a narrow entrance. Two rebel fighters were on sentry duty, their crossbows slung over their shoulders, and they both glanced at Bauchlie as he entered.

'Are the horses ready?' he said.

'Yes, sir,' said one of the rebels, her eyes on the scarred commander. 'The others are waiting outside.'

Bauchlie nodded at her, then he led Cisca through the narrow opening and out into the bright late-summer sunshine. Cisca shielded her eyes for a moment as a breeze blew off the ocean down to her left, then she gasped. Sailing past the northern coast of the Serpent Isle was the largest fleet she had ever seen; larger even than the one King Naghad had taken to invade Gunst. Their sails were full, and they were surging through the waves towards the east. Cisca tried to count them, but soon gave up.

Bauchlie stood by her side. 'Quite a sight. The Imperial Gunstian Fleet – all of it.'

'But… how many…?'

'A hundred and twenty-six ships altogether,' said Bauchlie. 'Warships, troopships and supply vessels. Every one of them has been sent here with a single purpose – to return the island to Gunstian control.'

'All of that is for the Serpent Isle?'

'One day,' he said, 'you might call it Zamata.'

He turned away, and began walking down a rough track. Cisca pulled her gaze away from the enormous fleet and followed him. They walked for ten minutes through a forest of spruce, the ruins of the ancient monastery buildings poking up through the ground, moss-covered and eroded. They came to a small dell, where six horses were waiting, along with four rebel officers – two men and two women.

'Good morning, sir,' said one of the officers, as he handed Bauchlie the reins of a horse. He glanced at Cisca, and gave her the reins of the sixth horse. Cisca placed a hand onto the animal's flank, then checked the straps of the saddle and bridle.

'Let's go,' said Bauchlie, as he pulled himself up into the saddle of his horse. 'We have over ten miles to ride, and we need to get to Tzalla Pen before the Gunstians reach the Cyasarta.'

The other rebels mounted their horses, and Cisca did the same. She placed her feet into the stirrups, and gripped the reins. The horse beneath her reared a little, her hooves lifting and stamping down onto the soft earth. Cisca dug her heels in and turned the horse to face the same way as the others. Bauchlie set off at a slow trot, guiding his mount down a steep path that ran along the eastern flank of Mount Medamuna. The forest stretched on for a mile or so as they descended to the lowlands, then they appeared by the ragged coast. The six riders gazed out at the vast Gunstian fleet for a few moments, saying nothing, then Bauchlie turned again, and led them on.

They stuck by the coastal paths, passing Wayston in the distance, then bore east until the hills rose again, blocking the view of the ocean. They diverted along the hill tracks, bypassing Belton, then joined a road for a mile as it snaked its way south towards Chesson. Before they reached the town, Bauchlie took another narrow path, and led them back into the hills. Despite the proximity of the Imperial Gunstian Fleet, Cisca allowed herself to relax. A few old familiar aches and pains appeared over her body, reminders of her time as a young officer cadet when she had been trained how to ride, and memories of those happier days seemed to soothe her. She had never seen a horse until she had joined the Dominion armed forces. There were none in the slums of Naeth, and were only plentiful out by the vast estates that surrounded the Aucterian capital of Teros City. The other cadets had teased her when she had first tried to mount a horse, her inexperience obvious to all; but the Dominion demanded that every officer in the service was taught the skills required, and Cisca had been a quick learner.

Bauchlie slowed their pace again as they wound their way up into the hills above Chesson. The land on the western-facing slopes had been formed into terraces many centuries before, and was covered in vineyards and citrus groves, but the inner valleys were untilled and under-populated. Hardy patches of grass and gnarly shrubs littered the way, and they disturbed a few goats grazing on a hillside.

Bauchlie glanced over his shoulder as they headed south, and then he waited for Cisca to catch him up.

'The chains will prevent the fleet from entering the Cyasarta,' he said.

'Then what are we going to watch?' she said.

'I was given an intelligence report yesterday evening,' he went on. 'It stated that Lady Abda is planning on leaving the island today.'

Cisca frowned. 'Lady Abda Min Gahad is on the Serpent Isle?'

'She has been in Igatz for a few days,' Bauchlie said. 'She forced Lord Rylan to give up his position as Governor, and intends to use the fleet Lahnos brought here to sail back to the Dominion.' He glanced at her. 'We are going to see if she is able to escape into the ocean before the Gunstians arrive. It's going to be tight.'

'The dragons are abandoning us?'

'Your faith in those beasts never fails to surprise me, Cisca,' he said. 'Of course they are going to abandon us. Well, they are going to try. We shall see if they succeed.'

'Do you want them to succeed?'

'The ideal outcome would be for the dragons and the Gunstians to annihilate each other. If each destroys the other's ships, then Zamata will be free once more.'

Cisca rolled her eyes. 'Until the next fleet arrives.'

'Which fleet?' he said.

'I don't know. The Dominion or the Gunstians – take your pick.'

He smiled. 'That is where you are wrong, Cisca. King Naghad

gambled everything on his invasion of Gunst, and his ships and army were almost wiped out. The small number of vessels under Abda's command is all that remains of the once-mighty Northern Fleet; and the Gunstians have brought every warship they possess to the island. If every ship is sunk today, there will be no more fleets coming to Zamata for a very long time. We will have years to make the island impregnable; perhaps decades.'

'You are obsessed,' she said.

'Is freedom not a worthy obsession?'

Cisca shook her head. 'Did other dragons arrive with Lady Abda?'

'Another three, I think,' he said. 'I don't know their names, but Abda is clearly the most senior. What do you know about her?'

'I met her in Nom Karta a few times.'

He glanced at her, waiting for her to continue.

'I was assigned to one of her sons for several months,' she said; 'a Lord Labran Mon Abda. We were trying to find him a mate from among the mortal dragons living in the palace complex. Lady Abda herself seemed... well, she was as arrogant as the others, I guess. I would imagine that she was a strong supporter of King Naghad. Is Lord Rylan on board one of the dragon carriers?'

'No. Abda ordered him to stay here.'

'Ah, so even if the fleet is destroyed, there will still be at least one dragon on the island?'

'Yes, but Rylan cannot fly, and he would be alone. Killing him shouldn't be too difficult. Abda is taking every Bullan soldier with her.'

Cisca's mood fell as she and Bauchlie followed the others down the long, narrow track. If the Bullan were also leaving, then the Dominion was not only abandoning the island, it was throwing away the strategy that had been followed for centuries. Lord Rylan was being left behind as a punishment, not because Abda had any hope that he might be able to prevent the Gunstians from reclaiming the Serpent Isle. And if the island fell, what would stop the Gunstians from re-conquering Irlan and Elso? Was the entire West to be left undefended? She glanced at Bauchlie, and the anger she felt increased. The only thing he cared about was the tiny speck of land where he had been born – did he not realise what would happen if the Dominion relinquished its dreams of ruling the world? Chaos and anarchy would be the consequence, not freedom.

They came to a halt by a stand of cedar trees and dismounted. One of the rebels took the reins from Cisca, and she followed Bauchlie down a steep track to the edge of a ridge. She turned past an outcrop of rock and saw the ocean spread out to the east. To her right were the vineyards of Tzalla Pen – acres of neat terraces that filled the land between Kaugatz and the shoreline. Beyond, in the distance, lay the northern Chain Castle, and then the narrow strip of water that marked the opening of the Cyasarta. Ships were moving along the inlet, their sails billowing in the westerly breeze as they raced towards the ocean. Only the hulls of the six dragon carriers were visible from the ridge, but Cisca could pick out the masts of the other vessels of the Dominion fleet.

'Lady Abda has stripped Handshore of every warship,' said Bauchlie.

'I don't understand,' said Cisca, as she sat down on the dusty ground. 'This is a disaster. A show of strength might have scared the Gunstians away, and then Lady Abda could have departed later. Now, it will be obvious that the island is undefended. Why? Why would she do this?'

'The politics of Inopei are of more importance to her,' said Bauchlie.

'I can see that,' said Cisca; 'but she is betraying everything King Gahad stood for.'

'Gahad was an imperialist, nothing more.'

Cisca said nothing, her eyes on the Dominion ships as they navigated the straits. She remembered when Lord Rufus had sent the fleet away during the Zamatan uprising. That had been hard to accept, but she had known that they would return – it had been a tactical manoeuvre, not a complete withdrawal. And when Lord Kheran had decided to leave the Serpent Isle – that, too, she had seen as temporary. The young dragon had been traumatised by his experiences; this time, it was Lady Abda – a Child of Gahad – who had taken the decision.

Bauchlie nudged her arm and pointed to the north-east. Her gaze followed the direction of his finger, and her despair deepened. The advance ships of the Imperial Gunstian fleet were racing south – a squadron of sleek frigates, their sails full as their bows cut through the waves. Behind them, the rest of the Gunstian vessels were rounding the rocky headland. Horns were sounded, their harsh peals drifting above the crash of the waves against the shore.

'The race has begun,' said Bauchlie.

Two dragons ascended into the air over the Dominion vessels. They circled once as they gained altitude, then they turned towards the approaching Gunstian frigates. The squadron of a dozen sleek-hulled vessels were aiming for the front of the Dominion column as it emerged from the straits. They veered towards the south-west, their pace outmatching the slower dragon carriers as they tried to pick up speed. The two dragons soared down, their wings shimmering in the sunlight, and twin streams of flame exploded from their jaws down onto the ocean. Two Gunstian frigates erupted, their masts and sails enveloped in fire, and their decks washed with flame. The dragons banked as ballista bolts spat through the air, then more flames hit another pair of frigates, leaving their hulls blazing as thin pillars of smoke began to stain the sky. The rest of the squadron reached the lead vessels of the escaping Dominion fleet. They darted among the larger ships, weaving between the huge carriers as each one was targeted by the two airborne dragons.

'Such sacrifice,' said one of the rebel fighters on the ridge. 'They are giving their lives to slow down the Aucterians.'

'The Gunstians have courage,' said Bauchlie; 'the courage of their faith.'

Another pair of frigates was engulfed in flames. Sailors leapt overboard, their clothes on fire, while one of the stricken vessels steered directly into the path of a dragon carrier. The Dominion fleet began to split apart. Two carriers had a clear path to the ocean, and took it; and they started to pull away from the others by the opening of the

Cyasarta, as, all the while, the bulk of the Imperial Gunstian Fleet drew nearer. Two more dragons ascended into the air. They soared over the Dominion ships, then circled above the ever-decreasing gap between the two fleets. The Gunstian heavy battleships approached, flanked by dozens of smaller war vessels, and the dragons struck, descending like spears amid the hail of ballista bolts. Flames raked over the exposed decks of a Gunstian flagship, but the momentum of the Gunstian fleet was unstoppable, and they closed with the part of the Dominion fleet still trying to escape the straits. The four dragons in the air wheeled and banked as they attacked, and each time they soared over the Gunstians more ships erupted into flames. A piercing cry ripped through the air as the dragons turned once more, and one of the four began to tumble through the sky, its wings ripped to shreds by the sheer number of ballista bolts that had passed through them. It collided with a Gunstian frigate in an explosion of noise and fire, then both sank beneath the waves in seconds. Another dragon screamed, her cry of agony reverberating off the high cliffs to the north of Tzalla Pen; then she spiralled downwards and slammed into the vineyards stretching away from the monastery buildings, gouging a great furrow through the dry earth.

The two dragon carriers that had fled through the gap in the Gunstian lines were pulling away from the mass of tangled vessels blocking the entrance of the Cyasarta; then a third carrier broke free, striking out for the south-east, as the Gunstian fleet surrounded what remained. None of the Gunstian ships made any attempt to pursue the Dominion vessels that had escaped the encirclement; instead, they concentrated on annihilating those who had fallen into their trap. Two more dragons took to the skies, joining the two still flying above the battle. One was brought down within seconds by the incessant hail of ballista bolts loosed by the Gunstian battleships, and he crashed into the deck of the carrier from which he had ascended. The other dragons aloft turned east in an attempt to flee in the direction of the carriers that had managed to escape, but the storm of ballistae bolts being loosed by the Gunstians was impenetrable, and all three were forced westward, soaring over the carnage at the mouth of the Cyasarta towards the safety of Igatz.

The Gunstians tightened the noose, their warships coming alongside the doomed Dominion vessels. Two of the remaining carriers were trapped in the centre of the massed tangle of vessels, but the one that had been the last to leave the inlet managed to execute a turn, and retreated back into the straits. Two Dominion destroyers moved into its wake, blocking the Gunstians from pursuing the fleeing carrier as it sailed back towards the chains. A battleship rammed one of the destroyers, its reinforced bow slicing through the beams along the ship's starboard flank and sinking it; but the retreating carrier reached the safety of the straits unharmed, the chains rising through the waves as soon as it had passed the two castles.

The rest of the fleet was picked off one by one. The two trapped dragon carriers held out the longest, the sailors and Bullan soldiers on board resisting to the end; but both went down, their sterns rising clear of the waves as each succumbed to the iron rams bolted onto the bows of the Gunstian battleships. A Dominion frigate attempted to surrender but it, too, was rammed beneath the waterline, and it sank in seconds.

'The battle is over,' said Bauchlie.

'The Dominion did better than I'd expected,' said a rebel fighter. 'Three of their carriers escaped into the ocean.'

'And a fourth is back in the Cyasarta,' said another fighter, 'along with three damn dragons.'

'Abda would have been on the lead carrier,' said Bauchlie. 'She could have saved more of the fleet had she risen into the air, but she preferred to live. Getting back to Inopei was all she cared about.'

'I counted at least two dozen Gunstian vessels destroyed.'

'It wasn't enough,' said Bauchlie. 'It was nowhere near enough.'

Cisca said nothing as the others talked, her gaze on the flotsam drifting over the mouth of the Cyasarta. Over a dozen vessels were on fire, while many more had disappeared forever beneath the waves. Gunstian vessels were sailing around, picking up the survivors from their own fleet from the water; while several had moved into a blocking formation a few hundred yards to the east of the chains. The carrier that had retreated into the straits had come to a halt a mile from Igatz – safe, but trapped within the inner waters of the Serpent Isle.

Thousands had died in less than an hour – burned to death, drowned, or struck down by bolts loosed from the decks of the warships.

'What a waste,' Cisca said. 'All those young sailors; and for what? This speck in the ocean? I hate this island.'

One of the fighters glared at her. 'Then maybe the Dominion should have left us alone in the first place, Aucterian. They had no right to be here.'

'You would rather be ruled by the Gunstians?'

'They don't belong here, either,' the fighter said.

Cisca swept her hand out in the direction of the dozens of Gunstian vessels anchored by the mouth of the Cyasarta. 'And yet here they are. What's your plan now, Bauchlie? Are you going to close your eyes and just hope the Gunstians decide to go home?'

'How dare you?' said one of the fighters. 'You Aucterian imperialists are all the same; you think you own this island. Bitch.'

'Leave her,' said Bauchlie. 'Cisca has earned the right to speak her mind. Thousands of her kinfolk from the East have just died in front of her; do not forget that.'

'You didn't answer my question,' said Cisca. 'What are you going to do?'

'The same as I have always done, Cisca,' he said. 'Resist.'

He got to his feet and turned his back to the ocean. He nodded to the other rebel fighters, and they began to make their way back up the steep slope towards the glade of cedars, where they had tied up the horses. Cisca remained where she was, her gaze on the bodies rising and falling on the ocean waves. The sound of lamentation reached her ears, and she glanced down. Monks had left the monastery buildings of Tzalla Pen, and had gathered round the corpse of the dragon that had crashed into the vineyards. The dragon's long neck had broken as she had landed, and her wings were splayed out at an awkward angle.

'Are you coming?'

Cisca turned, and saw Bauchlie waiting for her.

'Where?' she said.

'Back to Medamuna Gatzoun,' he said. 'Where else?'

'Maybe you should leave me here,' she said. 'I could walk to Kaugatz and get a ferry across to Igatz.'

'You are wanted by the Dominion authorities,' he said. 'You would be arrested.'

'So? It's over, Bauchlie. The dragons have gone, and the Gunstians are knocking on the front door.'

'Do not despair,' he said. 'There is always a way.'

'Not this time,' she said. 'Nothing can defeat the Gunstians. They will keep attacking until the island is theirs.'

Bauchlie extended his hand. 'I want you to come back with us,' he said.

'No, you don't. Your cause is all you care about. Compared to that, I mean nothing to you.'

'You are wrong,' he said.

She narrowed her eyes at him, then took his hand, and he pulled her to her feet. For a moment, she thought he was going to say something else, then he turned, and climbed up the track.

Cisca turned back to gaze at the mouth of the Cyasarta, then she lowered her eyes, and followed Bauchlie.

CHAPTER 6
A HEADACHE

Igatz, Serpent Isle – 19th Tuminch 1588

Leona moved through the thick crowds lining the shore of Igatz. Hundreds of Aucterian settlers were mingling with local Zamatans as each tried to catch a glimpse of the sole returning dragon carrier. The news of the battle that had taken place by the mouth of the Cyasarta had spread through the town, and the mood of the spectators was grim and nervous. Leona had her head uncovered, despite the advice given to her by Farakai. The agent had advised her to wear a hood whenever she ventured out of the house in Kaugatz, but Leona believed that such a garment would only serve to increase suspicion. When the colonel had walked the streets of either Igatz or Kaugatz, he had been recognised by many, but very few people knew what Leona looked like; and she felt safer than she had when she had been in the guise of Lady Takri.

Leona pushed her way past a small group of Aucterians and gazed at the sight of the dragon carrier as it sailed towards Handshore Naval Base. Apart from a few companies of Bullan soldiers, its long flight deck was empty. Three dragons were also rumoured to have survived the battle, excluding the ones who had managed to flee across the ocean, and Leona wondered who had made it back to Igatz.

Despite the air of anxiety drifting over the crowd, no one was weeping or lamenting the losses incurred during the battle. Lady Abda Min Gahad had abandoned everyone on the island, and that included the Aucterian settlers. Leona tried to imagine how they were feeling. For decades, the Dominion had encouraged the colonisation of Zamata by Aucterians; but they had been deserted in the moment of crisis, left behind among tens of thousands of native Zamatans.

Leona turned away from the shore and walked towards the centre of Igatz, wondering if she should still attempt to deliver the letter in her pocket. Like many on the island, she had assumed that Lords Rylan and Sigum would be the only dragons remaining in Igatz; but with the three who had retreated from the battle to contend with, Rylan's position as Governor was once again under threat. She slowed as she entered a small plaza ringed with palm trees, then she took a seat on a bench under the shade. She removed a book from her bag, and read while she waited.

Barely a minute had passed before an old man sat down on the bench next to her. He didn't look in her direction, but he also began reading from a book.

'Is he alive?' Leona whispered.

'Yes, ma'am,' said the old man. 'Lord Rylan has had him moved, though.'

'Where?'

'Zamata Gataza, ma'am. I heard Rylan with my own ears. He countermanded the execution order, and had the lad relocated instead. He'd already left the palace by the time the other dragons arrived.'

'And three have returned, yes?'

'That's right, ma'am. Three were on ships that managed to break through the Gunstian lines and get away; three were killed, and three have returned.'

'Do you have their names?'

'Yes, ma'am,' whispered the old man. 'Abda, Labran and Ecsin got away; Brotan, Gallus and Sengilla were slain; and Gradham, Givra and Natali have returned to the palace.'

'Has Rylan managed to retain control?'

'For now, ma'am. He is the most senior of them, and he has his sister to support him.'

'What does he plan to do about the Gunstian fleet?'

'I don't know, ma'am. The dragons were discussing it, but I had to leave in order to meet you here.'

'I'll let you go, then,' she said. She reached into a pocket and slid the letter across the bench. 'But first, take this, and deliver it to Rylan as soon as possible. Don't compromise your position, but ensure that no dragon sees this letter other than Rylan himself. Is that possible?'

'Yes, ma'am. I shall leave it where his personal aide will find it.'

'Thank you. Contact Farakai if there is a reply from Rylan, and he will arrange the meeting.'

The old man said nothing more. He placed the letter into the pages of his book, closed it, then rose to his feet and walked away. Leona waited a few minutes, then stood and walked in the opposite direction. She took a street that led to the deserted Fortress of Hortz, then turned left towards the Temple of the Undying Serpent, her mind going over everything the agent had told her.

Lahnos was still alive, though it puzzled her that Rylan had sent him to the monastery of Zamata Gataza. The monks there would no doubt be unsettled by the arrival of a part-Bullan prisoner, and none would wish to go near him; maybe that was the reason, she thought. As for the dragons, she was pleased that Abda and Ecsin had both left the island, as either would have tried to usurp Rylan's authority. She went over the three who had returned. Lady Natali presented no problems. As Rylan's younger full sister, she would be obligated to obey his orders. Lord Givra, on the other hand, had made his contempt for Rylan clear, and would need to be eliminated as quickly as possible. And Lord Gradham? Leona knew nothing about him, except that he had arrived at the same time as Lady Abda. She should have asked the agent about him, but that would have to wait. If Gradham was a mortal dragon, then his presence could be contained, but if he was a member of the Royal

Family, then he might decide to align himself with Givra. The possibilities were endless.

She reached the large open plaza in front of the temple, and passed by the monks standing by the front door. Leona knew she could pass for Aucterian, and none of the monks glanced in her direction as she entered the huge building. Like the spectators by the shore, the monks had also been abandoned by Lady Abda, and their unhappiness was evident in their hushed conversations by the main nave. Leona made her way to a small side chapel dedicated to Lady Nightsheen, King Gahad's second mate, and the mother of Abda and Tirna. She took a seat close to the front of the shrine, next to a young woman wearing a head scarf. Neither woman looked at each other, but both knelt and bowed their heads before the bronze statue of Nightsheen.

'Lahnos is alive,' Leona whispered. 'Rylan rescinded the execution order.'

The young woman kneeling next to her exhaled.

'There is a slight complication,' Leona went on. 'Rylan has had him moved to Zamata Gataza. I don't know why. If I had to guess, it is that his presence in Igatz might enflame the men of the Zamatan regiments. They would riot if they knew he was being held in the Dragon Palace.'

'Will he be safe in the monastery?' Reyn whispered.

'I imagine so. I would advise against trying to rescue him.'

Reyn narrowed her eyes. 'Why? We rescued you from Zamata Gataza.'

'I know, but it would be better if Rylan releases him without the rebels trying anything.'

'Better for who, Leona? You?'

'Better for the island, Reyn. You will have to trust me on this. A rescue attempt would ruin everything I am trying to achieve.'

'If they hurt him, I will come after you.'

'I know you will.'

'You have two days to do whatever it is that you are trying to do,' said Reyn. 'After that, I am getting Lahnos out of there. Do you understand?'

Leona nodded, then she got to her feet and left the side chapel. She passed the groups of whispering monks and emerged back into the strong sunlight of the Temple District. She walked past the repaired fence surrounding the Dragon Palace, and joined a small crowd of Aucterians who were staring into the gardens. Leona peered through the fence and saw a dragon in the sky over the palace, flying west from the direction of the Chain Castles. Her colouring was a brownish-grey with yellow streaks, and she began to descend into the gardens as the Aucterians gazed through the bars of the fence.

'Lady Natali,' one of the onlookers said.

'My lady!' another cried. 'Please! My lady!'

The dragon landed on a re-laid patch of lawn, and spoke to a few uniformed officers.

'My lady! Are we under attack?' one of the Aucterians called out.

Natali's head turned, and she gazed down at the group of humans crowded on the other side of the fence.

'We are safe, humans,' the dragon said. 'My brother the Governor will defend this island. The chains are holding.'

More Aucterians cried out, filling the air with their questions, but Natali turned away and strode towards the palace. She stopped when she reached the wide stairs leading up to the main entrance, as two more dragons appeared under the arched opening. The little crowd of Aucterians cheered at the sight of Lord Rylan, while next to him stood Lord Sigum. The three dragons conferred for a few moments, then Rylan and Sigum descended the steps into the garden.

'I think his lordship is going to talk to us,' cried an onlooker.

Leona tensed a little, and got ready to move away in case Rylan glanced in her direction.

'Don't talk rubbish,' said another Aucterian onlooker. 'He doesn't care about people like us.'

'His sister spoke to us; and what else would he be doing outside?'

Leona edged into the shadows and remained quiet as she watched the two male dragons speaking to each other on the lawn of the palace. A single Bullan squad was standing guard – the personal protection unit left behind by Abda when she had taken the rest of the Bullan with her on board the ships – and they were told by Rylan to stand back. The Bullan retreated a little, then Rylan extended his wings, his features grimacing as he did so. The crowd gasped, and then cheered as Rylan beat his wings and rose into the air. He ascended a few yards, then managed to circle once over the gardens before alighting again.

'Did you see that?' cried an Aucterian. 'He can fly again – Lord Rylan can fly.'

Natali joined Sigum and her brother on the lawn, and the three dragons leaned their heads together for a hushed conversation. Leona slipped away from the cheering crowd, and turned towards the nearest ferry terminal.

One hour later, Leona arrived back at her house in Kaugatz. Following Farakai's advice, she entered through the yard at the rear of the building, and walked into the kitchen, where her new housekeeper was chopping vegetables.

The old woman bowed her head. 'Ma'am.'

'Good afternoon, Kamasta,' said Leona, as she took off her coat. 'Anything to report?'

'Saewa was looking for you an hour ago, ma'am,' said the quarter-Gunstian housekeeper.

'Did he say what he wanted?'

'No, ma'am. He said he would come round later.'

Leona took a seat. 'And how has Lyla been?'

'She hasn't given me any trouble today, ma'am. Perhaps she is getting used to me. You know, it would help if I knew what was wrong with the girl.'

'I don't really know what's wrong with her,' said Leona. 'I am hoping that her memories will return. Has she spoken at all?'

Kamasta shook her head, her gaze on the onions in front of her. 'No, ma'am; though I'd swear that she was trying to say "I hate you" this morning.'

'Sorry about that.'

'That's fine. I think she hates you, too, ma'am.'

'I think you might be right. Did she eat any lunch?'

'Yes. Her appetite is the one thing I'd say is improving, ma'am. I put the plate of food in front of her, and she shovelled it into her mouth with her bare hands. I sat back and watched, and then I tried to show her how to use a fork, but she was having none of it. I also got her to put some weight onto her feet.'

'Why?'

Kamasta gave Leona a sideways look. 'I don't think we should be neglecting that aspect of her recovery, ma'am. Do you want her to be bedridden for the rest of her days? If I'm right, and her affliction is all in her mind, then we need to exercise her body; otherwise her muscles'll waste away.'

'Yes. That's a good idea. I should have realised it myself, but I was too busy thinking about her memories. Please continue with that. Was she able to stand?'

'She was unsteady, and she didn't like it; but yes. Do you know anything about her family, ma'am? It might be useful to prompt her with the right questions if we want her to remember things.'

'I'm afraid not. I think she was quite a secretive person.'

Kamasta nodded. 'She was an enemy, wasn't she, ma'am?'

'Why do you say that?'

'Well, you don't seem overly fond of her; all you're interested in, if you don't mind me saying, are her memories. So, I'm guessing that she bumped her head, or something like that; only she knows things that you want to know – and that's why she's here, and not in some infirmary with the monks looking after her.'

Leona said nothing for a moment, then she shook her head. 'No. She was... someone who was trying to help us – to help Zamata. I didn't know her very well, and she wasn't my friend; but she's not an enemy.' She got to her feet. 'I think I'll pay her a visit.'

'Dinner will be at the usual time, ma'am,' said Kamasta. 'Fish and vegetables again.'

'How was the market? Still stocked?'

Kamasta nodded. 'It had a few things, but no bread; and the prices... It's lucky you're rich, ma'am; that's all I'm saying.'

Leona walked from the kitchen and went to the room that had previously been used as a small study. A mattress had been placed against the wall where the desk had been, and Lyla was lying on it with a blanket covering her body. She was holding her hands above her head, and was staring at them as if she had never seen them before.

'Hello,' Leona said, as she entered.

Lyla ignored her.

Leona closed the door and sat in an old armchair. 'How are you?'

Lyla glanced at her. 'Sisss kaa?'

'No,' said Leona. 'Cisca isn't here. Do you remember your family? Your mother? Father? Did you have any brothers or sisters?'

Lyla stared at her, her eyes narrow.

'I had a sister once,' Leona said. She smiled. 'You know, I've never told anyone that before; not even the colonel. She died when I was little, and I have only a few memories of her. She looked after me for a while. She was tough, but she was kind, too.'

'Sisss kaa?'

'Do you remember Cisca before your... accident?'

Lyla gazed at Leona in confusion.

'You were friends with Cisca before you lost your memories,' Leona went on, 'but your new memories, if you have any, won't include her. Do you remember my name? No? Do you remember anyone else's name?'

Lyla opened her mouth. 'Aan... annoss.'

Leona leaned forward in her chair. 'Lahnos? You remember Lahnos?'

Lyla clenched her fists, then she extended the index finger on each hand and raised them to her head.

Leona frowned, then she laughed. 'He has horns,' she said. 'That's right; Lahnos has horns coming out of the top of his head.' She got to her feet. 'I have an idea.'

She went to the corner of the room, where the colonel's old desk was squeezed in among a few crates and boxes. She rummaged around in a desk drawer and removed some sheets of yellowed paper and a charcoal pencil. She sat back down again with the paper on her lap, and drew a rough outline of a head with horns, then wrote *Lahnos* underneath. She held it up to show Lyla.

'Lahnos,' she said.

'Laa-noss.'

'Yes. Lahnos Laimos. I hope to see him soon and, if I do, I will ask if he wants to come here to visit you. Would you like that?'

Lyla started to cry, but something had changed. Instead of the usual anguished sobs of rage or frustration, her tears seemed to Leona as though they had sprung from a sense of relief that, at last, she had managed to communicate something.

'Lahnos,' Lyla said again, though it came out a little clearer than before.

'I will ask him. I promise,' said Leona. She hesitated for a moment. 'I'm sorry. I haven't been a very good friend to you since you got here. Zamata is in deep trouble, and my mind has been occupied with a hundred plans and schemes.'

'Saa-maa-taa.'

'Zamata,' said Leona. 'That's the name of the island where we are. But did you already know that? Can you remember your own name?'

Lyla blinked twice, then seemed to grow angry. Her fists clenched again, and she made a strange, almost guttural, growling sound. Leona prepared herself for another scream, but Lyla seemed to calm herself, and her body relaxed.

'I wish I could help you more,' Leona said. 'I can see how frustrated you are. There are things going on inside your head that you want to tell me, but you can't remember how. Why don't you just listen for a while? Don't try to speak – just listen, and I'll talk to you about Zamata, and the other events going on in the world. Maybe we've been trying to talk to you as though you were a small child, so, instead, I'll speak to you adult to adult. Would you like that?'

Lyla blinked once.

. . .

Leona spent the next two hours talking. She spoke about the history of the island, and how it had become a prize to be fought over by Athumia's two largest empires. She detailed a few of the Gifts of Theodora, and went over Gahad's conquest of the lands that later became the Dominion. For the whole time, Lyla lay and said nothing, her eyes watching Leona from the mattress. Leona reached back further in time, and outlined the old legends regarding Gahad's first appearance on Athumia.

'It was a god called Nathaniel,' she said; 'that was his name. He turned Gahad into a dragon. Well, not exactly. He placed Gahad's... um, essence? His nature? I'm not sure how to explain it, but Gahad became a dragon, thanks to Nathaniel. I don't know if Nathaniel is a real god...'

Lyla gripped the blanket, the muscles in her face straining. 'He... is... dead,' she gasped.

Leona's eyes widened. 'What was that? Who is dead?'

'Na... Na... Nat...'

'Nathaniel?'

Lyla blinked once.

'Oh. I wasn't expecting that. The dragons would be quite upset to know that Nathaniel was dead; well, I think they would. What about Theodora? Have you heard of her?'

'Dead,' gasped Lyla.

'She's dead, too?' said Leona, raising an eyebrow. 'I wouldn't mention that in front of any Gunstians.'

There was a soft rap on the entrance to the study, and Leona turned to see the door open.

'Ma'am,' said Kamasta, 'Saewa is here to see you.'

'Thank you,' said Leona. 'Show him into the sitting room and I'll be there in a moment.'

'Right you are, ma'am,' said the housekeeper.

Leona stood as Kamasta left the room. 'I'm glad we've had the chance to spend more time together,' she said to Lyla. 'Once I've dealt with whatever Saewa wants, I'll try to come back. Would you like that?'

Lyla blinked, then opened her mouth. 'Yes.'

Leona smiled. She placed the paper and the charcoal onto the mattress next to Lyla, then walked out of the room. There were dozens of items on her mental list of things she needed to be doing, but she had no regrets about spending so much time with Lyla. She glanced out of the window at the position of the setting sun as she strode to the sitting room, then she walked in. Saewa was standing by the cold hearth, and next to him was a young girl.

'Good evening, Saewa,' Leona said. 'Is this your daughter?'

The man frowned. 'I don't have a daughter.'

The young girl snorted. 'He's not my father.'

'I didn't mean to offend either of you,' said Leona, suppressing a smile. 'Take a seat.'

'I think I'll stand, if it's all the same, miss,' said Saewa. He gestured towards the girl. 'I'm here to deliver her to you.'

'What was that?' said Leona. 'I... I wasn't expecting anyone to be... delivered here.'

'Farakai told me to bring her. And, frankly, the sooner she's off my hands, the better.'

'I have a name,' said the girl.

Leona smiled, then she paused. Did the girl have a Gunstian accent? 'Why would Farakai ask you to bring her here?' she said.

'You'd be better off asking Farakai that question, miss,' said Saewa. 'Anyway, I'd better go. I'll slip out the back.'

He nodded at Leona, then left the room.

Leona and the girl eyed each other for a few moments.

'How old are you?' said Leona.

'Eight,' said the girl. 'How old are you?'

'Twenty.'

'You're Gifted,' said the girl.

'Who told you that?'

'No one. I can sense it. I'm Gifted, too. Do you like Gunstians?'

'You are Gifted? The Gift of Kenning?'

'Answer my question – do you like Gunstians?'

'Not the ones currently besieging the island,' Leona said, 'but I have nothing against those Gunstians who already live on Zamata.'

The girl raised a hand to her head. 'Ow. You liar! If you lie to me again I'll run out this house and you'll never find me.'

Leona narrowed her eyes. 'I am actually thirty-five years old.'

The girl cried out again as though she was in pain. Tears came from her eyes, and she stared at Leona with pure loathing.

'Can you...?' said Leona. 'Do you have the Gift of Truth; but it hurts?'

'Please don't lie again,' sobbed the girl.

'I won't,' said Leona. 'I'm sorry.'

'Doesn't your Gift hurt?' said the girl.

'No.'

The girl squinted at her.

'So,' said Leona, 'you have the Gift of Kenning *and* the Gift of Truth?'

The girl shrugged.

'Sit down,' said Leona. 'Are you hungry? Do you like fish?'

'No,' said the girl, as she took a seat.

Leona sat on a chair a few yards away, while the girl eyed her warily.

'Let's talk,' said Leona. 'Why are you here? What is your name?'

The girl glanced away. 'My mother and father are dead.'

'Go on.'

'The demon dragons killed them.'

'Were they both Gunstian?'

'Yes. Like me.'

'And what happened then?'

'I hid.'

'And then?'

'Someone found me. They didn't like me. They said I scared them, so one of them told another one to bring me here. Are you going to look after me now?' She glanced around the room. 'I have one rule.'

'What rule?'

She stared at Leona. 'No lies.'

'You didn't tell me your name.'

'Who else lives here?'

'Kamasta, the housekeeper,' said Leona; 'and Lyla.'

'Ow!' the girl cried, placing both hands to the side of her head.

'That's what we call her,' said Leona, raising her palms. 'Damn it; sorry. It's not her real name, and I should have realised that you would see it as a lie. I didn't mean it.'

The girl sobbed for a moment, then wiped her eyes. 'What is her real name?'

'I don't know.'

'If I'm going to be living here, then I want to meet her.'

'Tell me your own name, and I'll take you to see her.'

'It's Ingla.'

Leona's head tingled. 'No, it's not. Tell me your real name.'

The girl frowned. 'I was trying to make your head hurt. Why doesn't it hurt when I lie?'

'I told you; my head never hurts when someone lies. It tingles; that's all. I didn't know that the Gift of Truth could make someone's head hurt.'

'People lie too much,' the girl said. 'My head is always hurting.'

'That sounds awful. Tell me your name.'

'Fine,' the girl said, as though she didn't care. 'It's Arrosa.'

'Thank you, Arrosa. Do you have any luggage?'

The girl nodded to a small leather bag tied with string that was sitting on the floor. 'Where am I going to sleep?'

'I don't know.'

'You don't want me here, do you?'

Leona hesitated and, for the first time in her life, she appreciated what it was like to be in the presence of someone who possessed the Gift of Truth.

'Your arrival has surprised me,' she said. 'I wasn't expecting this, and

I will need some time to adjust. Come on; I'll take you to... the person we call Lyla.'

They rose to their feet, and then Leona shepherded the girl through the ground floor of the house to the study. She opened the door, and they entered. Lyla looked up from several sheets of old paper that she had spread out on the mattress in front of her. A few had charcoal markings on them, but Leona could see nothing that made any sense to her.

'This is Arrosa,' she said.

Lyla stared blankly at the girl.

'Why do you live here?' said Arrosa. 'What's your real name?'

Lyla said nothing.

'Is something wrong with her?' said Arrosa. 'Can't she speak?'

'She can speak a little,' said Leona. 'She's learning, or rather, she's re-learning how to.'

Arrosa nodded, then she walked over and picked up a sheet of scrawled-on paper from the bed. Lyla snatched it off her, then Arrosa snatched it back.

'Don't fight,' said Leona.

A small cough sounded behind her, and Leona turned.

'You have another visitor, ma'am,' said Kamasta. 'Farakai this time.'

'Good,' said Leona. 'I need to speak to him.' She glanced at Lyla and Arrosa. 'I'll be back soon. Behave.'

She left the room, leaving the door open a few inches so that she would hear if a quarrel broke out, then she and the housekeeper walked to the rear of the townhouse.

'Will that young girl be staying, ma'am?' said Kamasta.

'That is a very good question,' said Leona; 'and one I intend to ask Farakai.'

They went to the kitchen, and found the agent leaning against the doorway.

'You have some explaining to do,' said Leona.

'Saewa just gave me the news,' Farakai said. 'Apologies, ma'am; he was supposed to wait for me before bringing the girl here.'

'It was a little awkward,' said Leona. 'Why here? What makes you think I have the time or inclination to look after an eight-year-old girl? I already have Lyla on my hands.'

'Sorry, ma'am,' said Farakai. 'There was nowhere else she could go. We've moved her about from house to house, but it has never worked out. Did she tell you what happened to her parents?'

'Yes; but this is not an orphanage.'

'The only orphanages on Zamata are run by monks, ma'am; and we could hardly send her to one of those places. You know how they feel about us Gunstians, especially the Gifted ones. I had her in my house for a while, but my wife couldn't stand it any more. Whereas you... well, you share the same Gift as her, ma'am. I thought that you might know how to deal with her. We couldn't leave her to roam the streets on her own.'

'You found her on the streets?'

'Not personally, ma'am. A lad I know in western Kaugatz discovered her raking through the bins in his back yard. He took pity on her. Could you please try – just for a while? You and I both know what it's like to live on the streets.'

'This is emotional blackmail, Farakai.'

'But you have a housekeeper, ma'am; and you have money. Perhaps the girl can keep Lyla company while you're out.'

Leona rubbed her forehead.

'She knows how to read and write, ma'am; she could teach Lyla,' Farakai went on. 'And the Zamatans... I think that... well, I think they owe the surviving Gunstians some charity for what happened to them. The girl's entire community has been wiped out, and things are going to get tougher, what with the Imperial Gunstian Fleet sitting outside the Cyasarta. Please, ma'am?'

'Very well,' said Leona. 'For a trial period – that's all I'm promising. If it doesn't work out, we can send her to Medamuna Gatzoun and let Bauchlie look after her.'

Farakai frowned.

'I'm joking,' said Leona. 'Do you want to see her before you go?'

'No, thanks, ma'am. She and I didn't exactly see eye to eye. I kept making her head hurt.'

'Fine. You'd better go, as I need to make sure that Lyla and Arrosa aren't scratching each other's eyes out. You owe me a favour for this, Farakai.'

The agent smiled, nodded, then slipped out into the darkness of the evening.

'Shall I prepare an extra plate for dinner, ma'am?' said Kamasta.

'That sounds like a sensible idea,' said Leona; 'and we'll need to find her somewhere to sleep. Let's put her in the main bedroom for now. She has a bag in the sitting-room; could you please take it upstairs?'

The housekeeper suppressed a grimace with some effort. 'Yes, ma'am.'

Leona strode back through the house, then listened for a moment at the door to the study. No shouting or crying was coming from within, so she opened the door. Arrosa was sitting on the mattress next to Lyla, the charcoal stick in her hand.

'And this is a goat,' Arrosa said, pointing to her drawing. 'Say *goat*.'

'Go... go... goat,' gasped Lyla.

Arrosa smiled, then she glanced up at Leona. 'Go away,' she said; 'we're busy.'

Leona raised an eyebrow. 'I'll call you when dinner is ready.'

'All right,' said Arrosa, but her attention had already drifted to the next little picture she was sketching for Lyla.

Leona smiled, then she retreated from the room.

CHAPTER 7
BURYING THE PAST

Zamata Gataza, Serpent Isle – 20th Tuminch 1588

The low droning of the monks' lamentations had kept Lahnos awake all night. The thick walls of the monastery were muffling the words, but there was no doubting the emotion they were conveying – it was grief. Lahnos hadn't seen any monks since he had arrived in the back of a guarded carriage on the previous day, but he had heard their intertwined voices mourn unceasingly for their fallen gods.

What would it be like, Lahnos wondered, to see beings you imagined to be all-powerful and immortal deities dying in front of you? How could it be possible to witness such things and retain your faith? It was different for the Gunstians – they worshipped a hidden invisible goddess; one whose existence was impossible to prove; but whose death was equally impossible to comprehend. For the followers of the serpent religion, their gods were made of flesh, scales and blood. It seemed ironic to Lahnos, as he lay on the cell's hard mattress, that the Gunstians had failed to destroy the beliefs of the Zamatans despite centuries of forced conversions and the suppression of their faith; no – all it had taken to prove the weakness of the serpent dogma was for the dragons to come to the island in person. Dragons could die, and that simple fact was wiping away a thousand years of faith. Had the Demon Witch not slain King Gahad, the serpent religion might have lasted another millennium, complacent and undisturbed in its certitudes.

The endless song of grief coming from the monks quietened a little. It didn't cease altogether, but its volume lessened, and Lahnos sat up, listening. More sounds came from the courtyard in front of the ten-storey building clinging on to the side of the cliff – the sound of movement. Lahnos got to his feet then stood on the narrow stone bench that ringed the cell. He peered out of the window slit and saw clouds drifting across the blue sky. He had no view of the courtyard, but the noises rising up from it grew clearer. Some of the monks were down there, and they were preparing for something. Lahnos wondered what it could be, then he saw a tiny speck in the sky. It soared down from the clouds, growing larger with every second, and its outline was unmistakeable – a dragon.

Lahnos watched the shape as it increased in size – the extended wings catching the rays of the afternoon sunshine. It was impressive, that was impossible to deny; godlike and terrible, beautiful and deadly. The dragon descended as it neared the mountainside where Zamata Gataza sat, and Lahnos recognised his grey and yellow colouring. It was Lord Rylan. When Lahnos had last seen the Governor of the island five days before, he had been unable to fly. He had stated that his injuries had been inflicted by the Demon Witch in the same confrontation that had claimed the lives of Malum and Macsin, and yet the dragon fast approaching the monastery was definitely him. He soared close to the window slit then descended out of sight, and the monks in the courtyard began a subdued song of praise for the god in their presence.

Lahnos stepped down from the window and sat on the bench. Had the grey and yellow dragon come to carry out Lady Abda's orders? The mighty daughter of Gahad had taken the ships of the fleet, and almost every dragon, and had set sail the previous day. Soldiers had then come to Lahnos's cell under the Dragon Palace, and he had believed that his execution was about to take place, but, instead, he had been bundled into a carriage and sent away.

He glanced at the cell door. If they came to kill him, he would resist.

It would be futile, but he would do it all the same. There would be no begging or weeping; he would fight to the end.

A key turned, the door swung open, and Lahnos leapt to his feet. He charged into the small group of Aucterian soldiers standing by the doorway, his head down. His right fist cracked off a chin, then the soldiers were on him, pushing him to the floor of the cell. Hands held him down, and his arms were twisted behind his back as he struggled.

'Stay still, lad,' one of the soldiers grunted.

Lahnos lashed out with his feet, and kicked one of the crouching soldiers in the stomach.

'Lahnos Laimos,' came a voice from the doorway, 'your execution order has been rescinded. There is no need to struggle.'

'You're lying,' Lahnos cried.

'Lord Rylan wishes to speak to you,' said the voice.

Lahnos glanced up, and saw an older Aucterian man wearing the uniform of a Dominion officer.

'What about Lady Abda?' Lahnos said. 'I heard her orders.'

'Lady Abda has departed the island,' said the officer. 'Lord Rylan is in charge again.' He gestured to the soldiers pinning Lahnos to the cell floor. 'Release him.'

The soldiers moved away, and Lahnos rolled onto his back, his wrists bound behind him.

'If you resist again,' said the officer, 'we shall be forced to bind your ankles and place a hood over your head.'

Lahnos narrowed his eyes. 'If this is a trick…'

'There's no trick,' said the officer. 'I was in Gunst, lad; I was one of those who survived on the ships that escaped with Lord Sigum. I know what you did. Everyone knows. If we execute you, every damn Zamatan on this island will riot.'

'You were in Gunst?'

The officer nodded. 'Every soldier guarding this monastery was on those ships, lad.'

'The dragons left you here?'

'Yes, lad; they did. They tried to take all of the Bullan, too, but they left a few Aucterians here.'

'What do you mean they *tried* to take them?' said Lahnos. 'I thought they had gone?'

'Three carriers made it past the Imperial Gunstian Fleet, lad,' said the officer; 'two were sunk, and one limped back to Handshore.'

'The Gunstian fleet arrived?'

'It certainly did, lad. Have you calmed yourself down now? If we loosen the cords binding your wrists will you try to punch us again?'

Lahnos eyed the soldiers in the cell, then he shook his head. The officer nodded to a sergeant, who leaned over Lahnos and untied the cords. Lahnos rubbed his wrists, then got to his feet.

'The Governor is down in the front courtyard,' said the officer. 'Follow me.'

The soldiers led Lahnos out of the cell, and they walked along a narrow passageway that ran the length of the monastery. They descended a set of stairs at the end and came into a large entrance hall. Double doors were lying open, letting in the fresh air, while the sound of the monks' lamentations grew, as if it was coming from somewhere below the ground level. A few monks were standing by the double doors, but none glanced in Lahnos's direction. The officer led the way, and the soldiers escorted Lahnos past the doors and into the open air. The courtyard was large, with a stone wall surrounding the perimeter, and the dragon had alighted onto the flagstones.

'My lord,' said the officer, his head inclined, 'I have brought Lahnos Laimos as ordered.'

'Thank you,' said the dragon, as he lowered his head to the level of Lahnos's eyes. He said nothing for a long moment as he stared at Lahnos, then he turned back to the soldiers. 'Leave us; I wish to speak to this man alone.'

The soldiers saluted, then they retreated back into the monastery building.

'Lahnos Laimos,' said the dragon, 'are you well after five days of captivity?'

'It was easier than being in Gunst,' Lahnos said.

'I am sure it was,' said Rylan. 'You have no doubt realised that you are still alive, despite the command issued by Lady Abda. According to my noble half-sister's decree, you were to be eviscerated, and your corpse was to be flung into the Cyasarta.'

'I had noticed, yes.'

'Lord Sigum has been petitioning me from the moment you were arrested,' Rylan said, 'requesting that I countermand Lady Abda's order as soon as she had departed this island; but that is not the reason why you remain alive. As much as I respect Lord Sigum, I did not spare you for his sake. Do you wish to know why you are not floating in the Cyasarta?'

'I do.'

'Are you aware of the battle by the Chain Castles?'

'The Aucterian officer mentioned something about it,' Lahnos said. 'He told me that two dragon carriers were sunk by the Gunstian fleet.'

'That is correct. Three dragons escaped into the East, three were slain, and three returned from the devastation by the mouth of the Cyasarta. Dozens of ships were destroyed, and thousands of humans perished in the encounter. This island is now being blockaded by the Gunstians. Do you know how many soldiers my blessed half-sister left here to defend the Serpent Isle?'

'No.'

'One thousand,' said the dragon. 'One thousand exhausted veterans, to face the tens of thousands amassed by the Gunstians. Lady Abda also took almost every Bullan with her, but two hundred were on the sixth dragon carrier, which managed to retreat into the safety of Handshore. Do you understand what I am saying, Lahnos Laimos? To attempt to defend this island with that many soldiers would be utterly futile. To have any chance of repelling the Gunstians, we need the seven thousand men of the Zamatan regiments. Do you think they would fight for me if I had eviscerated your body? Even now, rumours are circulating throughout the island that you have already been executed, and it would take a mere spark to ignite a new uprising in Kaugatz.'

Lahnos smiled. 'Are you saying that you need me?'

'I need you alive, Laimos,' said the dragon. 'I need you to show yourself to the Zamatans, to prove that I haven't slain you.' He leaned his head in closer. 'But more than that, I need you to persuade the Zamatans to fight against the Gunstians. Will you do this?'

'Why would any Zamatan want to fight for the Dominion after all they have done to us?'

The dragon tilted his head slightly. 'Have I mentioned the Dominion, Laimos? The mighty Dominion, in its wisdom, has abandoned this island to its fate. And they abandoned me. The Aucterian soldiers they left behind consisted of the old, the sick and the tired – men and woman worn out and traumatised by all they suffered in Gunst. They also abandoned thousands of Aucterian civilians.'

'Settlers and colonists,' said Lahnos.

'Yes. Settlers and colonists. I know you hold them in contempt, Laimos; but if we wish to endure, then we must forget all that has divided us in the past. Unless, of course, you would prefer the Gunstians to rule Zamata?'

'I think you know my answer to that.'

'Then you will help me?'

Lahnos glanced away from the dragon, as he tried to decide what to say. The image of what was happening struck him as ludicrous – was a Child of Gahad really begging a young part-Bullan for assistance? It was preposterous.

'What happens afterwards?' Lahnos said.

'What do you mean?'

'Let's say that the Zamatan regiments re-form, and ally with you and the Aucterians, and those Bullan you mentioned – let's say we do that, and we win. The Imperial Gunstian Fleet is defeated and sails home, and the island is left in peace – what happens then? Will you remain the sole authority? Will the Aucterians lord it over us as they have done in the past? I need to know what we would be fighting for, not just who we would be fighting against.'

'I cannot give you a definite answer, Laimos,' said the dragon, 'as the future is unknown. But, this I will say – if, somehow, we prevail against the Gunstians, then I pledge to defend this island against all comers; and I pledge to govern with laws that apply equally to all who reside here – Aucterians, Zamatans and Bullan alike. In other words, my allegiance shall be to the island.'

'You would betray the Dominion?'

'Do not insult me, human. I cannot betray the Dominion, for it has already betrayed me.'

'How many dragons are on Zamata?'

'Five, including myself.'

'And do they all feel the same way?'

'No. I shall not lie to you. Of the five, two support me, and two oppose me.'

'Lord Sigum is one of your supporters, I assume?'

'He is. He feels as betrayed by the Dominion as I do. He rescued the ships, sailors and soldiers from Gunst, and yet my noble half-sister Lady Abda decided to abandon him here – a slight that he will not soon forgive or forget. My full sister Lady Natali will also support me, despite having voted for Lord Naghad to become King.'

'Did you not do the same?'

The dragon eyed him. 'I did not.'

'You voted for the other guy – Tegru, was it?'

'I withheld my vote from Lord Tegru, also. Instead, in my naivety, I, along with another sister Lady Marda, proposed that the Children of Gahad form a legislative council, where all decisions would be put to a vote. The other dragons mocked us; they probably mock us still.'

'And yet Natali will support you now?'

'My sister has been thoroughly disillusioned by the disastrous invasion of Gunst, and though Lady Natali fought bravely in the battle by the mouth of the Cyasarta, she feels nothing but ire towards those who fled into the East. Lady Abda did not take to the air to defend the ships, nor did her son Lord Labran, nor the mighty Lord Ecsin – all three preferred to remain on their dragon carriers and escape.'

'What about the two who oppose you?'

'Both are junior members of the Royal Family – one a grandson of King Gahad, and the other a grandson of King Naghad. Their names are Lord Givra and Lord Gradham. They are strong, but I am stronger. If it comes to a fight, Lady Natali and I will tear them to shreds and rip out their throats.'

'You have left Lady Natali alone in Igatz – is she not in danger?'

'She is not alone. Lord Sigum stands by her side, awaiting my return. The two hundred Bullan who returned with the last dragon carrier are also under orders to protect them; but do you see how precarious my position is? I need the seven thousand Zamatans to rally to the united defence of this island; otherwise our internal divisions shall accomplish the purpose of the Gunstians without any need for them to invade. They could simply walk in, their boots grinding our bones into dust.' The dragon pulled his head back a little. 'There is one more thing I must tell you. The Gunstians have discovered what happened to their kin on this island during the rule of Lord Malum.'

Lahnos stared blankly at the dragon.

'Has no one told you what occurred here, Laimos?' the dragon went on. 'Two Gifted Gunstian agents destroyed hundreds of acres of wheat fields while you were with the invasion forces. In retaliation, Lord Malum and Lady Macsin annihilated every civilian of Gunstian heritage on this island.'

Lahnos took a step back, his eyes wide. 'No.'

'I wish it were not so, but it is true. I played no part in it, nor did I know in advance what Lord Malum was planning. Thousands of men, women and children lost their lives in Kaugatz – a collective punishment for the evil actions of two agents. It was a crime which has brought shame to the Dominion, and I renounce it utterly. However, as I said, the Gunstians aboard their fleet have discovered the truth, and they have proclaimed that they will do the same to every inhabitant of this island – the dragons, the Bullan, the Aucterians and, yes, even the Zamatans. Kneeling before Chadura will not save your people this time; the Gunstians will accept nothing but retribution for what Lord Malum and Lady Macsin did that dark day. Therefore, I ask you again –

no, I beg you – show yourself to the Zamatans, and urge them to unite under my government in order to defend the lives of everyone who dwells here. Will you do this?'

'What happens if I say yes?'

The dragon lifted a powerful forelimb and gestured toward the gates of the monastery. 'Then you walk away, free.'

'You will take me at my word?'

'I shall. In order for you to trust me, Laimos, I am prepared to trust you.'

'What about the rebels?'

'I am considering a general amnesty for all who are willing to put aside the past to aid the defence of this island. Did I not tell you I was naïve? I would rather assume the inherent goodness in people and be proved wrong, than presume the opposite out of pride and fear. This, I think, is the reason Lord Malum told me nothing about his planned massacre of the Gunstians – he knew I would have opposed him.'

'Tell me about the Demon Witch,' Lahnos said. 'Did she attack you?'

'She did. She grievously wounded Lady Lenta's mind, forcing Lord Malum to slay her. In return, Lord Malum set a trap to ensnare her, here, in this very monastery; but it went awry, and Lord Malum and Lady Macsin were also slain. I barely survived.'

'What happened to the Witch?'

'I do not know for certain. I was badly injured, and my memory of those events is confused. I must assume that she escaped. Why do you ask? I remember Colonel Friel Laimos, your uncle, telling us that the Demon Witch had assisted the Zamatan cause during the uprising. What do you know of this?'

'She helped us; that is true. Was my uncle in Zamata Gataza?'

'He was.'

'And?'

The dragon lowered his gaze. 'Yet again, I am forced to deliver bad news to you. Your uncle is dead. The rebels mounted an assault upon the monastery in the wake of the Demon Witch's attack, and Colonel Friel Laimos was killed trying to escape.'

Lahnos felt a tight ball of anger and grief form in the pit of his stomach, and his shoulders sagged.

'I am sorry for your loss,' said the dragon. 'We have all suffered; let us now come together. We can still save this island, Laimos; do not despair.'

'I will do as you ask,' said Lahnos, his gaze on the flagstones. 'I will prove to the Zamatans that I am alive, and I will try to persuade them to fight the Gunstians and serve under your command.'

The dragon closed his eyes for a moment. 'Thank you.' He turned to the soldiers standing by the building's main entrance. 'Give Lahnos Laimos a water skin and some food, and then open the gates. He is free to go.'

The soldiers saluted, then two emerged from the monastery building. One went to the gates and opened a smaller door cut into the large entrance, while the other handed Lahnos a water skin and a bag with a strap. Lahnos took them, and turned back to the dragon.

'When shall I see you again?' he said.

'That is up to you, Laimos,' said Rylan. 'I will now return to Igatz. It is a short journey, but my wings are still recovering from the injuries I received. I will need to practise more, in order to defend this isle. Good luck.'

Lahnos tilted his head in reply, then walked away. He passed the soldiers by the gates and stepped through the smaller entrance, ducking his head to avoid his horns snagging on the rest of the doorframe. The door swung shut behind him, and Lahnos gazed out at the view of the island. He hadn't noticed the wheat fields on his journey to the monastery, but he could see the devastation that stretched out in front of him. The fields had a greyish tinge, and an odour of decay reached his nostrils. He narrowed his eyes, then he turned a little to the south, and saw the blackened ruins of the town of Neeton. That had been Malum, too. Lahnos cursed the name of the pale red dragon, then set off down the track.

. . .

The eastern flank of the mountain was bathed in shadows as Lahnos strode away from the high monastery of Zamata Gataza. The sun had disappeared behind the bulk of Mount Hodzulat, though Kaugatz and Igatz were still shimmering in the daylight ahead of him, and the clear waters of the Hansarta were sparkling. He walked for a mile, then noticed a small group ascending the track in the opposite direction. Lahnos smiled, then he started to run. The three figures on the track below him heard the sound of his boots on the gravel and looked up.

'Lahnos!' Reyn cried. She sprinted up the slope, and Lahnos gathered her in his arms. He held her tight, closing his eyes as he buried his face in her hair.

He felt a slap on his back.

'Did you escape, Lahnos?' said Efizel.

Lahnos laughed, and looked at the Bullan renegade. Standing next to him was Karl, a crossbow slung over his shoulder, then Lahnos realised that Reyn and Efizel were also armed.

'No,' Lahnos said. 'The dragon let me go.' He pointed at the three crossbows. 'Were you planning on breaking me out?'

'Yes,' said Reyn. 'We were going to do it tomorrow, at dawn.'

'Just the three of you?' said Lahnos, shaking his head.

'Bauchlie is with thirty rebel fighters at the bottom of the hill,' said Efizel. 'We three were scouting the way.'

'You're working with Bauchlie?'

Efizel gave a gentle shrug. 'We found that, for once, our purposes aligned. It does not mean that I like the man; nor do I forgive him for his past transgressions.'

'And you, brother,' Lahnos said to Karl; 'are you a rebel now?'

'I'm with the sergeant on this,' said Karl. 'We came here for you, not to aid Bauchlie. The only proper rebel standing here is Reyn.'

Lahnos laughed, then he noticed Reyn's eyes tighten a fraction.

'Is that funny?' she said. 'What did you think we women were doing while every man on the island was taken to Gunst? We fought; that's what we did. Fought, bled and died.'

Lahnos blinked. 'I... All right. You always said you wanted to fight.' He eyed her bow. 'Have you used that thing much?'

'I have killed two Aucterians and three Bullan with it, Lahnos,' she said. 'And now I'm ready to use it against the Gunstians. Don't try to stop me.'

Lahnos said nothing.

'We have told Reyn all about Gunst,' said Karl. 'We stayed with her and Bauchlie under the ruins of Medamuna Gatzoun yesterday, planning this rescue attempt. I have to say that I'm relieved we won't have to go through with it now. Why did the dragon release you? Was it Lord Rylan? We saw a dragon flying overhead a short time ago, and we think it was him.'

'Yes, it was Rylan. He wants the Zamatan regiments to re-form and fight the Gunstians. He released me after I told him I would try to persuade them to unite with the Aucterians and Bullan.'

'Bauchlie isn't going to like that,' said Reyn.

'I couldn't give a shit what Bauchlie thinks,' said Lahnos.

Reyn frowned. 'Don't mention this to him until we get back to Medamuna Gatzoun.'

'Why are we going there? I need to go to Kaugatz to organise the regiments.'

'The Zamatans will come to you, wherever you are on this island,' said Reyn. 'Do you have the slightest idea what they're all saying about you, Lahnos? You're a damned hero to them. Every Zamatan family – the children, the wives, the mothers – they adore you for bringing the men back.'

Lahnos lowered his gaze. 'I didn't bring them all back.'

'I know. But seven thousand, Lahnos – we didn't think any would return. You saved the future of this island.'

'I didn't do it alone.'

'That's not what everyone is saying.'

'Then everyone is wrong.'

Efizel placed a hand onto his shoulder. 'Does it matter, my friend? The Gunstian fleet is blockading this island, and the Zamatans will listen to you. For my part, I am glad you came to an arrangement with Lord Rylan, but I also agree with Reyn, and advise that you keep this quiet until we have safely returned to the ruined monastery. The dozen Bullan you saved outside the gates of Great Gunst were among those left behind by Lady Abda. I will send out messages to them and they will join us there. They will also spread the word of your location to the men of the regiments. And then, we shall wait for them to come to you.'

Lahnos nodded, and they set off down the hillside track. Lahnos took Reyn's hand as they walked.

'Did you hear about your uncle?' she said.

'Rylan told me he was killed while trying to escape.'

'I was there, Lahnos. I saw it happen.'

'You were there?'

'We managed to rescue Leona and a couple of Dominion officers who had been condemned to death by the dragons. Friel was killed by a Bullan soldier, but we got Malum. Bauchlie drove a spear through the bastard's heart.'

'And the Demon Witch? Did she escape?'

Reyn eyed him. 'It depends who you ask.'

Lahnos met her glance. 'What does that mean?'

'Leona has a wild theory about what occurred in the caverns under Zamata Gataza,' she said. 'Would you like to hear it?'

'Yes,' said Lahnos. 'I think I would.'

CHAPTER 8
SPOILING FOR A FIGHT

Medamuna Gatzoun, Serpent Isle – 21st Tuminch 1588

Cisca glanced at the bag she had packed, her thoughts torn. She had very few possessions in the caverns under the ruined monastery of Medamuna Gatzoun, but she had filled the bag with enough food and water to last a couple of days – more than enough for the journey to Igatz. To her left, a small oil lamp was flickering, its tiny flames barely illuminating the tunnel that led to the centre of the cavern network. Oil rations had been cut, and many of the tunnels were in permanent darkness. On Cisca's right, the light of the waning moon was spilling in through one of the many entrances to the rebel lair.

That was her choice – left or right. Stay or go. When she had packed the bag an hour before, she had felt certain that her mind was made up – she was leaving. She would trek down the side of the mountain and walk all the way to the ferry terminal opposite Euzaru Naka; from there she would cross Kaugatz and take another ferry to Igatz, where she would hand herself in to the authorities. A rumour had reached the caverns that Lord Rylan was so desperate for soldiers that he was prepared to overlook a few minor transgressions; perhaps that would be enough to see Cisca reinstated into the Dominion armed forces. Or, the rumours were the usual nonsense that passed for news among the rebels, and she would be thrown into prison. The way she was feeling, she might prefer a jail cell to staying in a place where most people despised her. A few of the older rebels didn't seem to care about her presence in the caverns, but the new, youthful band of Zamatan women that Bauchlie had enlisted to his cause looked at Cisca with nothing but contempt. To them, she was just a failed Dominion officer, to be numbered among the enemies of the island. To flourish in such an environment, she would need to become more forceful and self-confident, or she would have to rely upon Bauchlie's unconditional support. At that moment in time, neither option felt likely. Her confidence had taken a battering during the events leading up to Lord Malum's brutal slaying, when she had been at the mercy of Lady Takri; blackmailed and vulnerable, always fearful of discovery, and unable to sleep through fear of being arrested. As for Bauchlie, would he even notice if she vanished? She had chosen to leave while he had departed the caverns with thirty young fighters earlier the previous day, on an operation to free his cousin Lahnos from Zamata Gataza. The caverns had been full of excited talk about the horned boy and what he had managed to achieve in the retreat from Gunst; and Bauchlie had made it clear that he intended to bring Lahnos into his rebel force. He would have no time for Cisca, but when had he ever had time for her?

Stay or go? A jail cell, or the prison of her own mind?

She heard footsteps in the darkness and glanced up to see a young rebel walking through the shadows towards her, a crossbow slung over her shoulder. The fighter's eyes went to Cisca, and then to the bag lying by her feet.

'What are you doing?' she said, as she came to a halt.

Cisca met her gaze. 'Waiting for Bauchlie to get back.'

'Why?' said the rebel. 'Me and the others feel sorry for you; did you know that? It's a little pathetic, the way you fawn over Commander Bauchlie – he'll never be interested in an Aucterian.'

Cisca said nothing.

'If I were you,' the rebel woman went on, 'I would give up trying to win his affections. In fact,' she said, lowering her voice, 'if you want to leave, I won't stop you. You could just slip out into the night. The moon is out, and the mountain paths will be clear. You could be back among your own folk by noon.'

'You would like that, wouldn't you?'

A small smirk traced the lips of the rebel fighter. 'I don't care what you do.'

'No? I thought you all wanted to remove every Aucterian from this island?'

'The dragons abandoned you here,' the rebel said. 'They don't want you, and we don't want you. How does it feel to be alone?'

Cisca felt her voice catch as she tried to respond. She closed her mouth. She would not weep in front of the young rebel.

'Nothing to say?' said the fighter. 'What a shame. I'm going now. That entrance is unguarded, and I will pretend that I never saw you.'

The young fighter turned and disappeared back into the shadows and gloom of the tunnel. Cisca waited until her footsteps had dwindled into silence, then she picked up her bag from the floor and pulled the strap over her shoulder. She took a last look down the tunnel, then turned right towards the moonlight. The entrance was narrow, and she squeezed through the gap in the rocks, then climbed out into the open air. The moon was high in the clear sky, and Cisca reckoned that midnight had come and gone. She ascended the steep path, then came to a spot from where she could see the entire island laid out before her. It was a beautiful sight; she couldn't deny it. The moonlight was reflecting off the whitewashed farm buildings at the bottom of the mountainside, and the Dragon Palace in the distance was gleaming like silver. Her gaze went to the Hansarta, and then to the Cyasarta. She would have to cross both to reach Igatz, but where else could she go? If only she had been on board Lady Abda's dragon carrier, then she would be well on her way to Inopei. The loathing she felt for Leona increased, and she imagined what might her life have been like had the duplicitous, blackmailing spy not intervened.

Cisca's eyes moved from the Cyasarta back to Kaugatz. The town was in darkness, with only a few streetlamps being supplied with enough oil to keep them burning throughout the night. Major Lyla was down there, hidden somewhere within the maze of narrow streets, at the mercy of the woman who had turned Cisca's existence into a nightmare. Cisca longed to find her old colleague, but had no idea where to begin. She could hardly start asking the local Zamatans if they knew where Leona might be living; her accent would give her away in seconds. She wondered how many Zamatans knew that Leona had been masquerading as Lady Takri. Did any of them realise that she had been assisting Lord Malum and Lady Macsin during the awful slaughter of the Gunstian civilians? Perhaps more should learn the truth, and perhaps Cisca should be the one to deliver it to them.

She began to walk down the steep path towards the village of Fidalaimos, the moonlight guiding her steps over the rough terrain. A low ruined wall stretched off to her left – a remnant of the once-mighty monastery that had dominated Mount Medamuna for centuries. Spruce trees were growing all over the ruins, their roots boring into and beneath the crumbling walls, hastening the day when nothing would remain to remind anyone that the buildings had ever been there. She reached a place where another path branched off, and paused, hearing low voices on the track ahead. Her heart sank. Bauchlie's thirty rebels were returning, and Cisca had squandered her opportunity to flee. She considered hiding among the tangled thickets of undergrowth on the right of the path but, instead, her feet remained frozen to the ground.

The first rebels came into view as they climbed the track up the hillside, the moon reflecting off their buckles and the steel components of their crossbows. They were talking in low voices, but their excitement was clear. Cisca stepped to the side of the track and waited for them to approach. More rebels came into view, and Cisca saw two pairs of horns among them. One of the sets belonged to the large and powerful Bullan soldier who had visited the caverns the day before, his presence causing an uproar until his identity as a friend of Lahnos Laimos had been made evident. The other set belonged to Lahnos himself. He looked older than the last time Cisca had seen him, and he was one of the few among the rebel group who didn't have a smile on his face. He was holding Reyn's hand as they ascended the path, and was ignoring the conversations going on around him. Behind him, Bauchlie was striding up the hill, a satisfied expression on his usually-dour features.

The first rebels reached Cisca, but they said nothing to her as they passed, then Lahnos caught her gaze and stopped.

His eyes narrowed a fraction. 'Lieutenant Cisca?'

'Hello, Lahnos.'

He glanced at Reyn. 'Why did you not tell me that the Dominion officer you rescued was Cisca?'

'It never occurred to me,' said Reyn.

Lahnos turned back to the Dragon Corps officer. 'You were condemned to death, weren't you? And now you have to live up here with Bauchlie?' He smiled. 'You have my pity, Cisca.'

'What's the hold up?' said Bauchlie, as he pushed his way through the crowd of rebels around Lahnos. He came to the junction in the path and saw Cisca. He smiled, then his eyes tightened as he noticed the bag over her shoulder. 'What were you doing out here?' he said.

'Taking a stroll in the moonlight,' she said.

'It's a nice night for it,' said Lahnos, his eyes going between Bauchlie and Cisca. 'But I'm hungry, and I need to eat something.'

'Just make sure they don't eat you,' Cisca said.

Lahnos laughed. 'I don't think I'm very palatable, but thanks for the warning.'

Reyn gave Cisca a funny look, then she pulled on Lahnos's hand. 'Let's go inside.'

Cisca remained where she was as Reyn led Lahnos away. The Bullan soldier followed them, tilting his head slightly at Cisca as he passed, and the crowd of rebel fighters moved on, leaving only Bauchlie standing in front of her.

'I don't understand,' he said. 'After all we've been through, you were going to leave us?'

'I didn't think you would notice.'

'But... I thought...'

'Yes? You thought what, Bauchlie?'

His eyes darkened. 'Never mind. Clearly, I was wrong. Do as you please. Go, or stay.'

He walked past her and followed the other rebels up the slope towards the entrance to the caverns. Cisca watched his back for a moment, then lowered her gaze. She had always thought of herself as decisive, but her mind agonised over the direction she should next take. Bauchlie was letting her go, but she had never been his prisoner in the ruins of Medamuna Gatzoun. On the other hand, she was curious to see what impact the arrival of Lahnos would have on the rebels. He didn't seem like someone who was in awe of the rebel commander, and it might be interesting to see the two men clash. For some reason, she felt a strange affinity with the horned part-Bullan. He had been an outcast upon the Serpent Isle since the day his horns had started to sprout from his head, while Cisca was nothing but an outcast in the ruined old monastery, surrounded by people who loathed her because of who she was. She also wanted to see how the Bullan soldier was treated. The rebels' hatred of the Bullan was well known, but they would be forced to suppress their true feelings if they wished to avoid alienating the island's new hero. That, too, Cisca would like to see.

She turned, and walked back up the path towards the caverns. She could always leave on another occasion; in fact, she could depart whenever she felt like doing so. The notion made her feel freer than she had in a long time. She was in control of her own destiny, just as Lahnos was, and all it had taken to show her this was a brief conversation with the part-Bullan. She squeezed back through the gap in the rocks, and re-entered the tunnel. She followed it down and began to hear the sound of raised voices, quiet at first, but growing louder with every step. She emerged into a large cavern, and saw Lahnos surrounded by what looked like every rebel in the complex. He was waving at them with a bemused expression on his face as they cheered his name, while both Reyn and Bauchlie stood to the side, the Bullan soldier next to them.

'Thank you,' Lahnos said, and the crowd hushed. 'A few stories are going around,' he went on, 'about how I single-handedly rescued every Zamatan man who returned from Gunst. Don't believe them. I couldn't have done it without the help of many others.' He gestured to the Bullan soldier. 'This man, for example, saved my life more than once, from the Gunstians, and sometimes from my own stupidity.' He laughed, then pointed at another man. 'And my brother Karl kept me sane. Thank you, brother. The friendship we forged in the mud of Gunst means more to me than I can say.' His voice choked a little, and he turned back to the crowd. 'You probably all want to know what I intend to do next.' He raised a finger in the air. 'I have a plan, but it will have to wait for now, as the sound of my stomach growling will soon start to drown out my words. But first, I want you to know that every Zamatan man who was sent to Gunst longed for the day when we could return to our loved ones.' He gazed at Reyn. 'We know that life was a struggle for you, just as it was for us; thank you for keeping the fires burning.'

The crowd cheered again, and Lahnos waved one more time, then he was led off by Bauchlie into another tunnel. Reyn, the Bullan soldier, and Lahnos's brother followed them, along with a handful of rebel officers, while guards blocked off the entrance to the tunnel they had taken. While the crowd talked, Cisca pushed her way through to the tunnel entrance.

The four rebels posted there barred her way.

'Let me through,' she said. 'I want to speak to Lahnos.'

'Everyone in this cavern wants to speak to Lahnos,' said a young rebel; 'you'll have to wait like the rest of us.'

Cisca peered over their shoulders. 'Lahnos!' she shouted.

The part-Bullan turned, then he nodded at the guards. 'Let her pass.'

The guards stared at Cisca, but moved out of the way. She resisted an urge to smirk at them, and hurried along the tunnel.

'You came back,' said Bauchlie, his face in the shadows of the dark tunnel.

'Yes,' she said. 'I want to hear Lahnos's plan.'

'As do I,' said Bauchlie.

They walked along the tunnel and entered a small, well-lit cavern, with wall-mounted oil lamps, a long table, and several chairs. Two of the four rebel officers opened a crate, and produced a variety of food and drink, which they laid out on the table as everyone else sat. Bauchlie took the place at the head of the table, and gestured for Lahnos to sit on his right. Reyn and the Bullan soldier sat down next to the horned part-Bullan, while Karl took a place opposite his brother. Cisca glanced at the other seats. The rebel officers were avoiding the Bullan soldier, so she sat down on his right, as far away from Bauchlie as it was possible to be. Wine was poured, and the table remained silent for a few minutes as everyone except Cisca ate.

'Thanks for the food,' Lahnos said, as he finished. He pushed his bowl away from him and took a drink of wine.

'My home is your home,' said Bauchlie.

Lahnos smiled. 'Is it? Perhaps you should wait to hear what I have to say before making such pronouncements.'

'We are all waiting to hear what you have to say,' said Bauchlie. 'The entire island wants to know what you will do. You have power, more power than you realise. At this precise moment, anything you say will be listened to – your actions in Gunst have earned you this privilege, and this opportunity. Do not spurn it.'

'I won't,' said Lahnos. He glanced at the rebel officers sitting across from him. 'So, have you killed any Aucterians recently?'

'The Zamatan resistance does what I order it to do,' said Bauchlie. 'I will never rest until the occupiers of this island have been destroyed.'

'Does that include Cisca?' said Lahnos. 'And what about the Bullan soldier sitting to my right? How about Lord Sigum? He led the Zamatan men home – do you intend to destroy him, too?'

'The dragon was doing his duty to the Dominion,' said Bauchlie. 'It was a mere coincidence that his actions have benefitted Zamata.'

Lahnos sat back and took another drink. 'What about the Gunstians?'

'We shall oppose them with all our strength,' said Bauchlie; 'you know this. I will not have one imperialist oppressor replace the other, not while I have a single breath left in my body.'

'That's not what I meant,' said Lahnos.

'Then explain yourself.'

Lahnos eyed the scarred commander. 'Will you continue to attack the Aucterians while this island is being blockaded by the Gunstians?'

Bauchlie laughed and shook his head. 'I think I can see where this is heading. Let me guess – you want me to pretend that the Dominion forces are not our enemy? You want me to forge some sort of coward's... agreement with the colonial powers sitting in the Dragon Palace?'

'I want you be pragmatic.'

'Is that what you're calling it?'

'If you continue to assault the Aucterians, Bullan and dragons while the Gunstians are trying to annihilate everyone on Zamata, then, effectively, you will be acting as a Gunstian agent. You will be carrying out their work for them.'

Bauchlie's face twisted with rage, then he took a breath. 'Is this what you came here to say? That we should serve the imperialists who have ground this island into the dirt?'

'Tell me *your* plan, Bauchlie,' said Lahnos. 'Tell me what you think I should be doing.'

'It is obvious,' said the commander. 'With you joining the rebellion, we shall have every Zamatan behind us. We can drive the Dominion usurpers from power and take the reins of government into our own hands – and then we shall repel the Gunstian invaders.'

Lahnos laughed, and the cavern stilled as the others stared at him.

'Do my words amuse you?' said Bauchlie.

'You are out of your mind,' said Lahnos. 'No wonder my uncle never let you lead the rebellion – at least he understood the truth.'

'And what truth is that?'

'The only way Zamata will flourish in peace is for everyone who lives here to put aside their differences and work together. Every Bullan soldier you kill is one fewer left to defend this island. Every Aucterian settler you terrorise off their property does nothing but add to the misery we all suffer.' He paused, his eyes on Bauchlie. 'It's time for my plan. Here is what I am going to do. I shall rally the men of the

Zamatan regiments, and ask them to serve under the command of Lord Rylan.'

The four rebel officers at the table all cried out at once, their fists clenching, while Bauchlie folded his arms across his broad chest, his mouth closed. Cisca smothered a smile.

'You filthy little traitor!' shouted one of the officers. 'We ought to throw you off the damn cliff.'

'I would advise against that,' said the Bullan soldier.

'Do you think you could stop us, you degenerate savage?'

'No,' said the Bullan, 'but the seven thousand Zamatans who returned from Gunst might have something to say if you kill the man who saved their lives.'

'Calm yourselves,' said Bauchlie. 'I want to hear what Reyn thinks.'

'Me?' said Reyn, her eyes widening.

'Yes, Reyn, you,' said Bauchlie. 'You are one of us – a rebel; a trusted comrade in the struggle against our enemies. You have killed Aucterians and Bullan, and your bravery is unquestioned. I have been harbouring thoughts about promoting you to become one of my officers, and so I would value your opinion. What do you think of Lahnos's plan?'

Reyn's face fell. 'I don't think I should say what I really think of it.'

'Why not?'

'Because you are trying to divide us, sir. You know my opinions, and you want me to announce that Lahnos is wrong and that you are right.'

'It was a simple question.'

'Then please allow me to ask another one.'

Bauchlie gestured for her to proceed.

She turned to Lahnos. 'If we follow your plan,' she said, 'and we are successful; I mean we manage to repel the Gunstians – then what happens next? Won't we be back in exactly the same position where we started, with the Dominion in control?'

Bauchlie smiled. 'That is a very good question, Reyn. Go on, Lahnos – tell us what happens next.'

'I will,' he said. 'To do so, I need to point out two facts. The first is that the Dominion won't be returning here any time soon. Lady Abda fled for a reason, and that reason is the prospect of a civil war raging across the lands of the Dominion. Lord Tegru will be fighting against those who supported King Naghad. They won't care what happens here, not when Inopei and Aucteran are in chaos. This island was a strategic stepping-stone that allowed the Dominion to invade Gunst. Do you seriously believe they will try that again in the foreseeable future? My second fact is this – Lord Rylan has renounced the Dominion. They abandoned him here, and he has not taken this kindly. If we support him, and unite under his rule, then Zamata will be free. Isn't that what you want?'

Cisca stared at him. 'Lord Rylan has renounced the Dominion?'

Lahnos turned to her. 'I heard him say it with my own ears. He knows that this island will fall to the Gunstians if we remain divided.'

'The word of a dragon whose reign is hanging by a thread means nothing,' said Bauchlie. 'He would promise you the whole of Athumia to get what he wants – and what does he want? Our submission. Your idea of freedom differs somewhat from mine, Lahnos, for I say we shall never be free if a dragon is ruling us from his palace in Igatz.'

'I disagree,' said Lahnos. 'I think we should give Lord Rylan a chance.'

The chamber fell into silence again, the atmosphere cold.

'You disappoint me, Lahnos,' Bauchlie said after a long pause. 'I had hoped for better from you.'

'I couldn't give a rat's ass what you think,' said Lahnos. 'The only important question left is this – are you going to try to stop me?'

'I could have you hanged for treason and cowardice,' said Bauchlie.

'Then try,' said Lahnos. 'I'm not frightened of you.'

Karl rubbed his face. 'Maybe, uh, this is getting out of hand. We came here in good faith, not to start a fight.'

'Lahnos cannot help himself,' said Bauchlie. 'He is always looking for a fight.'

'I won't argue with that,' said Reyn.

'I'm still waiting to hear your answer,' said Lahnos. 'Can we leave, or will you try to stop us?'

Bauchlie sipped his wine, then he glanced away. 'Go,' he said. 'No one will try to stop you. But remember this, boy – when Lord Rylan betrays you, don't come running to me for help.'

'I wouldn't dream of it,' said Lahnos, as he got to his feet. Karl and the Bullan soldier also stood, then Lahnos glanced down at Reyn. 'Are you coming?' he said.

'Where?' she said.

Lahnos raised his palms. 'I don't know.'

'What about the village?' said Karl. 'Fidalaimos is only a mile from here. We could stay there for the rest of the night and decide what to do in the morning.'

Lahnos smiled. 'You would accept me back into the village?'

'Of course,' said Karl. 'You are my brother.'

Reyn remained silent for a moment then she got to her feet. 'I'm sorry, Commander, but I'm leaving with Lahnos.'

Bauchlie waved his hand at her as if he didn't care, then Lahnos, Reyn, Karl and the Bullan soldier left the chamber. The four rebel officers started to speak, but Bauchlie glared at them.

'Leave me,' he said.

The officers saluted, and left the cavern by a different entrance. Cisca stood, and her eyes went to the tunnel that Lahnos had followed.

'Are you thinking about going after him?' said Bauchlie.

'Can you give me a reason not to?' she said. 'I think I would be safer with Lahnos; at least he doesn't believe that all Aucterians need to be destroyed.'

He stared at her. 'I don't think that about you.'

'Then tell me what you do think about me.'

Bauchlie leaned his elbows on the table and placed his head in his hands. 'Do you realise what that little idiot Lahnos is about to do? He plans to sell his own people to a damned dragon. I need to organise my agents to stop the Zamatans converting to his cause. I don't have time for... this.'

Cisca nodded then gave him a sad smile. 'You never have time for me. That tells me all I need to know.'

She turned for the tunnel.

'Wait,' said Bauchlie. 'Don't leave me, Cisca.'

'Why not?'

He stared at her, his dark eyes filled with pain and regret. 'I need you.'

She blinked. 'What?'

'Sit with me,' he said. 'My heart is burdened with the pain of trying to free this island, and I need you.'

Cisca placed her hands on her hips. 'You are not making this easy, Bauchlie.'

'I know,' he said. 'Sit with me. Please.'

She glanced at the tunnel entrance, then made her choice. It was a mistake, possibly the worst mistake she had ever made, but she couldn't help herself. She walked round the table, sat down next to Bauchlie, and took his hand.

CHAPTER 9
HAUNTED BY MEMORY

Kaugatz, Serpent Isle – 4th Luddinch 1588

A loud shriek echoed through the house. Leona dropped the papers she was working on and strode to the door of her upstairs room. Her anger at being disturbed for what felt like the hundredth time that morning rippled through her as she pushed open the door and walked to the top of the stairs.

'Would you be quiet,' she shouted. 'I am trying to work.'

The shrieking from Lyla's room stilled, and was followed by the sound of Arrosa's laughter. Leona turned, then halted again as a crash of broken glass sounded from the downstairs room. The housekeeper emerged from the kitchen, wiped her hands on her apron, and glanced upstairs.

'Can you deal with that, Kamasta?' said Leona. 'I am trying to read, and I can't think with all this noise.'

The housekeeper sighed and went to Lyla's room. She opened the door, then ducked as a shoe flew past her head.

'Girls!' Kamasta cried. 'Behave yourselves. Arrosa – put that down. Now. Lyla – stop that at once, or I'm taking all your books away.'

'Piss off,' Arrosa shouted back. 'You're not my mother.'

'And praise the serpent gods for that,' said Kamasta.

'There are no serpent gods, you stupid old woman,' said Arrosa. 'They're horrible lizard-demons.'

Kamasta rubbed her face, and Leona began to descend the stairs.

'They need more discipline, ma'am,' the housekeeper said, as Leona reached the ground floor.

'I'll take over for now,' Leona said. 'Thank you.'

Kamasta shook her head, then returned to the kitchen. Leona tried to calm her anger, knowing that it only made things worse, then she walked into Lyla's room. Lyla was in tears as she sat on her mattress, while Arrosa was holding a long pole used to open the tall shutters. She was aiming the pole at Lyla's chest, and prodding her with it.

'Arrosa!' Leona cried. 'What have I told you before? It's wrong to hurt other people – put that down.'

'She stole my book,' Arrosa said, 'and she won't give it back.'

Leona's eyes went to a broken vase on the floor of the room, knocked over by the pole clutched in the girl's hands.

'Put the pole down, and we'll discuss it,' Leona said.

Arrosa narrowed her eyes, then flung the pole onto the rug.

'Lyla,' Leona went on, 'did you take Arrosa's book?'

The woman blinked once, then her features twisted with frustration. 'Ye... ye... yes,' she said.

Leona walked over, avoiding the fragments of glass, and held out her hand. 'Give it to me.'

Lyla's right hand went under her pillow, and she retrieved a battered old leather-bound book. She stared at it for a moment, then she placed it on to Leona's palm.

'What book is this?' said Leona. 'I haven't seen it before.'

'It's mine,' said Arrosa, snatching it out of Leona's hand.

'Where did you get it?' said Leona.

'It was my papa's; and now it's mine.'

Leona glanced at the Gunstian writing down the spine. 'Is it one of Kitard's works? Is it about the Gifts of Theodora?'

'No. It's about the Gifts of Chadura.'

'I have a similar book, but it is much larger,' said Leona. 'If I let you borrow it, could I take a look at yours?'

The girl held the slim volume close to her chest, her eyes wary. 'It has things in it that foreigners shouldn't know.'

'It's the same with my book.'

Arrosa frowned. 'Can you read Gunstian?'

'Yes.'

Lyla stirred. 'I…,' she said, her voice low. 'I… want to read it.'

'But you can't read,' said Leona.

'She can,' said Arrosa. 'She can't read Zamatan, but she can read Gunstian.'

Leona blinked, feeling no twinge. How could that be possible?

'We don't speak Zamatan,' she said. 'There's no such language. We write, read and speak the Divine Tongue.'

'The lizard's language?' said Arrosa with contempt.

'Yes. The lizard's language.' She glanced at Lyla. 'Does this mean you have forgotten how to read your own language, but you can somehow remember Gunstian? How?'

'I… took it… from Lahnos,' Lyla said.

'How?'

'I don't know.'

'I have been teaching her the alphabet of the lizard's language,' Arrosa said.

'Yes. Thank you for that,' Leona said; 'but I want to know more about what else Lyla can remember.' She crouched down and began to pick up the pieces of broken glass from the rug. 'What other things are you hiding in your mind? Can you remember your family?'

Lyla glanced down. 'No.'

'What about where you come from?'

'I remember a… city,' Lyla said; 'and a… a…'

'Yes?'

'A desert,' Lyla said in Gunstian.

'A desert?' Leona said, keeping to the Divine Tongue.

'Yes. A house in the… desert. An old man.' She touched her eyes.

'Blind.'

'And the city?'

'Ter... Ter-osss.'

Leona dropped the fragments of broken vase into a small bin.

'Teros City,' Lyla repeated.

'No,' said Leona. 'That can't be right.'

'She's from Aucteran,' said Arrosa. 'Teros City is in Aucteran.'

'I know that,' said Leona.

'I dreamed of a house in the desert,' Lyla said in Gunstian, her accent fluent. 'A blind old man was teaching me; but I also dreamed of going to school in Teros City.'

'Your Gunstian is perfect,' Leona said. 'When did this start?'

'I woke up this morning,' Lyla went on, continuing to speak in the language of Gunst, 'and knew how to do it. How? Who am I?'

'Your memories must be starting to return,' Leona said.

'But how can I have two memories of the same time? Was I in the desert, or was I in Teros City?'

Leona stood up and scanned the books on the shelf above the colonel's old desk. She found a copy of a dictionary that translated words from Gunstian to the Divine Tongue, removed it, and handed it to Lyla.

'This should help,' she said, as Lyla stared at the cover of the book. 'Arrosa – come with me for a moment.'

'Why?'

'I want to show you that old book I mentioned.'

Leona and Arrosa left Lyla reading the dictionary and strode from the room. Leona led the girl upstairs and into the small chamber where she slept. She rummaged around in her possessions and found the Gunstian volume on Theodora's Gifts that she had read several times. She handed it to Arrosa.

'I know this book,' the girl said. 'This is *Volume One*. My papa had a copy.'

'Have you already read it?'

'Yes.'

'It is a very complex book – did you understand it?'

The girl narrowed her eyes. 'I'm not stupid.'

'I didn't say you were. You can borrow it. Now; tell me – what do you think of Lyla? You've been in this house for almost two weeks, and you have spent a lot of time with her.'

Arrosa shrugged. 'She changes from day to day.'

'What do you mean?'

'Every morning,' Arrosa said, 'I never know what to expect. I think she remembers more things whenever she dreams; and sometimes it confuses her, and sometimes it makes her sad.'

'Does she ever lie to you?'

Arrosa shrugged. 'No. You treat her like a child, but she's not.'

'I will try to do better. At least I now know she can speak fluent Gunstian. Do you like living here?'

'Kamasta is grumpy, and you're always busy.'

Leona frowned.

'But,' Arrosa went on, 'it's better than the last few places where I stayed, even though you're a demon-worshipper.'

'I am not a demon-worshipper. I don't believe that the dragons are gods.'

'Oh. Do you believe in Chadura?'

'I don't follow the Gunstian religion, either.'

'You should, or your soul will burn forever.'

Leona smiled. 'Has Lyla done anything... strange?'

'She's always strange.'

'I mean – has she...?'

'She's not Gifted like we are.'

'I know that. Do you like her?'

'Sometimes. When she's not crying.'

'Hitting her with a pole is not the best way to make friends.'

Arrosa laughed. 'No, but it was funny.'

'It was mean.'

'Shut up.'

'That was mean, too.'

'So? Are you going to kick me out and pass me on to someone else?'

'No. I promised to look after you, and I will; but I want you to try your best. No more hitting Lyla, and no more being rude to Kamasta. Now, I need to work. Go back downstairs to Lyla's room, and help her learn more of the Divine Tongue.'

The girl rolled her eyes and walked from the room. Leona closed the door and sat down by the pile of papers. She picked up a few and tried to concentrate, but Lyla's words were rattling round her mind. Leona had assumed that every last vestige of Major Lyla's memories had been obliterated when Lord Malum had overseen her death, but if that was so, then how could she have dreamed of going to school in Teros City, unless the Demon Witch also happened to have been brought up there? And what was the business about the blind old man in the desert? A possible solution presented itself, but Leona was loath to believe it.

Two hours later, Kamasta escorted Farakai upstairs and into Leona's room. The housekeeper departed again without a word, leaving the Gunstian-born agent standing by the door. Leona placed some papers on to the table in front of her and glanced up.

'I debated whether or not to come here, ma'am,' Farakai said, 'as I think this is a bad idea.'

'Go on.'

Farakai shook his head. 'Lord Rylan has sent a response to your letter.'

Leona's eyes widened. 'After two weeks?'

'Perhaps he is a slow reader, ma'am. He wants to meet you in person.'

'Where?'

'In the Dragon Palace, ma'am. It's a trap; it's obvious. If you set foot inside that place you'll be arrested and killed.'

'Perhaps.'

'He wants you to enter by the southern gate, and said that someone will be there to escort you to him.'

'When?'

'Today. Sunset.'

Leona nodded. 'If it is a trap, and I don't return, then I want you to report to Bauchlie and pass on everything we've been doing; and everyone we've been looking after.'

'You can't be serious, ma'am. You'd be throwing your life away; and Bauchlie? No offence, ma'am; but I've never agreed with his methods.'

'Who else is there?'

'Well, there's Lahnos, ma'am.'

'Lahnos is a boy.'

'Forgive me, ma'am, but isn't he the same age as you? Besides, the ordinary Zamatans love him, while no one trusts Bauchlie. I don't trust Bauchlie – he'd sell his own grandmother to further the cause.'

Leona gazed out of the window at the view of Kaugatz. 'Is Lahnos still in Fidalaimos?'

'As far as I know, ma'am.'

'All right. If I don't return then report to him, and not to Bauchlie.'

'I still think this is a mistake.'

'What alternative is there?'

'But you don't know anything about Lord Rylan, ma'am. The dragons cannot be trusted.'

Leona said nothing.

'Why would you risk everything, ma'am?' said Farakai.

'Because the risk is worth taking. You ran Kaugatz before I arrived, and you can do it again if I am killed.'

'Do you long for martyrdom?'

'No. I very much want to stay alive, but the Gunstians have been blockading Zamata for two weeks, and not a single ship can get in or out. Eventually, if nothing is done, everyone on this island will starve to death and the Gunstians will inherit the ruins. Would you call me a carriage?'

Farakai stared at her, then he bowed his head and left the room.

. . .

The weather was starting to turn; Leona could feel it. The warmth of the summer sun had lessened a little, and a mild breeze was blowing through her hair as she walked the short distance from the carriage to the gates outside the southern end of the Dragon Palace. Bullan soldiers were guarding the iron fence, and groups of anxious Aucterians were milling around, hoping to catch a glimpse of the dragons. Leona squeezed her way through the crowds and approached the gates.

'I have an appointment to see Lord Rylan,' she said to a Bullan sergeant on the other side of the thick bars.

'Name?'

'Leona of Kaugatz.'

The Bullan officer stared at her for a moment, then he gestured to the squad next to him. 'Let her through.'

Two soldiers swung open one of the gates, and Leona strode into the gardens, expecting to be arrested. Instead, an Aucterian army officer in a smart uniform approached from the left.

He nodded to the Bullan. 'I'll take her from here.'

'Yes, sir,' said the sergeant, as the gate was closed and barred.

'This must be kept quiet,' the officer went on. 'Not a word to anyone about our visitor, on the orders of Lord Rylan.'

The Bullan saluted, and went back to their posts.

'My name is Captain Jair,' the officer said to Leona. 'I am surprised you came.'

'Who else knows that I was invited here?'

'Apart from this squad, no one but me and Lord Rylan himself,' the captain said. 'We felt it better to keep it discreet. I trust that you have also told no one?'

'The agent who informed me knows, but I have told no one else. If this is a trick and I am to be executed, I hope you make it quick.'

The captain smiled. 'I was ordered to escort you to the Governor, miss. I have no idea what Lord Rylan intends to do with you once you are in his presence.'

Captain Jair led her through the quiet avenues of the large gardens as the sun began to set in the west. Great stretches of open lawn spread out to either side, lined by palm trees and decorative water courses. Leona was escorted to a small entrance in the side of the palace, and taken down a narrow flight of stairs. They emerged into a long passageway, close to where she had been imprisoned by Lord Malum before he had discovered that she was Gifted, but they passed the cells and entered a large chamber full of steam.

'My lord,' the captain said; 'Leona of Kaugatz is here to see you.'

An enormous grey and yellow head appeared through the clouds of warm mist. He eyed Leona, then tilted his head. 'Leave us, Captain. Wait outside, and let no one enter.'

The Aucterian officer bowed, then he left the chamber, closing the door behind him.

'Leona of Kaugatz,' Rylan said, 'or Lady Takri – which would you prefer?'

'I prefer Leona, my lord; as it is my real name.'

'You call me *lord*? That amuses me. You are a spy and a traitor, responsible for various crimes worthy of death; and yet you accepted my invitation – why?'

'To save Zamata,' she said. 'Kill me if that is your desire.'

'It is my desire,' the dragon said, 'but I shall, for now, suppress my longing to spill your blood.'

'I assume you read my letter?'

'I did. The agent who delivered it is resting in the dungeons. You would have passed him on your way here.'

'You arrested him?'

'Naturally. I needed to know the truth about your motivations. Tell me – how am I to ascertain the truth when you can resist my spells?'

'I see you recall that detail about me.'

'I recall everything about you, Takri; including your part in the massacre of the Gunstians who dwelt on this island. Part of me thought you would be too ashamed to show your face again, but then I saw you watching me through the palace fence some days ago. You were attempting to hide in the shadows, but I could sense your presence.'

'I saw you fly.'

'Indeed. Let us return to your letter. I would be interested to know why you think I could work with someone as reprehensible and treacherous as you.'

'Our purposes are aligned. My enemies are your enemies.'

'You are my enemy, Leona.'

'I disagree. What I did as Lady Takri was in service of this island. What I am doing now is in service of this island. I think, and I hope, that you also wish the best for Zamata. There is a rumour that you have denounced the Dominion.'

'I have not denounced anyone,' said Rylan. 'The Dominion abandoned me here, and I am no longer bound to its authority.'

'That amounts to much the same thing.'

'Perhaps. What can you offer me?'

'Information, and the cooperation of the Zamatan agents spread throughout this island. I control Kaugatz – its food supply, its deliveries of weapons; and every decision made there passes through me first. I would be your eyes and ears among the Zamatans. If you wish to defeat the Gunstians, then my help will be essential. Conversely, the same is true for me. I need your help if we are to prevail.'

'I have already brokered an agreement with Lahnos Laimos,' the dragon said. 'He pledged to speak to the men of the Zamatan regiments, to attempt to bring them under my authority.'

'I am aware of this deal,' Leona said. 'My people in Kaugatz have told me of this; but for Lahnos to be successful, he will also need my assistance. Before I give it to him, I need to know if I can do so without the fear that you will hunt me down and kill me.'

'Are you in league with Bauchlie?'

'I broke with Bauchlie some time ago. Lahnos has also parted ways with the rebel commander. Did you know that Bauchlie has sent his agents into Kaugatz? They are telling the Zamatans that any who ascend Mount Medamuna to look for Lahnos will be treated as traitors, and dealt with accordingly. Were you aware of that?'

'I was not. I had begun to fear that Lahnos had gone back on his word. He has spent many days on the mountain doing nothing.'

'Lahnos's promises can be trusted. He and I think alike on certain matters, but Bauchlie does not agree with us, nor does he understand our reasoning. He wishes to carry on in the same manner as before; it is all he knows.'

'Have you met with Lahnos since his return?'

'Not yet. I am waiting until I know that I can do so safely. My life, and the lives of my agents are not to be imperilled. Do you agree to this condition?'

'I, too, have conditions.'

'Then let us negotiate. What do you want?'

'Firstly, I need to know if the Demon Witch has plans to disrupt my defence of this island. I know that you have had dealings with her in the past. Do you have dealings with her now?'

'The Demon Witch will not intervene. You have my word.'

'And why is that? Did she perish in the events that took the life of Lady Macsin?'

'She is alive, but she will not intervene. That is all I am prepared to say on the matter.'

The dragon said nothing for a while, as steam billowed around his features, then he tilted his head.

'Secondly,' he went on, 'I need to know if you are able to neutralise the threat from Bauchlie. Will *he* attempt to intervene?'

'He might, but I will oppose him.'

'Will you kill him?'

'Only if that becomes absolutely necessary. Bauchlie can be contained and, once he learns that his methods are futile, he may change his mind.'

'Your responses to my conditions are unsatisfactory,' the dragon said. 'You remain vague regarding the Demon Witch, and you make no promises concerning Bauchlie. Perhaps I should open my jaws and remove your head, as punishment for the deaths of thousands of Gunstian civilians.'

'I did not kill a single Gunstian, and you know it.'

'You stood by Lord Malum's side and allowed it to happen.'

'It would have happened without me. My opposition would have merely resulted in my own death.' She lowered her gaze. 'All the same, that day will haunt me forever.'

'How I wish I could believe you, but Lady Takri was nothing if not a proficient liar. How do I know that you are not lying to me now?'

'You don't.'

'And yet you can sense every untruth uttered by another? What power.'

'I can offer you this power.'

'As you offered it to Lord Malum?'

'Lord Malum used my Gift for his own purposes, and I would allow you to do the same. However, if you truly wish to defend this island then I would give you my full support, not the evasive half-truths I gave to Malum. I could be a useful ally, but first I need to know if your intentions are honest. Tell me your plans for Zamata.'

'No. I do not trust you, Leona of Kaugatz.'

'Then we are doomed to fail. If I do not return to my home alive, then my agents will refuse to cooperate with your administration. Some may even desert to Bauchlie. How will you defeat the Gunstians if you cannot control Kaugatz?'

'You are bluffing. You are desperate, and you would say anything to leave this palace alive and with the assurance that I will not track you down and slay you.'

'I am desperate, yes. The island's food stocks are low, and the next harvest is many months away. Even if we are successful, people are going to starve over winter. You need someone in Kaugatz with the authority to enforce strict rationing, and I am the only person who can do it. You need someone to arm the men of the Zamatan regiments and, again, only I can do so. You need someone to contain Bauchlie, and to protect the island from any more Gifted Gunstians who may try to sabotage our defences – and yes, you will need me for that, too. Should I go on? Lahnos trusts me – did I mention that? By coming here today, despite the warnings of my most valued agents, I have proved that I am willing to compromise. Are you?'

'I have one more question. Will you accept my authority as Governor of the Serpent Isle?'

'No, but I will accept it as Governor of Zamata, if I can hear you pledge your loyalty to all who dwell here. Swear that you will defend this island and not hand it over to either the Dominion or to the Gunstians, and you will have my fidelity.'

'You push me too far, human.'

'I have hardly begun pushing you, Lord Rylan. If I swear allegiance, then rest assured that I will never stop pushing you.'

The dragon looked away.

'Give me something, my lord,' said Leona. 'Anything to set my mind at ease that you hold the best interests of this island close to your heart.'

'Very well, Leona of Kaugatz – I will give you this. As Governor of Zamata, I swear to defend this island against the Gunstians, and against anyone else who tries to invade. I swear to rule with justice. I swear to govern all inhabitants equally; the same laws will apply to Zamatans and Aucterians. There – did I lie?'

A low growling, groaning sound echoed off the chamber walls, and another dragon appeared through the steam, his red scales glistening.

'I have heard enough,' cried the red dragon, as he raised his claws. 'Rylan – you are a traitor. You have betrayed yourself with your own words.'

'Lord Gradham,' said Rylan, 'this was a private conversation. Were you skulking in the shadows and steam, listening? You dishonour yourself.'

'It is not I who have dishonoured myself,' roared Gradham. 'Your mighty father would be ashamed to hear such treachery! You debase yourself in front of this worthless spy, and for what – an insignificant speck in the vast ocean? Do you wish to be the king of a barren rock? The other dragons will rip you to shreds when I tell them what has transpired here.'

Rylan faced the red dragon. 'You shall not be telling them, Lord Gradham, for you will not be leaving the baths alive.'

Rylan lunged at Gradham, and the raised forelimbs of the two dragons locked together as each tried to push the other back. Rylan's jaws went for Gradham's throat, but the red dragon swerved away, his tail swinging round and catching Leona in the midriff. She was thrown through the steam-filled air, then collided with a tiled wall and fell into a pool of hot water. Her body plunged beneath the surface, then her head came back up as she gasped for air. A giant forelimb crashed down next to her, sending a great plume of water into her face, and she went under again, her lungs screaming in agony. She tried to swim, but she hit the smooth tiles of the back wall. A roar of noise filled her ears as she scrabbled backwards, but there was nothing on the wall to grip on to and she floundered.

The churned-up water around her turned red, then a ripped wing smashed into the wall above her, dislodging tiles as the two dragons wrestled and writhed in the enormous pool. Leona tried to breathe and instead filled her mouth with bloody water, as she choked and began to drown.

A man's hands gripped her shoulders and pulled her clear of the pool. She was dragged along the tiled floor and through a doorway, where she lay, panting and coughing up water. She opened her eyes and saw the Aucterian captain standing over her, his smart uniform sodden and dripping onto the floor of the passageway.

Leona rolled onto her knees and vomited red water over the ground as she hugged her chest. Next to her, Captain Jair crouched down and placed a hand on her back.

'Thank you,' she gasped.

'Don't thank me just yet,' Jair said. 'Both of our lives now depend upon which dragon walks through that door.'

He helped her sit.

'Why did you pull me out?'

He eyed her. 'Don't take this the wrong way, but I was listening to every word you and the Governor were saying. I don't like you, but if Lord Rylan wants you alive, then it was my duty to see that you didn't drown in there.'

'You were listening?'

'I was. You were Lady Takri? The Zamatans would kill you if they knew.'

'Are you going to tell them?'

He shrugged. 'I will if Lord Rylan orders me to.'

Leona shivered in the passageway, and drew her knees up to her chest, her body aching. The sounds of the two dragons stilled, and she and the Aucterian officer stared at the large doorway.

The door opened, and Lord Rylan's head appeared in the entranceway, his jaws dripping blood and gore onto the wet floor.

Jair gasped in relief and got to his feet, bowing. 'My lord.'

Rylan tilted his head. 'My faithful captain. Lord Gradham is no more.'

'What are your orders, my lord?'

'Get Leona of Kaugatz out of the palace as quickly as possible and without being seen. Ensure she is safely escorted to a carriage and return her to Kaugatz. She was never here.'

'And Lord Gradham, my lord? What will I say about that?'

'Tell anyone who asks that Lord Gradham attacked me as I bathed, in an attempt to usurp the governorship.' The grey and yellow dragon turned to Leona. 'And you, spy – go back to Kaugatz. I will ponder your offer. If I decide to accept, you will hear from me. If not, then your death will come swiftly in the night.'

'And my agent in the cells?'

'He will remain here for now. Go.'

The captain hauled Leona to her feet. She swayed, and he put his arm over her shoulders to steady her steps as they retreated along the stone passageway.

'You had some nerve coming here,' Jair murmured.

'What else was I supposed to do?' Leona gasped. 'Sit in Kaugatz and wait for the food to run out? Thank you again for saving my life.'

'I don't want your gratitude,' he said. 'Do you know why? Because if Lord Rylan refuses your offer, it will be me he sends to kill you.'

CHAPTER 10
FRUIT PICKING

Fidalaimos, Serpent Isle – 6th Luddinch 1588

Lahnos's back began to ache as he stooped down and filled the basket with ripe oranges. He had been picking fruit all day – oranges, lemons and limes from the extensive groves that surrounded Friel Laimos's mountainside cottage. The heat from the sun wasn't as strong as it had been in mid-summer, but it remained tiring work, and the fruit would be stored by the villagers of Fidalaimos to help tide them over the coming winter.

Perhaps manual labour was what he needed to take his mind off the crushing disappointment of the previous two weeks. Despite what Efizel and Reyn had assured him, only a trickle of people had made the journey up Mount Medamuna to see Lahnos, and he was starting to think that he had made a mistake. The life of the island had gone on despite the Gunstian blockade; and while the Zamatans might be grateful for what the young part-Bullan had achieved, few seemed grateful enough to leave their homes to seek Lahnos out.

He paused for a few moments to drink tepid water from a skin. To his right, the twelve Bullan he had rescued from the camp outside Great Gunst were busy gathering fruit, and Lahnos watched them at work, amused that they had shown more loyalty and devotion to him than the vast number of Zamatan men he had brought home.

Reyn glanced at him, and held out her hand for the water skin. He passed it to her and she drank, then she wiped the dust and sweat from her forehead.

'What's wrong?' she said.

'You know what's wrong,' Lahnos replied. 'What are we doing up here, Reyn?'

She smiled and looked around. 'Picking fruit?'

'You know what I mean. Should I have stayed with Bauchlie?'

'It's a bit late for that.'

'Is that your way of not answering the question?'

'You and I think differently these days,' she said. 'For me, this has been the best two weeks I've spent in...' She shrugged. 'I can't even remember when I was this happy. You and I spend every night together, just like we did before you were conscripted; and I feel free.'

'Free from Bauchlie?'

'He wasn't that bad. But, yes. Free from always worrying about the next operation. I learned a lot from him, but it was all about how to kill or maim people, or how to extract information from captives during interrogations. None of it made me feel good about myself, but this does. This is honest work.'

'I thought you wanted to be a fighter?'

'Yes, but there's a difference between being prepared to defend Zamata and actually enjoying what that means. Did you enjoy being a soldier?'

'I still consider myself a soldier.'

'Who's avoiding the question now?'

He took the water skin and slung it over his shoulder, then he stooped down to load the basket with more fallen oranges.

'Yes,' he said. 'No and yes. I enjoyed the feeling of being in a group that would fight to protect each other, but I hated the mud and the sight of death all around me. I would never tell the others in my squad this, but I think I might have loved every one of the stupid bastards. And, if it hadn't been for the army, I would never have been reconciled with Karl.'

'Apart from the bit about Karl,' Reyn said, as she leaned over next to him, 'I agree with all of that. Being in Bauchlie's band of rebels made me feel as though I was doing something important. I am ready to fight the Gunstians now – more prepared. I won't freeze or panic if someone points a crossbow at me, because I already know what it feels like.'

Lahnos threw a few more oranges into the basket. 'So, what's your advice?'

'Enjoy this,' she said. 'Try to relax and enjoy the freedom. It won't last.'

Lahnos picked up the full basket and grunted under its weight. Reyn walked by his side as they emerged from the grove, and they strode up to a line of carts. Lahnos deposited the basket onto the back of the closest one, and an old villager from Fidalaimos smiled at him.

'Thanks, lad,' she said. 'Just another five baskets, and this cart will be full. It was good of you to let us come up here to harvest Colonel Laimos's groves.'

'They're *my* groves now,' Lahnos said. 'My uncle didn't have any children, so the house will have come to me, Karl and our sisters.'

Something in Reyn's expression altered slightly as the words left Lahnos's mouth, but he ignored it and nodded at the old villager, and then began to head back to the neat rows of orange trees. He picked up an empty basket and he and Reyn re-entered the grove.

'What aren't you telling me, Reyn?' he said, as he placed the basket down by a tree.

Reyn glanced at him. 'What?'

'It's something to do with the house. Or my uncle and the house; I'm not sure.'

She shrugged.

'I know you too well,' he said. 'Can you say why you can't tell me?'

'It's none of my business,' she said.

'So there is something?'

Reyn crouched down in the shade of the trees and looked at him.

'Yes. There's something you don't know; but I don't think I should be the one to tell you. The only thing I will say is that you probably shouldn't go around telling people that you have inherited Friel's old mansion.'

'Right. That means that either Friel didn't actually own it or... he left it to someone else? Leona? Did my uncle write a will?'

'I have no idea, Lahnos.'

'If he left it to Leona, then you would tell me,' he went on, 'because that wouldn't be a secret.'

'Please stop this, Lahnos. Just leave it alone.'

'Why?'

'Because I'm asking you to.'

Lahnos frowned, but carried on gathering the fallen fruit from the dusty ground, while Reyn avoided meeting his gaze. A sense of frustration built within him about Reyn's time with Bauchlie and the rebels. They had killed Dominion soldiers together, and had shared a life that he had not seen or understood. And just who did Bauchlie think he was, gathering up two hundred of the island's young women to follow his orders and call him *sir*? It was as though he had been building the biggest harem in Zamata's history; and now every one of those women had been brutalised by violence. Would they ever be interested in settling down and having families after all that they had been through? Wars were for men to fight; they did it to spare the womenfolk from its horrors and pain, and part of Lahnos couldn't help but look differently at Reyn after she had admitted killing several Aucterian and Bullan soldiers.

When the Gunstians attacked, as they surely would, Lahnos knew he was going to have to watch Reyn fight them. He would have to override his protective instincts and allow her to put herself in danger, just as each member of his squad in Gunst had shared the same dangers together. Could he do it? After everything she had done with Bauchlie, he could hardly forbid it – and if he was foolish enough to try, he knew what her response would be.

Lahnos glanced up as he heard shouting coming from the other side of the cottage estate. He and Reyn got to their feet and peered through the lines of orange trees.

'Dragon! Dragon!' someone was calling out.

Lahnos cursed under his breath. Had Rylan come to see why he hadn't held up his end of the bargain they had struck? Or perhaps Rylan had been overthrown, and a different dragon was on their way to raze the ruins of Medamuna Gatzoun, in an attempt to destroy Bauchlie's rebel stronghold. Lahnos ran out from the orange grove, and saw several of the Bullan hurrying to pull on their armour and weapons, which had been set down by the main entrance to the mansion. Lahnos scanned the skies as he ran, but saw nothing but white clouds against the deep blue. He caught sight of a panicking villager and changed direction to intercept him.

'What's going on?' he cried.

'A dragon is climbing the mountainside!' the villager shouted.

Lahnos skidded to a halt. 'Did you say *climbing*? Not flying?'

'That's right,' panted the man.

'What colour are his scales?'

'They're green, but they shimmer like silver.'

Lahnos raised his hands in the air. 'Everyone – calm down. Listen to me! Calm yourselves.' He glanced at the Bullan. 'It's Lord Sigum. Come with me, to make sure no one is stupid enough to attack him.'

'Are you sure it's him?' said Reyn, catching up with him on the gravel at the rear of the mansion.

'I can't think who else it could be,' said Lahnos. 'Out of the five dragons on the island, only Sigum is silvery-green; and he's the only one who can't fly. Stay here, Reyn, and tell everyone that the approaching dragon is a friend of mine. I'll take the Bullan down the hill to meet him, and to make sure nothing disastrous happens.'

He raced away from Reyn, and gathered the twelve Bullan.

'Follow me,' he said. 'We'll meet Lord Sigum and escort him here.'

'Yes, sir,' said Efizel.

Lahnos narrowed his eyes. 'Don't call me that, not after everything we've been through.'

The Bullan soldier raised an eyebrow. 'That sounds like something I said when you insisted I become the squad sergeant in Gunst, sir.'

A couple of the other Bullan chuckled as they made their way through the gardens. They came to the path that led to Fidalaimos, and hurried down it. After a hundred yards, they ran into a small crowd of villagers who were streaming up the hillside towards them.

'Where is the dragon?' Efizel cried out.

The villagers halted at the sight of Lahnos with twelve Bullan.

One pointed down the slope. 'Uh, that way, sir.'

The crowd parted to let the Bullan through and Lahnos led them down the track. They passed through a thick stand of spruce trees, and then out the other side. On their left, the houses and buildings of Fidalaimos were nestling in a low valley, their red roofs visible through more trees. Lahnos pointed ahead. A dragon was moving up the valley towards them, his silvery-green scales reflecting the light of the afternoon sun.

Lahnos laughed. 'Are you lost?' he shouted.

Lord Sigum raised his head. 'Lahnos Laimos,' he said; 'at last.'

'Have you walked all the way from Igatz?'

'I have both walked and swam. I confess, it was a far longer journey than I had imagined. This island truly is a serpent, the way it snakes back and forth. Were I able to fly, I would have made the journey in under ten minutes. As it is, I have walked for many miles, after swimming both the Cyasarta and the Hansarta, and I am in dire need of some fresh water to drink.'

'Is there some emergency I should know about?'

'No, although I have a message for you from Lord Rylan.'

'Allow us to escort you,' Lahnos said. 'You may have frightened a few of the local villagers.'

Lahnos and the Bullan waited until the dragon reached them, then they set off up the hillside.

'How have you been, my friend?' said Lahnos.

'I am well,' said the dragon. 'Might I say how good it is to see you again? I feared for your life while Lady Abda was here, but I had every confidence that Lord Rylan would not have you executed as she commanded. Things have been tense in the Dragon Palace, however, and I did not think it wise to leave the Governor's side for a while.'

'He told me that you were helping to defend his rule.'

'I saw it as my duty, but I longed to be reunited with you.'

Lahnos raised an eyebrow at the dragon. 'Really? Why?'

'I cannot quite find the words to explain it, Lahnos. You... I mean, I... Well, you see, you are... dear to me.'

Lahnos stopped on the path. 'That means a lot to me, my lord.'

'Do not refer to me by that appellation again. I am not your lord, Lahnos – I am your friend.'

Lahnos raised a palm and placed it on to the side of the dragon's face. 'And I am yours.'

Sigum stared at him, then he looked away as though embarrassed.

'We should keep moving, sir,' said Efizel. 'The sooner we get back to the mansion, the sooner we can see to Lord Sigum's needs.'

They started moving again.

'Why was it safe to leave Lord Rylan's side now?' Lahnos said.

'The Governor slew Lord Gradham,' said Sigum.

'Rylan killed Gradham?'

'Yes. I did not see it, but the human servants in the palace took many hours to clean the baths where the slaying took place. Lord Gradham attacked Lord Rylan there, in an attempt to usurp power. It was a cowardly assault, and Gradham paid for his treachery. Needless to say, all opposition to Lord Rylan from Lord Givra ceased immediately, and so the Governor of Zamata gave me permission to look for you.'

'Did you just say the Governor of *Zamata*?'

'That is what Lord Rylan is calling himself. He wishes it to be known that he represents everyone upon this island. I concur with his decision on this. I feel intense bitterness about the way Lady Abda abandoned us here. The Dominion no longer has my allegiance; instead, my loyalty now lies with Lord Rylan and this island.'

A few of the Bullan glanced at each other.

They caught up with the crowd of villagers who had fled from the approach of the dragon, and they stood by the side of the road as Sigum, Lahnos and the Bullan passed, their eyes transfixed by the sight of the majestic creature.

'It was not my intention to scare you,' the dragon said. 'I sought my friend Lahnos Laimos, and I shall not hurt any of his kinfolk.'

The villagers said nothing, but several of them looked at Lahnos as though seeing him anew. They reached the edge of the gardens, and found that everyone who had been working in the groves had assembled by the side of the mansion.

Efizel gestured to three of the other Bullan. 'Fill the horse trough with fresh, cool water from the stream.'

The three saluted and hurried away.

'This is Lord Sigum Mon Sigel,' Lahnos said to the startled workers. 'He is my friend and an honoured guest. It was he who led the ships that brought the Zamatan men home.' He gestured for Reyn to come forward. 'Lord Sigum, this is Reyn.'

The dragon tilted his head. 'It is an honour to meet you, Reyn. Lahnos Laimos often spoke of you on our voyage from Gunst.'

Reyn flushed a little. She began to perform an awkward curtsy, then seemed to recall that the rebels hated the dragons, and stopped herself.

'It's... nice to meet you,' she said.

Sigum waited as though he assumed Reyn would say more, but she closed her mouth.

'The water is ready for you, my lord,' said a Bullan.

'Ah, thank you,' the dragon said. 'Please excuse me, everyone, while I take some refreshment.'

Sigum turned his enormous bulk through the gardens and leaned his long neck over the trough.

Reyn nudged Lahnos as the dragon began to drink. 'What's he doing here?'

'He came to find me.'

'Yes, but why?'

'It's what friends do.'

Reyn's tail swished, a sure sign that she was trying to suppress her annoyance.

When the dragon had finished drinking from the trough, he turned his head to gaze down at Lahnos.

'And now for the message,' he said. 'Lord Rylan, the Governor of Zamata, has this to say to you, Lahnos Laimos – he offers you his cordial greetings, and wishes to enquire if you have been unavoidably delayed in carrying out the actions that you agreed to in the monastery of Zamata Gataza. He has been assured by more than one source that your word can be trusted, and would like to offer his assistance in overcoming any obstacles you may face. He also suggests that it might be prudent to move your base of operations to a more central location; perhaps Kaugatz would be appropriate? Finally, he wishes you to know that you continue to have his support, but his lordship would also like to remind you that the Gunstian blockade tightens with every passing day, and that the time for action is pressing.' Lord Sigum tilted his head. 'That ends the message.'

Lahnos smiled. 'It sounded like a very polite reprimand.'

'Your interpretation may be correct, my friend,' said the dragon.

'In truth,' Lahnos went on, 'I had assumed that the men of the Zamatan regiments would come to me.' He gestured at the small crowd of Bullan, labourers, and local villagers from Fidalaimos. 'As you can see, I was wrong.'

'Do you wish to be made aware of the reasons for your error?'

'Do you know them?'

'I do,' said the dragon. 'Lord Rylan confided in me, and what I have to say is only for you to hear. May we go somewhere private?'

'Let's walk to the other side of the mansion,' Lahnos said. 'Sergeant, please keep everyone away while Lord Sigum and I speak.'

Efizel saluted. 'Yes, sir.'

Lahnos narrowed his eyes at his old friend, but said nothing. He led Sigum away from the crowd, and they walked until they were alone on the far side of the gardens.

'The information I am about to give you,' said the dragon, 'comes from a secret source that has been in contact with Lord Rylan. According to this source, the rebel leader Bauchlie has sent agents down into Kaugatz and the surrounding towns, forbidding them from coming up the mountainside to seek you out. Bauchlie has issued a warning that any who side with you shall be deemed traitors to the island, and the fear in which the rebel commander is held among the local populace has been enough to deter them.'

'It was Bauchlie?' said Lahnos. 'I should have known.'

'Hence Lord Rylan's request that you relocate. This mansion may be close to your old village, but it is also close to the ruins of Medamuna Gatzoun, where Bauchlie is based. I would advise that you move down from the mountain in the next day or so.'

Lahnos turned from the dragon and gazed out at the view of the island from the mansion's gardens.

'All right,' he said; 'I shall relocate to Kaugatz. I'm going to miss seeing this every day.'

Sigum followed his gaze. 'It is a magnificent spectacle. However, I flew over the island when I first arrived here with King Naghad's invasion force. That provided a view that was better than this.'

Lahnos laughed. 'You're making me jealous.'

'It is a pity that you do not have wings, my friend.'

'My horns will have to suffice. Let's go back to the others, and I'll tell them that we are moving to Kaugatz.'

'A sensible decision, my friend.'

They walked back round to the other side of the mansion.

'I have an announcement,' Lahnos said to the assembled workers. 'I'm leaving Fidalaimos as soon as we've finished gathering in the fruit. The Governor of Zamata has asked for our help to defend this island, and I can do that better down in Kaugatz. Anyone who wishes is free to come with me. Now, let's get back to work.'

Reyn approached him as the crowd dispersed.

'Does this mean our holiday is over?' she said.

'I'm afraid so,' he said. 'It's time to stop hiding in the mountains.'

. . .

A soft noise awoke Lahnos from a dreamless sleep, and he opened his eyes to the darkness of the room he shared with Reyn. He could hear the sound of her breathing next to him, but the rest of the mansion was shrouded in silence. The shutters were allowing in a little light from the crescent moon, and he wondered if Lord Sigum was used to sleeping out in the open air. He felt safe with the dragon down in the garden, and rolled onto his side. Something metallic glimmered for a fraction of a second, and a blade came down, striking the pillow where his head had been a moment before. Lahnos pushed out with his arms, sending Reyn flying off the bed. She landed on the floor as Lahnos threw his pillow at the figure leaning over the bed. The man dodged it, then raised his dagger again.

'You filthy little coward,' the man spat. 'This is what happens to traitors who betray their homeland to the dragons. For Bauchlie!'

The man's arm came down and Lahnos lashed out in a blind panic, his right hand grasping the man's wrist. The tip of the blade halted an inch from Lahnos's face as he struggled, but the other man was stronger. The blade grazed his cheek, and then a power within Lahnos that he hadn't known he possessed surged through his body, and entered the man via the skin of his fingertips.

Lahnos's vision went black.

Confused images rushed across his mind. He saw the groves of orange and lemon trees, and a half-filled basket by his feet; and then he felt a wave of anger and loathing pass through him as he watched the silvery-green dragon stride into the garden next to Lahnos and the twelve Bullan.

Disgusting demons.

He was delving through the man's memories, Lahnos realised, without understanding how it could be possible. He dug deeper and, through the man's eyes, saw his arrival at the mansion. He had hidden himself among a group of Zamatan labourers from Wayston, and was pretending to be an itinerant worker, moving from location to location for day jobs. Lahnos went back further, and found himself in a low-ceiling tavern.

'If he stays up in the mountains, then leave him be,' another man was saying. 'His inaction will discredit him among the Zamatans, and that would be as useful to us as his death. But, if he decides to move down to the inner island – take his life.'

'Yes, sir,' said the man.

'If possible, blame the killing on Bauchlie – let the Zamatans imagine that one of their own has murdered this so-called hero...'

The vision blurred and faded, and Lahnos opened his eyes, feeling wide awake and alert.

Had he dreamt the entire thing? Lahnos sat up. He saw Reyn staring at him, her hands on her face, and then he noticed the knife lying on the bed.

'What happened?' he said. 'Were we attacked?'

'You killed him, Lahnos,' Reyn said. 'I don't know how, but he was about to drive the knife into your face, and...'

Lahnos brought his glance down. A body was lying on the floor, his limbs twisted unnaturally. Lahnos lit the bedside lamp and jumped out of bed. He knelt down by the man and rolled him over on to his back. His face had frozen in an expression of pure agony, but more than that, his skin had withered like dried-up old leather.

'I think I recognise him,' Reyn said. 'He's been working in the groves for the last few days. I even talked to him this morning. But look at him now – it's as though he's been dead for days.'

'I didn't do this,' Lahnos said.

'I watched it happen,' said Reyn. 'You touched him, and he died.'

Lahnos remembered the wave of power that had passed through his fingertips. Some of that power still seemed to be surging through him, and his body felt almost giddy with energy.

'Bauchlie did not send him,' he said.

'How do you know that?'

'He was speaking in Gunstian. I mean, in his memories.'

Reyn pulled her gaze from the body. 'You read his memories?'

'That felt like death-reading,' he said, 'but the part before... I felt... something leave my fingers.'

Reyn reached out with a hand to touch him, then she pulled away.

'Fetch Efizel,' he said.

'What does it mean, Lahnos?'

'I don't know.'

Reyn pulled on a dressing gown to cover her nightshirt, then she ran from the room. Lahnos turned his gaze to stare at the withered-up body lying twisted on the wooden floorboards.

What had he done? From everything Leona and his uncle had told him about his Gift, he knew that the agent's death made no sense. In Toraq City, he had plunged a knife into the heart of a Gunstian officer, ending his life so that he could raid his memories; this time, his touch alone seemed to have killed the man trying to attack him. He looked at his hands. They seemed normal, as though nothing had happened.

When he reached Kaugatz, he would need to seek out Leona; perhaps she could explain what had occurred. Until then, it would be better if he touched no one. Reyn would understand. From the look on her face before she had rushed away to fetch Efizel, he doubted she would disagree.

CHAPTER 11
DOWN ON THE BEACH

Medamuna Gatzoun, Serpent Isle – 7th Luddinch 1588

'I can confirm it, Commander,' said one of Bauchlie's officers; 'our agent in Fidalaimos heard the lad announce it – he's going down to Kaugatz within the next few days.'

Bauchlie said nothing, his features obscured by the shadows of the flickering oil lamps.

'We should act swiftly, Commander,' said another officer. 'If Lahnos is able to talk to the peasants in Kaugatz, he could persuade many to bow before the dragons. We cannot allow this to happen; it would destroy all that we have worked for.'

'What do you recommend?' said Bauchlie.

'We have no choice, Commander. We should kill the boy.'

A few of the other officers lowered their gazes, but none spoke. Cisca remained quiet, aware that many objected to her presence in the hastily-called emergency meeting.

'Lahnos has a dragon and twelve Bullan protecting him,' Bauchlie said.

'Yes, Commander, but our agent has earned their trust. He has poison, and access to the mansion's kitchen. He only awaits your orders, sir, and the threat from Lahnos Laimos will be neutralised.'

Bauchlie shook his head. 'We cannot kill the man responsible for saving seven thousand Zamatans.'

'He is a traitor,' said the officer. 'He has sworn allegiance to Lord Rylan and betrayed this island. If you are concerned with the reactions of the ordinary Zamatans, Commander, then the answer is simple – we blame his death on the Gunstians.'

Bauchlie said nothing.

'If you wish, Commander,' the officer went on, 'you need not order anything. You can remain silent, in order to maintain deniability.'

'Then I forbid it,' said Bauchlie. 'Is that clear enough for you? Leave Lahnos Laimos alone. We will oppose him politically, but we shall not be poisoning his food, not while this island is surrounded by the entire Imperial Gunstian Fleet. Let the Zamatans have their hero. Let Lahnos descend from the mountain alive and unharmed. Our agent can follow him down to Kaugatz and report on his movements from there. That is my command. Dismissed.'

The officers stood without another word and filed from the dark, smoky underground chamber. Bauchlie exhaled as soon as they had gone, and placed his head in his hands.

'They will think I am going soft,' he muttered. 'Maybe I am.'

'Perhaps you should tell them the truth,' said Cisca.

Bauchlie emitted a low laugh. 'That would only make it worse. If they knew that Lahnos was my cousin, then they would accuse me of showing favouritism towards my family.'

Cisca edged a little closer to him. 'Is that the real reason?'

'Partly. I was never close to my father. I... regret that. He and I argued for many years about the best way to free this island, but we never spoke as father and son. Lahnos infuriates me, but how could I live with myself if I ordered his execution?'

'Did you know Lahnos's father – your uncle?'

Bauchlie shook his head.

'Do you want to know what I think?'

'Yes.'

Cisca pulled her gaze away from him. 'I think Lahnos is right to seek allies among the dragons who were abandoned here by the Dominion. The Gunstians cannot realise this, but if they were to land their troops along the Hansarta, then Zamata would be theirs within hours. One thousand Aucterian soldiers and two hundred Bullan cannot defend this island, even with four dragons aiding them. Lord Rylan has positioned the bulk of his forces to protect the two Chain Castles; the rest of the island is undefended. The best hope we have is that the Zamatan men re-enlist and help garrison the defences. Lahnos is the only person who can do this.'

'The Gunstians are waiting until hunger starts to bite,' said Bauchlie. 'They know how precarious our food supplies have become. In a few months, it won't matter how many men Lord Rylan has under his command. Lahnos is selling out his principles for nothing.'

'Do you really believe that? I don't think Lahnos views the cause in the same way that you do, Bauchlie. He isn't selling out his beliefs; he thinks he's doing the right thing.'

Bauchlie's dark eyes tightened.

'Will you call off your agents in Kaugatz?' Cisca went on.

'Why would I do that?'

'Your agents are part of the reason so few Zamatans climbed the mountain to seek out Lahnos. If they continue to go around threatening everyone, and telling them that they will be seen as traitors if they help your cousin, then you will divide the people you are trying to unite.'

'That would make it appear as though I was supporting the boy.'

'Would that be so bad?'

Bauchlie stared at her. 'Yes. I refuse to support a policy that will see Zamata remain in the hands of the colonial occupiers. Lord Rylan may talk about renouncing the Dominion, but I believe this to be a cynical and temporary manoeuvre on his part. He will fall back into line if the Dominion sends a new fleet to these shores.'

'But that could be decades away. You told me that you believe the dragons of the Dominion will be too busy fighting a civil war to care about the island.'

'Dragons live for centuries, Cisca. They can be patient. One day, the

Dominion might return, and if Lord Rylan remains in control of the government, then they will simply be able to walk back into power. We have to think of the long-term. We have to build a future in which the Dominion will fear to return to this island.'

'And in the meantime? We allow the Gunstians to take over? They would slaughter everyone on Zamata, and where would your future be then?'

'I know what you're saying, Cisca; but I cannot compromise on this. The cause is everything.'

'You would rather the island was reduced to smoking ruins than consider an alliance with Rylan?'

'Yes.'

Cisca sat back in her chair. How could she argue with such bloody-minded intransigence?

'Your agent with Lahnos,' she said; 'is it Reyn?'

He eyed her. 'Do you think I would order Reyn to betray the man she loves?'

Cisca shrugged. 'Yes.'

'Even if I had, she would have refused. She is a good fighter, but I know where her true loyalty lies. I wonder if it will last, though, once she sees Lahnos bow before Lord Rylan. That will hurt her deeply. And then, perhaps, she will come to me.'

'It sounds as though you like her.'

'I do like her. She has more patriotism in her little finger than Lahnos has in his entire body. If she ever returns to me, I would be proud to promote her. She would make a fine young officer.'

Cisca narrowed her eyes.

'What is it?' he said. 'Are you jealous?'

'No.'

'You have no need to be jealous, Cisca. You are the only person in this place that I would trust with this conversation. You are the only woman I can truly confide in; that has to mean something.'

'And what does it mean?' she said.

He glanced at her, and turned to face where she was sitting. His head moved a little closer, while his left hand took hers.

'Cisca,' he said. 'I...'

The door to the chamber swung open and a woman walked in. She eyed Bauchlie and Cisca sitting together, and a half-smile appeared on her lips.

Bauchlie blinked. 'Mother?'

'Good morning, son,' the woman said, as she leaned over the table and kissed Bauchlie on the forehead. 'How have you been? You seem to have recovered quickly from your father's death.'

'What are you doing here?' he said.

'Never mind that for now,' she said. 'Aren't you going to introduce me to your friend? I was led to believe that you were alone in here.'

Bauchlie said nothing for a moment, his eyes tight, then he gestured towards the former Dragon Corps officer.

'This is Cisca, mother.'

'Hello,' said Cisca. 'It is an honour to meet you.'

The smile vanished from Bauchlie's mother's lips. 'An Aucterian, son? You are... friends with an Aucterian woman?'

'We can discuss this later, mother,' said Bauchlie. 'Why are you in Medamuna Gatzoun?'

'I got your message about Friel Laimos. To be honest, the way he behaved, I'm surprised he lasted as long as he did. Were you on speaking terms with him before he died?'

'I was.'

'That's good.' She glanced at Cisca. 'Bauchlie's father and I didn't exactly see eye to eye. Still, I never tried to prevent Bauchlie from seeing him.' She held out her hand. 'My name is Abilo. Are you a settler or a soldier?'

Cisca stared at the woman's hand, then she shook it. 'Neither. I used to be a captain in the Dragon Corps.'

Abilo grimaced. 'That accent. So, have you betrayed the Dominion, or are you a spy trying to compromise my son's position?'

'The dragons sentenced her to death, mother,' said Bauchlie. 'Now, for the final time – why are you here?'

Abilo frowned at him as she withdrew her hand from Cisca's. 'You haven't changed, have you? I don't see you in over a year, and that's all you have to say to me? I've heard all about your recent exploits in the village, son, and the women there know that I am your mother.'

'Why?' said Bauchlie. 'We were supposed to be keeping that a secret. Why would you tell them?'

Abilo shrugged. 'Pride.'

'You are putting yourself in danger. If any Dominion or Gunstians agents discovered that you are my mother, they would hurt you to get to me.'

'That's one reason why I am here, son,' she said. 'Two days ago, some new men appeared in the village. They claimed to have been with the Zamatan regiments, but they were lying. I think they were Gunstians. They were asking questions, and it was only a matter of time before someone told them who I was.' She narrowed her eyes slightly. 'The other reason is to ask you for help.'

'What help do you need, mother? I can send a few fighters to deal with the men who arrived in your village; I'll just need someone who is able to identify them.'

'There is no need for that, as I have brought the village here.'

Bauchlie got to his feet. 'What? You brought the villagers up Mount Medamuna? Why?'

'Why do you think, son? There is no food left in the village. Our wheat fields were destroyed by the damn Gunstians, and we have no money to buy supplies from the other parts of the island; not at the prices they're charging. We were managing to get by before the men came home, but they've eaten through the last of our reserves. It was either bring the villagers here or take them all to Kaugatz, and I hear Kaugatz is about to implement a strict rationing regime. With everyone knowing that you are my son, the villagers voted to come here instead. You can feed them all, can't you? You must have been stockpiling food.'

Bauchlie shook his head, and Cisca thought he was about to start shouting. He took a breath.

'How many?' he said.

'Just under two hundred. They are all waiting up in the ruins. There are over a dozen young children among them – you can't let them starve.'

'You realise that there's no food coming into the island, mother? The Gunstians are preventing any ships from leaving or arriving. When the food's gone, it's gone.'

'But you will use what you have to feed them?'

'I have conditions.'

'You are the same old Bauchlie, son. Well? Let's hear your conditions.'

'The children are exempt,' he said, 'but everyone else will have to make themselves useful. Those of fighting age will join my rebel squads, while those too old or sick to fight will have to work here, in the caverns. There will be no more voting – what I say goes. If anyone breaks the rules, they will be expelled.'

Abilo said nothing for a moment, her sharp gaze matching her son's, then she nodded.

'I accept,' she said.

'Then wait here,' Bauchlie said. 'I will go up to the surface and take a look at what I am dealing with. You have doubled our numbers, mother. Instead of our supplies lasting four months, they will last two. Three, if we start cutting rations.'

'Three months is better than nothing, son. Thank you.'

Bauchlie strode from the chamber without another word, and Abilo sat down at the table next to Cisca.

'So, Dragon Corps officer,' she said; 'how do you know my son? I want to know everything.'

The caverns under the ruins of Medamuna Gatzoun were extensive, and the two hundred villagers spent the rest of the day moving their possessions down into the dark tunnels. Cisca had endured an awkward hour with Bauchlie's mother, answering her incessant questions, while attempting to hide her true feelings about Bauchlie from her. She doubted that the woman had been fooled, however, though she seemed to find it amusing rather than offensive that her son was showing interest in a mere Aucterian. A few of the rebels looked annoyed that Bauchlie had allowed so many civilians to enter their stronghold, aware that their presence would mean a cut in rations, and Cisca overheard a few whispering about leaving the caverns and going to Kaugatz.

Cisca set out to look for Bauchlie as the sun was setting outside, and she found him in an enormous cavern trying to organise the new arrivals. Several of the older villagers were eyeing the rebel commander with some suspicion as he doled out jobs and announced the rules that everyone would have to follow. A few children shouted at each other as they played by the side of the cavern, and Bauchlie glared at them.

'All children must remain underground unless supervised,' he said, 'and none shall be allowed to run or shout in the tunnels. This is a rebel base, not a school for infants.'

A young rebel fighter hurried into the cavern. She tried to reach Bauchlie, but he was surrounded by villagers, so she looked around and saw Cisca.

'Hey,' she said. 'I need someone to pass on a message to Commander Bauchlie.'

Cisca glanced over her shoulder to make sure that the rebel fighter was speaking to her and not to someone else.

'Yes, you,' said the fighter. 'You have the commander's ear, don't you? Tell him that three Gunstian warships have anchored just off the northern shoreline of Mount Medamuna, and one of them has launched rowing boats towards the coves on the cliffside. We need orders.'

Cisca nodded, then she squeezed through the press of villagers.

'I need a moment,' she whispered into Bauchlie's ear. 'It's urgent.'

Bauchlie nodded. 'Take your things to the caverns where you have been assigned,' he said to the crowd, 'and then meet back here for dinner, in one hour's time.'

Cisca relayed the message as soon as Bauchlie was clear of the crowd, and he nodded.

'You don't look surprised,' she said.

'I was expecting something like this to happen,' he said. 'The coves down by the coast have been used for centuries by Gunstian agents to deliver spies, weapons and messages from their government.'

'And which of those are they delivering tonight?'

'We shall see.' He turned to a rebel officer. 'Gather forty fighters; we have work to do.'

'Commander Bauchlie,' said the robed Gunstian; 'we meet again.'

'What do you want?' said Bauchlie.

'To talk,' said the agent. 'Shall we go somewhere less exposed to the elements?'

'The beach is fine,' said Bauchlie.

The Gunstian frowned. 'The last time I was here, you offered me a comfortable seat and some refreshments in one of those coves.'

'The last time you were here,' Bauchlie said, 'you were bringing me crates of weapons to help with the uprising.'

'Weapons that you misused,' the agent said. 'Our deal with Colonel Friel Laimos stated that those weapons were destined for the Gunstian civilians living on Zamata – instead, you handed them out to Zamatans.'

Cisca glanced at the dozen Gunstian soldiers lined up in a semi-circle behind the agent. Each was in leather armour, and had a crossbow clutched in their hands. Standing opposite them on the sand just yards from the lapping ocean stood only Bauchlie, Cisca and two young rebels. Overhead, the sky had darkened, and the quarter moon was shining out to the east.

'I don't trust you, Commander Bauchlie,' the Gunstian agent went on, 'but my superiors have decided to reach out and make contact with you nevertheless. We are aware that you continued the armed struggle against the Dominion occupiers throughout their ill-judged invasion of my homeland. You resisted the evil regime headed by Lord Malum. Indeed, we have also heard that you were the one to slay that vile beast. For this feat, you have earned the thanks of the Gunstian Empire.'

Bauchlie said nothing.

'Are you amenable to negotiating, Commander?' said the Gunstian.

'What do we have to negotiate about?' said Bauchlie. 'Your navy is blockading this island.'

'Let me attempt to sum up your position, Commander,' said the agent. 'Your food supplies are running out, and while none of your people are yet starving, that is inevitable, if nothing changes. You are confined to the mountains, while four winged demons remain ensconced within the palace in Igatz, surrounded by their Aucterian and Bullan slaves.'

'Get to the point,' said Bauchlie.

The Gunstian agent suppressed a low laugh. 'Colonel Friel Laimos was always so much more diplomatic in his dealings with us. He was devious, it is true, but he was never less than a gentleman. Very well, I shall be as abrupt as you. The Gunstian Empire is prepared to offer you a deal; one that would see the Zamatans survive the coming storm, with you as their leader.'

'Hasn't your government already sworn to annihilate every last man, woman and child upon this island?'

'That was our immediate reaction upon hearing the news of the massacre of our kinsfolk,' said the agent. 'Lord Malum and Lady Macsin slaughtered thousands of unarmed Gunstian civilians, while the impious Zamatans stood by and watched. However, we are prepared to relent. As long as the Zamatans pledge their faith and devotion to the Almighty Chadura, praise be Her name, then our retribution shall be limited to the winged demons, the Aucterians, and the Bullan. You see – we can compromise.'

'What about the part-Bullan?'

'They would be counted among the Bullan,' said the agent, 'as their blood is irredeemably tainted.'

Bauchlie showed no emotion on his face. 'What would you need me to do?'

'We would require you to convert to our religion, and then convert all those who shelter within the ruins of Medamuna Gatzoun. If you do this, then we shall supply food and weapons to your forces. With unlimited stocks of food, you will soon find your numbers increase. Everyone who comes under your protection shall also be required to convert and, in this way, the native population of this island will be saved. You shall take the war to the dragons, and attack them and their minions without cessation. The more enemies you kill, the more food we shall supply.'

'And when will your fleet land soldiers?'

'That will depend on how well your forces fight, Commander. When the soldiers of Gunst do land, it will be as a victory parade, hailed by the local Zamatans as their liberators, united in the faith of the divine Chadura.'

'Not even the idealists in your government can believe that all Zamatans will willingly convert.'

'You might be surprised at what hunger will persuade people to do. You are bound to have a few dissenters; such wicked people exist within every community. You will know how to deal with them.'

'And then the Gunstians rule?'

'The island would be formally annexed as an integral part of the Empire,' the agent said. 'A local government would be formed, with you at its head. Zamata would be treated as a city-state and, as I am sure you are aware, all city-states within the Empire have a degree of self-rule. Zamata would be no exception.'

Bauchlie turned his head to gaze at the three warships anchored off the coast. Each had lamps twinkling upon their decks in the night air.

'As a token of our goodwill,' the agent said, 'I am prepared to sanction an immediate delivery of food from those ships. All it will take is your solemn pledge to carry out the instructions I have given you.

Nothing more formal than that is required at present. Simply swear that you will join our faith, and promise to aid our cause, and the food will be yours.'

'What if I don't believe in your god?' Bauchlie said. 'Should I just pretend?'

'As I said, we shall take your words at face value if you kneel on this beach and recite a simple prayer to the divine Chadura. Believe me, Commander; you will not be presented with a better deal than this. If you set our plan in motion, you will rule this island.'

Bauchlie smiled. 'Until the Gifted arrive.'

'Do we not long for the same outcomes?' said the agent. 'To be rid of the Dominion scourge from the entire western half of Athumia? Or, if you wish to be purely pragmatic, what other choice do you have? Do you intend to ally yourself with the demons in the Dragon Palace? Do you wish to watch as your people slowly starve to death?'

'I intend to do neither of those things.'

'Good. Yes, that is good, Commander. Are we close to an agreement? Kneel, say a few words, and you will be on the path to power.'

'What if I have no desire for power?'

'Then tell me your desire.'

'I want Zamata to be free.'

'And this is how you will achieve it.'

'Being subsumed into the Gunstian Empire is not freedom.'

'It is the closest to freedom that Zamata will ever come. You cannot reasonably expect this little scrap of land to be a sovereign independent nation, of equal standing to the two empires that happen to be your neighbours. Even you, Commander, must realise that the time has come to choose a side. Who will it be – the decadent, tired old Dominion, a realm ravaged by doubt and civil war, its energies and vitality squandered in its futile invasion of the West; or your kinsfolk of Gunst? We are the same people, Commander – the Zamatans and Gunstians are one; indivisible. Steer this island to its home harbour, where it shall be welcomed and nurtured. Save the lives and souls of its people; feed their bodies and their spirits, and the blessings of the merciful and loving Chadura shall fall upon Zamata like rain from the sky.'

'And if I refuse?'

'Then the blockade shall grind on to its painful and necessary conclusion. Your granaries shall empty, and your children shall starve in the streets. Law and order will break down, slowly at first, and then as quickly as the on-coming tide. Everyone you know and love will die, their souls damned for eternity. That is the choice you face, Commander.'

'Then here is my decision,' Bauchlie said. 'I shall prostrate myself on these sands in front of you.'

'Excellent,' said the agent, clapping his hands together. 'You have chosen wisely, Commander.'

Bauchlie turned to Cisca and the two young rebels standing next to her. 'You three shall also prostrate yourselves,' he said, lowering his voice, 'and keep your damn heads down.'

Bauchlie fell to his knees, and the two rebel fighters did the same. Cisca frowned, then Bauchlie caught her eye, and she lowered herself to the wet sand. Bauchlie prostrated himself, and Cisca lay down next to him, her guts churning with nausea. She looked at Bauchlie at that moment, and loathed him.

'Now,' said the agent; 'repeat these words – Oh Blessed Chadura, I solemnly swear that...'

He got no further as the air thickened with crossbow bolts. Cisca almost leapt up in alarm, and Bauchlie placed a hand on her back, forcing her back down into the sand as the agent screamed. Cisca glanced up, as the Gunstian agent and his dozen guards were cut down, the bolts piercing their leathers.

Within a minute it was over, and Bauchlie stood. He brushed the sand from the front of his clothes as four dozen rebel fighters emerged from the thick shadows by the cliffside, their crossbows held in their arms. They went by the bodies of the fallen Gunstians, and any who had survived were shot in the back of the head.

'Bring thirteen stakes, and enough wood for a large fire,' Bauchlie said.

Cisca got back to her feet, her eyes on the blood mingling with the foam from the waves on the shore. The Gunstian agent was lying on his back with three crossbow bolts embedded in his chest, while his left hand was still grasping a piece of paper. Cisca leaned over and plucked it from the dead fingers, then she held it up to the moonlight. On the paper were the words of a prayer.

'Dig thirteen holes in the sand and place the stakes along the length of the cove,' Bauchlie said to his fighters, 'then impale the Gunstians, one to each stake. Light the fire behind them, so that the Gunstians on the warships can see my response to their offer. Let's not leave any room for doubt.'

Cisca turned away as the fighters began to drag the corpses towards the line of thick, sharpened stakes. Other fighters had brought shovels, and they began to dig out deep post holes along the beach; while others constructed the bonfire.

Bauchlie walked to her side. 'You probably don't want to watch the next part,' he said. 'It's going to get messy.'

She stared at him.

He frowned. 'Did you think I was going to submit?'

'For a split second, yes.'

'Good. I needed to sound convincing, and the look on your face helped persuade the Gunstians that I was being truthful.'

'You used me?'

'It was necessary. That agent might have possessed the Gift of Truth. I needed to act accordingly.'

Cisca glanced away, but her eyes were drawn to the sight of a Gunstian soldier being impaled onto the end of one of the stakes, and she vomited onto the sand. Bauchlie placed a hand on her shoulder, but she turned and rushed away, desperate to be as far from the bloody beach as possible. She ran towards the path that led up the side of the cliffs towards Medamuna Gatzoun, then came to a halt, falling to her knees and clutching her stomach as she wept.

She understood why Bauchlie was doing what he was doing, but the sheer barbarism of his actions repelled her. She heard a noise as the bonfire was lit and, against her better judgement, she turned to look. The flames were rising into the night sky, illuminating the thirteen stakes that had been placed upright into the sand of the beach. Upon each hung a body of a Gunstian, while, beyond, the three warships sat in silence, their deck lights twinkling.

CHAPTER 12
INDISPENSABLE

Kaugatz, Serpent Isle – 8th Luddinch 1588

Thousands of Zamatans were lining the streets of Kaugatz to see the young man with horns. To Leona's mind, it looked like a victory parade, rather than a procession in the midst of a blockade. Despite the anxiety shared by many on the island, the faces of the Zamatans were filled with hope, as though Lahnos Laimos had appeared as the answer to their prayers. Men and women were openly weeping as they cheered his name, while every child seemed to have been hoisted up onto an adult's shoulders.

Lahnos was walking down the middle of the road with his twelve Bullan bodyguards flanking him, and the mighty silver-green dragon strode behind them, his long neck raised high, and his eyes on the teeming crowds. The dragon was also being flanked, but by human soldiers rather than those from the land of the Bullan. Zamatan veterans from the Gunst campaign were walking alongside the procession, and more were joining them with every moment that passed. Lahnos would sometimes lift an arm and wave at one side of the street or the other, a slightly bewildered expression on his features as he gazed at the screaming masses.

'They certainly seem to love him, ma'am,' Farakai whispered, as he and Leona edged their way through the crowds.

'In hindsight,' Leona said, 'perhaps it was better that he remained on Mount Medamuna for so long – the anticipation couldn't have been better stage-managed. Every man in Kaugatz will be clamouring to join his band by the end of the day.'

'And a few women, too, by the looks of them,' Farakai said.

'I wonder where Reyn is.'

Farakai pointed through the crowds at a young woman with stubby horns, who was walking with the Zamatan soldiers next to the dragon.

'Is that her, ma'am?'

'Yes,' said Leona. 'Strange. Why isn't she by Lahnos's side? I would like to know whose choice that was.'

'Shall I ask, ma'am?'

'No. Just deliver the letter to one of the Bullan and slip back into the crowds. I'll take Saewa and go on ahead.'

Farakai nodded, then he glanced at Saewa, who was trailing them a few yards away.

'Don't lose sight of her; understand? There could be Gunstians, or rebels from Bauchlie's lot in this crowd.'

'Got it, boss,' Saewa said, as he caught up with them.

Farakai squeezed through the joyous mass of people, a folded slip of paper clutched in his left hand. He skirted the procession of Zamatan soldiers, then darted forwards, his right palm raised. Several of the Bullan tensed, then Farakai bowed his head and held out the letter. Leona watched as one of the Bullan took it, then she nodded to Saewa and hurried down a side street to the right, away from the main road.

They reached a quiet alleyway, and kept up their quick pace.

'What was in the letter, miss?' said Saewa.

'I was welcoming Lahnos back to Kaugatz, and recommending a suitable base of operations for his regiments. That is our objective now – to reach Tsallon Anura before he does. Are you ready to run?'

'What if he decides to ignore your advice, miss?'

'Then we shall be returning home disappointed,' said Leona. 'Let's hope that doesn't happen.'

'But it's two miles to the monastery,' said Saewa. 'What if...?'

Leona rolled her eyes and began to run down the alley. Saewa was trustworthy, but perhaps not the fittest among her agents in Kaugatz. They took a road running parallel to the main thoroughfare that bisected Kaugatz, passing the central ferry terminal to their right. A few of the braver Aucterians had crossed the Cyasarta to catch a glimpse of Lahnos and the dragon, and over a hundred of them were making their way west from the ferry terminal. Leona and Saewa weaved their way through them and kept running, keeping the banks of the Cyasarta on their right. The road veered a little to the east, and the towering walls and battlements of the ancient monastery came into view. Leona slowed a little to allow Saewa to catch his breath, and they walked the last three-quarters of a mile to the western edge of the monastery. Seeing the gates closed, Leona halted for a moment, listening. The roar of the crowds was steadily increasing behind them, and she judged that they had a few minutes before Lahnos would arrive.

Leona strode up the main gate in the western wall of Tsallon Anura and banged on the wooden doors.

'Open up!' she cried.

Nothing happened for a few moments, then a small square hatch opened at eye-level and a monk peered through.

'Alms-giving is at sunrise and sunset, girl,' he said. 'Visitors are not permitted inside the monastery at any other time.'

'I'll make this brief, brother,' said Leona. 'You and the other monks inside Tsallon Anura have ten minutes to vacate the property. In the name of Lord Rylan, Governor of Zamata, I am confiscating Tsallon Anura for use as a military site during the defence of this island. Your personal possessions shall not be touched, and the chapel will be locked for the duration of the occupation. If you have any complaints, the prelate in Zamata Gataza can lodge them with the Governor in the Dragon Palace in Igatz.'

The monk stared at her through the hatch. 'Is this a joke? Who are you?'

'I am Leona of Kaugatz, and if that name means anything to you, you will know what I am capable of. Open the gates, and start packing.'

The monk closed the hatch, and Leona waited, while Saewa raised an eyebrow.

The hatch opened again, and three monks tried to peer through at the same time.

'Do not make me repeat myself,' said Leona. 'Open the gates, or I shall have a dragon tear them down.'

'What dragon?' said one.

'Lord Sigum Mon Sigel,' said Leona. 'Do you hear the crowds approaching? Do not embarrass yourselves, brothers. Open the gates, and let the humble residents of Kaugatz think that it was your idea to donate the use of Tsallon Anura to Lahnos Laimos. That way, you might be able to reclaim some of the respect you have recently lost.'

The hatch closed again.

Leona waited, and then the gates began to move. She and Saewa took a few steps back, and watched as several monks wedged the twin doors open at their fullest extent. An older monk approached, his eyes troubled.

'Leona of Kaugatz?'

'Yes, brother?'

'Might we negotiate?'

'I'm listening.'

'As you know, the wicked criminal Bauchlie murdered the monks who previously dwelt here. However, that does not frighten us. Might I ask that we be allowed to stay?'

Leona narrowed her eyes. 'Would you promise not to interfere in the defence of the island against the Gunstians?'

'Of course, ma'am,' said the old monk. 'We are loyal to Zamata, and have no desire to see the idolatrous Gunstians take over. There is also the matter of our daily alms-giving. Without our charity, many local families would go hungry.'

'And would your monks refrain from casting any aspersions on to the good name of Lahnos Laimos?' Leona said, as the roar of the crowd grew louder. 'He is, as you know, part-Bullan. I would take it as a personal insult if any of the good brothers under your authority were to refer to him as a demon while he resides here.'

'We shall do no such thing,' said the old monk. 'You have my word.'

Leona smiled. 'Then I shall permit you to stay.'

The gathered monks exhaled in relief.

'Thank you,' said the old monk, bowing his head. 'We shall pray for your soul this evening.'

Leona tilted her head a fraction, then she turned and waited next to Saewa as Lahnos came into sight at the end of the street. The dragon's head was rising above the horned young man, and Leona heard a few gasped prayers come from the monks behind her. The crowds had followed Lahnos and the dragon, and many spilled into the area by the open gates, as Leona stood in the middle of the road.

Lahnos smiled as he saw her, and the procession slowed, then came to a halt in front of the walls of the monastery.

'Welcome home,' said Leona.

'It's good to see you again, Leona,' said Lahnos, above the noise of the crowd. 'Tsallon Anura? Are the monks happy with this arrangement?'

'Why don't you ask them?' Leona said, gesturing to the gathered men in brown robes.

The old monk stepped forward, and bowed low. 'You are welcome here, Lahnos of Fidalaimos; and you also, my Lord Sigum Mon Sigel; most welcome.'

The huge dragon tilted his silvery head. 'You have my thanks, monks of the serpent religion. It shall be an honour and a privilege to dwell among you.'

The monks bowed, then Leona led Lahnos over the threshold and into the grounds of the monastery. Half of the cloister remained in disrepair, and the rubble of the tower destroyed by Lord Meer Mon Adal was still lying where it had fallen, but the open ground had been cleared, and the skull of Lord Meer removed. Lord Sigum squeezed through the tall entrance, and then the twelve Bullan followed. The monks and the Bullan eyed each other with suspicion for a few moments, then Lahnos turned to the crowds and raised his right arm.

'This will be my new home,' he said, to a roar from the assembled masses. 'Let me get settled in, and then we shall start re-admitting soldiers from the regiments back into the service of Zamata. For now, I am only going to allow those who have signed up over the last few days to enter Tsallon Anura, so that we don't overwhelm our hosts. Registration for those who wish to re-join the regiments starts at dawn tomorrow.' He smiled, and his face opened up. 'Thank you all for welcoming me and my friends back to Kaugatz. I will never forget this moment. Thank you.'

The crowd roared again, and then over a hundred Zamatans began to file through the gates, while the others remained outside.

'We need to talk,' said Leona.

Lahnos nodded. 'Let me find Reyn first.'

Twenty minutes later, Leona, Lahnos, Reyn and the twelve Bullan were seated by the intact eastern flank of the cloister, while Lord Sigum sat on the flagstones in front of them. The gates of Tsallon Anura had been closed, and the hundred and twenty soldiers who had entered the monastery were taking up positions by the gates and curtain wall. Monks had served coffee, chilled wine and smoked fish for Lahnos and the others, before retiring to pray in the chapel. The sun felt strong for an autumnal afternoon, but an awning was providing some shade for those who were seated.

'Let's get down to business,' said Leona, as she set her glass of wine onto a low table. 'I assume your regiments shall require weapons and uniforms?'

Lahnos nodded. 'Yes. Do you know how we can get them?'

'I shall provide all that you need,' Leona said. 'Wagonloads of uniforms are on their way, and will arrive within the next few hours, while the first deliveries of crossbows and bolts should be here by sunrise tomorrow. How many thousands of soldiers can we anticipate?'

Lahnos's eyes tightened a little. 'It's as easy as that? You will just give us uniforms and weapons?'

'I control access to the old militia depots, Lahnos,' she said. 'I shall also be providing food for your men. So, how many?'

'I'm not sure. If everyone comes, then seven thousand, but I have to assume that some won't want to re-join. They will have farms and families to look after, and growing food is as important as manning the defences.'

'I am glad we agree on that point,' said Leona. 'Perhaps we should cap the numbers at four thousand? Or maybe five?'

'What about women who want to join?' said Reyn.

'I have no objection to that,' said Leona, 'but it seems like an operational matter, and so I will leave it to Lahnos.'

Lahnos frowned. 'Am I the commander? No one has appointed me, or given me any authority over the Zamatans. What will Lord Rylan say about it?'

'Perhaps we can ask him when he gets here,' said Leona. 'I took the liberty of informing the Governor of your arrival today, and he is keen to meet you again.'

'Lord Rylan is coming here?' said Sigum, his head rising. 'That is excellent news, Leona of Kaugatz. I assume that you have received a pardon for your previous offences?'

'If he doesn't kill me upon arrival, then I would say that the answer to that is probably *yes*. The truth is that I have not seen Lord Rylan since I visited him in secret in the Dragon Palace. However, assisting Lahnos was one of his lordship's conditions for my rehabilitation, so I rather hope that my head will remain upon its shoulders.'

'I've already had more help from you than I ever got from Bauchlie,' said Lahnos.

'There was little I could do for you while you remained upon the slopes of Mount Medamuna,' said Leona; 'but, now that you are here, I would like us to work closely together.'

'Are you happy to submit to Lord Rylan's overall authority?' he said.

'For the sake of Zamata – yes, I am.'

Lord Sigum tilted his head. 'Well said, Leona.'

'This is... unbelievable,' said Reyn. 'You, Leona – submitting to a dragon? I would never have thought it possible.'

'Things change, Reyn,' Leona said. 'Circumstances alter. At this present moment in Zamata's long and troubled history, we are facing a blockade determined to squeeze the life out of everyone living here. If that leads me to forge alliances with those who have previously been my enemies, then so be it. I will leave it to the future to judge my actions. Now, I want to talk about rationing. I would advise that the recruits are processed in batches of one thousand, with a day between each new group of arrivals. That will allow me to coordinate the movement of supplies. Five thousand soldiers will eat a lot of food, and it is important that the civilians do not feel that they are being treated unfairly. As of tomorrow, I am implementing the strictest rationing regime yet seen in Kaugatz, and tempers might fray. Therefore, Lahnos, I am asking you for soldiers to defend the stores where the town's stocks are being held. There are four main depots, and each will require fifty men to protect them from looters.'

'Are we anticipating a looting spree?' said Lahnos.

'Not yet,' said Leona, 'but we must be prepared. Hunger will drive many ordinary, sane people to perform desperate acts. I elect to be the one the people shall hate. The rationing decrees shall be in my name, and my name alone, to shield you from the wrath of the populace.'

'That doesn't seem fair,' said Lahnos.

'That is immaterial. The only thing that matters is that our supplies are eked out for as long as possible. We must also ensure that children are prioritised. Nothing will demoralise the people more than seeing children starving on the streets. This next part is going to sound selfish, but there is a cruel logic behind it – the leadership must remain reasonably well-fed. Hunger will lead to bad decisions, and bad decisions will lead to our defeat.'

Reyn narrowed her eyes at Leona, then she glanced away, muttering something under her breath.

'Leona of Kaugatz is correct,' said one of the Bullan. 'It sounds dishonourable, but it is far better for the population as a whole that the leaders remain competent.'

'A dragon is approaching,' said Lord Sigum, as he pushed himself to his feet. 'It is Lord Rylan.'

Leona stood, and then the others did the same. She turned towards the east, and saw a dragon flying low over the Cyasarta. He soared past the single dragon carrier anchored off Handshore Naval Base, then he turned for the walls of the monastery. Leona steadied her breathing. The moment was arriving when she would see if her actions had secured her life. She had left instructions with Farakai about what to do if Lord Rylan proved unforgiving, or if he decided to name her *Lady Takri* in front of the Zamatans. She watched his grey and yellow scales catch the rays of the setting sun as he banked through the air, then he glided down and alighted in the centre of the large open cloister.

Lord Sigum bowed his head. 'Greetings, my lord.'

Rylan glanced at the silvery-green dragon. 'And to you, Lord Sigum. I am glad that you were able to pass my message on to Lahnos Laimos.' He turned to the part-Bullan. 'You did well to come to Kaugatz, I think, Laimos. Already, I can see the effect your presence has had upon the Zamatan civilians. How was your stay in the mountains?'

'It was peaceful,' said Lahnos. 'I think I needed some time after Gunst; time to recover – but I am ready to do my duty.'

'That pleases me,' said the dragon; 'and I would not begrudge you a little rest after all you have done. Tell me – what is your plan?'

'I intend to recruit five thousand men within the re-constituted Zamatan regiments, my lord,' said Lahnos, as Reyn suppressed another frown. 'Their deployment will be for you to decide. However, I am only a corporal. Should someone else not lead?'

'No, Laimos; it shall be you,' said Rylan. 'Surround yourself with experienced veterans and listen to their advice; but you will command the Zamatan regiments when they go into battle. I hereby appoint you as sole general of said regiments, and my only condition is that you appoint Lord Sigum as your chief of staff and deputy.'

Lahnos shook his head and laughed. 'Do you know how old I am?'

'That matters not to me,' said the dragon. 'You are an adult; a man – and all humans appear young to me. The important point is that the Zamatans will listen to you, and they will follow your orders. That outweighs your lack of age and experience. Now, here are my requirements. All recruits will swear fealty to the island of Zamata, and to me as its Governor. I shall need one thousand men within four days, to relieve the exhausted Aucterian soldiers garrisoning the Chain Castles; and a further two thousand to re-garrison the fortresses of Atzoun and Hortz. Another one thousand are to be dispersed to the coasts, while the remainder shall be employed in keeping the peace within Kaugatz and Igatz. Is this feasible?'

'Yes, my lord,' said Lahnos.

'Good. You have made a fine, if belated, start, young Laimos. Tsallon Anura was an excellent choice.'

Lahnos smiled. 'You should thank Leona for that,' he said. 'It was her idea, and she has already pledged to provide weapons, food and uniforms for every soldier under my command.'

Lord Rylan said nothing for a moment, then he turned his long neck until his head was directly facing Leona.

'And so we come to you, spy,' the dragon said. 'Did I not tell you to await my decision, Leona of Kaugatz? And yet you are here.'

'I fully intended to remain at home, my lord,' said Leona; 'but when I heard that Lahnos was on his way, I made a decision. I acted. If that... displeases you, then I am at your mercy. Even if every soldier in this monastery tried to defend me, you could kill me if you wished.'

'Perhaps I should,' said Rylan; 'your crimes demand it, do they not?'

Lahnos stepped forward. 'If you kill her, then kill me, too,' he said. 'I know Leona, and I trust her.'

The dragon eyed him. 'But you do not know all that she has done, young Laimos. Perhaps if I told you, then you would not be so quick to leap to her defence.'

'Lahnos has a good heart,' said Leona, 'and I would ask that you spare his life if you decide to end mine. However, my lord, if you are in a conciliatory mood, then I wish to offer you my full cooperation. Tomorrow marks the beginning of the new rationing regime, and my preparations are well underway.'

'And don't forget the food, uniforms and weapons she is providing us,' said Lahnos. 'We need her.'

Lord Rylan stared at Leona, his iron gaze piercing her, then he tilted his head slightly.

'Very well; I shall relent,' he said. 'Well played, Leona of Kaugatz; it appears that I do need you. You have managed to make yourself indispensable to the defence of this island. Your next task shall be more difficult, for I wish you to find a way to bring Bauchlie to his senses. His agents remain active in Kaugatz, and he presents a danger to the unity of this island. Meet with him, and negotiate a settlement that will prevent me from having to fly to Medamuna Gatzoun to destroy his stronghold. Is that understood?'

Leona bowed her head. 'Yes, my lord.'

'You may leave us now,' said Rylan. 'I wish to speak to General Laimos without having to worry about being stabbed in the back.'

Leona glanced at Lahnos, who gave her a shrug and a smile, then she pulled Saewa from the crowd of watching soldiers and they strode through the cloister towards the main gates of the monastery. The Zamatans on duty allowed them to pass, and they re-entered the crowded streets outside Tsallon Anura.

Saewa shook his head at her as they hurried away. 'That was as reckless as anything I've ever seen, miss. You bullshitted your way into the largest monastery on the island, and then you bullshitted a dragon into receiving a pardon. The colonel would have been proud.'

'I learned from the best,' she said. 'Come on; let's go home while we still can.'

. . .

Arrosa and Lyla were arguing in Gunstian when Leona entered her home in the suburbs of Kaugatz. Leona smiled as she hung her coat on a peg, the familiar sound of raised voices comforting her after the stress and anxiety of her outing to Tsallon Anura. She walked into the old study and found Arrosa standing on the colonel's desk, waving a charcoal drawing in her left hand.

'Give that back to me,' Lyla said, her clear Gunstian accent never failing to impress Leona; 'or I shall be obliged to take it by force.'

'Shut up, you crazy old woman,' yelled Arrosa.

'Old? I'm... I'm...' Lyla frowned, and her gaze fell.

'You don't even know how old you are,' Arrosa shrieked.

'Get down from there,' said Leona. 'And stop this at once.'

Arrosa turned, and saw Leona by the doorway. 'Or what?'

'Or you don't get any supper,' said Leona.

Arrosa scowled, then she jumped off the desk. She held out the drawing, but Lyla seemed too distracted to even notice.

'How old am I?' said Lyla, reverting to the Divine Tongue in Leona's presence.

'That's not an easy question to answer,' said Leona.

'Why not?' said Lyla. 'It sounds easy.'

'Let's say mid-twenties for now,' said Leona. 'Sit down. Tell me if you had any more dreams last night.'

Lyla sat in a chair, and Arrosa walked over and perched on one of its upholstered arms, the drawing still in her hand.

'I dreamt of horses,' Lyla said.

'That sounds nice,' said Leona.

'It wasn't. Can I tell you in Gunstian? It's... easier.'

'You are supposed to be learning the Divine Tongue,' said Leona.

'I know, but... it is hard.'

'All right. Just this once.'

'The dream kept changing,' Lyla went on, switching to Gunstian. 'One moment, I was riding a grey mare over an endless plain, where no mountains were visible. It was hot; I mean the weather was hot and sunny. Hotter than Zamata. And the next moment, I was riding a dappled brown gelding in the foothills of a mountain range, with a large city behind me – Teros City, I think. It's a city that I have often seen in my dreams – the city where I went to school.'

Leona said nothing.

'Am I... am I two different people?' Lyla said.

Arrosa laughed. 'I told you she was crazy.'

'Why don't you answer me, Leona?' Lyla went on. 'If you thought it was a silly idea, then you would say so.'

'Here is the truth,' said Leona; 'I don't know who you are.'

Arrosa glared at her and rubbed her head. 'That wasn't the complete truth.'

'Tell me,' said Lyla, switching back to the Divine Tongue.

'You're not ready to hear it,' said Leona. 'What I know would only confuse you even more. Keep learning – that's what I advise. Your body is getting stronger and healthier, and your mind is improving, too. And, best of all, your memories are slowly returning, piece by piece.'

Lyla looked unconvinced, and she lowered her head.

'I met Lahnos today,' Leona said.

'Did you... ask him to... come here?' said Lyla, her voice faltering again.

'No. There were dragons and soldiers, and it was very busy. However, he's living in the same town as us now, and I intend to visit him again, soon. I will mention it next time.'

Lyla glanced up at her. 'What is a... dragon?'

CHAPTER 13
THE THIRTEENTH GIFT

Kaugatz, Serpent Isle – 14th Luddinch 1588

Lahnos hadn't touched another person in eight days. Apart from Reyn, he didn't think anyone had noticed, but he still worried that someone would try to shake his hand.

He spread his blanket over the chair, as Reyn closed the shutters of their room within Tsallon Anura. They were staying in the same small apartment where they had lived during the uprising, its whitewashed walls and sparse furniture reassuringly familiar to them both.

'Come to bed, Lahnos,' Reyn said, as she watched him prepare the chair.

'I can't,' he said. 'You know I can't.'

She narrowed her eyes. 'Is this the way it's going to be from now on?'

'What choice do we have? I have no idea what caused the Gift to come from my fingertips, and if I can't control it, then I can't risk touching you.'

'Then learn how to control it,' she said. She sat on the bed. 'I thought you were going to try to find out more about this new Gift.'

'I was going to ask Leona, but I've been too busy. And when have I had any time to leave the monastery? If I tried, I would be mobbed by the crowds outside. If they got close enough to touch me, I might have killed a few dozen people by the time I got to Leona's house.'

She got into bed and pulled the blanket over her. 'Why do you have to see *her*? There must be other people on Zamata who know about the Gifts.'

'No doubt. Can you name any of them?'

'You'd think of something if you tried hard enough.'

He glared at her from the other side of the room. 'Is this why you've been so angry with me?'

'It's part of the reason,' she said. 'You refuse to touch me, but you don't seem to care; and...'

'I do care.'

'I hadn't finished,' she said. 'You kept calling a dragon *my lord*, as if nothing we did in the uprising meant anything. I understand that we have to defend Zamata against the Gunstians, but did you have to make the regiments swear loyalty to a damn dragon? And you were lying about allowing me to fight. As soon as you got here, you decided that every soldier in your little army would be a man.'

'I'm picking veterans, and every veteran from the Zamatan regiments happens to be a man.'

'What about me? I've fought – am I not a veteran? Bauchlie allowed me to fight.'

'Then go back to Bauchlie.'

'I might,' she said. 'You don't seem to mind that we're living together like brother and sister, so why should I stay? You care more about Sigum than you do about me.' She reached out and extinguished the lamp. 'Good night.'

Lahnos stood in the darkness, still dressed in his militia uniform. 'You're wrong,' he said.

'Then prove it.'

'I will.'

'It's the middle of the night, Lahnos.'

'It's not even midnight yet. And it's a full moon; it'll be light enough.'

She sat up as he walked towards the door. 'What are you going to do?'

'If I try hard enough,' he said, 'I'll think of something.' He went through the bedroom door and closed it behind him. His anger had got him that far, but he hesitated as he pictured trying to walk through the streets of Kaugatz at night. Hundreds of Zamatans were camped outside the monastery walls. Some were there to be close to the men who had re-enlisted, while others seemed only interested in catching a glimpse of Lahnos. He could take a carriage, but it would still have to navigate its way through the crowds.

He walked out of the apartment, went down the stairs to the ground level, and walked to the room where Efizel slept.

He knocked on the door, and it opened a few moments later.

'Yes, sir?' Efizel said.

'Get dressed,' Lahnos said, as he strode inside. 'We're going to visit Leona.'

Efizel closed the door and frowned as he lit a lamp. 'Now, sir?'

'I don't want to be seen,' Lahnos said, 'so I thought going at night would be better. Any ideas on how to get there undetected?'

Efizel shrugged, then picked up his uniform. 'We could take a boat, sir.'

Lahnos laughed. 'Of course, yes. The monastery has a jetty. Do you, uh, know where Leona lives?'

'I do, sir,' Efizel said, as he pulled his boots on. 'One of her agents passed me her address. Leona lives in a townhouse close to the central ferry terminal. The district should be quiet at this time of night.'

Lahnos nodded as the Bullan got ready.

'Perhaps we should wake up a couple of the lads from the old squad,' Efizel went on. 'If we want to keep this quiet, the fewer who know, the better. We can trust the men from Fidalaimos, and they would not stand out in Kaugatz compared to my kinsfolk.'

'Wake Smithy and Jancke,' said Lahnos. 'They can row.'

'I am sure they would be delighted to row you down the Cyasarta in the middle of the night, sir.'

Lahnos smiled. 'I'm sure they would.'

Lahnos waited in the Bullan's room as Efizel left to gather up the old squadmates, then the four of them set off for the jetty. Jancke yawned as they walked by the ancient cloister, his eyes bleary, while Smithy looked wide awake.

'Where are we off to?' the former blacksmith said, as he peered up at the full moon.

'The other end of Kaugatz,' said Lahnos. 'The sergeant knows the address.'

A pair of Zamatan soldiers was on duty by the postern gate leading to the jetty, and they saluted as Lahnos approached. Efizel spoke to them for a few moments, then they opened the door. Lahnos strode through and stepped onto the narrow jetty. A couple of rowing boats were tied up next to a fishing vessel, and Jancke yawned again as they untied the ropes leading to one. Smithy and Jancke attached the oars to the side of the small craft, and Lahnos sat down on the bench facing them.

'Where to, boss?' said Smithy.

'The central ferry terminal,' said Lahnos, as Efizel pushed the boat away from the jetty and stepped in.

The Bullan sat next to Lahnos as Smithy and Jancke started rowing.

'When we arrive,' said Efizel, 'I shall remain by the docks to watch the boat. I will attract too much attention walking the streets of Kaugatz at this hour.'

'What about me?' said Lahnos. 'I'm not going to hide my horns. I can't, even if I wanted to.'

'The townhouse is next to the part-Bullan district,' Efizel said. 'With any luck, you will blend in.' He passed Lahnos a slip of paper. 'The address is written down for you.'

Lahnos scanned the piece of paper. 'I know this street. I think Reyn and I might have robbed one of the neighbouring townhouses.'

Smithy chuckled as he rowed. 'From thief to conscript to general, eh? I see I was wasting my time trying to work at an honest living.'

The rowing boat started to veer a little to the left.

'Keep up, lad,' Smithy said to Jancke, 'or we'll end up going in circles.'

Jancke yawned again. 'I can hardly keep my eyes open.'

'When you get there,' Efizel said to Lahnos, his voice low, 'go through the rear gate and knock on the back door. There is a good chance that Bauchlie's agents will be watching the front of the townhouse.'

'Gunstians, too?'

'No, sir. If the Gunstians knew where Leona lived, they would send assassins to kill her.'

Lahnos nodded. Efizel knew about the attempt made on Lahnos's life, although he remained ignorant about the means by which Lahnos had killed the agent who had infiltrated his bedroom. He glanced at the passing shoreline for a while, then he turned to gaze at the enormous dragon carrier anchored off Handshore. Apart from a few guards, the huge vessel was empty, its crew deployed alongside the Aucterian soldiers protecting Igatz. There was a rumour circulating that Lord Rylan was going to scuttle the ship to prove his loyalty to the island, but Lahnos hoped it wasn't true. One day, maybe, if they survived the blockade, he imagined boarding that ship with Sigum, and using it to see the world. It was a foolish fantasy, so foolish that he had never mentioned it to Reyn; but the sight of the carrier gave him hope for the future.

The central ferry terminal lay shrouded in silence, its vessels tied up for the night, and Smithy and Jancke guided the rowing boat to one of the long piers that jutted out into the calm waters of the Cyasarta.

'I will remain here with Jancke,' said Efizel. 'Smithy, go with General Laimos and watch his back.'

Smithy laughed at Lahnos's new title as they stepped up onto the wooden pier.

'Good luck, sir,' said Efizel.

Lahnos nodded, then he and Smithy set off towards the main street. Lahnos knew every back lane in the district, and he could see the warren of narrow streets that marked the edge of the area where the part-Bullan had lived in Kaugatz for generations. He thought back to those days, when he had walked around in a permanent state of defiance, staring at anyone who even glanced at his horns, and daring them to make a comment. Now, for the first time in his life, he was sneaking around his old neighbourhood, keeping to the thick shadows out of the light of the full moon. He led Smithy to a cobbled lane, and counted the back yards until they reached the correct one. He tried the handle of the gate, but it was locked, so he gestured to Smithy to give him a boost. Smithy clasped his hands together, and Lahnos placed a foot into his grip and pulled himself up and over the gate. He dropped into a square courtyard, with a stable along one side.

'Wait here for me,' he whispered through the gate to Smithy. 'If anyone comes, go back to the ferry terminal and I'll catch up with you there.'

'No problem, boss,' the soldier replied.

Lahnos turned to the large townhouse. The ground floor was in darkness, but a few slivers of light were coming through the shutters of an upstairs window. Lahnos crept up to the back door of the house and listened. He raised his fingers towards the handle, then the door swung open and an old woman armed with a wooden bat sprang at him.

Lahnos leapt backwards, and the bat struck his right shoulder.

'Get out of here, thief!' the woman cried.

'Wait; I'm here to see Leona. I'm a friend.'

'A friend who skulks about in the dark, eh?'

He pointed to his horns. 'I'm Lahnos Laimos. It wasn't safe to come here during the day.'

'Yeah, right,' said the woman, as she advanced. 'The general of the bloody army goes wandering the streets alone at night? Do you think I was born yesterday?'

'Kamasta, stop,' said a voice from the rear entrance of the house. 'He's telling the truth.'

Lahnos glanced up and saw Leona standing in the doorway, a dressing gown wrapped round her.

The old woman narrowed her eyes at Lahnos. 'Next time – make a bloody appointment, General.'

'I will,' said Lahnos. He laughed. 'You nearly knocked my head off with that thing.'

'Come in,' said Leona, 'before you wake up the entire street.'

Kamasta ushered Lahnos into the house and shut the door behind her. She placed the bat against the wall, frowned at Lahnos, then smiled at Leona.

'Coffee, ma'am?' she said.

'Yes, thank you,' said Leona. She waited until the housekeeper had left the room, then she shook her head at Lahnos. 'She's right, you know; why didn't you tell me you were coming? Send me a message, and I'll be waiting for you. Did you get seen on your way here?'

'I got a couple of lads to row me here from the monastery.'

She smiled. 'I assume this must be urgent?'

'It might be,' he said. 'I need to talk to you about the Gifts of Theodora. You know all about them, don't you? You've studied them?'

'I have read a Gunstian book about them,' she said. 'Let's go to my bedroom.'

'Doesn't this house have a study?'

'It does, yes; but someone is sleeping in there. I won't eat you, Lahnos; you will be perfectly safe.'

She led him out of the hallway, then poked her head into the kitchen.

'Bring the coffee upstairs to my room, please, Kamasta.'

'Yes, ma'am.'

Leona and Lahnos climbed the stairs to the upper storey, and then she escorted him to a small bedchamber filled with papers, maps and books.

'You run Kaugatz from here?' said Lahnos, as he glanced at the chaotic mess. 'I imagined that you would at least have a bigger bedroom.'

'I do, but someone else is sleeping there.'

'How many people live in this house?'

'There are four of us,' said Leona, as she cleared a space on the room's only chair. 'You sit here; I'll take the bed.'

Lahnos sat. 'There's you,' he said, 'and Kamasta, who is your housekeeper and bodyguard, by the looks of things.' He glanced at Leona. 'And Lyla?'

'That's right,' she said, sitting on the edge of the bed. 'Did Cisca tell you that she was here?'

'It was Reyn. She also told me who you believe is inside Lyla's head. Do you still believe it?'

'Yes, but it seems to be more complicated than that. She remembers you.'

'I've never met Lyla,' he said, his eyes narrowing, 'and I find it a little hard to believe that the Demon Witch is inside her head.'

'I understand. Regardless, she will be very disappointed in the morning if I tell her that you were here and didn't see her. Would you mind if I woke her?'

'Can we talk first? I need your advice.'

'About death-reading?'

'No. About something else. Another Gift.'

She nodded.

'You don't seem surprised,' he said.

'Were you aware that your uncle was Gifted?'

'Was he? Uncle Friel was Gifted?'

'Yes. He had the Gift of Kenning. Do you know what that does?'

He shook his head.

'It grants someone the power to sense other people's Gifts. It's how he found me, and it's how he knew that you were Gifted.'

'Ah,' said Lahnos. 'That makes sense. When I woke up in my grandmother's house, he was there. I always wondered how he knew.'

'I was with him when he died, Lahnos,' Leona went on. 'He said something to me that I can clearly remember. He told me that you had... another Gift. I presume that you have discovered this?'

Lahnos glanced at the floor. 'Yes.'

'Do you want to talk about it?'

'That's why I'm here. The only person I've told is Reyn, and I don't know if I would have told her if she hadn't been there at the time. She saw me... use it.'

'Go on.'

'I... Well, there was an intruder. We were in Uncle Friel's old cottage – do you remember the place?'

'Yes.'

'Someone broke into my room at night, and...' He paused as the housekeeper entered with a tray.

'Your coffee,' Kamasta said, setting the tray down onto the bed, as there was no space for it anywhere else.

'Thank you,' said Leona.

'Lyla has awoken, ma'am,' the housekeeper said. 'She followed me upstairs, after she heard the voices.'

'Where is she now?'

'Standing outside this room, ma'am. Should I send her back to bed?'

Leona glanced at Lahnos, and he shrugged.

'Send her in, please,' said Leona.

'Right you are, ma'am.'

Kamasta left the room, and Leona eyed Lahnos. 'Be careful what you say to her, and don't mention the Demon Witch. She is liable to get confused.'

Lahnos nodded, then he turned as a young woman entered the room.

'Look who's here,' said Leona, as she moved along on the bed to make space. 'Come in and sit down.'

Lyla kept her gaze on the carpet, then she crossed the room and sat down next to Leona. She raised her eyes, and stared at Lahnos.

'Do you recognise him?' Leona said.

'Yes.'

'Who is it?'

'Lahnos.'

'What do you remember about him?'

The young woman shrugged, but she held her gaze, and Lahnos started to feel a little awkward. Why was she staring at him like that? He had never seen the woman before in his life, and he couldn't accept the story that Reyn had told him.

'Lyla,' said Leona. 'I asked you a question. Do you remember anything about Lahnos?'

Lyla broke off her stare. 'I... I killed his father.'

The room fell into silence.

'Is this a trick?' said Lahnos. 'Why would you say that?'

'I'm... sorry,' said the young woman. 'It was a... It was...'

Lahnos frowned.

'It was an accident,' the woman said in Gunstian. 'The volcano. An accident.'

'Who are you?' said Lahnos.

'I can't remember,' Lyla said, continuing in Gunstian. 'I might be two people. I have a memory of you, Lahnos. You were trapped under a mound of dead bodies, and the rain was pouring down from the sky. I woke you up, and told you to escape. Why did I do that?'

Lahnos narrowed his eyes. He had never mentioned those details of Gunst to anyone before. Could it be true? Was the Demon Witch somewhere inside the mind of the young Aucterian woman sitting opposite him?

'Can you answer her, Lahnos?' said Leona.

He nodded, his eyes still on Lyla. 'You said that you were trying to make amends. You were helping me because you felt guilty about my father. You helped me lots of times, and I was rude to you. I told you to leave me alone. I'm glad you didn't. I would be dead if you hadn't woken me, and thousands of Zamatans would still be prisoners in Gunst. Are you the...?'

'Don't say it,' said Leona.

Lyla turned to her. 'Don't say what?'

'Why doesn't she know?' said Lahnos. 'Why haven't you told her?'

'She is fragile, Lahnos,' said Leona. 'I want her memories to return naturally. If I try to explain what happened to her, she would only get more upset.'

Lahnos shook his head. 'It sounds as though whatever Lord Malum did to her didn't work properly. She thinks she's two different people. I assume that one of those is Major Lyla of the Dragon Corps, and the other is the Demon Witch?'

Leona's eyes tightened. 'What did I just say, Lahnos?'

'Major Lyla and the Demon Witch?' said the young woman. 'A witch? Am I a witch? What happened to me?'

'The dragons did this to you,' said Lahnos. 'They killed Lyla and put the Demon Witch into your mind.'

Lyla's face paled and she started to cry.

'That's enough, Lahnos!' cried Leona, getting to her feet. 'Hold your tongue or get out!'

'I'm not sorry,' Lahnos said. 'She deserves to know the truth.'

'She's not ready,' said Leona.

'Is that why I have two memories of school?' Lyla wept. 'Two memories of riding horses? I have the memories of a dead woman inside my head?'

'Two dead women,' said Lahnos. 'The Demon Witch was also dead.'

Lyla wailed, her hands going to her face.

Leona glared at Lahnos and pointed towards the door. 'Out!'

Lahnos got to his feet, picked up a cup of coffee from the tray, and left the room. He stood on the landing by the top of the stairs, his back to a wall, and listened as Leona tried to calm the young woman down. He felt sorry for Lyla, but he didn't regret what he had said to her. The sooner she knew the truth, the sooner she would accept it. He shook his head – what was he thinking? Did he believe it? Could one body contain the memories of two different women? Reyn had told him everything she had heard about the strange ritual enacted by Lord Malum. Lady Macsin had also been involved, and Lord Rylan, too, although he had claimed not to have remembered what had occurred. Had the grey and yellow dragon been lying to him? More importantly, had the ritual partly worked?

Another door opened, and a young girl walked out, rubbing her eyes.

'What's going on?' she said. 'Why is Lyla crying again?'

'I might have told her about the dragon ritual,' said Lahnos.

The girl glanced up at him, and her eyes widened.

'Demon!' she cried. 'Demon! Help! A demon death-seer! Help!'

Kamasta came bounding up the stairs with the wooden bat in her hand as Leona opened the door to her small bedroom. The girl ran to Leona and hid behind her.

Lahnos raised his palms. 'I didn't do anything. The girl took one look at my horns and started yelling.'

The girl pointed at him, her hand trembling. 'He has three Gifts, and one of them is the Thirteenth. Make him leave! Make him go away. Don't let him touch you.'

'Perhaps you'd better go, Lahnos,' said Leona.

'But I need to talk to you about my Gift. What did the girl call it – the Thirteenth? I need to learn how to control it.' He paused. 'And did she say that I have *three* Gifts?'

'Hit him with the bat, Kamasta!' the girl yelled. 'Hit him hard.'

Lahnos glanced at the others. 'This house is full of crazy women,' he said. 'I'm leaving.'

'I will speak to you about this,' said Leona; 'but not here, and not now. Go back to Tsallon Anura.'

'And don't touch anyone, death-seer!' the girl shrieked.

Lahnos's shoulders slumped, and he walked past the housekeeper and down the stairs.

An hour later, Lahnos was walking up the steps to his apartment. He had said nothing to Efizel or his two old squad mates as the rowing boat had ferried him back to the monastery, and they had respected his sullen silence. He opened the front door of the apartment, pulled off his boots and went into the bedroom. Reyn moved on the bed, and lit a lamp.

'You're back,' she said. 'How did it go? Did you find out anything useful?'

'Not really,' he said, sitting in the blanket-covered armchair. 'It looks as though I'll be sleeping down here for a while. Sorry.'

'Well, you tried,' she said. 'Where did you go?'

'Leona's house.'

Reyn said nothing, her expression masked by the shadows in the room.

'I got screamed at by Lyla,' Lahnos went on, 'and then I got screamed at by a little girl, while an old woman threatened me with a wooden bat.'

'You met Lyla? How was she?'

'Awake, walking and talking. Leona told me not to say anything to her about the Demon Witch, but I couldn't help myself. And then the little girl called me a demon.'

'A little girl?'

'Yes.'

'Was she Gunstian?'

'I didn't stay long enough to find out. She muttered something about me having three Gifts, and then she called me something – a death-seer. She said I had the Thirteenth Gift.'

'At least you now have a name for what happened. A death-seer? I've never heard of death-seers. It sounds as though the Thirteenth Gift is related to being a death-reader, but I guess we already knew that.' She frowned. 'Three Gifts?'

'That's what she said.'

'Did the girl mention anything about the third Gift – the one that's not death-reader or death-seer?'

He shook his head. 'She was a little hysterical at the time. I don't know what she meant.' He glanced at Reyn. 'Lyla mentioned something that happened to me in Gunst,' he went on; 'something that only the Demon Witch knew about.'

Reyn frowned. 'Could Leona have told her?'

'Leona didn't know about it. I think she might be right about what happened – I think the Demon Witch might be inside Lyla's head. She's confused, and doesn't remember much, and she seems to recall some things that happened to the real Major Lyla. I don't know. I don't understand any of it.'

'It seems impossible.'

'I know.'

'Back to your problem,' Reyn said. 'What are we going to do now?'

'I think Leona is going to look into it,' he said.

'And will she?'

'I'm supposed to go up to Fidalaimos in a few days for the meeting,' he said. 'Leona will be there. If you come, you can ask her.'

'I will,' said Reyn. Her gaze lingered on him. 'It's lonely up here in this huge bed. I miss you.'

'I miss you, too.'

Reyn leaned over and extinguished the lamp. 'Goodnight, Lahnos.'

He gazed at her in the darkness. 'Goodnight, Reyn.'

CHAPTER 14
LEVERAGE

Fidalaimos, Serpent Isle – 16th Luddinch 1588

Cisca, Bauchlie and his mother walked along the mountain track, the spruce trees shielding them from the glare of the sun. Over to the north-west, a long low bank of dark clouds was moving slowly across the blue sky towards the island, heralding the first of the autumnal rains. A light shower had fallen that morning, but the heavier rains would finally wash away the mess in the wheat fields left behind by the Gift of Famine, filling the seasonal rivers and watering the newly-sown crops.

To the rear of Bauchlie walked several young rebel fighters, each leading a horse along the track. Bauchlie had insisted that they accompany him, in case the meeting was a trap. His eyes were on the skies most of the time, watching for any approaching dragons, and it was his mother who was leading the way down the mountain slopes towards the village of Fidalaimos.

Bauchlie's mother had moved into a cavern next to where her son slept, and she had assumed the role of gatekeeper, filtering out those she deemed unsuitable from reaching the commander's quarters. She had never refused entry to Cisca, but had chaperoned her instead. It was for the good of the island, she had told Cisca – her son required the time and space to be able to lead the rebels without any unnecessary distractions. Bauchlie had accepted this without any comment. He had also called a temporary halt to any offensive operations against the Aucterian and Bullan forces on Zamata. His stated reason for this change of strategy was that the enemy soldiers and settlers were now all confined to Igatz, leaving the rest of the island free of the occupying forces; but Cisca suspected that he was searching for a compromise that would allow him to keep his honour.

'There are soldiers ahead of us,' Bauchlie's mother said, coming to a halt on the track.

Bauchlie lowered his gaze and stared through the trees at the three men blocking the way to the village.

'They're Zamatans,' said Cisca. 'Look at their uniforms.'

'I know who they are,' said Bauchlie. 'One of them is Karl Laimos – Lahnos's brother.'

'And your cousin,' said his mother.

'He doesn't know that, mother. None of them do.'

'I understand why you kept it a secret while your father was alive,' Abilo said; 'but it might help with the negotiations if they knew you were Lahnos's cousin.'

'Say nothing about it, mother. The cause is more important than family blood.'

His mother narrowed her eyes at him as he strode forward in the direction of the three soldiers. Karl extended a hand when Bauchlie reached him, but the rebel commander ignored it.

'Are you three my escort?' he said.

'We are,' said Karl, lowering his hand. 'The others are waiting for you in the village tavern.'

'We're meeting in the tavern?'

'Yes.'

'Does that mean no dragons will be present?'

'That's right,' said Karl. 'That was the agreement.'

Bauchlie eyed him. 'Do you think I trust any agreement brokered by the so-called Governor of Zamata? And look at you three – all dressed as members of the old militia. The uniforms suit you, as the militia were also collaborators.'

Karl and the other two Zamatan soldiers tensed, but said nothing.

'Let's not stand here like fools,' said Abilo. 'I believe we have a meeting to attend.'

'Yes, ma'am,' said Karl. He gestured down the track. 'Follow me.'

The soldiers led them through the forest, and Cisca saw smoke rising from the chimneys of the houses in the village. They joined a wider track and passed the first cottage, where an old man was leaning on the fence, his eyes on Bauchlie. The commander ignored the stare, and Karl continued on until they reached a low building in the centre of the village.

'You can tie up your horses by the side of the tavern,' Karl said.

'Keep them ready,' said Bauchlie.

'Yes, sir,' nodded a fighter.

Cisca glanced at the small houses lining each side of the unpaved street, as the rebel fighters led the horses out of sight. Despite its proximity to the ruins of Medamuna Gatzoun, she had never set foot inside Fidalaimos before. It was pretty, almost idyllic, but the people watching looked as though they had led hard lives, eking their livelihoods from the unsparing soil.

Karl gestured to the front door of the low building, and Bauchlie strode forwards, Cisca and Abilo flanking him. The rebel commander pushed the door, and it swung open. He peered into the gloom of the interior for a few moments, then he crossed the threshold. Behind him, Cisca and Bauchlie's mother also entered the tavern, while Karl and the two other soldiers remained outside with the horses and rebel fighters.

Two windows opened out on to the main street, but the tavern was wreathed in shadows, and it took a moment for Cisca's eyes to adjust. A long table had been set with drinks and food, and several people were sitting along one side. She recognised Lahnos and Reyn, and the tall Bullan sergeant who never seemed to leave Lahnos's side; then she frowned as she saw Leona sitting next to them. The young woman was next to a man Cisca had never seen before, but he had the familiar air of an agent; a type she was becoming accustomed to. Next to him sat another man Cisca didn't know, wearing the uniform of a Dominion army captain.

Leona got to her feet. 'Welcome,' she said. 'Please, be seated. Help yourselves to food and drink.'

Bauchlie approached the table then came to stop. 'What do you want?'

'To talk,' said Leona; 'to see if there is any way that we can set aside our differences.'

'Judging by the company you have brought with you, Leona,' Bauchlie said, 'I very much doubt that. A Bullan? An Aucterian officer? Are these the people you now associate yourself with? Colonel Friel would be ashamed of you, Leona.'

'Colonel Friel had many friends, Bauchlie,' said Leona, 'including Bullan and Aucterians. Will you not sit? Will you not at least pretend to be civil for a short while?'

Bauchlie stared at her, then Abilo stepped forward and sat down opposite Lahnos. She smiled at the six people sitting on the other side of the table and poured herself a mug of wine.

'I am Bauchlie's mother,' she said. 'Please believe me – I did not raise him to be so impolite.' She glanced at her son. 'Sit.'

Bauchlie and Cisca pulled out chairs and sat down, Bauchlie facing Leona, while Cisca was opposite Reyn, who gave her a brief nod.

'Do we require any introductions?' said Leona, as she also took her seat. 'You know Lahnos and Reyn, of course, and you will have met Lahnos's Bullan friend before...'

'Get to the point,' said Bauchlie. 'State your demands so that I can refuse them, politely, and then we can all go home.'

Lahnos laughed. 'You're still an ignorant bully, I see, Bauchlie.'

'What does that make you, Lahnos?' said the commander. 'I hear you sold yourself and the Zamatans for a general's uniform. Do you think that ridiculous title endows you with any kind of authority? You are a dragon's pet, boy; nothing more. When Rylan tires of you, as he will, you will find yourself friendless and tainted by cowardice and treachery.'

Lahnos glanced at Cisca. 'I admire you. Who else could put up with this bullshit all day long?'

'Hold your tongue, Lahnos,' said Leona. 'I know you sometimes struggle with that, but I would ask that you refrain from squabbling with Bauchlie.'

Lahnos gave her a wry look, then raised his empty palms.

'How have you been, Reyn?' said Bauchlie. 'The caverns under Medamuna Gatzoun are poorer without you.'

Reyn shrugged.

Bauchlie smiled, and folded his arms across his broad chest. 'I see.'

'You asked me to get to the point,' Leona said; 'so let us proceed. The Imperial Gunstian Fleet has been blockading this island for a little under one month. In that time, no ships have been allowed to arrive or leave, and we all know what that means. Zamata does not grow enough food to feed everyone who dwells here, and after the devastation of the western wheat fields, we will soon be entering a crisis.'

'Zamata grows enough food for the Zamatans,' said Bauchlie. 'It is the influx of Aucterian settlers, sailors and soldiers that is the cause of this crisis. Moreover, the four dragons will consume enough food to feed twenty families. Were we to rid ourselves of foreigners, Leona, there would be no crisis.'

'Speak plainly,' said Leona, 'so that there is no misunderstanding. Are you advocating the slaughter of every Aucterian, Bullan and dragon on Zamata? Is that your stated policy?'

Bauchlie rolled his eyes. 'Do not put words into my mouth.'

'I wasn't aware I was doing that,' she said. 'Did you not say *were we to rid ourselves of foreigners*? How exactly were you proposing to do such a thing without bloodshed?'

Bauchlie said nothing.

Leona nodded. 'Let us continue. I have a proposal for you, Commander Bauchlie.'

'One that a dragon has dictated to you?' he said.

'No. Lord Rylan has delegated responsibility to me to...'

'Delegated?' said Bauchlie, his eyes dark. 'The true power lies with him, and you know it. Any authority the usurping Governor can delegate, he can remove. What happened to you, Leona? The colonel had such faith in you; and so did I, for a while. I considered you a patriot. I genuinely believed that you were an asset to the rebellion; and yet here you sit, under the command of a dragon, doing his bidding, debasing yourself for a sliver of power over your fellow Zamatans. What a disgrace you are.'

'You can insult me all you like,' said Leona, 'but the fact remains that the only way for this island to survive is if we band together against the Gunstians. I am not asking you to swear allegiance to Lord Rylan, nor am I requesting that you join forces with Lahnos's regiments. All I require is your pledge not to attack us while the blockade remains in place.'

Bauchlie smiled. 'I want to hear you beg.'

Lahnos opened his mouth, but Leona shot him a fierce look.

'I am a patriot,' she said. 'I love this island, and I love the people who call it their home. Have I done things that have compromised my ideals? Yes, and I would do so again if it was necessary to save the things I hold dear to my heart. I am not afraid to compromise, Bauchlie, and that is the difference between us. Therefore, I beg you to proclaim a truce for the sake of the island. Order your rebel fighters to cease their attacks upon the administration headed by Lord Rylan, and permit them only to engage with the enemy Gunstian forces. If you do this, your base at Medamuna Gatzoun will not be assaulted, and your fighters and agents will not be arrested.'

Bauchlie laughed, then he stood. 'No.'

The others at the table watched in silence as Bauchlie turned and strode from the tavern.

'You shouldn't have begged,' said Abilo. 'My son will perceive that as a sign of weakness.'

'I am trying to save your son,' said Leona. 'If these negotiations fail, then the dragons will incinerate the ruins of Medamuna Gatzoun, and all who live in the caverns beneath them will burn. Lord Rylan cannot defend this island if he has to constantly look over his shoulder.'

Abilo placed her mug onto the table. 'Bauchlie was right – you are a traitor.'

'And whom have I betrayed?'

'My son, for one.'

'Compromise is not betrayal,' said Leona. 'What I do, I do for the good of every Zamatan, not one man too obstinate to see the truth.'

'Am I a traitor, too?' said Lahnos, his eyes on Abilo.

The older woman returned his glance. 'You are a foolish boy, too young to understand the consequences of your actions. You did a marvellous thing for this island; no one can deny it, and I will not even try. But you have allowed your heightened sense of entitlement to lead you astray. Have you bowed before the dragons? Do you call Rylan *my lord*?'

'You're talking shit,' said Lahnos. 'I was never interested in Bauchlie's stupid cause. My notion of what is right has not changed since the day the uprising began. Bauchlie has also remained true to his principles; but now, his heightened sense of self-righteousness is about to lead to our complete annihilation at the hands of the Gunstians. All we are asking for is a truce, not his surrender. Are you sure it is I who has gone astray?'

'I will speak to him,' said Cisca.

'No,' said Abilo, rising to her feet. 'Stay here, girl; let me talk to my son.'

She walked from the tavern, and the others on the far side of the table from Cisca relaxed a little.

The agent next to Leona shook his head. 'That went exactly as I expected, ma'am.'

'Yes,' said Leona, 'but we had to try.' She glanced at Cisca. 'How is the food supply under the ruins?'

Cisca narrowed her eyes. 'Are you forgetting what I know about you, Leona of Kaugatz?' She pretended to look puzzled. 'Is that the name you are going by these days? It would be easy to let slip your other name.'

'What other name?' said Lahnos.

'The reason I asked about the food,' said Leona, 'is that I am prepared to divert supplies to Bauchlie, if he agrees to a truce. Do you want to know how your friend the major is progressing?'

Cisca stared at her, her ire battling with her curiosity. 'Tell me.'

Leona stood. 'I shall, but only in the presence of Lahnos. Come with me, both of you.'

Lahnos eyed Reyn, then he got to his feet. Cisca did the same, and they followed Leona into the quiet shadows at the other end of the empty tavern.

'Lyla is doing very well,' Leona said in a low voice. 'She dreamed that she could speak fluent Gunstian, and when she awoke, she found herself able to converse freely in that language. It has made things considerably easier, as she still struggles with the Divine Tongue.'

'She dreamed it?' said Cisca.

'It seems that her memory is returning slowly in her dreams,' Leona said.

'But... Gunstian? Major Lyla did not speak Gunstian, as far as I am aware.'

'She did not, but Lahnos here taught the Demon Witch that language. Is that not true, Lahnos?'

'It's not completely true,' he said. 'I didn't teach her – she pulled it out of my mind.'

Cisca felt a strange sadness grip her. 'Then Lyla is really dead?'

'No,' said Lahnos. 'I spoke to her a couple of nights ago, and she told me that she has memories of being the Demon Witch, and of being Major Lyla.'

'How?'

'You were there, Cisca,' said Leona. 'You saw what Lord Malum did. The dragons tried to invoke a ritual that probably hasn't been used in millennia, not since Nathaniel placed Gahad into the body of a dragon. Wouldn't it seem reasonable to assume that he might have erred? That some of Lyla's mind remained when he placed the Demon Witch into her body? Do you want to visit her? She remembers you fondly, and I think it would please her greatly if you paid her a visit.'

Cisca glared at her. 'You treacherous, devious little bitch. You stole her from me, and now you have the cheek to invite me round for a chat?'

'I did what I had to. I believe it was the right thing. You were caring and kind, but you refused to believe that the ritual had changed anything, other than transforming Lyla into a permanent invalid. She spent over twenty days in Medamuna Gatzoun and, for most of that time, she lay alone in an underground chamber, confined to a bed. For her own good, I had to remove Lyla from that environment. She is flourishing, Cisca. She is up and about, walking again, and her speech improves day by day. She has books, and paper and charcoal with which to draw and sketch; and she has fresh air and sunlight.'

Cisca felt tears well in her eyes, but she hardened her heart, refusing to weep in front of Leona.

'Does she know about the ritual?' she whispered.

'Unfortunately, yes,' said Leona. 'I was keeping it back from her until more of her memories returned, but a certain young part-Bullan standing here with us blurted it out when he visited.'

'I didn't blurt it out,' said Lahnos. 'She needed to know, and so I told her. I don't regret it. Has she spoken about it since?'

'It is all she has spoken about, Lahnos,' said Leona. 'Worse, it has created a rift between her and Arrosa.'

'Is that the little girl's name?' he said.

'Yes. As you saw, she has an aversion to anyone going by the name of *demon*.'

'That doesn't make sense. The Demon Witch killed Gahad – I thought the girl would admire her for that. She's Gunstian, isn't she? A Chadura-worshipper?'

'She is.'

'You have a Gunstian girl living in your home?' said Cisca. 'Ironic.'

Leona seemed to ignore the comment. 'I am trying to convince

Arrosa that the Demon Witch is on our side, but I have had little success so far. She is a very stubborn girl.'

'I might visit,' said Cisca. 'And if I do, I might mention to this Arrosa the truth about what happened to the other Gunstians who used to live on the island.'

'What is that supposed to mean?' said Lahnos. 'Lord Malum and Lady Macsin slaughtered the Gunstians, didn't they?'

'They did,' said Leona. 'Might we speak alone, Cisca?'

'Why?' she said. 'Don't you want Lahnos to know what you did? You seemed very proud of yourself at the time.'

'You are mistaken,' said Leona. 'I was never proud of that.'

Lahnos rolled his eyes. 'Why are you both talking in riddles? Leona has done some bad stuff, Cisca – I get it. Are we not here to put the past behind us?'

Leona smiled. 'Well said. How about it, Cisca? We will probably never be friends, but perhaps we can treat each other with decency and civility.'

'There is no *probably* about it, Leona,' said Cisca. 'I will never trust you again.'

The tavern door opened, and Bauchlie strode inside, his mother walking next to him. He glanced over into the shadows where Leona, Cisca and Lahnos were gathered, and raised an eyebrow.

'Leona wants to offer us food supplies,' said Cisca.

Bauchlie nodded, then he sat, retaking his old seat. His mother sat down next to him, and Leona returned to the table with Cisca and Lahnos.

'Cisca is correct,' Leona said, as they took their seats. 'I am prepared to divert several tons of supplies from Kaugatz to Medamuna Gatzoun, if you agree a temporary truce.'

'Lay out the conditions clearly,' Bauchlie said.

'Very well. You will order every agent and fighter under your command not to initiate any hostilities against the forces under the authority of Lord Rylan. That includes the dragons, the Bullan, the Aucterians, both those in the military, and the civilians; and it also includes the Zamatans enlisted into Lahnos's regiments, and any property held or used by any of those I have already named. You will also order your forces not to raid the food depots, and to refrain from stealing anything from the inhabitants of this island. Finally, you will call off the agents operating in Kaugatz. You may keep them in place, even the ones who watch my home; but they must desist from threatening any Zamatan who offers their cooperation to Lord Rylan's administration. In return, I will deliver five tons of foodstuffs to Medamuna Gatzoun. I will also ensure that none of your forces are assaulted, harassed or arrested.' She paused. 'Do we have an agreement?'

'What if one of my fighters goes rogue and disobeys orders?'

'If either party suspects that the other has violated the agreement, we shall send delegates here to Fidalaimos to establish the truth before any hostile action is undertaken. Karl Laimos shall be your point of contact. He shall remain here in the village, ready to pass on messages in either direction.'

'If my brother comes to any harm,' said Lahnos, 'I will hold you responsible, Bauchlie.'

'I'm sure you will,' said the rebel commander; 'but you needn't be concerned about that. Karl Laimos will be safe; none of my forces will touch him.'

'Then, we are agreed?' said Leona.

'No,' said Bauchlie. 'I want ten tons of food, and five crates of militia crossbow bolts.'

'Deal,' said Leona, extending her hand across the table.

Bauchlie stared at her. 'I hadn't finished. The truce shall last for one month, after which I expect to renegotiate our terms.'

'The truce shall last for one month,' Leona repeated. 'Shake my damn hand, Bauchlie, then we can all go home.'

Bauchlie looked down, his eyes seeming defeated despite all that he had extracted from Leona; then he lifted his arm and took Leona's hand.

'Thank you,' she said. 'I shall organise the delivery of food and munitions as soon as I return to Kaugatz.'

Bauchlie withdrew his hand and rose to his feet. 'And I shall see you all here one month from now, if you keep your end of the bargain. If you do not, then I shall revenge myself upon all of you.'

He glanced at Cisca and his mother, and they got to their feet and followed him out of the tavern and into the afternoon sunshine.

Abilo shook her head. 'Ten tons, son? You just couldn't resist, could you?'

'I should have asked for twenty,' he muttered. He nodded to the young rebel fighters loitering by the horses. 'We're leaving.'

Karl Laimos and the two other soldiers nodded to them, and Bauchlie led the way back through the village. Dozens of eyes watched them as they made their way along the main street, and none of the glances seemed sympathetic.

'You did the right thing,' said Cisca.

'I knew you would think that,' Bauchlie said.

'I would have been even happier with a formal alliance.'

'I thought you hated Leona?'

'I do,' she said, 'but she has become predictably sly. She is dependant upon Lord Rylan, and she will do whatever it takes to maintain that relationship. I would worry more about Lahnos. Lord Rylan needs him, rather than the other way around; and there's no telling what he might do.'

'I agree,' said Abilo. 'That boy holds you in contempt, son. Perhaps if he knew you were cousins, that might change his opinion of you.'

'I don't care if he hates me,' said Bauchlie, as they left the village behind. 'I'm more concerned with how the rebels in Medamuna Gatzoun will take the news. It will appear to some that I have sold out the island for ten tons of food and a few crossbow bolts.'

'You don't need to adhere to every condition laid out by Leona of Kaugatz, son.'

Cisca frowned. 'Are you suggesting that we break the agreement?'

Abilo gave a gentle shrug. 'You heard what that woman said. Suspected breaches will go to arbitration before hostilities recommence. I am surprised that she left such a gaping loophole for one who is supposedly so surefooted. Enforce the truce, son; but leave enough room for true patriots to continue working for the cause.'

'I think you might be right, mother,' said Bauchlie.

Cisca blinked. 'But...'

'But what, girl?' said Abilo. 'The word of a dragon cannot be trusted, and Leona has become a slave of Lord Rylan – his little pet Zamatan.'

'My mother is correct, Cisca,' said Bauchlie. 'We can make this *truce* work in our favour. The imperialists' guard will be lowered, and they will keep Medamuna Gatzoun supplied with food. And then, once the threat from the Gunstians has been overcome, we will be in a strong position to assert our authority over the island. Let Lord Rylan exhaust his own forces battling the Gunstians, while we sit, and wait.'

'Cisca does not need to know every detail, son,' said Abilo.

Bauchlie shrugged.

'You need to make up your mind,' his mother said. 'Thanks to you, Cisca now knows what we intend to do, and you must decide what to do with her. At the moment, she is at risk from anyone with a grudge against Aucterians; and, let's face it, there are plenty of rebels and villagers under the ruins who loathe Captain Cisca, and who would be only too willing to stick a knife into her back. At the same time, you cannot allow her to go running back to the Aucterians with the knowledge she possesses.' Abilo glanced around at the forest. No one was in sight apart from the young rebel fighters leading the horses behind them. She stopped on the path, and Bauchlie also halted, his eyes narrow.

'This is my advice, son,' Abilo went on. 'You must choose – either declare to all who follow you that Cisca is yours, and that she falls under your personal protection; or admit that it is time to let her go. Hold her close or cast her aside, son; but do not leave her in this middle ground.'

'And are you one of those who would be happy to stick a knife into her back, mother?' Bauchlie said. 'Are you suggesting that I kill her on this forest track?'

'Cisca may be Aucterian,' she said, 'but if you love her, then I will protect her as though she were my own kin. To be honest, I had come to believe that you would never find anyone that you could share your life with, such was your devotion to the cause. But, if you do not love her, then she is nothing but unnecessary baggage; and here would be as good a place as any to dispose of her.'

'Cisca is not baggage, mother,' said Bauchlie. 'If anyone tries to harm her, I will throw them from the cliffs.'

'Then you have made your decision, son,' said Abilo. 'For better or worse, Cisca is now part of our family.'

Bauchlie rolled his eyes and continued down the track.

Cisca turned to Abilo. 'Have you ever thought to ask what I want?'

'I know what you want, girl,' said Abilo. 'You want my son. He has had many admirers over the years, but you are the first he has shown any interest in.'

Cisca said nothing.

'I said I would protect you, girl,' Abilo went on, 'but trust has to be earned, and you have not yet shown that you deserve to be trusted. If you behave yourself, and prove to be loyal and dependable, then everything will be fine.' Her gaze hardened. 'But, if you betray my son, then I will make you suffer.'

CHAPTER 15
ILL REPUTE

Hansarta, Serpent Isle – 17th Luddinch 1588

Leona stood on deck with her hands clutching the side railings of the ferry, as a cool breeze gusted across her face.

'Bauchlie will break the deal as soon as he believes he can get away with it,' murmured Captain Jair, who was standing by her side. 'Not in any major way; nothing that will make it obvious. Instead, he will nibble around its edges, going a little further each time, while he watches to see how you react.'

'I am aware of this,' Leona said.

'And yet you still agreed,' said the Aucterian officer. 'Lord Rylan will not be pleased.'

'I am also aware of that. However, I believe that what we negotiated yesterday will hold, in the main, for a few weeks. The most important thing was to be seen trying. The second most important thing was to show the people of Zamata that even Bauchlie can compromise. The one man on the island that everyone assumed to be utterly immovable has just moved, albeit a few inches. It will be enough to shatter the illusion he has built around himself. That was worth the handful of assassinations and food raids that he will no doubt blame upon rogue elements out of his control.'

Jair smiled. 'You have a virulent strain of ruthlessness about you. I'm not sure if that makes you very likeable, but it certainly makes you dangerous.'

'What will you recommend to Lord Rylan?'

'That's none of your business. Will you be at home this evening?'

'Why – are you planning on cutting my throat as I sleep?'

'If ordered to; however, I was intending to let you know the Governor's opinion of your deal.'

'I will be in. I assume you know my address?'

'Yes.'

'How?'

'That is also none of your business.'

Leona laughed and shook her head. 'It seems there are four rival networks of spies and agents roaming the streets of Igatz and Kaugatz these days – yours, mine, Bauchlie's, and the Gunstians. I wonder how many are members of more than one group?'

'I wouldn't like to hazard an answer to that.' He glanced at the approaching shoreline. 'We'll be in Kaugatz in a few minutes. I'm going to get back on board my carriage, so no one sees you speaking to an Aucterian officer when we land.'

'How thoughtful of you.'

Jair turned away and strode along the deck of the ferry to the carriage that had borne him from Igatz the previous day. Standing by a different carriage was Lahnos, Reyn, and their Bullan guard, while Farakai was sitting on his own by a third carriage at the stern. Leona walked over to Lahnos.

'Could I have a word, alone?'

Lahnos nodded, and followed her to the railings.

'I'll make it brief,' Leona said. 'I have managed to obtain a copy of a book with information pertaining to the Thirteenth Gift.'

'I thought you already had a book about the Gifts.'

'The book you are thinking of is Kitard's *Discourse on the Gifts of Theodora, Volume One*,' she said. 'It is a classic Gunstian text, but it only discusses twelve Gifts, not thirteen. I had always imagined the Thirteenth Gift to be legendary, as the work mentions nothing about it. This new book appears to be *Volume Two*. It is devoted to a few more esoteric theories surrounding the Gifts, and it includes some information regarding your condition. There are pages missing, but…'

'It has parts missing?'

'Yes. The book is very old, and the pages may have fallen out. However, here is what I can tell you – firstly, it appears that only death-readers can progress to becoming death-seers. That is why the Thirteenth Gift is not regarded as a true, individual Gift by some authorities. Secondly, it works in reverse. Instead of taking the memories of a recently-deceased person, the Thirteenth Gift rips the memories from the living and, in the process, it kills them. Does that sound right to you?'

Lahnos lowered his gaze. 'Yes. I touched the man who was trying to kill me, and his memories flooded my mind. When I came out of the trance, he was lying dead on the floor.'

'Did you feel the Gift leave you?'

'I did. He was trying to drive a knife into my face, and my fingers were round his wrist.'

'You were desperate and in fear of your life?'

He nodded.

'This next question is a little more delicate, so you don't have to answer – have you touched anyone since?'

Lahnos did not raise his eyes and Leona guessed the answer.

'I see,' she said. 'Well, that explains Reyn's current mood. I had wondered if you and she had been arguing. And I noticed that you haven't been holding hands – I'm used to seeing the two of you doing that, and it struck me as odd.'

Lahnos gazed out at the waters of the Hansarta. 'We have been arguing – a lot. Not being able to touch each other hasn't helped, but I wish that was the only problem we had. She fundamentally disagrees with every decision I've made since I got back from Gunst.'

'I can't help with that,' Leona said, 'but I can put your mind at ease about your Gift.' She held out her hand. 'Touch my palm.'

'Why?'

'To prove to you that it's safe. To show you that you don't have to withhold physical contact.'

'If I kill you, then sorry in advance.'

He reached out and placed a finger onto Leona's palm.

'Do you feel anything?' she said.

'No.'

'From what I have learned, Gifts that involve physical contact are not triggered by mere touch. There also has to be a strong emotional reaction. You thought you were about to die, and your latent Gift revealed itself. Unfortunately, you will not be able to control it until you practise more, and the Thirteenth Gift is not one that easily lends itself to practice. If you wish, I can grant you access to a group of condemned criminals – ones who are destined to hang for their crimes, and…'

'No,' he said, grimacing. 'No, thanks.'

'The offer is there if you reconsider.'

He nodded. 'I also wanted to ask you about what Arrosa said – she mentioned I had three Gifts. Is she right?'

'I don't know for certain,' she said. 'Arrosa has the Gift of Kenning, but not everything she says should be taken at face value. Have you sensed any other Gift?'

'No. How would I go about looking for it?'

'I don't know. Do you want me to ask Arrosa?'

'Yes.'

Leona smiled. 'Of course, there's no guarantee that Arrosa will tell me anything; you know her opinion on the part-Bullan.' She glanced at the approaching shore. 'The ferry is about to dock in Kaugatz, and then you and I will go our separate ways. If you need to visit me again, send advance word.'

'All right. Thanks for the advice.'

'We're partners, Lahnos,' she said. 'If you need anything that I can provide, just ask.'

She watched as he walked back to Reyn and the Bullan. Reyn asked him something, but instead of responding, he placed a hand on her waist and kissed her. Reyn pushed him away, and then she said something that made Lahnos scowl. Leona turned away as the two part-Bullan began to argue, and she wondered why she had omitted to tell Lahnos everything that Friel had said about him. The colonel had mentioned *other Gifts*, and Arrosa had merely confirmed it. Lahnos had the Gift of Death Reading, and the Gift of Death Seeing. His third Gift couldn't be Truth or Kenning; so what was it?

The ferry bumped against the pier, and sailors threw ropes to the waiting dockhands. Leona strolled to her carriage by the stern, and Farakai stood and opened the door for her.

She climbed into her seat, then Farakai joined her and closed the door.

'Did you enjoy our trip up the mountain?' she said.

'All apart from the meeting with Bauchlie, ma'am,' he said. 'It was the first time I've ever been that far from Kaugatz. It seems a quaint old life up there, but the villagers were hospitable enough.'

'I would have thought that the colonel would have taken you there at least once.'

'He never did, ma'am. In fact, he barely ever mentioned his family or his personal life to me. I was aware he was originally from Fidalaimos, but only due to his name.'

'He used to tell me that a Zamatan surname was a sign of nobility,' she said. 'Needless to say, that wasn't entirely true.'

Their driver pulled on the reins and the carriage bumped its way over the flat deck of the ferry. Its wheels rolled onto solid ground, and they ascended the ramp to the street. Leona leaned back in her seat as they passed through the busy thoroughfares of Kaugatz, her eyes on the Zamatans. How could Bauchlie so misunderstand the situation? He wasn't a stupid man, but his unwillingness to compromise endangered everyone he was supposedly trying to help. All three of the people they had met with in Fidalaimos despised her – Bauchlie, his mother, and Cisca. Of those, the only one that mattered was Bauchlie. She and the rebel commander had forged a useful business relationship while she had been in Zamata Gataza pretending to be Lady Takri, but he had thrown that away by his refusal to see her recent actions as anything other than base treachery.

'Captain Jair might be visiting this evening,' she said. 'He will presumably not be wearing his uniform; inform the others to allow him to reach the house.'

'He might be coming to kill you, ma'am.'

'Yes, possibly; but he is my conduit to Lord Rylan. I suspect that the dragon relies on his judgement and opinion, especially where humans are concerned. If I can earn his trust, then Lord Rylan might continue to allow me to live. Could you procure me a couple of bottles of wine?'

'Certainly, ma'am.'

'Don't look at me like that; I'm not going to seduce him.'

'Why not, ma'am? It might be a good tactical move on your part. The colonel forged all kinds of relationships with women he wished to influence; I don't see why you couldn't do the same. I could send round a girl to do your hair and make-up for you; something that will make an impression on the captain.'

Leona frowned at him. 'No. That's not how I am going to do things. Men like the colonel can get away with that sort of behaviour in Zamata; but I don't think it works in the same manner for women.' She glanced back out of the window. 'Do you think I need my hair and make-up done? Do I appear plain to you?'

Farakai stifled a groan. 'No, ma'am.'

'I wasn't trying to entrap you. I have never given much thought to my appearance, but perhaps I should. When I was on the streets, I would deliberately try to make myself look repulsive to men, to avoid their attention. It didn't take much of an effort; I was filthy most of the time as it was. I wished to be overlooked. But now? I'm certainly cleaner than I was in those days, but I hardly dress like aristocracy. Do the people of Zamata expect a female leader to appear glamorous?'

'I wouldn't know, ma'am,' he said. 'We've not had many female leaders. Besides, you're in an odd position, so to speak. Most Zamatans in Kaugatz are aware that a certain Leona is in charge, but very few would recognise you if you walked past them on the street. Do you wish that to change? It could bring risks.'

'I don't know,' she said. 'They have Lahnos to worship, so perhaps I should remain in the shadows. I will give it some thought.'

They fell into silence as the carriage took them deeper into Kaugatz. They stopped at a pre-arranged location two hundred yards from the house, climbed down from the carriage, and then followed a series of twisting alleyways until they reached the back yard.

'Thank you for your company over the last two days, Farakai,' she said. 'Once you drop off the wine, take the rest of the evening off.'

He bowed slightly. 'Thank you, ma'am.'

Leona waited until he had disappeared around a corner, then she unlocked the gate and strode into the empty yard. After re-locking it, she hurried across the yard and into the house.

'It's just me,' she cried, as she took off her coat.

'Good morning, ma'am,' said Kamasta, as she appeared by the hall door. 'Pleasant trip?'

'Useful rather than pleasant,' Leona said. 'How were things last night? Did any fights break out?'

'It wasn't too bad, ma'am, though Arrosa seems quite upset about a book she says you borrowed. She wanted to search your room for it, but I said no, so there was a tantrum. You should get a lock on your bedroom door. I had to guard it all night to stop her sneaking in.'

Leona nodded. 'And Lyla?'

'Fairly quiet, ma'am. There were a few tears when Arrosa called her a demon, but no worse than usual.'

'We might have company this evening.'

Kamasta frowned. 'Not that horned boy again, ma'am?'

'No. An Aucterian army captain. Discretion will be required, so please don't mention anything about demons in his presence. If he does come round, I will pick the correct moment to introduce him to our two lodgers.'

Kamasta raised an eyebrow. 'A gentleman officer, ma'am?'

'It will be a business meeting, nothing more.'

'Right you are.'

Leona rolled her eyes and went through to the old study. She knocked and entered, to find Lyla and Arrosa sitting on the low bed, talking in whispers.

The girl's eyes narrowed when she saw Leona by the door. 'Where's my book, you thief?'

'How can I be a thief when you lent me the book?'

'You've had it for ages. You must have read it by now. What did you want it for? Did you speak to that demon death-seer about what was written inside? You shouldn't have. It's not right that a demon has Gifts – they're not for his kind.'

Leona smiled as she walked in and took a seat. 'That was a lot of questions, and they raise an interesting dilemma as regards your faith.'

Arrosa glared at her.

'You believe the Gifts were bestowed upon the people of Athumia by Chadura, whom we call Theodora,' Leona went on, 'and yet here is a part-Bullan with Gifts. Why would Chadura give Gifts to a demon? Hmm? Any ideas?'

'Shut up.'

'Is it possible that Chadura doesn't perceive the Bullan or part-Bullan to be demonic, Arrosa?'

'The Bullan don't have Gifts; everyone knows that.'

'And the part-Bullan?'

Arrosa shrugged, her eyes aflame with anger.

'We know that Lahnos has the Twelfth Gift – Death Reading; and the Thirteenth – Death Seeing,' said Leona. 'What is his other Gift? You mentioned that he had three.'

'Why should I tell you?'

'Because the knowledge may help us.'

'It won't,' said the girl. 'There's no point in knowing, not if that stupid demon doesn't know how to make it work.'

'Stop talking about demons,' said Lyla. 'It makes me feel sick.'

'Well, that's because you are one,' said Arrosa. 'A demon and a witch.'

'The Demon Witch is just a silly name invented by the dragons,' said Leona. 'It doesn't mean what you think it means, Arrosa. The dragons knew that someone had killed King Gahad, but they couldn't explain how it was done, and they only knew that it was a woman – so, that's the name they came up with.'

Arrosa frowned. 'The dragons invented the name?'

'Yes.'

'I, uh... didn't know that. Why didn't you tell me that?'

'I tried to tell you a couple of days ago, but you were too busy hurling abuse to listen.'

Arrosa eyed Lyla. 'Did you really kill that horrible Gahad?'

'I think so,' said Lyla. 'I remember a palace on the side of a volcano, and I remember a huge dragon. Lahnos's father was there, and I think I might have killed everyone who was in the palace. If the dragon's name was Gahad, then yes – I killed him.'

'Good,' said Arrosa.

'Perhaps you owe Lyla an apology, Arrosa,' said Leona. 'You have been quite mean to her about this Demon Witch business.'

Leona blinked in surprise as Arrosa started to cry.

'It wasn't my fault,' the girl sobbed; 'I thought she was a demon.'

'Saying sorry can be hard,' Leona said. 'It would mean a lot to me if you could, though. It's just one small word.'

Arrosa sniffled. 'Sorry.'

Lyla smiled. She gave Arrosa a hug and, for a tiny moment, Leona thought she might start crying as well. She got to her feet.

'I'll find that book for you,' she said. 'And thank you.'

Kamasta lit a few lamps as evening fell over Kaugatz, but much of the house remained in shadow, as the price of oil had become too expensive for even Leona to waste any. Farakai dropped off two bottles of fine red wine from the vineyards of Chesson after supper, and then Leona had remained in her room, reading reports about the various shortages that were afflicting the island. Some items remained cheap and plentiful, while others were becoming rarer by the day. Her rationing regime was causing much anger, but it was working, and the date when starvation would begin to take hold had been postponed for another month. The more she read, the more she was convinced that she should remain in the background. Farakai had included excerpts of conversations overheard at a depleted marketplace, where one of his agents had been mingling, and it was clear who the vast majority of people blamed for going hungry. The Gunstians, naturally, incurred the greatest amount of anger, but after that it was Leona. While most people had nothing but good things to say about Lahnos Laimos, it was Leona they were blaming for a perception of unfairness in the rationing regime. Wild rumours that the Aucterians in Igatz were receiving more than their fair share of bread and meat seemed to have taken hold, while many were under the impression that Leona was living like a queen in the Dragon Palace, dining nightly with the Governor and laughing about the poverty of the Zamatans.

Was it worth it? Leona had a thick skin, but the reports made for hard reading, and she felt unjustly maligned by those she was doing her best to help. She glanced at the two bottles of wine sitting on her little table, and a sense of guilt settled in her half-empty stomach. She was hardly living like a queen, but she still had the wealth and means to access luxuries that were outwith the reach of most people living in Kaugatz. Should she throw the bottles out? But, what would be the point? Who was she trying to impress?

A soft knock rapped against her door, and it opened.

'A Captain Jair is here to see you, ma'am,' Kamasta said. 'He is waiting in the dining room.'

Leona nodded. 'Thank you.' She got to her feet. 'Could you bring one bottle of wine down to us in a few minutes?'

'Certainly, ma'am.'

Leona left her room and walked downstairs, hearing no sounds coming from the old study. She entered the dining room and saw the Aucterian officer standing by the long table, wearing a dark cloak over a set of civilian clothing.

'Good news,' he said. 'Lord Rylan has decided not to kill you today.'

'Or perhaps you are trying to lull me into a false sense of security before you attempt to assassinate me.'

'I wouldn't make the effort,' he said. 'I would come at a later hour than this, and I wouldn't bother knocking on the front door.'

She gestured to a chair. 'Sit.'

They both sat by the table, and he eyed her for a moment.

'That was the only good news I had,' he said. 'The Governor understands that the deal you made with Bauchlie was better than nothing, but he is unhappy about some of the details. His lordship considers that you were too lenient with the rebel commander, and I agree. However, he has decided to let it be known that a truce is in force. That way, when Bauchlie inevitably breaks the agreement, Lord Rylan will be able to say that he tried his best.'

'Is that all Lord Rylan had to say?'

'Regarding the deal, yes. Between you and me, he is impressed at how well you have organised things here in Kaugatz. Lahnos's regiments are expanding smoothly, and there have been no riots over rationing. He worries about your end goal, however. If we defeat the Gunstians, then what's to prevent you from allying yourself with Bauchlie and trying to remove his lordship from power?'

'After yesterday's meeting, do you really believe that Bauchlie would wish to make me his ally?'

'He would do anything for his cause – he made that clear.' He narrowed his eyes. 'You hide it well, but I believe that you want the same thing that Bauchlie wants.'

'I want Zamata to be free; I've never made a secret of that. If you are loyal to Lord Rylan, Captain, then aren't we working towards the same goal? Or is the Governor planning to hand this island over to the Dominion if they come calling?'

'He would never do that.'

'Never? Not even in a century or two, when every human currently living on this island is dead?'

Jair said nothing.

'And what about you?' she went on. 'Do you have no desire to go home? I assume you are from Aucteran and have a home there, and possibly a family? How do I know that you are loyal to Zamata?'

'My personal life is none of your concern.'

'You are hardly allowing me to build any trust in you, Captain.'

Kamasta's familiar soft rap at the door sounded.

'Enter,' said Leona.

The housekeeper opened the door and walked in, bearing a silver tray with a bottle and two rounded glasses.

'Your wine, ma'am,' she said, bowing as she placed the tray onto the little table. 'Shall I pour?'

'Yes, please.'

Kamasta lifted the bottle and half-filled each glass, then she bowed again and left the room.

Leona picked up her glass and took a sip.

'Drink,' she said.

'Not while I'm on duty.'

'Duty? I thought we were having a chat.'

He eyed the glass.

'I haven't drugged it,' she said, taking another sip. 'See?'

He raised the other glass from the tray and brought it to his lips.

'Trust has to run both ways, Captain,' she went on. 'I am trying to prove trustworthy to Lord Rylan, and my recent actions have shown that. In order for me to trust you, I want you to answer my questions.'

'You have an unfair advantage.'

'Only if you were thinking about lying to me. Let's start with a simple question – you are not Dragon Corps, are you?'

'No. Army.'

'Then how was it that you were assigned to Lord Rylan?'

'The Dragon Corps has been gutted out. King Naghad removed most of the officers from their positions some time ago, and very few remain. I was in the Dragon Palace when Lord Rylan returned wounded from Zamata Gataza, and I was selected to attend to his needs. All of this is a matter of public record.'

'Why didn't you sail away with Lady Abda?'

'I was one of a small number who volunteered to stay with Lord Rylan. That decision saved my life, as I was due to depart on Lady Sengilla's dragon carrier, which is currently lying at the bottom of the ocean.'

'And your home?'

'Tell me about your home first.'

'I am from Zamata,' she said.

'I knew that. Where did you grow up?'

'Kaugatz.'

'Again, that was known to me. Give me something, and I will reciprocate.'

'All right. I don't remember my parents. A sister brought me up, but she died when I was ten and I was thrown on to the streets. The next few years were chaotic, but I survived.'

He narrowed his eyes. 'If you were on the streets for years, then where did you receive your education?'

'From my sister when I was young, and then from Colonel Laimos, after he came across me one day, begging in an alleyway. He sensed my Gift and took me in. In order to become useful to him, I required knowledge, and he provided it.' She glanced at him. 'I have just given you more than I give to most people. It's your turn.'

'I am from Teros City,' he said. 'I have parents and siblings living there, but I haven't seen any of them in over five years. I was serving in Irlan before being sent here as part of King Naghad's grand invasion force. My home is wherever I am posted.'

'Are you still loyal to the Dominion?'

He smiled. 'I cannot answer that question properly without in some way triggering your Gift. My feelings are mixed. Did I like King Naghad? Not particularly. Was I loyal to him? Of course. I have no wish to become embroiled in a civil war; and if I was in Aucteran, I would have to choose between Lord Tegru and the adherents of the late King Naghad. Fighting the Gunstians seems a lot more straightforward, and I won't have to kill fellow Aucterians. In truth, this island means little to me, but I made my choice when I decided to remain by Lord Rylan's side. For better or worse, I am stuck here.'

'That wasn't so difficult,' she said. 'Do you trust me now?'

'No, but Lord Rylan has chosen to work with you, and so I will do the same. If you betray him, then I will kill you. If you ally yourself to Bauchlie, I will kill you. I would take no pleasure from it, but I am charged with maintaining stability on this island, and I will do whatever it takes to fulfil my duty.' He drained his glass and got to his feet.

'Are you leaving?' she said.

'Yes, before I drink more wine and am tempted to fall into your trap.'

'What trap?'

'Do you think I am stupid? Wine and pleasant conversation may seem innocent, but I know you are trying to seduce me. You are beautiful, but I can see through your lies. If I stay, then I would be in danger of... well, let's not talk about that.'

She stared at him. 'I am not trying to seduce you.'

He smiled. 'I know your reputation.'

'What are you talking about?'

'You were Colonel Laimos's little whore, were you not? There are rumours that he lent you out to his friends, and now you are attempting to ensnare me. You are proficient at blackmail, I believe?'

Her eyes tightened. 'Get out.'

He tilted his head. 'I shall see myself to the door. Good night.'

'I don't want you to come here again,' she said.

'Then don't give me any reason to.'

He strode to the door and left the dining room. Leona hurled her empty glass against the wall, where it shattered into a hundred pieces.

'Bastard!' she cried, hoping Jair would hear it.

How dare he? Had he assumed all along that she was attempting to drag him into her bed? Had he come to her house thinking that in advance? And she had a reputation? She felt sick, though she was too angry to cry. She thought about sending Saewa and some men after Jair, to ram a knife into his back as he made his way home to Igatz, but Lord

Rylan would assume that she was responsible if his favourite officer was found dead in a backstreet in Kaugatz.

She put her head in her hands, the thought that people were discussing her private life with Friel Laimos churning her stomach. She remembered when Reyn had accused her of the same thing; did everyone think that? Did Farakai? What about Kamasta?

The door opened and the housekeeper walked in. Her eyes went to the broken fragments of glass, and then she frowned at Leona.

'I heard the captain leave, ma'am,' she said.

'If he comes here again, lock the doors and don't let him in.'

Kamasta walked over to her. 'What did he do to you, ma'am?'

'He called me a whore. He thought I was trying to seduce him.'

Kamasta said nothing.

'You believe it, too, don't you?' said Leona. 'Is that what everyone says about me?'

'I don't pay any heed to rumours, ma'am.'

'But there are rumours?'

'You are an attractive young woman, ma'am,' Kamasta said, 'and you were with Colonel Laimos for a long time; and it's no secret what he got up to. People are liable to see what they want to see.'

Leona glanced up at the older woman, feeling an urge to tell her everything – to open her heart, as though the housekeeper could take the place of her mother or sister. She clamped her mouth shut. She could trust no one. She was on her own, and she would have to take care of herself, as she had always done.

She got to her feet and picked up the bottle of wine.

'Will that be everything for this evening, ma'am?' said Kamasta.

'Yes,' she said. 'That will be all.'

CHAPTER 16
DASHED

Kaugatz, Serpent Isle – 20th Luddinch 1588

Lahnos was leaving the training up to the experts. Two thousand men from the Zamatan regiments were lined up in company-sized groups across the empty fields south of the farmstead monastery of Tzalla Pen, just below the terraces that held a large proportion of the island's vines. Overseen by experienced old hands from among the Aucterians, newly-appointed Zamatan sergeants were drilling the soldiers, and their boots were trampling over the damp soil. The soldiers had marched the four miles from Tsallon Anura that morning, and were conducting their manoeuvres in full view of the blockading Gunstian fleet. Lahnos wondered if they were watching. He hoped the Gunstians would see the Zamatans out training and realise that they were in for a long siege. And maybe, just maybe, it would dispirit them a little.

Efizel coughed, and Lahnos turned away from the sight of the soldiers marching through the fields.

'Lord Sigum should be making his attempt around now, sir.'

Lahnos nodded, and squinted in the direction of Kaugatz. He couldn't see the walls of Tsallon Anura, but he could make out the built-up area of Kaugatz stretching along the shore of the Cyasarta. He willed the dragon to succeed.

Further to the south-west, Lord Rylan was circling over the Dragon Palace.

'The Governor has come to watch,' Lahnos said.

'Yes, sir,' said Efizel. 'His lordship will understand how Lord Sigum has been feeling these past months. He will wish for Lord Sigum's success as much as you do.'

Lahnos waited, and then he saw it – a small black speck rising above the roofs of Kaugatz, and he clenched his fists, his nerves jangling.

'You can do it,' he whispered, as the tiny speck rose higher and higher into the cloudy sky. The speck moved out over the waters of the Cyasarta, then plummeted downwards and soared above the surface of the inlet, his long silvery wings reflecting the light of the afternoon sun. The dragon raced eastwards, his underside barely clearing the Cyasarta. Lord Rylan dived down to meet him as he passed the palace, and the two dragons sped towards the land where Lahnos had brought the Zamatan regiments. The soldiers had been given permission to stop their drills, and they roared at the sight of the dragons flying towards them. Rylan and Sigum circled together as they cleared the shoreline, then they soared over the vineyards and landed by the edge of the long field, their claws gouging furrows through the earth.

Lord Sigum raised his head, his eyes gleaming as the Zamatan soldiers cheered.

'Well done, my old friend,' said Lord Rylan. 'Your recovery is complete, and you can now savour the feel of the wind under your wings again.'

'Thank you, my lord,' said Sigum. 'I had almost forgotten how good it is to fly; and now I feel better prepared to aid you in the defence of this island.'

The two dragons turned to gaze at the ships of the Imperial Gunstian Fleet anchored off the coastline, and Lahnos strode up to them.

'Congratulations,' he said.

Sigum glanced down at him. 'Your encouragement has hastened my progress, Lahnos. I will be sorry to leave you on the ground whenever I go flying.'

'Now that we have four dragons capable of flight,' said Rylan, 'I would like to propose that we commence some modest offensive actions against the Gunstians. We cannot attack their main fleet, as the Gifted on board would bring us down, but we can scout for their supply vessels, and target them. After all, our besiegers also need to eat, and they are dependent upon ships reaching them from Gunst. Lord Sigum, would you be prepared to search the ocean with my sister Lady Natali? You would have free rein to destroy any Gunstian vessel you came across.'

The silvery-green dragon bowed his head. 'I would be honoured, my lord.'

'Let us give it a few more days,' said Rylan, 'to give you time to exercise your wings. I will return now to the palace, and speak to my sister. She is feeling a little claustrophobic on Zamata, and I think a few long flights would do her some good.' He glanced at Lahnos. 'Carry on with the training, General Laimos; your troops are in fine shape.'

The grey and yellow dragon took to the air again. He banked over the coastline, and soared back towards the Dragon Palace.

'A flight over the ocean hunting Gunstians sounds like fun,' said Lahnos. 'Once again, I am a little jealous.'

'It does sound good,' said Sigum, 'but it leaves me with a few concerns.'

'You don't have to do it until your wings are ready.'

'My concerns are not for my own safety,' said Sigum. 'It is Lord Givra who worries me. Were it not for him, we could have been hunting Gunstian vessels long before now. I fear that, without Lady Natali's presence in the palace, Lord Givra may be tempted to strike.'

Lahnos frowned. 'Should you be telling me this?'

'You are a general in Lord Rylan's armed forces, Lahnos; you should be aware of every threat faced by this island. Lord Givra has sat in sullen silence ever since Lord Rylan took the life of Lord Gradham in the bath house. He has not directly disobeyed any command, but as

Lord Rylan does not trust his nephew, no vital orders have ever been issued to him. Were Lord Givra to seize power, I think it likely that he would try to negotiate his escape with the Gunstians.'

'Would they allow him to leave?'

'If he ensured that the chains barring the Cyasarta were lowered – then, yes, they might. He could take the last remaining dragon carrier and sail into the East, enabling the Gunstians to enter the Cyasarta unopposed.'

Lahnos turned to gaze at the vast fleet stretching out along the coast of Zamata.

'Why hasn't Lord Rylan killed him?'

'For several reasons. The first is honour. It would be shameful to kill Lord Givra without due process, and he has committed no crimes. The second is Lady Natali. She is of the opinion that Lord Givra will change his mind in time, and she would be incensed if her noble brother took his life.'

Lahnos gave the dragon a wry smile. 'I think I might know why Lord Rylan wants you and Lady Natali off the island for a while.'

Lord Sigum lowered his neck and stared at Lahnos. 'I do not like what you are insinuating, but that does not make it untrue. After all, there were no witnesses to what occurred in the bath house, only Lord Rylan's solemn word that he was the victim of an unprovoked attack by Lord Gradham.'

'Do you believe him?'

'I choose to believe him, Lahnos. There is no alternative.'

Lahnos nodded, and decided it was time to change the subject. 'Did you see Reyn in Tsallon Anura before you left?'

'I did not,' the dragon said. 'I mean no offence by this, but I do not believe that Reyn particularly likes dragons.'

'She sees you and your kin as occupiers, oppressing the island.'

'I can understand why, having seen the manner in which Lord Malum conducted his affairs. Does she not realise that, like humans, we are not all the same?'

'One bad dragon can wipe out large numbers of humans,' Lahnos said; 'the way that Lord Malum destroyed the entire town of Neeton. Bad humans don't possess that kind of power.'

'What about the Gunstians? They have pledged to destroy all life upon this island.'

'Reyn hates them more than she dislikes dragons,' Lahnos said. 'I think she's coming round, slowly. Give her time to change her mind.'

'Now you sound like Lady Natali talking about Lord Givra. I also think... no. Perhaps I shouldn't say it.'

Lahnos narrowed his eyes. 'You'll have to say it now.'

'Very well, although it will sound foolish when spoken aloud. I think that perhaps Reyn is a little envious of your friendship with me.'

'That doesn't sound foolish. She is envious. For a long time, it felt like it was me and Reyn against the entire world. Walking around this island as part-Bullan, knowing that most people hated or mistrusted us, made us reliant on each other. Then I was taken away to Gunst, and everything changed. She made new friends among Bauchlie's rebels, and found a purpose of her own; while I had the squad, and then I became friends with you. We joined different circles, and those circles don't mix well.'

'But you still love her?'

'Yes.'

'Good. I do not wish to be the reason why you separate. I want to see you raise strong children together, and still be holding hands when you are old and grey. If I remain upon this island, then I will never find a mate, and I will die childless, but I will take joy from protecting your little ones.'

'How old are you, Sigurn? I feel a little embarrassed that I don't already know this.'

'I am four hundred and fifty-three years old, Lahnos; just twenty-three years younger than Lord Rylan. However, unlike him, I am a mortal dragon, with none of King Gahad's divine blood in my veins. Lord Rylan could go on to live for another millennium, perhaps longer; I will not.'

'How long do mortal dragons live for?'

'If I remain healthy, then I should reach six hundred. I am perhaps the equivalent of a human in their forties or fifties, Lahnos.'

'Four and a half centuries? Did you live on Inopei for that whole time?'

'Mostly. My father has a cliff-top castle on that continent's western extremity, far from Nom Karta. He is elderly, having passed his six-hundredth year a decade ago. I am his eldest child, and his greatest disappointment.'

'I find that hard to believe.'

'Three hundred years ago, I was betrothed to a Lady Minula Min Famula, a granddaughter of the great King Gahad. My father's heart nearly burst with pride, and then it broke in despair when I ended the betrothal. Lady Minula was a deeply unpleasant dragon – arrogant and selfish, and I was loath to tie myself to her for life. She despised me in turn but, as she is immortal, I would have been but the first in a succession of mates that would have provided her with offspring throughout her long life. That is what the Royal Family do – they select mortal dragons to help them further the royal bloodline. When I announced that I was breaking off our engagement, her mother Lady Famula Min Gahad banished me from her palace in Nom Karta, and I had to return to my father's castle in disgrace. He did not speak to me for fifty years. I was his way into the upper echelons of dragon society, and I had ruined everything. My younger brothers and sisters were also affected by my actions, as they each struggled to find mates from among the other mortal dragon households, such was the shame I had brought upon my family. Today, Lady Famula is Princess Regent of the Dominion, ruling the empire after the death of her brother King Naghad. Hence, I would be unwelcome in Nom Karta even now.'

'All that, over a broken engagement? And you never found another mate?'

'None would have me, Lahnos. The Royal Family took my actions as an insult against them, and none of the mortal families wished to risk their ire by providing a daughter I could court. Had I realised this at the time, I might have made a different choice.'

'But then you would have been unhappy.'

'I would have spared my siblings much angst and worry. There are only a few thousand dragons on this world, and every family knows the others' business.'

'I know how Gahad got here, but where did the mortal dragons come from?'

'King Gahad brought them with him.'

'From the same place where he brought the Aucterians?'

'No, Lahnos. Gahad visited a world where my kind dwell in great numbers – the home of the dragons. There, he selected two thousand young followers to accompany him to Athumia. I am of the fifth generation, descended from those same dragons.'

Sigum raised his head as if hearing something, and his eyes stared into the east.

'What is it?' said Lahnos.

'I sense human cries from afar, drifting across the ocean waves. I think I shall take a look.'

The dragon extended his great wings and ascended into the sky, then he banked and turned towards the ocean. Lahnos watched him soar away, then he walked the short distance to where Efizel was standing with a couple of other Bullan as they watched the Zamatans drill.

'Something could be happening at sea,' he said. 'Lord Sigum heard a noise and flew off.'

The Bullan glanced at each other.

'It could be the latest supply convoy from Aucteran, sir,' said one. 'Lady Abda Min Gahad will still be crossing the ocean towards Inopei, and no one in Naeth will have heard of the disaster that befell King Naghad.'

'A supply convoy?' said Lahnos.

'The Aucterians were under orders to send monthly convoys to the invasion force in Gunst, sir,' said the Bullan. 'I assume that they will continue to do so until they learn the truth.'

'Shit,' muttered Lahnos. 'The Gunstian fleet will slaughter them. Come on; it's a mile to the shores of the ocean. We should take a look.'

The Bullan issued a few orders, and then they set off, flanking Lahnos as they ran east along a farm track. Several companies of Zamatan soldiers were ordered to about-turn, and they also headed east. They passed a succession of empty fields and, when they were halfway to the coast, Lord Sigum passed over them, flying back towards Igatz. The soldiers kept running until they reached the ragged shoreline, where a series of short cliffs fell down into the waters of the vast ocean. Lahnos squinted into the distance. He could see plenty of masts, but it was hard to tell what was happening. Shadows streaked over the ground, and four dragons soared overhead, with Lord Rylan in the lead. They crossed the line of cliffs and flew on, approaching the ships of the Gunstian blockade.

Lahnos stared. Ships were moving, their sails filled with the wind, and large vessels were peeling away from the main blockade line, but, beyond that, it was impossible to see what the movements signified. In the sky, the four dragons had diminished into specks, black against the grey clouds, then they wheeled and turned, and retreated back to the coast.

'They cannot get past the Gifted,' said Efizel.

As the four dragons returned, they passed a Gunstian destroyer that had got itself separated from the others in the complicated manoeuvres. Lord Rylan dived, and a burst of flames swept over the deck of the warship. Its masts and furled sails blazed in the inferno, and the ship began to drift towards the shore. The dragons then soared over the crashing waves and landed on the cliffs next to the gathering Zamatan soldiers. Each dragon turned to stare into the east, their anger palpable.

Sigum saw Lahnos and the Bullan, and strode up to them.

'This is a dark day,' he said. 'The Gunstians are sinking every ship of a supply convoy that made it this far from Aucteran; and there is nothing we can do to stop them.'

'The humans of this island are doomed,' cried Lord Givra; 'all will starve. Lord Rylan, will you listen to me now? We have but one choice, or the Serpent Isle shall be our grave.'

'I will never surrender this island to the Gunstians,' said Lord Rylan; 'and you will cease this defeatist talk in front of our soldiers.'

'The life of a dragon of the royal household is worth a million wretched humans,' said Givra, 'and there are three of us here. You are consigning us to dust and ash – shame on you!'

Givra rose into the air, and turned for Igatz. A few moments later, Lady Natali also ascended, and she followed Lord Givra back to the Dragon Palace.

Lord Rylan glanced down at the hundreds of Zamatan soldiers who had reached the shore.

'Let not your hearts be downcast by what you have witnessed,' he said, 'for I will never abandon you to the Gunstians. I will fight to my last breath to defend Zamata, come what may. If they land on our beaches, we shall destroy them; if they attack the Chain Castles, we shall lay their corpses in heaps. We shall show the invader no mercy, for they will show us none. They will know death, and fear, and fire. I will be with you, to the end!'

The Zamatan soldiers raised their arms and cheered, but several had their gazes fixed in the direction of the burning destroyer that was approaching the line of cliffs. With its masts and sails destroyed in the inferno, the ocean currents were pushing it closer to the island. The fires on the deck had been brought under control, and sailors were rushing around. Some were at the burnt remains of the wheel by the stern of the vessel, while others were trying to repair the bow, where the thick anchor cables had fused together in the heat of the blaze. Lord Rylan took off again. He sped towards the stricken vessel, hovered over it, then he gripped the bow in his giant forelimbs and pulled it through the waves. Sailors loosed crossbow bolts at him, and several struck the dragon's flank, but Rylan ignored the pain. He heaved again, and the bow of the ship crashed into the cliffs with a roar of splitting beams amid the screams of the sailors. Sigum went to assist the Governor, and they dragged the vessel up onto the shore. The dragons released it, and it fell onto its port side, its hull torn and ruined.

'Take your revenge, my soldiers!' Rylan cried. 'Let the Gunstian navy see what happens to any of their kin who reach our shores!'

The Zamatans on the cliff-top roared again, and charged the vessel. Swords were drawn, and the panicking sailors close to the main deck were cut down in minutes, as the Zamatans stormed the ship.

Lahnos glanced at the Bullan. 'Find me a Gunstian officer,' he said. 'Get him out of there before the soldiers kill everyone.'

The Bullan raced away, sprinting towards the wrecked destroyer as the two dragons landed again. Lahnos folded his arms across his chest as he watched the carnage unfold. Sailors were being pulled from hatches and then butchered on the ragged cliffs, their blood staining the dark rocks. A few Gunstians pleaded for their lives, but after watching the destruction of the supply convoy, no Zamatans were in the mood to be merciful. After a few minutes had passed, the Bullan emerged back into the open, dragging a single Gunstian prisoner through the crowds of Zamatans. They formed a tight circle around the man, and brought him over the cliffs to where Lahnos was standing; then they forced him to his knees.

'Name and rank?' said Lahnos in Gunstian.

'I will tell you nothing, demon,' spat the officer.

Lahnos smiled. 'You are wrong; you will tell me everything.'

Two hours later, Lahnos was back in the monastery of Tsallon Anura. Seated in the dark chamber opposite him was the Gunstian prisoner, his hands bound behind his back.

'Kill me if you wish, demon,' said the Gunstian; 'for I know that Chadura's holy embrace awaits me after death.'

'Your choice is simple,' said Lahnos. 'You can tell me what I want to know, and you will be placed into a cell; or I will rip your memories from your head and you will die.'

The Gunstian stared at him.

'Have you heard of the Thirteenth Gift?' Lahnos went on.

'You are lying,' said the Gunstian. 'The divine Chadura would not bestow such power onto one who possesses no soul.'

'What is the fleet planning?' he said. 'Do they intend to land soldiers soon?'

The Gunstian spat on the stone floor of the chamber.

'You are a second lieutenant, by your uniform,' Lahnos went on. 'I doubt you know much, but you must have a vague idea of what your fleet is going to do. You can't blockade this island indefinitely.'

'We can blockade it for as long as we wish,' said the officer. 'Our supply lines to Gunst are open – what about yours? Has anyone starved to death yet?'

'Last chance,' said Lahnos. 'What are you planning?'

'You will burn for all eternity, demon.'

Lahnos nodded and got to his feet. 'I don't know if this will be painful. When I did it before, I didn't actually see the other man die – my mind was full of his memories. You know, I'm not even sure if it will work, but as all death-seers are also death-readers, then it doesn't matter. Either way, you will die and I will take your memories.'

He walked behind the officer, then he gripped the man's neck with his right hand.

'You can scream all you like,' Lahnos said; 'I won't hear you.'

He closed his eyes and searched for his Gifts, as the Gunstian struggled to free himself from his grip. Lahnos tried to remember how it felt to death-read a corpse, and then he felt a tingling in his fingertips. The two Gifts were closely related, and he concentrated. His fingers tingled again, then his vision went blank.

The first thing he saw was the shape of Lord Rylan diving towards the destroyer. The officer had been up on the quarter deck with the captain, and they had scattered as the flames burst from the dragon's open jaws. Lahnos pushed backwards in time, and felt boredom and the long hours of waiting aboard the ship as it sat anchored outside the opening of the Cyasarta. The blockade was working, or so the officer believed, but it was taking a long time, and some of the sailors were getting restless. Lahnos sifted through the monotony, then stopped when he came to a conversation with the captain of the ship. The second lieutenant was on the quarter deck again, and a handful of officers were gazing at the shoreline of Zamata as the sun set over the two mountains in the distance.

'A few of the lads are starting to complain,' said one of the other officers. 'What should we tell them, sir?'

The captain frowned. 'What is the nature of their complaints, Lieutenant?'

'We've been sat here for nearly a month, sir,' the lieutenant said. 'The lower ranks want to know how long we can expect to remain in position. There's a rumour that we have over fifty thousand marines sitting on board the troopships – why haven't they landed?'

'We have twenty thousand marines, not fifty,' said the captain, 'and the admiral does not want to risk them; not yet. Our instructions state that we are to remain here until the island is on its knees, and that will take time. We have agents posted on Zamata, and several operations are underway to sabotage the remaining food stocks. That will speed things along, if they are successful. More importantly, tell the sailors this – taking Zamata will guarantee that Gunst shall never again be invaded by the Dominion. That alone is worth the wait. Ask them to be patient. Once this is over, we can all go home.'

Lahnos tried to pull away, but he found himself mired in the officer's memories. Another scene opened before his eyes, of the officer kissing a woman on the quayside of Toraq City, the ruins of the harbour visible behind her.

'Take care, husband,' she said. 'I love you.'

'Don't worry about me,' said the second lieutenant. 'We'll be back as soon as we've kicked the Aucterians out of Zamata. I'll see you and the children within a month – I promise.'

Lahnos forced his hand away from the prisoner, and his eyes opened. He looked down. Just as before, the victim of his Gift seemed to have withered and shrunk, his leathery flesh tough and dry. His mouth was open as though he had been screaming, but Lahnos could remember no sound being made.

He gazed at his right hand. Something was different, as though some of the Gift he had released remained within his body. He felt strong, and whole. Was this a side-effect of the Thirteenth Gift? He had never felt so energised after death-reading; on the contrary, the experiences had always left him feeling a little nauseous and dizzy.

Lahnos turned and left the chamber. Two Bullan were standing guard outside, and both glanced at him.

'Did you hear anything?' Lahnos asked them.

'Yes, sir,' said one. 'The prisoner was calling out a woman's name.'

Lahnos lowered his glance. 'Get rid of the body,' he said. 'I need to speak to Lord Rylan.'

CHAPTER 17
CENTRE OF THE WEB

Medamuna Gatzoun, Serpent Isle – 27th Luddinch 1588

Cisca gazed at the four walls of her tiny new room, deep within the caverns under Medamuna Gatzoun. It reminded her of the small chamber where she had looked after Lyla, except, this time, it was Cisca who was unable to leave. No one, least of all Bauchlie's mother, had referred to the room as a prison cell, but that was what it felt like, and Cisca was growing desperate for a glimpse of the sun and some fresh air.

Two young rebel fighters stood guard outside the ill-fitting wooden door. They were there for Cisca's protection, or so she had been repeatedly informed. With Bauchlie busy dealing with the four hundred people living in the caverns, he was seldom around, and Cisca could spend days on end without seeing him. She suspected that Abilo had engineered the situation to keep them apart, but as Bauchlie had rarely been available prior to his mother's arrival, Cisca couldn't be sure.

She stared at the streaks of smoke staining the walls from the two small oil lamps that were providing the dim illumination. It was too dark to read, but as she hadn't been provided with any books, that hardly mattered.

She had missed her chance. Lulled into complacency, she had overlooked her best opportunity to flee the caverns during the meeting with Lahnos and Leona. If she had requested that they take her away with them, then Leona might have refused, but she was sure that Lahnos would have agreed.

She turned on the straw mattress as the door was opened.

'We've got today's food for you,' said one of the young guards, carrying a basket.

Cisca sat up. 'I would rather eat in the main canteen.'

'You're not allowed to,' said the other guard. 'Orders. There are people up there who want you dead. It's too dangerous.'

'But you could stay close to me. You could protect me.'

'Sorry,' said the one holding the basket. 'The commander wants you kept safe and alive.'

'Where is he?'

They both shrugged.

'No idea,' said one.

The other lowered the basket to the floor of the cavern. 'At least there's plenty of food, eh?' she said, as she unpacked the basket. 'A big delivery arrived yesterday; courtesy of Leona of Kaugatz. As a celebration, the commander has ordered that today's ration allowance be increased a little.' She picked up a sealed ceramic jug. 'There's even fresh ale; can you believe it?'

'I don't want fresh ale, I want fresh air. The smoke in this room is giving me a headache.'

'There's nothing we can do,' said the guard. 'You can complain all you like, but until our orders change, you're stuck in here. Still, it's better than being attacked, eh? These caverns aren't safe for Aucterians.'

'I walked these caverns for weeks without being attacked.'

'Abilo said that there have been credible threats made against you. She told us that if you died while under our protection, she would rip our heads off.' She smiled. 'I'm not going to argue with the commander's mother, no matter what you say.' She stood. 'Enjoy the ale. Knock on the door if you need to pee.'

The two guards left the room and the door was closed. Cisca crouched down by the contents of the basket. As well as the jug of ale, there was fresh bread, two smoked fish, olives, a block of soft goats' cheese and a ripe orange. Cisca picked up the bread and sniffed it. It was the first time she had seen fresh bread in a long time, and she tore into the small loaf, devouring it in minutes. Thirsty, her eyes went to the jug of ale. She picked it up, then placed it back down again, and instead opened the fresh water skin that had been left for her. That much ale would make her drunk, and being inebriated alone in her small chamber held no attractions. She sipped from the water skin, then peeled the orange.

If she and Bauchlie had been alone somewhere, away from the never-ending politics and strife of the island, then she imagined that they might have stood a chance. Even before his mother had arrived, the possibility of something happening between them had been present, but Cisca had lost all hope. Regardless of her feelings towards him, it was never going to work. In the best possible scenario, he was blithely unaware that she had been confined to a small room on her own, but even if that was the case, what did it say about his priorities? He had told her that he needed her, but that seemed laughable.

She listened as the guards talked outside her room. Their voices were louder than normal, and she suspected that they had opened their own jug of ale. Cisca could hardly blame them for that; they must be bored senseless having to watch over their charge every day. A few laughs echoed through the gaps in the doorframe, and Cisca lay down onto her mattress to eat the orange.

When she had finished, she dozed for a while, her stomach full for once. She dreamed about being on a sinking ship amid the endless waves of the vast ocean. A raging storm had brought the mast crashing down, and the rain was falling from the dark skies as the vessel began to capsize.

Her eyes shot open, and she sat up, her breath ragged. She listened, but heard nothing, and she relaxed. It was only a nightmare, she told herself, then she noticed a thin stream of liquid that was seeping into her room from under the closed door. She eyed it, then went down onto a knee and sniffed. Ale. She listened again, but could hear no sound coming from the two guards outside her room. Were they so drunk that they had fallen asleep and knocked over the jug of ale? Cisca crept towards the door. She knew the tunnels in that part of the cavern network well, and a faint hope began to arise in her. If the guards were sleeping, then she might be able to slip past them unobserved.

She placed her palm on to the door and gently pushed. The edge scraped against the wall, and she stopped, cursing herself. Nothing happened. She pushed again, and the door opened a few inches. The two guards were lying on the floor of the passageway, but they weren't sleeping. Cisca stared at their faces. Each had turned a shade of greyish-green, and their eyes were wide open. Next to them, the over-turned jug of ale was dripping the last of its contents onto the ground. Cisca eased her body through the gap and crouched down next to the closest guard. She placed a finger onto the woman's neck, but there was no need – she was clearly dead. Cisca stared at the two bodies, transfixed and nauseous.

Poison – it had to be. Leona. The guards had mentioned her name, and Cisca remembered her promise to send food as part of the deal brokered with Bauchlie. Leona had sent poison instead. Her thoughts went to the rebel commander. If he had also drunk the ale, he would be as dead as the two guards; then she pictured the likely scene in the upstairs canteen, where most of the cavern's inhabitants would have gathered to eat and drink, and she almost vomited.

She needed to get out of the caverns. She got to her feet, using a hand to reach for the side wall to steady herself, then she set off, climbing a set of stairs that led up to the main cavern network. She halted in the shadows at the top of the stairs as two rebel fighters sprinted past, heading towards one of the larger caverns. They disappeared from sight, and then a long scream pierced the air.

Cisca turned in the other direction. She came to a lamplit chamber cut into the bedrock to her right, and peered in. Inside, four rebels and a handful of older civilians were sitting with their heads slumped over a long table. Several jugs of ale were sitting open next to them, and one of the fighter's hands was still gripping onto a mug.

More screams came from another passageway, and the sound of boots followed a few moments later. Cisca hid against the wall by the open doorway, her heart racing. How many more corpses were lying within the caverns? Had Leona known that two hundred civilians had sought sanctuary beneath the ruins? On Zamata, even children were given ale from time to time, especially if the water wasn't fresh. Part of her wanted to find Bauchlie, but she knew she would break down if confronted by the sight of a poisoned child. If Bauchlie was alive, he would be consumed with horror and rage; perhaps it would be better to leave him alone. She found herself hoping that Abilo had drunk the ale, then felt guilty at entertaining such a thought. Did she hate Bauchlie's mother so much that she wanted her dead? Instead of answering her own question, she left the chamber and ran.

The nearest way out from the cavern network was open and deserted, and Cisca clambered into the open air, feeling the autumn rains upon her face. Amid the downpour, she heard the sound of raised voices, and she crouched into the undergrowth. Twenty yards away, a small group was huddled together, weeping and lamenting under the branches of a tall cypress tree. Cisca listened to their angry curses, and she realised from their words that they had been in the canteen when the first people had begun to die from the effects of the poison. In the confusion, rebel fighters had ordered them to leave, and had forbidden them from taking any food or drink.

Cisca crept away, her clothes drenched from the rain. She found the path that led down the southern flank of the mountain, turned her back to the ruins, and fled.

The rain had ceased by the time Cisca had reached the town of Wayston by the shores of the Hansarta. She had bypassed Fidalaimos and the other small villages that clung to the slopes of Mount Medamuna, but to get to the ferry terminal she would have to walk through Wayston. She tried to act normally, but no one glanced in her direction. From her shabby and patched-up clothes, she would look like an ordinary Zamatan, but she knew that her accent would give her away if she was forced to speak to anyone. Overhead, the clouds were breaking up, and the afternoon sun was shining down on the wet streets. A few locals were working by the small docks, readying their fishing vessels, but Cisca had no money to pay them to carry her across the Hansarta. The harbour where the ferry docked was another four miles away, but it was free, so she joined the main road that led south towards the ruins of Neeton. The ferry terminal was located halfway between the two towns, and if she hurried, she would reach it before sunset; but then what? She wanted to see Lyla, but had no idea where in Kaugatz Leona lived, and besides, she had no desire to meet the woman who had sent poison to destroy Bauchlie's rebels. It would have to be Igatz. Her heart sank as she trudged along the road. Did she wish to walk into another prison so soon after escaping the last? But what choice did she have? Perhaps her fellow Aucterians would take pity on her.

It was evening when Cisca walked off the ferry that had taken her over the Cyasarta. She had managed not to speak to anyone during her entire journey from Wayston to Igatz, and her feet were sore from all the walking. Getting through Kaugatz had been the worst part, but her spirits rose a little as she made her way along the wide boulevards of Igatz. Every Aucterian on the island was now clustered within the limits of the innermost town of the island. They might hate her if they discovered what she had been doing for the previous few months, but at least she could open her mouth without the fear of being lynched.

A few people glanced at her as she walked along the main road past Handshore Naval Base. They probably assumed that she was Zamatan, as the same peasant clothing that had shielded her in Wayston and Kaugatz now made people turn and stare.

Two Aucterian soldiers noticed her and approached.

'Excuse me,' said one. 'What business do you have in Igatz?'

'I am walking to the Temple of the Undying Serpent,' she said, 'to pay my respects.'

The soldiers' eyes widened at her Naeth accent.

'Sorry, ma'am,' said one, as they got out of her way.

She was stopped another three times before she reached the Palace District. She stared through the iron fence into the wide gardens surrounding the Dragon Palace, her gaze taking in the palm trees and the grass, and the lamps that shone from the white marble façade of the building. The last time she had been there, she had been the highest-ranking Dragon Corps officer on the entire island, and the soldiers from the army and Bullan units had saluted her whenever she had passed.

'Can we help you, miss?' said a voice.

She turned, and saw two Bullan soldiers standing close by.

'Are you lost?' said the other Bullan.

'No, I am not lost,' she said.

The two Bullan glanced at each other.

'My name is Cisca, formerly a captain in the Dragon Corps, and I wish to surrender myself.'

Cisca spent the next few hours in a holding cell under the ground floor of the Dragon Palace, as a succession of junior officers interviewed her. Each seemed to ask the same questions, and she answered them fully, only avoiding topics concerned with the events in Zamata Gataza that had claimed the life of Lady Macsin and Lord Malum. None of her questioners seemed interested in that, however, their queries focussed solely on Bauchlie and his rebel operations. She told them that she had been held against her will, and she also detailed what she knew about the poisoned ale that had been brought into the caverns. The officers had seemed surprised by that; either that, or they were convincing liars.

When her cell door was unlocked again, Cisca prepared herself for another round of questions. A captain strode in clutching a sheaf of papers, and Cisca's eyes narrowed. She recognised the man from the meeting in Fidalaimos; he had been sitting close to Leona, but had not spoken the entire time.

'Cisca,' he said, a faint smile on his lips; 'my name is Captain Jair. Lord Rylan has requested that I take ownership of your case. Your future is now in my hands.'

He gestured to the guards standing out in the passageway, and they closed the cell door. The captain sat in a chair opposite Cisca and scanned a few of the papers.

'These are the transcripts of your interviews,' he murmured. 'Some of your answers are clearly false; let's start with those.'

Cisca said nothing.

'This part here,' he said, pointing at a sheet of paper; 'where you say that you were held prisoner in Medamuna Gatzoun – that's a lie. I saw you in Fidalaimos, Cisca. Were your hands bound? Did Bauchlie force you to attend a meeting, and then force you to walk back to the ruins with him? I think not.'

'My imprisonment started after we returned to the caverns,' Cisca said.

'And before that you were a willing accomplice to the most notorious criminal on the island?'

'A criminal you negotiated with.'

'Did you hear me negotiate? Did I utter a single word to Bauchlie in your presence? I was there as an observer, to ensure that Lord Rylan had a truthful account presented to him. Why were you there?'

'I was trying to persuade Bauchlie to accept a deal.'

'A convenient response. Unlikely, but convenient. Why don't you tell me the real reason you left the ruins? Did Bauchlie send you here to spy on us?'

'I have already answered that question. I was being held prisoner, but a shipment of poisoned ale arrived, and it killed the two rebels who were guarding me. I ran away.'

'I see. I've read what you have reported about the alleged poisoning, and we are looking into it.'

'I suggest that you ask Leona, as it was she who delivered the ale.'

Jair laughed. 'Do you think Leona sent the poison? That would be amusing if it were true; however, despite our best efforts, Leona has refused to contemplate assassinating Bauchlie on our behalf. No, if it happened, then I would think that the Gunstians might be involved. There was no ale included in the delivery sent by Leona yesterday, and we have evidence that Gunstian agents have been trying to sabotage the food and drink on this island. Tell me – is there any reason why the Gunstians would wish to target Bauchlie?'

'The Gunstians sent a dozen soldiers and an agent to talk to Bauchlie,' she said. 'They offered him power over the island if he helped them.'

'And how did Bauchlie respond?'

'He had them impaled along the beach.'

'So, we have motive and means. How many of Bauchlie's people died from poison in the ruins?'

'I don't know. I saw... maybe a score of bodies, and there were screams coming from the canteen. I didn't linger long enough to find out. All I wanted to do was escape.'

'Why? I mean, why now? You have been assisting Bauchlie for over two months.'

'When we returned from the meeting in Fidalaimos, I was placed into a cell and told I was forbidden to leave.'

'I see. Why did Bauchlie do this?'

'He said it was to protect me. He said that there were people in the caverns who wished to kill me.'

'Is that true?'

'I don't know. I was never very popular with the other rebels.'

The captain looked through more of the papers. 'There is no mention here of you seeing Bauchlie during your alleged escape. I assume therefore that you do not know if he drank any of the poisoned ale?'

'That's right. He could be dead for all I know.'

'Would that upset you?'

'Yes.'

'Why?'

'Because I thought I could see something good in him. Maybe I was wrong, but nevertheless, I don't want him to die.'

'Tell me, Cisca – what do you want?'

'I… I want to come home.'

'Home? You mean Naeth?'

'I doubt I will be seeing Naeth again. I meant I want to be among Aucterians.'

'Do you consider yourself to be a traitor?'

'Against whom – the Dominion? Hasn't Lord Rylan publically renounced the Dominion? If I committed any crimes, it was against them, not Lord Rylan.'

'The Governor remembers you,' Jair said. 'You neglected to mention much about Zamata Gataza in your interviews, but Lord Rylan recalls that you were working there as a double agent. You were being blackmailed by Leona; correct?'

'Yes, but she wasn't known by that name in Zamata Gataza.'

'What name was she using?'

'Lady Takri.'

Jair nodded. 'You are one of the very few people on this island who know that Leona and Takri were the same person. How does that make you feel?'

'Worried. I believe Leona would kill me if she could.'

'You don't seem to like Leona very much.'

'I hate her,' said Cisca. 'After what she put me through in Zamata Gataza, I… I loathe her.'

'Leona is hiding something from us,' he went on. 'She is resistant to the dragons' truth spell – were you aware of that?'

'Yes. I saw Lady Macsin try to use the spell on her; it didn't work.'

'This means that Lord Rylan cannot rely upon his powers to get the truth from her. Listen to me carefully, Cisca – if you wish to be rehabilitated among the Aucterians, then I am going to need something from you. I have the power to send you to the gallows, but I also have the authority to have you pardoned, and to wipe your record clean. Imagine that – you could be reinstated as a captain in the Dragon Corps, as if the last few months never happened. However, if you refuse to answer my next question, I will have you brought in chains upstairs to Lord Rylan, and he will force you to reveal everything before your appointment with the gallows. It is up to you.'

Cisca narrowed her eyes.

Jair leaned forward. 'What is Leona hiding? It has something to do with the Demon Witch. Think, Cisca. Your entire future depends upon what you say in the next few seconds.'

A wave of guilt and anxiety surged over her. Could she betray Lyla to save herself? But did the Lyla she knew even exist any more? She imagined the pain of being placed under the truth spell by Lord Rylan, followed by a shameful death from the noose, and made her choice.

'Leona is harbouring someone.'

'Who?' said the army captain.

'A woman called Major Lyla of Teros City.'

'Our records show that she was killed in Zamata Gataza – are they wrong?'

'No; they are correct. Lord Rylan was there; doesn't he remember?'

'If he did, then do you imagine I would be down here asking you these questions?'

Cisca glanced at the floor of the cell. 'What I am about to say may sound crazy, but I am only repeating what Leona believes to be true.'

'Go on.'

'Leona thinks that the dragons placed the... soul of the Demon Witch into the body of Major Lyla.'

Jair raised an eyebrow. 'But Major Lyla was executed.'

'I know. Lord Malum revived her after he ordered her death. She is alive. I know this because I cared for her for a while. She couldn't speak or move, or even feed herself, but she was most certainly alive.'

'And then?'

'Then Leona stole her from me and took her away. As I said, she believes that the Demon Witch is inside Lyla's mind.'

'Do you know where Major Lyla's body is now?'

'No. I assume that Leona still has her. During the meeting, do you recall that I spoke with Leona and Lahnos alone for a few minutes?'

Jair nodded.

'Leona told me that Lyla was making progress; that she was walking and talking. Therefore, Leona must be keeping her somewhere close.'

'That implies that General Lahnos Laimos is also aware of the possibility that the Demon Witch is dwelling inside Major Lyla's body.'

Cisca nodded, then she frowned. 'What are you going to do with this information?'

'First of all, I'm going to say thank you, Cisca – you have been very useful. I have no doubt that Lord Rylan will be most grateful for this information.'

'I meant what are you going to do with Lyla?'

'That is none of your concern.'

'You're going to kill her, aren't you? Even if you don't believe the Demon Witch is in her mind, you need to be sure.'

'The Demon Witch is a mighty adversary. It would be negligent of us if we failed to intervene if she has been weakened.'

Cisca put her head in her hands. 'Please don't kill her. Lyla was my friend.'

'I am going to recommend your release, Cisca,' Jair said, 'but not yet. I have a feeling that you might try to do something foolish if I were to let you go now.'

'Such as? I have no idea where Leona lives.'

'All the same, I need to be prudent. Here is my offer. We shall move you to a nice clean apartment upstairs with a decent view of the Cyasarta, where you shall be kept under house arrest until this Lyla business has been taken care of. And then, I will bring you before Lord Rylan, and you will have a chance to beg for his lordship's forgiveness. That will be a formality but, for the sake of good form, it will have to be done. After that, you will be reinstated at your former rank of captain within the Dragon Corps and assigned to one of the dragons within the palace. Your record will be cleansed, and I could probably even issue a few months' back pay. Before you accept this generous offer, I have one or two conditions.'

'Yes?'

'Firstly, you are not to tell anyone that Leona and Takri were the same person. No matter your personal thoughts regarding Leona, she has become essential to the defence of this island, and Lord Rylan does not wish her life to be endangered.'

'Leona will never allow you to harm Lyla.'

'Let me worry about that. Secondly, if anyone asks, you will tell them that Bauchlie held you against your will for the entire duration of your stay in Medamuna Gatzoun. There's no point in admitting the truth; it will only get you into trouble. Thirdly, before being reinstated, you will have to swear a new oath – not to the Dominion, but to Lord Rylan as the sole sovereign authority over Zamata. You will take your orders from me, but Lord Rylan shall require your complete loyalty.'

Cisca hung her head. 'Anything else?'

'Yes. My final condition is this – you will be assigned to serve Lord Givra Mon Girvine. Then, when the time comes, I will call upon you, and you and I will help Lord Rylan kill him, and then cover up the evidence.'

Cisca stared at the army captain.

'I own you now, Cisca,' he said. 'Your crimes are such that I could snap my fingers and have you executed any time I please. Your life is conditional upon obeying my orders and keeping my secrets. I can see the anger you feel for me in your eyes, but I will do whatever it takes to ensure Lord Rylan is able to unite this island, and defend it against all enemies, both external and internal. Do you understand, Cisca?'

'I understand.'

Jair got to his feet. 'I shall arrange your new accommodation once I have relayed your news about the Demon Witch to Lord Rylan. You chose well, Cisca, and I can see a bright future for you on this island. If you continue to help me, you will be greatly rewarded.'

He knocked on the cell door, and it opened. He took one last look at

Cisca, then he left the small chamber and the door was closed and locked.

Cisca buried her face in her hands. Not only had she sold out Lyla, she had sold herself to Jair, a man who seemed capable of anything. She examined her choices. If she assisted Jair, and did as he bid, then she had no doubt that she would rise in his service; but she would become a traitor not only to Bauchlie, but to the entire Dominion. She would never be able to go back to Aucteran. Igatz and Zamata would be her home, forever.

CHAPTER 18
FORCED OUT

Kaugatz, Serpent Isle – 3rd Kolinch 1588

Leona's townhouse in Kaugatz had a small basement, which the colonel had used to store vital supplies. Friel's idea of *vital*, however, had differed from Leona's, and much of the space was taken up by dusty old crates of fine brandy, confiscated jewellery and works of art. There were also several boxes of smart uniforms and fashionable clothes, all in the colonel's size. Leona had seldom ventured down the narrow stairs to explore the space, but with a bound and gagged agent lying on the floor of her dining room, she decided it was time to find a new use for the most neglected part of her home.

She, Saewa and Kamasta took less than an hour to move the clothes, brandy and paintings up into the main area of the house. The jewellery was set aside, the small pouches of diamonds, emeralds and rubies placed into a locked box within Leona's bedchamber. It was portable wealth, and Leona could imagine all kinds of possible uses for it, as the food stocks dwindled by the day, and even basic supplies like fish and olive oil were becoming harder to find. Arrosa and Lyla were told to remain in the study while the prisoner was carried downstairs into Leona's new makeshift dungeon and, for once, they did as they were told. Leona had no chains or shackles, but Saewa tied the man's wrists and legs to the sides of a wooden chair, as Kamasta brought down and lit a few oil lamps.

'Thank you,' Leona said, as her two helpers paused to survey the results of their labour. 'This will do perfectly for now.'

'Do you need me here for the... interrogation, miss?' said Saewa, his eyes going to the hooded figure on the chair.

'No, but I would like you to wait upstairs,' Leona said. 'Once I've finished with him then, one way or another, he will need to be carried out of the basement. Kamasta will make you some coffee – I think we still have a little left over.'

'Right you are, ma'am,' said the housekeeper.

'Please keep the girls from disturbing me while I remain down here,' Leona said.

'Of course, ma'am. Will there be any screaming?'

Leona glanced over the chamber. 'These walls seem quite thick. I'll try to keep it quiet.'

Saewa and Kamasta bowed their heads, then they retreated up the creaky old wooden staircase. Saewa closed the door at the top of the steps, and the basement fell into dim shadows. Leona walked towards the chair, then checked that her knife was securely fastened to the belt round her waist.

She reached forward and pulled the hood from the man's head, and his eyes stared at her with a mixture of fear and defiance.

'I am going to remove your gag,' she said. 'If you scream or shout, then your opportunity to walk out of here will have been squandered. I don't wish to kill you, but I shall, if only to shut you up. This is a respectable neighbourhood, after all. But, if you answer my questions, then I will let you go. Nod if you understand.'

The man's head remained motionless for a while, then it inclined slightly.

Leona walked round to the rear of the prisoner and untied the gag. The man spluttered and gasped for air, and Leona took a step away from the chair.

'I know you're going to kill me,' the man said. 'Just get it over with.'

'Why would you think that?' she said, as she faced him again. 'Is it because you believe that it was I who sent the poisoned ale to Medamuna Gatzoun? That's the story you and the rest of Bauchlie's people have been spreading in Kaugatz. Normally, I don't pay much heed to rumours, but this one is starting to damage my standing in this town.'

'You murdered three hundred people, you wicked piece of shit,' the man cried. 'Women and children; civilians.'

'No, I did not,' she said. 'There was no ale in the shipment sent by me to the ruined monastery, and the cargo receipts at the ferry terminal documented that fact. I have conducted my own investigation, and it seems that by the time the shipment reached Wayston, the jugs of poisoned ale had been added to the back of a wagon. Furthermore, the four men who delivered the supplies to Wayston have gone missing. At least one of them, I suspect, was working for either Lord Rylan or the Gunstians – I can't decide which, because both parties want Bauchlie dead. I, on the other hand, would prefer to keep him alive.'

'Why are you telling me this?'

'Because I want you to pass on my words to Bauchlie. I know he survived the attack. Whoever planned it clearly didn't realise that Bauchlie never drinks alcohol when he is on duty. Have you seen him recently?'

'How do I know that you're telling the truth?'

'I have had several opportunities to kill Bauchlie, had I wished to do so. We have had our differences, but I see him as an ally in the fight against the Gunstians. If and when our mutual enemy decides to land soldiers onto this island, I was relying on Bauchlie's forces to aid our defences. Why would I wish to remove such a tactical asset? You have been watching this house, haven't you? Did you see me on the day of the poisoning? Was I in hiding? No, I was coming and going as normal. Would I have been so careless if I had just sent poison to Bauchlie?'

'I know how devious you are,' said the man. 'You could brazen it out.'

'Perhaps. Nevertheless, I want you to think of this not as an interrogation, but more as a chance for me to set the record straight. Tell Bauchlie that I did not send the poison. Tell him that I feel nothing but sympathy for his losses. And tell him this – if he continues to send agents to undermine my authority in Kaugatz, then I will not hesitate to protect my interests. I have refrained from having his agents eliminated, but if they become a serious nuisance then that state of affairs shall end.'

The agent said nothing.

'Did his mother also survive?' Leona said.

'Yes.'

'And Cisca?'

The agent glanced away.

'Is the Aucterian woman dead?' said Leona.

'I'm not sure. I haven't spoken to the commander since the attack, not in person, as I've been in Kaugatz the whole time. I get my news from a courier who comes down from the mountain every few days, as I'm sure you know. But, I heard a rumour that an Aucterian fled from the ruins of Medamuna Gatzoun, but that's all it is – a rumour.'

Leona narrowed her eyes. Why would Cisca have fled from Bauchlie? Wasn't she besotted with him?

'If Bauchlie wishes to meet me on neutral ground,' she said, 'then I would be open to the idea, as long as he came with no hostile intentions.'

The agent snorted. 'The way I hear it, he's furious with you. He believes you conspired with Rylan to have him and his fighters killed. The rest of the food you delivered was thrown off the cliffs; he said he would rather starve than take any of your so-called charity.'

'But he hasn't ordered my assassination?'

'You're too well protected,' the agent said. 'I knew your agents were watching me watching you; they see everyone who tries to get close to this house; but I saw that Aucterian captain arrive here a couple of weeks ago, the one who works for Rylan – you can't deny it.'

'I wasn't going to deny it. He was here. We were discussing the deal I brokered with Bauchlie.'

'And you conspired to poison the commander at the same time? You can see how it looks.'

'This is exactly what the Gunstians want,' she said. 'The more I think on it, the more I am tending to reject the theory that it was Rylan who sent the poison. He would have guessed that Bauchlie would blame me, and might even try to have me killed in retaliation. Rylan hates me, but I am too useful to him at the moment for him to want to have me killed. Without me, Kaugatz would fall into chaos, and that's the last thing the Governor wants to see. All right. I'm going to let you go now.'

The man stared at her. 'Is that it? You bundled me into a wagon and dragged me down here for that?'

'Yes.' She walked round to the back of the chair and pulled the hood over the man's head. He struggled, moving his head back and forth, but she managed to tie the cords around his neck. She turned to the stairs. 'Some assistance, please.'

Saewa opened the door and hurried down the steps. 'He's still alive, then, miss?'

'He is. Have him taken from the house, and then dump him close to the Hansarta ferry terminal.'

'Unharmed?'

'Yes. We remain at peace with Bauchlie's agents for the moment, despite their provocations.'

'I'll need some help, miss,' Saewa said. 'I'll be back in a minute or two.'

He ascended the staircase, and Leona followed him up to the ground floor. Kamasta was in the hallway, standing outside the door that led to the study. Leona watched Saewa leave by the front door, then she walked up to the housekeeper.

'I have finished downstairs,' she said. 'You can relax; he is still alive. There is no corpse in the basement. Is there any of that coffee left?'

'Yes, ma'am.'

'Fetch me a cup, would you?'

Kamasta strode away towards the kitchens, and Leona waited in the hallway. Saewa returned before Kamasta did, bringing two other men with him. They each bowed to Leona, then they descended the stairs to the basement. A minute later, they appeared again, and they escorted Bauchlie's agent from the townhouse. Kamasta came back as they were closing the front door, and handed Leona a mug. Leona took it, and entered the study. Lyla was sitting at the colonel's old desk, while Arrosa was peering through the shutters of the window.

'What were you doing to that hooded man?' the girl said.

'I was asking him a few questions,' Leona said. 'He wouldn't have come here if I had invited him, so a little persuasion was required.'

Arrosa narrowed her eyes. 'What job do you have? I see you working, and strange people are always showing up here.'

'I organise things,' she said.

'Why do we have food, when there is nothing in the markets?'

'How do you know there's nothing in the markets?'

'I hear what Kamasta says. She was complaining yesterday about there being no bread left on the entire island; but we had some for breakfast.'

'I think that might have been the last of it. There will be plenty of meat soon.'

'Why?'

'Because orders have been sent out from the Dragon Palace. The last of the cattle and horses are to be slaughtered.'

Lyla turned from the desk. 'The horses are being killed?'

'Unfortunately,' said Leona. 'We don't have enough grain to feed them any more; and the food they would have eaten can go to poor families. And, their meat shall be distributed all over Zamata.'

Lyla looked upset. 'Are all the animals going to die?'

'The cats and dogs are safe for now,' Leona said, 'but their days are probably numbered. There are still goats up in the hills to the west, and above Chesson. They will be more difficult to catch.'

'I don't want to eat goat,' said Arrosa.

'And I don't want to eat horse,' said Lyla.

Leona took a seat. 'It is my duty to make sure that neither of you starves. When the meat runs out, there will be little left but expensive fish and a few oranges. And olives – we still have a few of those. Lyla, did you have any more dreams last night?'

The woman nodded. 'Can I tell you in Gunstian?'

'Keep speaking the Divine Tongue for now – you are getting better at it.'

Lyla frowned, and her brows furrowed in concentration. 'I dream in...' She hesitated, and opened her dictionary, flicking through the pages, her finger tracing the columns of printed words. 'I dream in pairs,' she said. 'The horses. The schools. Pairs. One dream of Lyla of Teros City; one... not.'

Arrosa turned and sat down on the mattress, listening.

'And did you have another pair of dreams last night?' said Leona.

'Yes,' said Lyla. She looked through the dictionary again, then glanced up, her eyes mournful. 'Brothers. I think I dreamed of brothers.'

'Did Lyla and the Demon Witch have brothers?' said Arrosa.

'Don't call me that,' said Lyla.

Arrosa shrugged. 'Then what's her real name?'

'I don't know. Call her the... other one. In one dream I was in Teros City, walking with a boy...'

Arrosa laughed. 'Are you sure he wasn't your boyfriend?'

'I am sure,' said Lyla. 'I knew it; my... memory told me he was my brother. We were walking to the school, and he was upset about something. Our parents...' She flicked through the pages, then stopped and scanned the lines. 'Our parents were... divorced. My brother was sad.'

Lyla stopped talking, her gaze lowered.

'All right,' said Leona. 'And the other dream?'

Lyla shuddered and closed her eyes. 'I hurt him.'

'Who? Your... other brother?'

'He was only a baby...' Lyla said. She started to cry. 'My mother screamed.'

'Did you see your mother?'

'No. I heard her scream, and I saw the baby. I hurt him.'

Leona and Arrosa shared a glance as Lyla wept.

'Did you kill him?' whispered Arrosa.

Lyla shook her head. 'No.'

'Do you remember how old you were at the time?' said Leona.

'I was young, but I knew it was wrong.'

Leona said nothing, her eyes on Lyla. She heard a low cough and turned to see Kamasta standing by the door.

'May I speak to you in private, ma'am?'

Leona got to her feet, left the room and closed the door. 'Yes.'

'That Aucterian captain is outside, ma'am; the one you told me not to let in. Two of your agents have apprehended him.'

'Where?'

'They are in the back yard, ma'am.'

Leona took a breath, then strode through to the rear of the house as Kamasta followed her. They reached the back door, and Leona opened it. Outside, two cloaked Zamatans were aiming crossbows at Captain Jair. The officer was dressed in civilian clothing, and his hands were raised.

'Is he armed?' Leona said.

'No, ma'am,' said one of the agents.

Leona frowned at the officer. 'Well? What do you want?'

'May we speak alone?' Jair said.

'Are you here to harm or kill me?'

'No.'

There was no tingle.

'Are you here to apologise?'

He half-smiled. 'No.'

'Then you can leave. I have no desire to be insulted by you again.'

'I am under orders from Lord Rylan to speak to you,' he said. 'It is urgent, but private. I did not want to come here, but if you send me back to the Governor without letting me in, he will not be pleased.'

Leona tapped her foot on the back step. 'Five minutes.' She glanced at the two agents. 'Remain here. If you hear me scream, come inside and kill him.'

She turned and walked back into the house, then heard footsteps behind her. She led Jair to the dining room, then closed the door.

'Aren't you going to offer me a seat and a glass of wine this time?' he said.

'No. Get on with whatever you have to say.'

'Very well. Where is Major Lyla? Is she in this house?'

Leona blinked.

Jair lunged at her, his reactions faster than her response. He placed a hand over her mouth and an arm round her throat, and squeezed.

'Where?' he whispered in her ear. 'I don't wish to hurt you, Leona. Tell me where she is.'

She struggled in his grip, but he was too strong for her. She kicked backwards, and her heel scraped down his shin. He stifled a cry, then dragged her to the door. He opened it an inch and peered out. Faint voices were coming from the back door, from where Kamasta was talking to the two agents in the yard. Jair scanned the other doorways, then headed straight for the old study. He pushed the door open with a shoulder and shoved Leona into the room. He closed the door with his foot, as Arrosa leapt up from the bed.

'Stay quiet,' Jair told Lyla and the girl, 'or Leona gets hurt.'

He released Leona's throat and whipped the knife from her belt, his other hand still placed firmly over her mouth. His gaze went to the young woman staring at him from the desk.

'Major Lyla?' he said.

Lyla froze, her mouth opening.

Arrosa jumped forward, her fists clenched. She punched Jair in his stomach, and he raised the knife to Leona's throat.

'Don't touch me, girl. I don't want to hurt Leona, but I will if you come anywhere near me; it's Lyla I'm here for.'

'Me?' said Lyla.

'I need to know who I am speaking to,' he said. 'Are you Lyla, or are you someone else?'

Lyla said nothing.

Jair threw Leona to the side, and she landed on the floor next to the mattress as he darted forward. He held the tip of the knife against Lyla's neck.

'Nobody breathe a word,' he hissed. 'If you do, I will slit her throat.'

'My men will kill you,' Leona gasped.

'I accepted that risk when Lord Rylan ordered me to come here. He told me that I had to make sure that the Demon Witch would not be returning.' He swallowed as he gazed into Lyla's terrified face. 'I'm sorry about this. I don't want to do it, but if there's even the slightest chance that the Demon Witch is in there, then I must.'

Leona felt no tingle as she stared at the knife in Jair's right hand.

'Don't kill her,' she whispered. 'Please.'

Lyla gazed into Jair's dark eyes. 'I am not the Demon Witch,' she said. 'You have made a mistake.'

Jair's eyes narrowed. Leona tried to speak, but her mind seemed clouded, as though she was dizzy or drunk. She glanced at Arrosa, but the girl was swaying on her feet, and she looked stupefied.

'I am not the Demon Witch,' Lyla repeated. 'The dragon ritual failed. I am Major Lyla of Teros City. Go back to Lord Rylan and tell him that you are certain of this. You have done your duty. There is nothing else for you here.'

Jair took a step back, the knife falling from his fingers. He staggered, then collided with the wall of the study, almost falling.

'Say it,' said Lyla.

He stared at her. 'You are not the Demon Witch. You are Major Lyla.'

'Go back to your dragon,' she said, her gaze never leaving him.

His hand went to the door, and he rushed out of the room, his boots clattering off the wooden floor. Leona pulled herself up, her nerves fraying and her mind groggy.

'What happened?' she said.

Lyla turned to her, then she fell off the chair and onto the floor, her eyes closing. Arrosa seemed to snap back to life, as though coming out of a trance. She stared at the body of Lyla, and crouched down by her.

Leona did the same, her hand grasping the knife and hiding it beneath her robes.

'Is she all right?' said Arrosa. 'What did she do to that man?'

'I don't know,' said Leona. She placed a hand on her neck and lowered her face. 'She's breathing, and I can feel a pulse.'

The door opened again. 'Is everything all right in here? Ma'am?'

'Has the captain left, Kamasta?' Leona said.

'He came out of the back door looking dazed, ma'am. The agent lads are holding him in the yard. What should they do with him?'

'Let him go,' said Leona. 'No; have him safely escorted to the nearest ferry terminal and make sure he crosses the Cyasarta.'

'Yes, ma'am.'

Kamasta ran from the room as Lyla opened her eyes and groaned.

'The bed,' she gasped. 'I need to sleep.'

Leona and Arrosa dragged Lyla onto the mattress, and the girl covered her with a blanket. Lyla closed her eyes again and seemed to drift into a deep sleep within moments.

'She *is* a witch,' Arrosa whispered. 'I could feel her power in the room.'

'I also felt it,' said Leona. 'And when she told Jair that she wasn't the Demon Witch, I even believed it for a moment.'

'Me, too. She told lies, but they didn't hurt my head.'

'Lahnos told me that the Demon Witch had the ability to... influence the minds of others. I think some of her powers might be returning, along with her memories. All the same, perhaps we should find Lyla somewhere else to stay. I'm not sure that Lord Rylan will be convinced, not if Jair turns up at the Dragon Palace staggering and groggy. He might suspect the same thing that we suspect.'

'I don't want her to leave,' said Arrosa.

'I know, but we must keep her safe. You saw how easily Jair was able to get to her.'

'That's because you invited him in.'

'I won't make the same mistake, but what if Rylan sends twenty men next time?' She stood. 'Let's leave Lyla to sleep, while I think about what to do.'

Leona called for more of her agents to patrol the local neighbourhood, but the rest of the afternoon passed in peace. Lyla continued to sleep, as though the ordeal had exhausted her, while Leona found it impossible to concentrate on her increasing workload. She moved her papers down to the study and sat at the desk, but her mind kept going back to the way she had felt while Lyla had spoken to the Aucterian captain. Every few moments, she would glance at the sleeping young woman, as Arrosa sat on the floor reading a book about dragons.

Kamasta came by to light some lamps for the evening, then the house reverted to a still quiet, and Leona gave up trying to read the same report for the tenth time. Her mind went to alternative places to stay. The colonel had owned several properties, and she knew of at least two that remained unoccupied. Neither was as spacious or as comfortable as the townhouse, and she would miss it if they had to relocate. She wondered if Jair's agents knew of the other addresses. Even if they didn't, it wouldn't take them too long to discover where she had gone.

A shout from the street outside the front of the house made her jump. She walked over to the shutters and peered between the slats. A solitary man was being restrained by two of her agents just yards from her front door.

'They have my little girl!' the man cried. 'She's not Zamatan – she's Gunstian, and I want her back!'

Arrosa jumped to her feet and stood next to Leona at the window. The girl gasped. 'Uncle Luka?'

'Do you recognise him?' said Leona.

'I thought he was dead,' said the girl, then she ran from the room.

Leona rushed out after her, and then she blocked the girl's way to the front door.

'Let me pass!' Arrosa cried. 'That's my uncle outside.'

'It could be a trick,' said Leona.

'I want to see him; he's my uncle!'

Kamasta joined them.

'Tell the agents to bring that man to the back yard; quickly,' Leona said. She gripped Arrosa's arm as the housekeeper opened the front door of the house. 'I will let him speak to you,' she said to the girl, 'but we must be careful.'

'Why?' said Arrosa.

'Because... because he's a Gunstian. If he knows you're here, then other Gunstians might know it, too. The Gunstians want to kill me.'

'My uncle won't hurt you. Let me go!'

'Come with me to the back yard,' Leona said. 'You can talk to him there.'

She pushed the girl away from the front door, then clutched her hand and pulled her through the house. She waited by a window close to the back door, her eyes on the gates. They swung open, and the two agents escorted the Gunstian into the yard, a crossbow aimed at his back.

'Where is she?' the man said. 'Where's my niece?'

Leona considered having the man executed where he stood, but Arrosa had already seen him and was trying to get to the back door. Leona opened it, and Arrosa ran out into the yard. A broad smile developed across the man's face, and he crouched down as Arrosa reached him.

'You are alive!' the man said in Gunstian. 'Little Arrosa! Have they treated you well?'

Arrosa hesitated for a moment, then hugged him. 'The lady has been nice to me, uncle,' she said.

'What lady?' said Luka.

Arrosa turned and pointed at Leona, who was standing by the doorway.

Luka glanced up, and his eyes widened. He grabbed hold of Arrosa, his thick arms pulling her back towards him.

'Stay where you are,' said Leona.

'She's here!' Luka yelled, his voice booming out. 'It's Leona; she's here!'

There was a low thrum, and several crossbow bolts spat through the air, loosed from the upper storey of the house facing the back lane. One struck an agent in the left leg, and he fell, while others were aimed at Leona. One hit the doorframe as she threw herself to the ground.

'What have you done, uncle?' Arrosa cried, as Luka dragged the girl towards the gate.

'They're not after us,' he said.

'Let me go!' Arrosa screamed.

The uninjured agent in the yard turned to loose at Luka, but was struck in the left eye by a bolt. More bolts ricocheted off the cobbles, and then Kamasta emerged from the back door. She ran in front of Leona, shielding her from the upper windows of the house on the other side of the lane. Kamasta leaned over to pick Leona up, but groaned as a bolt struck her back.

'No!' cried Arrosa. 'Let me go!'

Another bolt hit Kamasta, and she fell forwards onto Leona, her weight pinning her to the cobbles.

'Stop struggling, girl,' Luka shouted. 'You belong with the Gunstians.'

The girl reached up with a hand and tried to push Luka away. Her palm touched the side of his face, and his features contorted for a second; then he emitted a scream that tore above the sounds of footsteps and cries; a scream that echoed off the buildings.

The scream cut short. Leona moved Kamasta's arm, and stared. Luka was still crouching in exactly the same spot, his arm round Arrosa, and his mouth open, but his skin had changed, as though his body had transformed from flesh and bone into a hard, translucent green substance like coloured glass. Arrosa's eyes were wide with panic. She struggled in her uncle's cold grip, then wriggled free and crawled backwards across the cobbles away from him. The gates burst open, and Farakai entered, along with several agents, and then Leona noticed that the hail of crossbow bolts had ceased.

'Are you all right, ma'am?' Farakai yelled, as he ran to Leona. He pulled the body of Kamasta away, and knelt by Leona. Arrosa arrived at the same moment, and threw her arms round Leona's neck. The girl was sobbing and shaking as though in a blind panic, her eyes clenched shut.

'Kamasta is dead,' Farakai muttered. 'Are you injured, ma'am?'

Leona sat up and embraced the weeping girl. 'No,' she said. 'I'm fine.'

'We killed four Gunstians in the building across the street, ma'am,' Farakai went on. 'They were waiting to get a clear shot at you. They know where you live.'

'Kamasta saved me,' she said, 'and then Arrosa...'

She and Farakai stared at the frozen, sculpture-like figure of Luka. Several agents were peering closely at it, and one reached out with a finger and touched the Gunstian's arm.

'He's cold,' the agent said; 'like glass.'

Farakai narrowed his eyes, then he turned to Arrosa. 'The Gift of Vitrification,' he whispered. 'How many damn Gifts has this girl got?'

'Help me take her inside,' Leona said.

She stood, then she and Farakai lifted the girl onto her feet. Arrosa kept her arms round Leona's waist, her head buried into her dress.

'What will we do with the... ah... body?' said one of the agents.

'Dump it in the Cyasarta,' said Farakai. 'Do it quietly.'

He and Leona eased Arrosa over the threshold and then into the kitchen, where they sat her down.

'It's over,' said Leona, crouching by her. 'You're safe.'

'I killed my uncle,' the girl sobbed. 'I used my bad Gift; the one mummy told me never to use.'

'It's all right,' Leona said. 'Everything's going to be all right.' She turned to Farakai. 'We need to find a new home,' she said. 'Somewhere Bauchlie's agents, Captain Jair, and the Gunstians can't reach us.'

'I don't think there is anywhere on the island that fits that description, ma'am.'

'There must be a safe house somewhere.'

'None that will remain hidden for long.'

Leona lowered her gaze, and then it came to her. 'Perhaps we should hide in plain sight.'

'Where?' said Farakai.

'Fetch a carriage,' said Leona. 'I'm taking Arrosa and Lyla to Tsallon Anura. Lahnos will protect us.'

CHAPTER 19
COMING AND GOING

Kaugatz, Serpent Isle – 4th Kolinch 1588

'Of course it was her,' said Reyn; 'it's obvious.'

'I don't believe it,' said Lahnos. 'I refuse to accept that Leona would try to poison hundreds of Zamatans.'

'There's a lot we don't know about her, Lahnos,' she said. 'She's more ruthless than you think. She would do anything to impress Lord Rylan, and that damn dragon also wants Bauchlie dead. You're too naïve to see it.'

He laughed, and gazed out at the view from their apartment's balcony. 'It's good to know you think I'm naïve. Thanks.'

'Only about certain things – other people's motivations, for example. Do you think that Leona is your friend? She's not. And Lord Rylan – do you think he sees you as anything more than a useful tool with which to control the Zamatans? They are both using you, Lahnos. I mean, you're a twenty year old general of an army – can you not hear how stupid that sounds?'

'I didn't ask to be made general.'

'No, but you didn't refuse it, either. Rylan knew that you would accept. You're a figurehead, that's all – a way for that damn dragon to exert authority over the Zamatans. They might not do what he says; but they'll follow you. Why can't you see it?'

'What if I can see it, Reyn? What if I am perfectly aware of Rylan's motives, and yet I still agree to obey him? What does that make me?'

She glared at him. 'Do you want me to say it?'

'Bauchlie already has; several times. I am a traitor and a dragon's pet, according to him; and sometimes I think you agree.'

'Then why are you doing it?'

'Because the alternative is even worse. Imagine I had sided with Bauchlie, and told the Zamatans to fight the dragons. By now, the Gunstians would be in charge of the island, and people like you and me would be burned at the stake. Look; I know that Rylan thinks he is manipulating me, and perhaps Leona is doing the same thing. Does it matter? Should I allow my pride to overrule my common sense, or should I play the role I have been given? Which choice is more likely to lead to our survival?'

'If we beat the Gunstians, then Rylan will reduce us all to slavery.'

'I don't believe that.'

'Why not? The evidence is right in front of us. Rylan is a Child of Gahad, and his father's dream was to subdue this entire world. The dragons don't see humans as their equals, and they never will. For them, it's all about power. Rylan knows that if he defeats the Gunstians, and has the Zamatans firmly under his control, then he can negotiate from a position of strength when the Dominion next sends a fleet to the island. He will be able to dictate terms, and return home a hero; no matter which side wins their civil war.'

Lahnos said nothing.

'Rylan's next move will be against Givra,' Reyn went on. 'Just wait and see. Lord Givra is the only dragon left who opposes him.'

'It was me who told you about that.'

'I know. Yet somehow you keep putting two and two together and getting five.'

Lahnos frowned. 'This is not how I wanted breakfast to go. I'm sick of us arguing all the time, Reyn.'

'So am I; but would you rather I stayed quiet like a good Zamatan girl, when I think you're making a terrible mistake?'

'Is it too much to expect a little support?'

'I am supporting you. I'm saying all this because I care.'

'All right; what do you think I should do? I mean now – don't bring up anything I have done in the past – what do you advise I do now?'

Reyn edged closer. 'Get close to Rylan, and kill him.'

Lahnos shook his head. 'Are you out of your mind? Firstly, how could I possibly kill him? He's a damn dragon, Reyn.'

'Bauchlie managed to kill Lord Malum, and he was bigger and stronger than Rylan. Use your new Gift on him, Lahnos. Drain his memories and take his life. Imagine the things you would learn.'

'And then what? Presumably, Lady Natali might be a little upset that I killed her brother.'

'Then kill her, too. Once the dragons have been eliminated, unite the island and defeat the Gunstians.'

'You're forgetting about Sigum.'

'No, Lahnos; I'm not.'

'So, according to you, I should kill him, too? Kill the dragon that brought us all home from Gunst? Sigum is my friend, Reyn.'

'Dragons don't have human friends. At best, they see us as useful, short-lived pets – the way some people see horses and dogs.'

Lahnos narrowed his eyes. 'I think you spent too much time with Bauchlie.'

'And you spent too long with Sigum.'

He got to his feet. 'I'm going to work.'

'And I guess I'll just sit here all day, because I'm not allowed to fight.'

He walked from the balcony without another word, and left the apartment through the front door, his mood dark. He thought back to the short weeks they had spent in Friel's old mansion on the slopes of Mount Medamuna – Reyn had been right. It had been like a holiday, and nothing had been the same between them since. They were growing apart before his eyes, neither happy with the other's advice or decisions; or their choice of friends. He passed the guards at the main doors and walked out into the interior of the monastery. The ground was still wet from the rain that had passed over the island during the night, and puddles had formed on the uneven and worn flagstones. Lahnos had an office next to the old refectory, where his twelve Bullan worked as his staff, and he walked through the cloisters towards it. When he was just a few yards away, he saw a carriage approach through the monastery's western gates, and he paused for a moment. Zamatan soldiers had surrounded the carriage and brought it to a halt, and a junior officer was talking to someone through the side window. The officer nodded, then he glanced around and saw Lahnos.

'Sir!' he cried. 'We have visitors to see you.'

Lahnos walked towards the carriage as the side door was opened, then he smiled.

'Leona? What are you doing here?'

Leona's eyes went to him, then she helped a young girl clamber down from the carriage, and Lahnos's smile faded. After Arrosa disembarked, Lyla followed, her eyes wide as she stared at the ancient monastery buildings. Leona ushered the others along, and they walked up to Lahnos.

'We need your help,' Leona said. 'The Gunstians have discovered where I live.'

'Have you eaten?'

'Yes, thank you. Can we go somewhere to talk?'

He eyed the girl. 'Am I liable to be screamed at again?'

Arrosa scowled at him, and made a strange hissing sound, like an angry cat.

'Behave yourself,' said Leona. 'I want no shouting, and certainly no hissing.'

'Hello, Lahnos,' said Lyla.

Lahnos smiled at the young woman, unsure what to say to her.

'Let's go somewhere quiet,' he said.

He led them through the grounds of Tsallon Anura, to a meeting room in the back of an ancient accommodation block. No one was in the room, and Lahnos opened the tall shutters to let in the morning light. They took seats by a small table, and Arrosa made sure that Leona was sitting between her and Lahnos. The girl hadn't stopped scowling since she had arrived, and her eyes never left him.

'The Gunstians know where you live?' Lahnos said.

'Yes,' said Leona. 'They attacked the house yesterday evening, and killed my housekeeper. We need somewhere to stay, but there is nowhere on this island that will remain hidden from their agents. So, we would like to ask if we can stay here, under your protection.'

'You want to stay in the monastery? I'm sorry to say this, but there are bound to be a few Gunstian agents embedded within the staff who work here; there might even be one or two serving in the Zamatan regiments. They are probably already aware that you are here.'

'We know that,' said Leona. 'I think that I should be out in the open, as hiding in the shadows no longer works. If we were here, then everyone would know, but we would probably be safer. All I would need is a place to work, and some rooms for Arrosa and Lyla.'

'And, presumably, some guards to watch over you?'

'Yes.'

'Tell the thrice-Gifted demon about Captain Jair,' muttered Arrosa. 'Why are you not mentioning him?'

Lahnos glanced at the girl.

'He tried to kill Lyla.'

'Who did? The captain? What happened?'

'Do you know Captain Jair?' said Leona.

'The name seems familiar,' said Lahnos. 'Was he the officer that came with us to Fidalaimos?'

'Yes. He also came round to the townhouse yesterday. Somehow, he has discovered that the Demon Witch might be residing inside Lyla's mind; and he was under Rylan's orders to dispose of her, in case the Demon Witch resurfaces.'

Lahnos frowned. 'Then it isn't just the Gunstians you need shielding from? How did Rylan find out?'

'I don't know. As far as I am aware, the only people who knew were us four sitting here, as well as Bauchlie, Reyn and Cisca.'

'Well, I haven't mentioned it,' he said; 'and I doubt Reyn or Bauchlie would ever speak to Lord Rylan. Did Cisca survive the poisoning?'

'Perhaps. One of Bauchlie's agents said he heard a rumour she had fled Medamuna Gatzoun.'

'Do you think she went straight to Lord Rylan?'

Leona shrugged.

Lyla narrowed her eyes. 'Did Cisca tell the dragon about me?'

'Without any evidence, I wouldn't like to say,' said Leona. 'Does this change things, Lahnos? Would you be prepared to protect us from Lord Rylan if he comes for Lyla?'

Lahnos gazed at the young woman sitting next to Leona. 'Yes.'

Leona puffed out her cheeks. 'Thank you, Lahnos.'

'Why would you do that, demon?' said Arrosa.

'Because I owe the Demon Witch my life,' he said.

'Please don't call me that,' said Lyla. 'Did I ever tell you my real name?'

'No. You were quite secretive about those sorts of questions. You did tell me that...' He glanced at Leona. 'Are you going to shout at me if I give her more details?'

Leona raised her palms. 'No. Tell her.'

'All right. I'll call you Lyla for now, even though that sounds strange. Well, Lyla, you told me that you had two children – twins.'

Lyla stared at him. 'Twins? What does that mean?'

Arrosa said *twins* in Gunstian, and Lyla's eyes widened.

'I don't remember them,' Lyla whispered. 'What else did I say about them, Lahnos?'

'Um, let me try to remember. I think you said that one was a boy and the other a girl. Your sister is looking after them... and you refused to discuss their father. That was all, I think. No – you also said that they were eight years old.'

Lyla put a hand on her face and started to cry, but they were no longer the sobs of a child's tantrum. Lyla seemed older, more of an adult, compared to when Lahnos had last seen her.

'I'm sorry,' he said.

'No. Thank you, Lahnos,' Lyla whispered. 'Even though I can't remember them, I feel better knowing the truth.'

'Then try to remember more about the volcano, when you killed Gahad and... and my father; because you also said that your children were there. That's why you had to slay Gahad – to save your children.'

Lahnos closed his mouth as Lyla's tears spilled down her cheeks.

'Maybe you will dream about them,' said Arrosa.

'Did, uh, did Major Lyla have any children?' said Lahnos.

'I don't know,' said Leona. 'If I had to guess, then I would say no; but that's purely based on what Cisca told me. Cisca said that Lyla never mentioned having any children, and she wasn't married. I think she served in the Dominion army for years before joining the Dragon Corps.'

'Did I mention the names of my children?' whispered Lyla.

'No,' said Lahnos.

'They are the same age as me,' said Arrosa. 'I'm eight.'

'I will protect you all,' said Lahnos, 'even eight-year-olds who think I'm a demon.' He got to his feet. 'Wait here.'

He walked out of the meeting room, and found a young soldier. 'Go to my office and tell all of the Bullan to come here.'

'Yes, sir,' said the soldier.

Lahnos went back into the room and closed the door. He glanced at Lyla, who was still quietly crying, and then at Arrosa, who was regarding him with deep suspicion.

'You're not going to like who I have assigned to guard you, Arrosa,' he said, 'but they are the best and most loyal soldiers I have. I want you to be polite to them – can you do that?'

The girl scowled.

'Answer him,' said Leona. 'He is putting himself in danger to help us.'

Arrosa shrugged then, unexpectedly, she also started to cry.

Lahnos narrowed his eyes, as Leona put an arm over the girl's shoulder.

'What's wrong with her now?' he said.

Leona shot him a look. 'Her uncle died last night; he was one of the Gunstians who attacked us.'

Lahnos knelt by Arrosa. 'I'm sorry. My uncle died, too.'

The door opened, and all twelve Bullan strode into the room.

'You asked us to come here, sir?' said Efizel, as the Bullan eyed the two women and the girl.

Lahnos stood. 'Leona, Lyla and Arrosa will be staying in Tsallon Anura from now on, and they will need close protection. The Gunstians are after them, and Lord Rylan might also try to harm them.'

'Lord Rylan, sir?'

'Yes. The Governor has made a simple mistake about the identity of Major Lyla, and one of his agents tried to kill her. I will clear this error up with the Dragon Palace; I intend to go there today and tell Lord Rylan that Major Lyla is not the woman he is looking for. In the meantime, though, there is a chance that the Governor's agents may attempt to strike again. I am relying on you to prevent that from happening. I want one Bullan per guest, day and night.'

Efizel saluted. 'Yes, sir.'

The Bullan sergeant turned to the others and they began to speak in their own language.

'Listen!' cried Arrosa. 'The language of the demons!'

The Bullan paused to look at her.

Lahnos shrugged. 'She says the same thing about me.'

Leona eyed Lahnos as the Bullan resumed their conversation. 'Come with me,' she said.

They walked to a quiet corner of the meeting room, and Leona lowered her voice.

'There's more,' she whispered. 'When Captain Jair tried to kill Lyla yesterday, she used... powers to stop him.'

'What kind of powers?' Lahnos said.

'Demon Witch powers. She looked him in the eye and told him that she wasn't the Demon Witch, and he seemed to believe her. She then told him to go back to Rylan, and he did.'

Lahnos nodded. 'I think I know what you mean. We needn't worry, then. If this Jair believes that he made a mistake, then Lyla will be safe.'

Leona shook her head. 'We should be careful all the same. I'm not sure if her little trick will work for long. Jair seemed dizzy and dazed; he could barely walk. It might wear off.'

'I'll hold off on the visit to the palace for now,' he said, 'and send a message instead, announcing to Lord Rylan that you have relocated to the monastery following a Gunstian attack. Then, we'll see where we stand.'

'Thank you again, Lahnos.'

'It's fine. You and I need to work together more, anyway. Reyn won't be pleased, though; she thinks you poisoned the rebels in Medamuna Gatzoun.'

'I didn't, Lahnos; that wasn't me.'

'I know. I believe you, but Reyn... she doesn't trust you.'

Leona narrowed her eyes a little, but said nothing. Lahnos noticed Efizel trying to catch his attention, and they walked back to the Bullan.

'We have worked out a schedule, sir,' the Bullan sergeant said. 'Might I suggest that we place all three of the new arrivals into the same building where you and I live? There is an empty apartment on the second floor, and the building is already under constant supervision. It would simplify matters.'

'That seems sensible,' said Lahnos. 'I'll take them there now; this morning's briefing can wait.'

Efizel voiced a few commands in his own language, and eight of the Bullan saluted and returned to their posts.

'We shall escort you there, sir. The protection starts immediately.' He glanced at Leona. 'These three Bullan soldiers shall take the first shift, ma'am. Where you go, they go; but I would ask that you inform me if you intend to leave the grounds of the monastery.'

'Thank you,' said Leona. 'Lyla, Arrosa; let's go. These soldiers will be looking after us.'

Lyla got to her feet, but Arrosa glared at the four Bullan. 'No. I don't want a demon to be watching me all of the time.'

'You will do as you're told,' said Leona; 'and they are not demons. They are Bullan.'

'They are bullies, not Bullan,' said Arrosa. 'My papa told me never to trust them.'

'The Bullan are like everyone else,' said Efizel. 'Some are good, some are bad. We are all good ones.'

'That's what a bad one would say.'

Leona looked angry, but softened her tone. 'We are very lucky to find somewhere safe to stay. No one will hurt Lyla here, and no one will come to try to take you away.'

The girl looked down at the floor. 'No.'

Lyla crouched down by Arrosa's chair. 'Will you do it for me?' she said in Gunstian. 'I can't go back to the townhouse. That man who wanted to kill me might return.'

'But you used your powers on him.'

'I tried to,' Lyla said. 'I dreamt about having strange powers, but I'm not sure if I still have them, or how to use them, and I think I might have done it wrong yesterday.' She took the girl's hand. 'If we stay here, then I can look after you, and you can look after me. And we don't want anyone to hurt Miss Leona now, do we? They tried to kill her, too. Poor Kamasta died to protect her.'

Arrosa stared at the young woman. 'Why did my uncle try to trick me? I thought he liked me.'

'Maybe they threatened him,' said Lyla. 'There are bad people on this island, but they can't get us here. There are hundreds of soldiers, and the Bullan, to stand in the way; and you and I can use our powers to help each other. Shall we give it a try?'

Arrosa glanced at Lahnos, her eyes tight. 'Is it a nice apartment?'

'Yes,' he said. 'It's small, but it has an indoor bathroom, and there's hot water every evening for a whole hour; and there's a balcony with a view of the Cyasarta.'

'A balcony?' said Arrosa, her eyes lighting up. She started to stand, then hesitated. 'But this is a monastery – are there monks here? I hate monks; they think Gunstians are all evil.'

'They think I'm evil, too,' said Lahnos; 'and they don't like the Bullan, either. The monks will stay out of our way. They're not allowed into the building where you will be living.'

'Do you promise?'

Lahnos nodded. 'I promise.'

Arrosa got to her feet. 'I will try it here, death-seer.'

Leona smiled. 'Thank you.'

Lahnos gestured to the door, and then led the others outside. Three of the Bullan shadowed the new arrivals, while Efizel strode next to Lahnos, as they negotiated the narrow twisting lanes through the monastery compound. They passed the chapel, where Bauchlie had slaughtered the previous batch of monks, and could hear the faint sound of chanted prayers and responses coming from within. Arrosa put fingers in her ears to block out the noise until they had reached the cloister, then they turned for the large accommodation block.

They came to a halt by the carriage that had brought Leona and the others to Tsallon Anura. It had been parked close to the entrance of the accommodation block, and soldiers were unloading the luggage onto the ground. The four ponies that had pulled the carriage had already been removed to be butchered for their meat, and the sight of the empty harnesses made Lahnos queasy and sad at the same time.

'Take everything to the apartment on the second floor,' Lahnos said to the soldiers.

They saluted, then got to work.

'This is going to make my job easier,' Leona said, as she gazed upwards at the tall building. 'I will have to provide you with a list of people who are permitted to come and go.'

'Write it all down for me,' said Lahnos.

Leona raised an eyebrow. 'That might not be wise. The Gunstians would dearly love to get their hands on a written list of my agents in Kaugatz. The names will have to remain in your memory.'

'All right. I recommend that you work out of your apartment for now. Are you expecting any of your agents to visit you today?'

'No. I told them to give me a day to settle in.'

They waited until all of the baggage had been taken into the building. When the soldiers returned, Lahnos led the others inside, the four Bullan following. Efizel gave him a set of keys, and he handed them to Leona as they reached the front door of their new apartment.

She slid the key into the lock and opened the door.

'Stay outside,' Lahnos said to the Bullan, and they saluted.

Leona ushered Lyla and Arrosa into the apartment, and Lahnos followed them in and closed the door. Piles of luggage had been neatly stacked up close to the entrance, and the soldiers had also brought a crate of fresh food.

'You have this living area,' Lahnos said, 'and there is a large bedroom, a dining area, a bathroom and the balcony.'

'It's not as big as the townhouse,' said Arrosa. 'I had my own bedroom there.'

'Did the townhouse have a balcony?' he said.

He drew a set of curtains, revealing a large balcony door. The sunlight spilled into the room as he opened the door, and Arrosa rushed out. The others followed her, and they stood on the balcony in silence for a few minutes, gazing out across the monastery towards the glistening waters of the Cyasarta. Half a mile away was the shore of Igatz, and its roofs and streets were visible, along with high domes and steeples.

Arrosa nudged Lyla and pointed at an enormous building of white marble. 'That's the Dragon Palace. It's where the scaly demons live.'

'Apart from Lord Sigum,' said Lahnos. 'He's over at the palace just now, but he sleeps in Tsallon Anura.'

Lyla nodded, then she turned to look down at the monastery compound. 'A dragon died here,' she said in Gunstian, as her eyes scanned the ancient buildings.

'Can you sense it?' said Arrosa.

Lyla smiled. 'No. I remember seeing a huge dragon skull mounted on a tall post. And I can remember Lahnos living here. It's an odd feeling, as though I was looking down on the monastery from above.' She glanced up at the sky. 'How did I get up there?'

'You didn't have a body,' said Lahnos. 'You were a ghost.'

Lyla stared at him, then she started to laugh. 'That was a joke, yes? There are no such things as ghosts, and I...' She paused, and her smile faded. 'I had no body?'

'I think that was the entire point of the dragon ritual,' Lahnos said; 'to give you a body so that they could kill you. Is that right, Leona?'

'Yes,' she said. 'That's right. You spoke in our minds, Lyla; you had no physical form.'

Lyla gripped the balcony railing with both hands. 'I must have had a body once,' she said. 'Another body, I mean. How else could I have had twins?'

'Do you remember I told you that the Demon Witch was dead?' said Lahnos. 'Therefore, you must have been alive at some point. In fact, from what you told me, I think you were alive when you killed King Gahad, and that was only, um...'

'It was a little over nine months ago,' said Leona.

'So I was only a... ghost for a short while?'

'You told me you hated that word,' Lahnos said. 'You told me that you were lonely, because there were no other ghosts around – you were the only one. You used to watch over your children, which is why you couldn't always be here to help us. I'm guessing that you must have been extremely powerful when you had a body. As powerful as a god.'

Arrosa snorted. 'There is only one god, and it's not Lyla.'

'My... other memories are starting to feel more real than Major Lyla's,' she said; 'as though the Demon Witch is my true self.' She shook her head. 'I wish I could remember my name, and I wish I could remember what my children look like. There are deserts in Aucteran, aren't there? On the other side of the great mountains from Teros City. Maybe the Demon Witch is from that part of Aucteran. I mean, maybe that's where I am from. If that is true, then my children might still be there.'

'I don't think that's the case,' said Leona.

'Why not?'

'Because no humans on Aucteran have powers. None of the original inhabitants survived, so there are no Gifted there, or anywhere else in the East.

'Lyla isn't Gifted,' said Arrosa. 'Her powers are different.'

'You told me that the great god Nathaniel was dead,' Leona went on; 'Theodora, too, though Arrosa refuses to believe that part. Do you remember that?'

Lyla shook her head, then frowned. 'Maybe. A lot of my memories are vague from those days. I can't remember anything from before I arrived in Kaugatz; but my memory is improving.' She glanced at Arrosa. 'I can remember everything since you arrived.'

'That's good,' said Leona, 'but it's not the point I was trying to get across. You are a human with powers that are reserved for immortal dragons, and you have knowledge about the fate of other powerful gods. What I am trying to say is this – I don't think you come from Athumia.'

'That seems impossible,' Lyla said. 'How did I get here?'

'Lord Sigum told me that King Gahad gathered dragons from another world,' said Lahnos. 'And the Aucterians also came from somewhere else. It's not impossible.'

'So,' said Arrosa, pointing upwards at the sky; 'Lyla is a demon from the stars?'

Lahnos laughed. 'Maybe. Right; I'll leave you to unpack. Reyn and I share the apartment upstairs from you. Come and ask if you need anything.'

'Thank you,' said Leona.

Lyla smiled. 'Yes, Lahnos; thank you.'

Arrosa narrowed her eyes at him.

Lahnos strode from the apartment. Efizel had left the three Bullan soldiers outside the door, and they were positioned by the entrance. They saluted Lahnos as he took the stairs up to his own quarters. He opened the front door, and saw Reyn in the living area, throwing clothes into a bag.

'What are you doing?' he said.

'What does it look like, Lahnos?'

'Are you leaving?'

'Yes. I heard you laughing downstairs with Leona. I looked over the balcony, and could hear you talking. You're letting her stay, aren't you? You're an idiot. She poisoned hundreds of people in Medamuna Gatzoun, but all she has to do is bat her eyelashes at you and you give her an apartment.'

'The Gunstians tried to assassinate her.'

'What a pity they didn't succeed.'

'Lord Rylan sent someone to kill Lyla; what was I supposed to do?'

Reyn hesitated for a moment. 'Lord Rylan? You are going against that lizard for Leona, but you wouldn't do it for me?'

'All I am doing is protecting them; you wanted me to kill Rylan.'

'I can't do it,' she said. 'I can't live above Leona. How am I supposed to walk past her on the stairs every day, or sit on the balcony and overhear her laughing? I'm already jealous of Sigum, and now I have to be jealous of Leona, too.'

'There's nothing to be jealous about. I would never go with Leona, and she isn't interested in me, either.'

'There are other ways to be unfaithful,' she said. 'You spend all of your time with Sigum when he is here, and now you will spend the rest of your time with Leona. You prefer being in their company; and you trust them.' Her eyes darkened. 'I hate them both.'

She crammed more clothes into the bag, and tied the cord at the opening.

'Where are you going?' he said.

'None of your business.'

'Is that it? Is it over? I don't want it to be over, Reyn. Stay, and we'll work on it. I love you.'

'It's not enough,' she said. 'I can't stand watching you change into someone else. There was a time when you and I did everything together; now I barely see you. And when we are together, all we do is argue.' She shouldered the bag and walked to the door. 'Come and find me, if you ever decide to leave all this behind. Otherwise, goodbye, Lahnos.'

She left the apartment and Lahnos remained where he was. Part of him wanted to run after her; but he had sworn oaths, and others were dependent upon him. How could he abandon them all? He sat on the long couch, hardly able to believe what had happened. He loved Reyn, but she was asking him to give up his friends and his responsibilities – Sigum, Efizel and the other Bullan, the Fidalaimos squad; even Leona, Lyla and Arrosa. He had to stay – why couldn't she understand that?

Someone knocked on the door.

'Yes?'

Efizel opened the door and glanced at Lahnos. 'I just saw Reyn walk out of the building with a bag, sir. Is everything all right?'

'She has left me,' he said.

'I see. Sorry, sir. Should I cancel your appointments? Do you wish to be left alone?'

Lahnos got to his feet. 'No,' he said. 'I have work to do.'

CHAPTER 20
PROSTRATED

Igatz, Serpent Isle – 6th Kolinch 1588

For seven days, Cisca had been confined to her new quarters in the Dragon Palace. Despite being unable to leave the three-roomed apartment, it was a world away from the house arrest she had experienced in the caverns under Medamuna Gatzoun. She had been supplied with clean uniforms and a selection of off-duty clothes from the quartermaster's stores, and her rooms were bright and airy. Best of all, she had her own private balcony. It was small, but it had a beautiful view facing the west, from where she could watch the sun set over Igatz. Kaugatz was also visible, and she could see the ancient battlements of Tsallon Anura in the distance. Her guards were not beyond sharing gossip with her when they delivered her meals twice a day, and she had learned that Lahnos and Leona were both now living in the old monastery. The new king and queen of Kaugatz – that's what the guards had called them, and Cisca had laughed along.

From the balcony, she had often watched Lord Sigum make the short journey between Tsallon Anura and the Dragon Palace, his great wings carrying him over the Cyasarta. That morning, however, she had noticed the silvery-green dragon fly away in a different direction, accompanied by Lady Natali. They had gone north together, crossing eastern Kaugatz before disappearing in the direction of Belton.

That left only Lords Rylan and Givra within the palace, and Cisca's nerves had been thrumming since dawn. She had seen nothing of Captain Jair since he had interviewed her in the basement cells, and she hoped that something terrible had happened to him. And, if something bad had occurred, then she hoped it had been before he had made any attempt to find Major Lyla. If she had been hurt or killed because of what Cisca had told him, then she doubted she would be able to live with the guilt.

Lyla wasn't the only person she was feeling guilty about. She had often tried to picture Bauchlie's reaction to her escape. Amid his grief and rage over the poisoning, would he care that she had gone? Part of her hoped so, but the other part did not wish to add to his misery. She wondered if his mother was trying to persuade him to send rebels after her, to hunt her down and kill her, either as a punishment for leaving, or to prevent her from passing on any of their secrets. The irony was that Captain Jair had seemed uninterested in any aspect of Bauchlie's operations when he had questioned her, and so Cisca hadn't been faced with the dilemma of whether to reveal anything to him. Weighed against the threat of the Gunstian blockade, Bauchlie's terrorist group seemed almost irrelevant, and the mass poisoning had reduced their influence further.

Her front door opened without any warning, and Cisca turned from the balcony to see her two guards walk in. She stood.

'You're wanted downstairs,' said one of the guards. 'Governor's orders.'

Cisca's nerves heightened. 'The Governor?'

'That's right. Come with us.'

Cisca glanced down at the informal naval uniform she was wearing. 'Do I need to put on my full dress uniform?'

'No. What you have on will do.'

She followed them out of her apartment and down the wide stairs to the ground floor of the palace. The building was being heavily guarded, and a mixture of Aucterian and Bullan soldiers were on duty at regular intervals along every main passageway. Her escort took her to the entrance leading into the grand central audience hall, and came to a halt next to Captain Jair, who was leaning against the tall archway.

'I'll take it from here, lads,' Jair said.

The two guards saluted, then about-turned and strode away.

'Good morning, Cisca,' Jair said. 'Are you ready for this?'

'Ready for what, exactly?'

'It's time to get on your knees and beg for the Governor's forgiveness. As I told you – it will be a formality. As soon as it's over, I have permission to fully reinstate you in the Dragon Corps.' He pulled a set of keys from a pocket. 'Do you like your current apartment?'

'Yes.'

He threw her the keys. 'In ten minutes, your period of house arrest will be over, as long as you get this next part right.'

She pocketed the keys. 'What do I have to do?'

'You will prostrate yourself, and then confess your crimes. Then you wait. Come on.'

'But... what crimes? I thought I was to tell everyone that I had been held in Medamuna Gatzoun against my will.'

'Talk about Takri blackmailing you, but keep it short and don't mention Leona.'

He set off into the hall, and Cisca hurried to keep up. Inside, Lord Rylan was reclining upon a great mound of cushions in the centre of the hall, while a dozen Aucterian officers were also in attendance. Jair led her to a position in front of the dragon, and bowed.

'My lord,' he said; 'I have brought Cisca of Naeth before you. As you know, she was formerly a captain in the Dragon Corps, and she is here to beg for your forgiveness.'

The huge dragon turned his head to stare at Cisca. 'Oh yes – you. I recall that Lord Malum used to hold you in high regard, before you deserted.'

Cisca bowed her head, then fell to her knees.

'Lower,' whispered Jair.

She gave a slight nod and then fully prostrated herself on the cold marble floor.

'I beg your forgiveness, my noble and blessed lord,' she said. 'I was being blackmailed by Lady Takri, but I should have reported it to the dragons, and I should not have left Zamata Gataza. I am sorry, my lord. I have made some terrible mistakes, and all I wish for is the chance to be able to return to your service.'

'And where have you been these past few months, Cisca?' said the dragon, as the Aucterian officers watched in silence.

'I was being held prisoner by Bauchlie under the ruins of Medamuna Gatzoun, my lord,' she said. 'The poisoning incident gave me an opportunity to escape, and I took it. As soon as I was free, I handed myself over to the soldiers guarding the Dragon Palace.'

'Well, well,' said the dragon. He raised his head. 'And what should I do with this woman? Do any of the officers here present have anything to say? Captain Jair?'

'I believe that Cisca still has much to offer, my lord,' said the captain.

'I see. Anyone else?'

'Captain Cisca always seemed to be a competent officer,' said an army major. 'When Lord Malum retook this island prior to the invasion of Gunst, it was Captain Cisca who organised the capture of Handshore Naval Base.'

'I recall hearing about that,' said the dragon. 'Does anyone here wish to speak against her?'

The hall fell into silence, as Cisca's heart pounded.

'Very well,' the dragon went on. 'Cisca, I forgive your previous transgressions and hereby issue you with a full pardon. My administration has need of good officers, and it would be a waste to see you hang. You may stand.'

Cisca got to her feet, though she kept her head bowed.

'Now swear to serve me, Cisca,' said the dragon. 'Swear that you will be my faithful and obedient servant, from this day until your death.'

'I swear it, my lord.'

'Good. Your loyalty now belongs to the island of Zamata, and to me. Say it.'

'My loyalty belongs to you, my lord, and to the island of Zamata.'

'Captain Jair,' Rylan said, 'see that Cisca has her old rank reinstated, and assign her to the service of Lord Givra. His lordship has been without a close human assistant for some time, and I am sure that someone of Cisca's experience will serve him well.'

'Thank you, my lord,' said Cisca, to a smattering of applause from the assembled officers.

Jair took her elbow in his hand and steered her away from the dragon.

'That was quick,' she said, as they left the hall.

'Quick, and stage-managed,' said the captain. 'Even that major's little contribution was scripted; but it had to be done, and done in public.'

'What now?'

'I want you to return to your apartment and change out of those naval clothes. You are a captain in the Dragon Corps, and you need to look the part before I introduce you to Lord Givra.'

'Is that it? I am a captain again?'

'You are.'

She smiled. 'The same rank as you?'

'My official rank is meaningless. You will take my orders, and do exactly as I say. Go. I'll give you ten minutes to get ready, and then you can meet me by the entrance to Lord Givra's quarters.'

Cisca lowered her voice. 'And... is Lord Rylan still planning on killing him?'

Captain Jair looked at her as though she had lost her mind. 'I don't know what you're talking about. Go.'

Cisca hurried away. She climbed the stairs to the first floor, and returned to her apartment. The door had been locked, and she opened it with her new keys, while going over what Jair had said to her. She could understand why she had needed to beg in front of the dragon in the presence of witnesses. That part hadn't concerned her – she had prostrated herself before dragons on many occasions in Nom Karta – but why had the captain denied knowledge of any plan to slay Lord Givra? She was certain that he had told her of the plan during the interview – had they changed their minds? Or perhaps telling her had been a test, to see if she could be trusted with secrets. If so, she had passed, as she hadn't breathed a word of it to anyone.

She threw off the informal navy clothes and changed into a clean Dragon Corps uniform, then she paused by the mirror on her way back out of the apartment.

Cisca smiled at the reflection. She was in the Dragon Corps again, and a sense of belonging settled upon her. After so many months of fear and uncertainty, she was back in her old job, and she almost wept with relief. The Dominion was no longer the supreme authority in her life, but Lord Rylan's administration felt familiar, and serving dragons was what she had been trained to do. The natural order of her life had been restored, and she could forget all about Lady Takri and the dark, claustrophobic caverns under the ruins of Medamuna Gatzoun. It would take longer to forget about Bauchlie, but given enough time, the memory of him would fade. Wouldn't it? She pushed him from her mind and left the apartment, locking the door behind her. She raced back down to the ground floor, and smiled as a pair of Bullan soldiers saluted her.

Lord Givra was staying in the same quarters that Lord Meer Mon Adal had once inhabited, and Cisca met Captain Jair outside a set of tall doors.

He eyed her up and down. 'That's better. Before we go inside, I want to give you a couple of tips.'

Cisca suppressed another smile. Was an army officer about to lecture her on how to look after a dragon?

'Lord Givra is a little discontented at present,' he said. 'He disagrees with some of the fundamental principles of the Governor's rule of this island, and he is liable to make his feelings known to you. Allow him to rant. Your main task will be to win his trust; but the filthy state of his living quarters will also be keeping you busy.'

'Why has no one been cleaning his quarters?'

'He has refused to allow any humans to touch the place. He insisted that he wanted a high-ranking Dragon Corps officer to serve him, and that no one else would do. Frankly, I think he was just being difficult, as he knew there were no Dragon Corps officers present in the palace. Your arrival here has fulfilled several of our needs; but his lordship may well be surprised to see your uniform.'

'Does Lord Givra possess the ability to use the truth spell, sir?'

'He does not. Do you think I would send you into his quarters if he did?' He placed a hand on the door. 'Are you ready, Captain?'

'Yes, sir.'

Jair pushed at the tall door, and it opened a couple of feet. Beyond, the interior was shrouded in darkness, and he led her into the dragon's rooms. A wave of noxious odour assaulted her nostrils, and she almost gagged.

'My lord?' Jair called out into the gloom. 'May I speak to you, my lord?'

An enormous head emerged from the shadows. 'You, again? What do you want? If you are summoning me into that usurper's presence, tell him that I am ill. I have no desire to debase myself in front of a pretender.'

'I have brought you someone, my lord,' said Jair, gesturing to Cisca.

The dragon's eyes turned to stare at her.

'This is Captain Cisca of the Dragon Corps,' Jair said. 'She has been assigned to see to your needs, my lord.'

'Have you dressed someone up in a Dragon Corps uniform to trick me?' said the dragon.

'No, my lord. Captain Cisca was being held captive by a band of rebels, and has not long escaped. She is the most senior Dragon Corps officer on the island; no – she is the only Dragon Corps officer on the island.'

Givra said nothing for a long time as his eyes seemed to pierce Cisca, and then, finally, he turned to Jair.

'Get out,' he said. 'Leave me alone with this woman.'

Jair bowed. 'Yes, my lord.'

The army officer backed away, then he disappeared through the door and swung it shut.

'Are you the genuine article, woman?' said the dragon.

'I am, my lord,' said Cisca. 'I served in Nom Karta prior to being posted to this island.'

'Which dragons have you served?'

'Most recently, I served Lord Malum, both here and in Zamata Gataza, where I was captured by the rebels who slew the noble lord. Before that, I was in the service of Lord Kheran, and...'

'Lady Tirna's son?' said Givra. 'You served that little traitor? Wait – I think I know who you are. I recall you being discussed during Kheran's interrogation. If my memory is accurate, didn't you try to persuade Kheran to remain at his post?'

'I did, my lord.'

'Why?'

'I thought it was... I thought...'

'You can speak bluntly in front of me, woman. What Lord Kheran did was nothing short of a dereliction of duty.'

'Yes, my lord. I urged him to remain here, upon the Serpent Isle, and await reinforcements. He did not take my advice.'

The dragon laughed. 'Had you named it Zamata, I would have ripped your head off. I assume you have heard Rylan refer to himself as Governor of Zamata?'

'Yes, my lord.'

'And what is your opinion of this?'

'I prefer the name King Gahad bestowed upon the island, my lord.'

'Yes; good answer. However, to get through those doors, I must also assume that Rylan made you swear a new oath – to him, and not to the Dominion?'

Cisca bowed her head. 'Yes, my lord. If I hadn't, I would be dead.'

The dragon tilted his head. 'Then you are tainted. A pity. All the same, I shall allow you to clean my quarters. You may start immediately.'

. . .

Cisca found everything that she needed in a large storeroom at the rear of the cavernous chamber. There were taps, and she filled buckets with soap and water and mopped the marble floor for several hours. Lord Givra had a long balcony, and she opened its wide doors, letting in the light from the overcast sky, while the fresh breeze removed some of the odour. The soiled blankets were piled up and taken away by a couple of servants via the rear door. Cisca also ordered the servants to remove a large manger filled with rotten, maggot-infested meat, and then she cleaned the fresh water trough, scrubbing away layers of pale green mould. All the while, Lord Givra sat and watched without comment, his eyes following her as she moved through his quarters. It was growing dark when the servants returned with fresh blankets, and Cisca had them piled up over the clean floor into a mound where the dragon could sleep. Her back and hands aching, she then started to scrub the walls, using a ladder to reach as high as she was able. She had decided that she wasn't going to stop until the dragon told her to, and the stars appeared in the evening sky as she continued to scrub.

'That will do for today, Captain,' said Givra. 'Come down from the ladder and put everything away for the night.'

'Yes, my lord,' she said.

She carried the ladder to the storeroom, then tidied away the buckets, mops and scrubbing brushes and bowed in front of Lord Givra.

'Do you require anything else this evening, my lord?'

The dragon surveyed his quarters. 'You have done well. I had almost forgotten how pleasant it is to dwell in a clean environment.' He tilted his head a fraction. 'It is good to have a proper Dragon Corps officer attend to me again, even one who has sworn an oath that betrays the Dominion. Tell me, Captain; how do you feel about our new Governor?'

'I am still adjusting, my lord,' she said. 'I had no news while being held captive, and was unaware of the... changes made by Lord Rylan.'

The dragon laughed. 'You have been well-trained, Captain – such a diplomatic response. I do not yet trust you, but you have made a good start, and I will allow you to return here tomorrow to continue cleaning.'

'Thank you, my lord.'

'Leave me.'

Cisca bowed low, then walked from the chamber. She eased herself through the tall doors, and found Jair waiting for her outside. She swung the doors closed, and they began to walk away from the dragon's lair.

'You have made it through your first day, Cisca – well done.'

'Did you think he was going to kill me?'

'It was a possibility. How did he take to you?'

'He was disappointed that I have sworn an oath to Lord Rylan.'

'Naturally. Are you allowed to come back tomorrow?'

'Yes.'

'Yes what?'

'Yes, sir.'

They stopped at the bottom of the stairs.

'I will meet you here at dawn, Captain,' Jair said. 'Don't be late.'

Exhausted by the day's labour, Cisca slept well, and a soldier awoke her before dawn with a sharp rap on the front door of her apartment. She washed and dressed in silence, then brushed her hair while the sky was still dark. She opened her front door, and Jair shoved her back into the apartment. He closed the door and gripped her wrist.

'Let me go,' she whispered.

'Shut up,' he said, pushing her into the living area. He shoved her again, and she fell onto the couch. She stared up at him, and saw how tired he looked.

'I think... something, or someone... my mind...'

'What?' she said.

'I need to know something,' he said. 'What powers does the Demon Witch possess?'

She blinked. 'I... I'm not sure.'

'Can she twist your thoughts? Shape your memories? I must know.'

'Did you speak to her? Did you find Major Lyla, sir?'

'I found her. She was in Leona's townhouse, and now they are in Tsallon Anura with the Laimos boy.' He began to pace up and down the room. 'I spoke to Major Lyla. And then... I was so sure.'

'Sure of what, sir?'

'That she wasn't the Demon Witch; that the ritual hadn't worked. And that's what I told Lord Rylan. But... last night, I couldn't sleep. My mind felt... well, it felt as though a fog had lifted.' He stopped and stared at Cisca. 'I think I was deceived.'

'The Demon Witch could read minds; I know that,' Cisca said. 'And she could manipulate thoughts – she destroyed Lady Lenta's mind, and forced Lady Macsin to attack her brother.'

'The Demon Witch forced her to attack Lord Malum?'

'Yes. Lord Rylan was unconscious at the time; he didn't see it happen, but I remember it clearly. If she could do that to dragons, sir, then...'

'Then what she did to me was simple in comparison. Why didn't you warn me?'

'You didn't tell me what you intended to do, sir.'

He shook his head at her, then he glanced at the growing light in the sky through the balcony doors.

'Shit,' he muttered. 'I will have to inform Lord Rylan immediately. Now I understand why Leona is sheltering with the Laimos boy. The two of them are conspiring with the Demon Witch against us.'

Cisca said nothing.

'If you utter a word of this, I will kill you,' Jair said. 'Go to Lord Givra, and ingratiate yourself with him. You have my permission to make a few treacherous comments about Lord Rylan in his presence. Make him think that you disagree with the Governor's policies, especially his policy to renounce the Dominion.'

Cisca got to her feet. 'Yes, sir.'

They left the apartment, locked the door, and then went downstairs to the ground floor of the palace. Jair strode away in the direction of

Lord Rylan's chambers, and Cisca smoothed down the front of her uniform and carried on towards Lord Givra.

The huge dragon was awake when she knocked and entered his quarters.

'Today, Captain,' he said, 'I want you to talk about your life in Inopei while you work. Perhaps you served some dragons in Nom Karta that I know, and I would like to be reminded of my home.'

'Yes, my lord,' she said. She went to the storeroom and collected her supplies, then she began cleaning the smears and dirt from the glass in the balcony doors.

'The most important dragon I served in the palaces of Nom Karta was Lady Shana Min Gahad,' she said, as she wrung out the cloth in a bucket.

The dragon's eyes flashed. 'That traitor? Were you aware that Lady Shana voted for Lord Tegru? The last I heard, she was on the run with that coward! How I wish I was there, rather than trapped upon this barren rock. Tegru and his minions could be assaulting Nom Karta right now, and yet here we are, thanks to that oaf Rylan.' He paused. 'Do you intend to report my words to the Governor?'

'No, my lord,' she said. 'Whatever you say to me while we are alone I will keep to myself. I still feel bound by the oaths I swore when I joined the Dragon Corps. To be truthful, my lord, I also feel bound by my oath to the Dominion, regardless of the words I was forced to say to Lord Rylan.'

The dragon eyed her.

'I did not serve Lady Shana for long,' she went on, as she wiped the glass doors, 'and I was the most junior member of her staff. After that, I was assigned to serve one of her ladyship's daughters – to assist her in the selection of a suitable mate. I was still doing that when the news arrived about King Gahad's demise.'

'I was also in Nom Karta on that dark day,' the dragon said. 'That was when everything started to go wrong. I greatly admired King Naghad, and my most noble father voted for him, but perhaps his invasion of Gunst was ill-judged. If it hadn't been for Kheran's treachery, then I believe that King Naghad would have planned the invasion with more care. Instead, he was rushed into sending a fleet to retake this island; and now look at us. Naghad, Malum and Macsin are dead, along with many other fine and noble dragons. We are weakened and divided, and the future of the Dominion is in great peril. I would do anything to return to Inopei at this moment, to assist my father and Lady Famula in the defence of Nom Karta against that coward Tegru. Anything.'

Cisca kept her eyes on the balcony doors. 'There is only one way for a dragon to leave the Serpent Isle, my lord.'

'Indeed. But how would I gather sailors to crew the dragon carrier? And how would I be able to leave the Cyasarta if Rylan's soldiers are occupying the Chain Castles? And then, how would I pierce the Gunstian blockade? It cannot be done; not unless I first take power, and Rylan is in a strong position. With Lord Sigum's assistance and Lady Natali's neutrality, he would outnumber and overpower me.'

'Lord Sigum and Lady Natali are frequently off the island, my lord.'

'Is that so? Why?'

'The Governor has asked them to patrol the ocean, my lord; to hunt down and sink any Gunstian supply ships that they find.'

'Are they both absent at the present moment?'

'They flew away yesterday, my lord, so they will be due back this morning.'

The dragon tilted his head. 'You will inform me the next time they leave; is that understood?'

'Yes, my lord.'

'Tell me, Captain – has Lord Rylan used the truth spell upon you?'

'No, my lord; he hasn't.'

'Good. Give him no reason to. Fulfil your duties and do nothing to draw attention to yourself. I am beginning to think that he might have erred by sending you here, Captain. Where does your true loyalty lie?'

Cisca turned, and met his gaze. 'To the Dominion, my lord.'

'And would you like to spend the rest of your short life upon this island?'

'No, my lord,' she said. 'I want to go home.'

'Then you and I seem to have much in common, my Dragon Corps officer. When the time comes, whose orders will you obey – the usurping Governor's, or my own?'

'I am assigned to you, my lord,' Cisca said. 'It is you I serve.'

The dragon smiled, tilted his head, then settled down to watch her work.

CHAPTER 21
ARREST WARRANT

Kaugatz, Serpent Isle – 9th Kolinch 1588

Leona signed her name at the bottom of each page, then she slipped the papers into an envelope and sealed it shut.

'Take this to the western gate of the monastery,' she said to the waiting soldier, 'and give it to the man reading a book on a bench in the shade of the cypress tree.'

'The same man as before, ma'am?' said the young Zamatan, taking the thick envelope.

'Yes. Be discreet, if possible.'

The soldier saluted, then left the apartment. Leona stretched her arms and yawned, then she got to her feet and strode towards the balcony. Arrosa was sitting on a chair outside, her gaze on the view. Leona glanced up at the clouds, then walked to the railings.

'Where's Lyla?' she said. 'I thought she was out here with you.'

'She went for a walk,' said the girl. 'She asked me to come, but I don't want to walk about if one of those disgusting Bullan demons is going to follow me everywhere.'

'Is that why you've hardly left the apartment?'

Arrosa nodded.

'Did Lyla say where she was going?'

'No,' said the girl, 'but it's obvious. She will be with Lahnos. She feels sorry for him after his girlfriend left.' She turned her head to look at Leona. 'Did she leave because of us?'

'I don't know. Maybe.'

'Are you going to be Lahnos's girlfriend now?'

Leona laughed. 'No.'

'Good. Never kiss a demon; they steal your soul. My mummy told me that. She made me take a bath every time we saw a part-Bullan on the streets of Kaugatz.'

'You must have taken a lot of baths.'

'Not really. We avoided the places where they lived. There were whole streets full of Gunstian families in Kaugatz; some days, we spoke Gunstian to everyone we met, and we never saw a single Zamatan. Are those houses empty now?'

'Yes. This is a difficult question, Arrosa, but how did you survive the massacre?'

'Bullan soldiers came to our street and put everyone onto wagons,' she said. 'One old man refused, and they killed him, so everyone else did what they were told. We heard screams when we got close to the town square, and my father pushed me off the wagon and I ran away. The Bullan didn't see me.'

'Did you... go to the square?'

'No, but I could hear the dragons and knew what they were doing.' She turned to Leona. 'And now you think I should like the Bullan and the dragons; but I hate them, and I always will.'

'What about the Zamatans?'

Arrosa shrugged. 'It wasn't the Zamatans who killed everyone I knew; it wasn't even the Aucterians, or the part-Bullan. The dragons were looking for the Gifted who ruined the crops, but why did they have to kill my parents?'

'Lord Malum was evil,' Leona said. 'There's no other word for it. I think I will look for Lyla; do you want to come?'

Arrosa shook her head.

Leona walked to the balcony doors, then she stopped and turned.

'The Bullan are not evil,' she said. 'I know you might find that hard to believe. Their greatest fault is blind loyalty to whomever is giving them orders. The twelve Bullan in Tsallon Anura obey Lahnos – they would die to protect you, Arrosa.'

The girl said nothing, her gaze back on the view, and Leona went through their apartment and left by the front door. Two Bullan were standing at their posts outside in the hallway, and they saluted.

'Do you know where Lyla went?' she said to them.

'No, ma'am,' said one, 'but her guard went with her when she left.'

'Arrosa is alone in the apartment just now,' Leona said.

'Understood, ma'am. One of us will remain here at all times. Are you leaving the building?'

'I want to look for Lyla, and she is probably with Lahnos; so, yes.'

One of the soldiers stepped forward. 'I shall accompany you, ma'am.'

The soldier followed Leona down the stairs and out through the building's main entrance. The sun was breaking through the gaps in the autumnal clouds, and the air felt warm and still. Leona made her way through the grounds of the monastery. Small vegetable gardens had been planted in several locations, though their produce wouldn't be ready for another few months. On the far side of the cloister, the stables were lying empty. The meat had been sent all around the island, with each family receiving a small amount. The only farm animals that had been spared were a few large oxen that were needed to plough the fields in spring; but they, too, were under threat from the hungry populace. Many goats had also survived, but that was due to their ability to scamper up near vertical cliffs in order to escape their pursuers. Some households were fiercely protecting their dogs, but Leona knew that when starvation began to bite hard, then they would also be sacrificed to stave off death. Leona's signature that morning had authorised money to be spent on refurbishing some old boats so that they could be added to the fishing fleet, but it was an action that bordered on futile, as the reserves of fish in the Hansarta were plummeting due to the large increase in the daily catch. When the fish ran out, it would be over.

The Bullan soldier glanced at Leona and pointed towards the gate that led to the jetty. She turned to look in that direction and saw Lahnos arguing with six Bullan soldiers. Leona narrowed her eyes. She couldn't tell the difference between the Bullan, but the six by the jetty were wearing slightly different uniforms to the twelve who lived in Tsallon Anura. Lyla was standing a few paces behind Lahnos, and one of the new Bullan pointed at her. Leona picked up her pace, and ran the last few yards.

'What's going on, General?' she said.

Lahnos had his fists clenched. 'These idiots think they can just come in here and demand that we hand Lyla over to them.'

'I have a warrant signed by Captain Jair,' said one of the new Bullan, holding up a document. 'Major Lyla of the Dragon Corps is under arrest. Are you trying to prevent us from upholding the law, General Laimos?'

Lahnos snatched the sheet of paper from the soldier's hand and tore it to pieces. 'Does that answer your question, sergeant?'

The Bullan glanced at each other.

'If Captain Jair wants Major Lyla,' said Leona, 'then he should come here in person. We would be happy to sit down and talk to him.'

'The captain's orders were that we were to escort her to the Dragon Palace, ma'am,' said the sergeant. 'He stated that if you resist, then we were also to take you into custody, Leona of Kaugatz.'

'You're not touching her, either,' said Lahnos. 'This is my damn monastery, and you have no rights here.'

One of the new Bullan reached out to grab Lyla, but her Bullan guard shoved him away. Several of the Bullan squared off against each other, some snarling in their own language.

'You should leave before you get hurt,' said Lahnos.

'Pull back,' said the sergeant. 'This is not over, General. Tell the twelve Bullan under your command that they will be formally expelled from the soldiers' guild at midnight tonight unless they sail to Igatz and hand themselves in. Our kin have no use for traitors and cowards.'

Lyla's guard raised a finger and started shouting something that sounded like a tirade of angry insults at the Bullan sergeant. The sergeant said nothing in return, and herded his men through the gate and down the jetty, where a small sailing vessel had berthed. The six soldiers boarded the vessel, the ropes were loosened, and the craft began to move away from the shore.

'What is the soldiers' guild?' said Lyla.

Her guard turned to her. 'It is the community that all Bullan soldiers belong to, ma'am. It takes care of pensions, and payments to the relatives of fallen and maimed soldiers. That sergeant had no right to say what he did. Every Bullan on this island has sworn a new oath to Lord Rylan. If our kin back in our homeland knew this, we would all be expelled.'

'Thank you for protecting me,' she said.

'No problem, ma'am.'

Leona noticed a few scraps of paper by her feet and she leaned over to look at them. She found a piece bearing Jair's signature, and slipped it into a pocket. She stood, and glanced at Lahnos, who was watching the sailing vessel cross the Cyasarta in the direction of the Dragon Palace.

'We should talk, Lahnos,' she said.

He nodded, and then they walked with Lyla and their Bullan guards to the old refectory building. They entered the ancient structure and walked into Lahnos's office, where his Bullan sergeant was working at a desk.

'I need to speak to Leona and Lyla alone for a moment,' Lahnos said.

The Bullan soldiers saluted and left the room, closing the door behind them.

'I think Jair has recovered from whatever I did to him,' said Lyla in Gunstian.

'If he comes here, could you do it again?' said Lahnos.

'Yes. Why does he want to kill the Demon Witch?'

Leona sat. 'He knows what you did to Lady Lenta and Lady Macsin.'

'What did I do to them?'

'You destroyed Lenta's mind, and then you took control of her body and made her speak. With Macsin, you went into her mind as well, and forced her to attack Lord Malum. Rylan was there, although he was badly injured and was unconscious for part of it. He fears you.'

'But I have no desire to hurt him.'

'Lord Rylan sees you as a threat to his rule,' said Leona. 'How do we change that?'

Lahnos frowned. 'Whose side are you on, Lyla?'

'I don't know,' said Lyla, 'but I can't be on the same side as a dragon who wants to kill me.'

'What about the island? You have helped it in the past; could you help it again? If you did, then Rylan might see you as an asset, not a threat.'

'I don't want to be an asset,' she said. 'The people on this island have not been very nice to me. Why should I be nice to them?'

'Do you remember anything about the politics of this world?' said Leona.

'I remember what you told me,' said Lyla, 'and I have tried to read a few books, but my grasp of the Divine Tongue is still weak. I know about the Gunstians and the Dominion, but I can't tell which side is better than the other. If I am from a different world, then maybe I should stay out of the wars on this one.'

Lahnos rubbed his face. 'It's too late for that. You killed King Gahad, along with other dragons and plenty of Gunstians and Aucterians.'

'I don't want to hurt anyone,' she said. 'Hurting people is wrong. Violence never solves anything.'

'I'm afraid I have to disagree with that,' said Lahnos. 'Perhaps violence shouldn't solve anything, but sometimes it does. Sometimes, only the threat of violence can deter bad folk from trampling all over you. And Zamata is surrounded by empires that want to trample all over us. Right now, it's the Gunstians' turn. If we don't resist them, they will kill everyone on the island, including the pacifists.'

Lyla sat and put her head in her hands. 'The part of me that remembers Major Lyla agrees with every word you just said, Lahnos; but the other part, the Demon Witch part, is telling me that violence is wrong.'

Lahnos walked over to a cabinet and picked up a crossbow. 'Can I try something?'

Leona smiled. 'As long as it doesn't involve shooting either of us.'

Lahnos laughed.

'That's the first time I've heard you laugh since Reyn left,' Lyla said.

His face fell. 'Thanks for reminding me,' he said. 'Do you have any memories of the Demon Witch using a crossbow?'

Lyla shrugged. 'I don't think so.'

He handed the weapon to her. 'Load it and loose at... that patch of damp in the corner of the wall.'

She looked down at the bow on her lap. 'I don't know how.'

'Don't think,' he said; 'just do it.'

Lyla ran her hand down the stock of the bow, then she closed her eyes. Her fingers pulled the loading lever, and the bolt slotted into place. She stood, raised the bow to her shoulder, opened one eye, and loosed. The bolt flew past Lahnos and Leona and embedded itself in the centre of the small damp patch.

She lowered the bow, her eyes wide. 'How did you know I could do that?'

'Major Lyla was in the army for years,' said Lahnos. 'She probably did what you've just done a thousand times; so often that it's burned itself into your memory, whether you can find it or not. You know, I bet that you would also be handy with a sword. You should start training, and then you would be able to defend yourself.'

Leona raised an eyebrow. 'Are you suggesting that a mere woman trains to be a soldier, Lahnos?'

'Part of her is Aucterian,' Lahnos said, 'and she used to be a soldier. She couldn't have reached the rank of major without being half-decent.'

'I was a lieutenant in the army,' Lyla said. 'I dreamt about that a few nights ago. I was on a ship going to a place called Irlan, and I had thirty soldiers under my command.'

'You went to Irlan?' said Lahnos.

'I didn't see Irlan in the dream; only the ship.'

'And what was the dream's pair?' said Leona.

'I was travelling,' Lyla said; 'just as I was in the first dream, but I was crossing a desert, not the ocean. The blind old man was with me, and we were going to see my family; but the dream ended before we arrived, just as the desert was turning into grasslands.'

'We know you have a brother.'

'And a sister,' said Lyla. 'Lahnos told me that my sister was looking after my children.'

'I was thinking about that,' Lahnos said, 'and I remembered another detail. It was your adopted sister who has the twins; that's what you said to me.'

Lyla nodded. 'When I go sleep every night, I hope that I will dream about the twins. I wish I had told you their names even more than I wish I had told you my own. I did what you suggested, Lahnos, and tried to recall more about the volcano palace where I killed King Gahad, and was able to remember the face of a young woman who was with me, but she wasn't eight years old; more like twenty.'

'Perhaps all of your memories will return,' said Leona, 'but could we return to the current situation? If Lord Rylan decides to come here in person, then it could prove difficult to keep you safe. The Demon Witch had several powers, and you have shown that you can use at least one of them – what you did to Captain Jair, for example. The Demon Witch could also read other people's minds; have you tried that?'

Lyla nodded. 'I have tried, but I don't know how it is supposed to work.'

'And,' Leona went on, 'in the caverns under Zamata Gataza, you neutralised Lord Malum's power over life and death. He attempted to kill us all, but you stopped him. You also stopped him from being able to breathe fire. Could you do that again? It might save our lives if Lord Rylan tries to take you by force.'

'I don't remember doing that.'

'It wasn't long after the ritual had taken place,' Leona said. 'You were unconscious most of the time, but you cried out when Malum tried to use his powers on us, as though you had sensed them.'

Lyla shook her head.

'One last thing,' Leona said. 'You did something to my mind, to protect me from the dragons' truth spell. I'm not sure if it still works, but that would also be very useful.'

Lyla lowered her gaze. 'I'm sorry. I can't remember. There is another way to keep you all safe from Rylan – hand me over to him. That's what he wants.'

'We are not going to surrender you, Lyla,' said Lahnos. 'Lord Rylan will kill you to make sure that the Demon Witch never returns. You helped us so many times in the past that we owe you. I owe you. You saved my life in Gunst, even after I was rude and told you to leave me alone.'

'You had every right to do that. I killed your father.'

'I know. But, it was an accident. It's taken me a long time to accept it, but I believe you. You didn't mean to kill my father, and you could have walked away; but you didn't. You kept coming back to help me, again and again – and look where it got you. Your reward was to be confined inside Major Lyla's body, your memories stripped and tangled, your powers forgotten. Now that you are vulnerable, it is our turn to help you. I swear it, Lyla – I will never let Lord Rylan take you, not while I am still breathing.'

Lyla looked at him, her sad eyes seeming to pierce his soul.

'Sir?' said a Bullan by the door. 'Lord Sigum has just landed in the cloister.'

Lahnos nodded. 'Shall we talk to our dragon?'

'How close is Sigum to the Governor?' said Leona.

'Apparently, they are old acquaintances,' Lahnos said, as he began to walk towards the door. 'We can trust him, if that's what you were getting at. Come on.'

Leona and Lyla followed him out of the office, and their Bullan guards moved in to flank them as they walked through the building. They emerged into the sunshine, and Leona gazed up at the huge dragon in the square courtyard in the middle of the cloisters. His silvery-green scales were glimmering in the light, as he tucked in his great wings.

'Lahnos,' he said, 'it is good to be back.'

'How did it go?' Lahnos said.

'This expedition was more of a success than our first,' the dragon said. 'Lady Natali and I came across four Gunstian galleys about eighty miles off the western coast of the island. None had Gifted aboard, and we sank them all.'

'Were they carrying supplies for the fleet?' said Leona.

The dragon turned his head to regard her. 'Not food, unfortunately,' he said. 'The decks of the ships were heavily laden with munitions for the fleet's ballistae.'

'That definitely counts as a success,' said Lahnos.

'Lord Rylan wishes us to depart again tomorrow,' Sigum said. 'I have just come from the Dragon Palace after reporting to the Governor. He led me to believe that Major Lyla would no longer be in Tsallon Anura, but I see that he was mistaken.'

'They tried to arrest her while you were gone,' Lahnos said. 'I refused to allow it.'

Sigum's eyes flashed. 'You disobeyed an order from the Governor? Why?'

'Lord Rylan does not understand what he is doing, my friend. Lyla is innocent.'

'Then let her plead her case in the Dragon Palace. The Governor would give her a fair hearing, regardless of the charges made against her.'

'Do you know the charges?' said Leona.

'I do not, Leona of Kaugatz. However, Lord Rylan seemed agitated when he mentioned her name. What crime is she being accused of committing?'

Lahnos and Leona shared a glance, then Lyla took a pace towards the dragon.

'He believes me to be the Demon Witch,' she said, 'and he is correct.'

Lahnos put an arm out to shield her, his eyes on Sigum.

'I will not hurt her, my friend,' said the dragon, 'but this news disheartens me greatly. The Demon Witch is a murderer and a spy; her assassination of King Gahad set in motion the events we are now living through, and she should be held accountable. Lahnos, I advise you to surrender her to Lord Rylan immediately.'

Lahnos smiled up at the dragon. 'That will not be happening. She is under my protection.'

'But why would you align yourself with a notorious criminal? This bodes ill for the future of Zamata.'

Lahnos glanced at Leona. 'Take Lyla back to your apartment. I will speak to Sigum alone, and tell him everything. He deserves to know the whole truth.'

'If you think that wise,' said Leona.

'I do.'

Leona took Lyla's arm, and guided her away from the silvery-green dragon. Their two Bullan guards shadowed them back to the apartment block, and they ascended the stairs. Arrosa's guard was standing outside the front door, and the three Bullan exchanged a few words in their own language.

'May I ask you something?' said Leona.

The soldiers turned to her.

'If Lord Rylan issues an order that Lahnos disregards,' she went on, 'whose side will you take?'

'All twelve of our kinfolk in this monastery have each taken three oaths,' said one of the Bullan: 'to the Dominion, to Lahnos, and now also to the new Governor of Zamata. These oaths are incompatible with each other, and swearing one does not negate the others.'

'I understand your difficulty,' Leona said, 'but who, then, would you obey?'

'By usurping the sovereignty of this island,' said the Bullan soldier, 'it seems clear to us that Lord Rylan has broken his word; therefore, we twelve shall obey Lahnos.'

'And what will you do if the Dominion returns?'

The Bullan glanced at each other.

'Opinions are divided, ma'am,' said one of them. 'Some of our kinfolk would revert to the oath they swore to King Gahad; while others believe that oath expired with His Majesty's death.'

'But you served King Naghad.'

'Many now think that was a mistake, ma'am. King Naghad's brief reign, and his unwise invasion of Gunst, led to the slaughter of thousands of our people. Some of us are now questioning if we should continue to serve the Dominion under a new monarch.'

Leona narrowed her eyes a little, then she opened the front door.

'Thank you,' she said, as she stepped inside. Lyla followed her into the living area and then out on to the balcony, where Arrosa was still sitting. The girl glanced up at them, then she returned to gazing down at the sight of Lord Sigum talking to Lahnos in the middle of the cloister.

'The silver-green demon has returned,' she hissed.

'Bullan soldiers tried to arrest me,' said Lyla, as she sat down next to Arrosa.

The girl's eyes widened. 'I told you not to trust them!'

'Not the Bullan in the monastery,' said Leona. 'Lord Rylan sent others from the Dragon Palace. The Bullan here defended us, and Lahnos tore up the arrest warrant and made the others leave.'

'Did he? Good. He's all right for a demon, I suppose. But I don't trust that dragon. Why does Lahnos like him so much?'

'They are friends,' said Lyla.

'Ha!' Arrosa cried. 'Impossible. He is probably imagining what Lahnos tastes like.'

Leona walked to the railings, and gazed out at the view of Igatz across the Cyasarta inlet. She frowned. A small dark speck was racing through the sky towards Tsallon Anura. A wave of fear passed through her, and she suppressed it. If it was Lord Rylan, then she would have to remain clear-headed, and not show any fear in front of Lyla and Arrosa.

'Who is that coming?' said Lyla.

'It's another demon!' Arrosa cried.

'It's Lady Natali,' said Leona, recognising the dragon's form. Her anxiety eased a little, though she knew it was possible that Rylan had sent his sister to carry out his orders.

The dragon soared over the clear waters of the Cyasarta, and then ascended over the monastery battlements. She circled once, and her eyes caught sight of Leona, Lyla and Arrosa on the balcony. Leona tensed, but the dragon veered away, and landed next to Lord Sigum in the centre of the cloister. The two dragons conversed, then Lahnos stepped back as they both rose into the air and sped off into the east. Lahnos began shouting out commands to the soldiers close to the cloisters, and a low rumble of voices and bustle started to envelop the grounds of the ancient monastery.

A few moments later, someone pounded upon the front door of the apartment, and Leona went inside and strode to the entrance. She opened the door, and saw a fourth Bullan standing next to the three guards.

'Ma'am,' he said, 'General Laimos wishes you to know that he is leaving Tsallon Anura immediately. He requests that you remain in your apartment.'

'Where is he going?' said Leona.

'He shall be leading the Zamatan regiments east, ma'am, towards the northern Chain Castle.'

'Why?'

The Bullan's eyes tightened. 'Because the Gunstians have landed, ma'am. The invasion has begun.'

CHAPTER 22
MUTUAL LOATHING

Northern Chain Castle, Serpent Isle – 10th Kolinch 1588

The four dragons soared low over the glistening waters of the Cyasarta as the sun split the horizon to the east. The soldiers of the two Zamatan regiments by the northern Chain Castle hushed as they watched the sight – Lord Rylan was in the lead, with Lady Natali to his left and Lord Givra to his right, while Lord Sigum flew behind, as the only mortal dragon among the descendants of the mighty Gahad. The Gunstian marines also quietened, pausing from their siege work around the base of the castle as the dragons approached.

'Keep moving!' a Bullan soldier cried at the Zamatans. 'Encircle the invaders! Let the dragons do their job.'

Few paid the soldier any heed as Lord Rylan opened his jaws. The grey and yellow dragon ascended from the level of the Cyasarta and rose above the line of cliffs on the northern shore, where the besieged companies of Zamatans in the Chain Castle had been holding out all night. The garrison cheered, their raised arms and weapons visible on the roof of the northern Chain Castle's main keep. The dragons banked, swooping down towards the thousand Gunstian marines besieging the castle. At the last moment, just as Lahnos was waiting for the flames to burst from the dragons' jaws, Lord Rylan and Lady Natali roared out in pain, and were buffeted backwards as though struck by an invisible force. Givra was the next to suffer. He spiralled down to the right, almost plummeting into the Cyasarta; then Sigum was hit by the same force, and peeled away to the left.

'The Gift of Pain,' said Efizel, as he stood next to Lahnos. 'The dragons will not be able to dislodge the marines, not while the Gifted one lives.'

Rylan flew to his sister's side, and they retreated out of range, circling over the two great chains that hung suspended across the narrow straits. Givra and Sigum joined them, and they pulled back further, and landed on the opposite shore, a hundred yards from the southern Chain Castle. By the base of the northern castle, the Gunstian marines resumed their work. They were constructing a squat wooden tower, and assembling several small catapults that had been dropped off for them when they had landed on the island the previous day. They had also dug a line of deep ditches along their northern flank, to protect them from counter attack while they brought the Chain Castle under siege.

'What are your orders, sir?' said Efizel.

Lahnos gazed at the bustling activity of the Gunstian marines. Several hundred were deployed to defend the line of ditches, and each marine was pointing a crossbow at the ranks of Zamatans who had marched out from Kaugatz. If Lahnos ordered a frontal attack, then hundreds of Zamatans would be cut down before they reached the ditches.

'I have never faced Gunstian marines before,' he said. 'Are they well trained?'

'They travel with the fleet,' Efizel said; 'and yes, they have received excellent training. They are as proficient as the elite army units we came up against in Gunst.' He frowned. 'The Zamatans are no match for them, sir.'

'Then we hem them in,' said Lahnos. 'We have already cut off their supply route to the coast. How much food could they have brought with them? And where will they find fresh water?'

'But, sir,' said the Bullan, 'they mean to assault the Chain Castle as soon as their preparations are complete. If they breach the walls of the keep, the chains will be lowered and...'

'I know that,' Lahnos spat. He gazed at the two Zamatan regiments spread out across the muddy fields north of the Chain Castle. They outnumbered the Gunstians two-to-one, but with the marines dug in along their narrower front, any attack across the flat fields would result in carnage.

'Lord Sigum and Lady Natali are approaching, sir,' Efizel said.

Lahnos glanced up, and saw the two dragons flying at speed over the Cyasarta. They diverted around the Gunstian lines in a wide arc, then landed behind the Zamatan command post, where Lahnos and his officers were standing.

Lahnos strode across the field towards them, Efizel by his side. The dragons had alighted next to the terraces of a huge vineyard farmed by the monks of Tzalla Pen. They saw Lahnos approach, and waited.

'My friend,' said Sigum, as Lahnos and Efizel got closer; 'Lord Rylan has called off the dragon attack. We cannot get close enough to burn the Gunstians besieging the northern Chain Castle.'

'Are you hurt?' said Lahnos.

'It will pass,' said Sigum. 'The Gift of Pain does no permanent damage...'

'It does not need to,' said Natali, her green eyes burning with anger. 'It blinds us with agony. If we had continued onward for another few yards, we would have been overcome, and rendered unconscious. Those of us who were in Gunst remember this well. The humans must kill the Gifted before we can burn the others. You should order the attack at once, Laimos.'

'Are those Lord Rylan's orders, ma'am?' said Lahnos.

'The Governor was in too much pain to issue you with any fresh orders, human,' said Natali. 'His only command concerned myself and Lord Sigum.'

Lahnos narrowed his eyes. 'Does he want you to assault the castle, ma'am?'

'Do not be ridiculous, human,' said Natali. 'Were you not listening? My noble brother has ordered us both to leave the island and resume our task of hunting down Gunstian supply vessels. The Governor feels that our best chance of success is to starve out the fleet, to force them to abandon their blockade. He and Lord Givra will guard the chains while we do this.'

'I don't understand,' said Lahnos. 'Lord Rylan is sending you away? But the Gunstians have landed.'

'I can see that!' Natali cried. 'However, I shall obey the commands of the Governor of this miserable rock. Shall you, horned boy? I know that you defied my brother yesterday, when you refused to hand over a prisoner into his custody. If it were up to me, you would be stripped of your rank and thrown from a cliff.' She turned to Sigum. 'Let us go; this treacherous little horned creature is beginning to distress me.'

Sigum said nothing, but tilted his head a fraction in Lahnos's direction; then the two dragons extended their wings and soared away to the north, eliciting a wave of complaints and groans from the watching Zamatans.

'There is a certain logic to the Governor's orders, sir,' said Efizel.

Lahnos frowned as he gazed at the diminishing specks in the cloudy sky. 'Is that right?'

'Yes, sir. If the dragons cannot pierce the defences of the Gunstian marines, then they should be redeployed to perform a different task. Sinking the Imperial Fleet's supply vessels will hasten the end of the blockade.'

'Eventually,' said Lahnos, 'but what about right now? If we do nothing, then the marines will only take a day or two to break into the Chain Castle, and then the fleet will be able to enter the Cyasarta. What should I do?'

'You are the commanding officer, sir.'

'Yes, but you know I was only appointed as a figurehead. I am twenty years old, and I was a terrible corporal. How am I supposed to act as a damn general? What would you do, Efizel, were you in my position?'

Efizel turned, and surveyed the various formations of soldiers and marines clustered before the walls of the Chain Castle. The terraces of the vineyard were slightly elevated above the fields that ran down to the Cyasarta, and both the besieged and the besiegers could be seen.

'Each battalion within the two Zamatan regiments is led by an experienced Aucterian officer, sir,' he said. 'Allow them to use their initiative when the battle commences. Tell them they are free to make decisions as they see fit, so that they don't have to send messengers back here to ask permission to retreat or advance. You have capable men under your command – let them do their jobs.'

'You think we should attack the marines?'

'If we wish to prevent them from assaulting the Chain Castle, then yes, sir.'

'Many will die.'

'Yes, sir. That is the nature of a battle.'

Lahnos watched as the Gunstian marines toiled under the overcast sky. A few catapults seemed operational, but none had yet been loosed against the walls of the keep. The wooden tower had reached the height of two yards, and the sounds of hammering and sawing were drifting over the headland in the easterly breeze.

'Summon the battalion commanders,' he said. 'We shall attack.'

'I suggest that we organise skirmish lines, sir,' said an Aucterian captain ten years older than Lahnos, 'and probe the Gunstian defences for weaknesses. Platoon-strength attacks, staggered across the entire front, with the main body of soldiers in reserve, ready to move into any gaps that can be exploited.'

'That's too complicated,' said another officer. 'It might succeed if we had properly-trained Aucterians or Bullan carrying out the assault, but the Zamatans will make a mess of such manoeuvres.'

'But a full frontal assault could fail,' said the captain. 'The Gunstians have five hundred men in those ditches, and the Zamatans will have to charge across open ground. Any that make it as far as the ditch will be incapacitated by the Gifted agent.'

'We should wait for the hours of darkness,' said another officer; 'and launch a diversionary attack from the west, while the rest of the first wave crawls across the fields.'

'If the Zamatans aren't up to daytime manoeuvres,' said another, 'then what makes you think they'll manage it in the dark?'

The four battalion commanders turned to Lahnos, waiting for him to say something.

'Might I ask, sir,' said a captain; 'what is the purpose of the assault you wish us to carry out? Are we trying to destroy the Gunstians marines, or merely tie them down?'

'We are trying to prevent them from attacking the walls of the Chain Castle,' said Lahnos. 'Their attention needs to be on us. We all know what will happen if the chains are lowered.'

The officer nodded. 'Then I recommend that you order a full frontal assault, sir. That will certainly draw their attention.'

'It will also lead to an unacceptable number of casualties.'

'Unfortunately, sir, with the resources at our command, casualties will be unavoidable. If we try to be too clever, the Zamatan regiments will be slaughtered; if we do nothing, then the chains will be lowered and that fate will befall us all; but if we attack, hard and fast, and then pull back again, then only some will be killed. It is a cruel formula, sir, and the decision is yours.'

Lahnos lowered his gaze. Already, the time taken to summon the battalion commanders and discuss their options had seen the Gunstian siege tower almost double in height. A row of six catapults were also aiming at the Chain Castle, and heaps of rubble taken from the dry stone walls that criss-crossed the fields sat behind each. Ringing the artillery, the semi-circular ditch network had been extended, and half of the Gunstian marines were occupying the trenches, their weapons ready. Across the gap of no-man's-land, the four Zamatan battalions – two from each regiment – were lined up, their shields facing the enemy positions.

'We could have some of the men carry torches and fuel, sir,' the captain went on. 'If there is a breakthrough, we could set that tower ablaze.'

'The attack will proceed,' said Lahnos. 'How long do you need to get ready?'

The four officers glanced at each other.

'Half an hour, sir?' said one.

Lahnos nodded, as a sickened feeling grew in the pit of his stomach. 'Do it. Attack the Gunstian lines with all four battalions. Kill as many of the bastards as you can.'

The officers saluted.

'A whistle shall be blown thirty minutes from now, gentlemen,' said Efizel. 'Ensure your battalions are in position by then.'

The four officers strode away, talking among themselves as they crossed the fields towards the Zamatan regiments.

'Is Lord Rylan setting me up to fail?' Lahnos whispered.

'Perhaps, sir,' said Efizel; 'but it is equally possible that he has given your predicament not a moment's consideration.'

'I would rather be in the front lines. I don't want this responsibility.'

'You took the advice of your officers, sir. That is more than some generals ever manage to do.'

'I need to clear my head,' he said. 'I'm going for a walk for a few minutes.'

Efizel nodded, then began to walk with him as he strode towards the shoreline of the Cyasarta. Lahnos thought about telling the Bullan that he wanted to be alone, but perhaps his presence would prevent him from wallowing in despair. They reached the high line of cliffs that overlooked the Cyasarta and came to a halt. Below them snaked a narrow path that led from the keep of the Chain Castle to a small jetty at the base of the cliffs. The jetty was located on the inner side of the great double chains that stretched across the inlet, and three small vessels were tied up there, delivering supplies to the garrison holding out in the castle. On the far side of the chains, several Gunstian warships were anchored across the full width of the straits, with the bulk of the Imperial Fleet positioned half a mile to the east. Lahnos turned his gaze to the south. The Chain Castle on the opposite side of the Cyasarta had not yet been attacked, but an entire Zamatan battalion had been sent to reinforce its garrison, and was camped outside the castle walls.

'I cannot see any sign of Lords Rylan and Givra, sir,' said Efizel.

'They have probably returned to Igatz,' said Lahnos. 'Rylan must have a plan.'

'I hope you are right, sir.'

'What do we need to win today?'

'Artillery, sir.'

Lahnos narrowed his eyes. 'We have none; you know this. My uncle destroyed the entire stock of artillery when he launched his night attack on Lord Malum's fleet. What about something that isn't an impossibility?'

'Luck, sir. A few Gifted of our own would also help. If we could kill or capture the Gifted Gunstian embedded among the marines, then the dragons could burn the rest of them.'

'All right; how is this for a plan? I get myself captured. The Gifted will question me, and I touch his skin and kill him. Then the dragons return and take care of the rest.'

Efizel eyed him. 'Is that a serious proposition, sir?'

'Not really.'

'Its greatest flaw is not its recklessness; I am used to you behaving recklessly, sir. No, it is its reliance upon Lord Rylan. After yesterday, when you refused to hand over Major Lyla, I fear that you have become a liability to our new Governor. Were your plan to succeed, then I suspect that he would wait until you have been executed before unleashing an inferno; either that, or he would simply burn you, too.'

'Do you really believe that?'

'You are harbouring the Demon Witch, sir – the greatest enemy the dragons have ever faced. Not even the mightiest among the Gifted could have slain King Gahad, such was his strength; and his children and grandchildren are each weak in comparison. Yet Rylan dare not move against you openly, not while the majority of the soldiers upon this island follow you.'

'We'll see if they still follow me after four battalions charge the enemy lines,' said Lahnos. 'I don't think I can watch.'

'You must, sir. Do not turn away; keep your gaze upon your soldiers as they fight and die. It is the least they deserve.'

Lahnos was back by the elevated edge of the vineyards when the Bullan soldiers blew the whistles to mark the start of the attack. The Gunstians had been watching the Zamatans prepare their charge, and were waiting in the ditches, ready. Work had paused on the construction of the siege tower to allow more marines to defend the site, and their lines were bristling with crossbows as the Zamatans began their advance. The ground between the two forces was flat and without cover, excepting the remains of a few dry stone walls denuded by the Gunstians for their catapults. The lead Zamatan ranks picked up their pace, their shields raised, while a second wave set off after them, their boots thumping off the ground. The first soldiers entered crossbow range, and the shooting began. The Gunstians were aiming at a slight incline, and the bolts were dropping among the soldiers crossing the field; and Lahnos forced himself to watch as the Zamatans started to fall in numbers. Over by the left of the Gunstian defences, a tall man in robes raised his arm, and four Zamatans fell screaming to the ground, dropping their weapons and shields and rolling in agony. The garrison manning the Chain Castle also began loosing, sending bolts and rocks down into any Gunstian who had ventured too close to the curtain walls.

The battle lasted twenty minutes. Three times the Zamatans reached the ditches and engaged in ferocious hand-to-hand fighting with the Gunstian marines, and three times they were repulsed. Someone managed to throw a lit torch at a cluster of catapults and two were set alight, the smoke and flames rising into the grey sky. The Gifted agent moved around the front line, appearing in places where the Gunstian defences were close to collapsing, and Zamatans tortured by the Gift of Pain were dragged back to safety by their comrades. When they had been repulsed for a third time, Lahnos signalled to the Bullan, and the whistles were blown to sound the general retreat. The Zamatans pulled back, leaving over a hundred dead and wounded littering the field.

Lahnos stared at the bodies lying amid the mud and the drifting smoke. Each dead soldier had survived Gunst only to have their blood stain a battlefield in Zamata; while the cries of the wounded tore at his ears.

'Should I summon the battalion commanders, sir?' said Efizel.

Before Lahnos could respond, a large shadow passed overhead, and he turned to see Lord Rylan land by the vineyard.

'Explain yourself, General Laimos,' the dragon said. 'Why have you ceased your offensive?'

'I just lost over a hundred soldiers in twenty minutes, my lord,' said Lahnos.

'You need to press home the attack,' said Rylan. 'Don't give the Gunstians time to regroup and rest.'

'And will you help us, my lord?'

Rylan stared at him.

'If you were to join the attack, my lord, then your presence might be enough to tip the scales.'

'You saw what that Gifted agent did to me and my kin, did you not?' said Rylan.

'Yes, but you could draw the agent's attention while we charge the marines.'

'Do you secretly crave my death, Laimos? Are you in league with the Demon Witch; are you conspiring with her to usurp my power over this island?'

Lahnos's gaze tightened. 'No. I am trying to defend this island. Why aren't you doing the same?'

'How dare you?' growled Rylan. 'I am the Governor of Zamata. This is my island, Laimos, not yours.'

'Then fight for it,' said Lahnos, 'or are you all talk? Are you happy to watch us bleed while you sit in your palace?'

Rylan raised a forelimb, and extended his long, razor-sharp talons towards Lahnos, who remained where he was, his fists clenched.

'You filthy little wretch,' Rylan growled. 'I think you may have outlived your usefulness.'

'The regiments are watching, my lord,' said Efizel.

The dragon turned his neck, and his gaze roamed over the masses of Zamatan soldiers who had returned to their starting positions. Some were attending to the wounds of their comrades, but most were staring at the dragon.

Rylan lowered his claws. 'General Laimos,' he said, 'I expect your regiments to attack the Gunstian positions until you have driven them into the sea. While you do this, I shall continue to protect the chains, to prevent any Gunstian ship from trying to cut through them.' He turned to Efizel. 'And, you, Bullan – inform your renegade kin in Tsallon Anura that I shall greatly reward the soldier who brings me the head of Major Lyla.'

He extended his great wings and took off, sending a wave of dust from the vineyards gusting into Lahnos's face.

'You have a talent for angering the high and mighty, sir,' said Efizel.

'At least I can do something right. Order the battalions to regroup, form up their lines, and continue the assault. If we have no dragon to help us, then we will have to do the job ourselves.'

The battle raged on in fits and starts throughout the rest of the day. The casualties sustained by the Zamatans rose inexorably, but each attack wore away more of the Gunstians. As the sun was almost touching the mountains in the west, a squad of Zamatans managed to set fire to the wooden siege tower, and Lahnos ordered a withdrawal. As they pulled back, the Gunstians extinguished the flames, but the structure collapsed a few minutes later, eliciting a loud cheer from the exhausted Zamatans. Orders were given for the regiments to camp for the night, and the battlefield settled down into silence, as both sides nursed their losses.

Throughout the day, Lahnos had kept half an eye on Lord Rylan, who had periodically swooped over the chains in the centre of the Cyasarta, demonstrating his presence to the watching Gunstian fleet. He departed the straits when he saw the Zamatans pull back, and Lahnos prepared to do the same.

'I have a casualty report, sir,' said Efizel. 'I have spoken to each of the battalion commanders, and they have provided me with estimates.'

Lahnos said nothing. It was a five mile walk to Tsallon Anura, and he was impatient to leave.

'Approximately three hundred dead,' Efizel went on, 'and the same number injured. Half of those wounded are still on the battlefield; should we approach the Gunstians and request a truce to collect our dead and wounded, sir?'

Lahnos nodded, his mind a foggy blur. Six hundred casualties out of two thousand?

'We have also estimated the Gunstian losses, sir,' Efizel said. 'We think they have suffered roughly two hundred dead, perhaps two hundred and fifty; with maybe another hundred too wounded to fight tomorrow. We destroyed three catapults and the siege engine, but the Gunstians have enough wood to begin the construction of another tower.'

'Appoint the most experienced battalion officer to take command of the camp tonight.'

'Why, sir?'

'Because I am going back to the monastery.'

'You are leaving the regiments, sir?'

'Yes. I don't trust Rylan. I think he may attempt to snatch Major Lyla tonight, and I need to be there to stop him. Tell the other Bullan here to come with me; we will return at dawn.'

. . .

The road to Kaugatz was busy. Heading west along with Lahnos and the Bullan were carts loaded with wounded soldiers, while, in the other direction, wagons were being sent to the front with supplies for the two regiments. The oxen spared for the ploughing season were hitched to each vehicle, and the going was slow. Amid all the hornless Zamatans, Lahnos and the Bullan were easy to recognise, and many civilians glanced at them with troubled eyes, the rumours of the day's losses having spread quickly through the streets of Kaugatz. A few cheered Lahnos when they saw him, but others were already mourning their fallen kin, and the carts full of the injured were swamped by anxious relatives as soon as they reached the built-up area.

Five hundred Zamatans had been left behind to garrison the monastery, and they opened the gates to Lahnos and the Bullan. Lahnos ignored the worried soldiers inside the compound and made straight for Leona's apartment. He bounded up the stairs, Efizel just a pace behind, and almost staggered in relief when Leona opened her front door.

'Is everyone all right?' he said.

'We're fine,' said Leona, her eyes narrowing. 'I heard about the battle. You destroyed the siege tower?'

'I didn't do anything,' Lahnos said, as he entered. 'I'm going to sleep here tonight; I'll take the couch.'

Leona eyed him as she closed the door. 'Why?'

'Because Rylan thinks I'm conspiring with the Demon Witch to remove him from power. He nearly killed me today. He might come here. I'm going to place soldiers all around this apartment block, and we should stay clear of the balcony.'

Leona turned to the balcony. 'Arrosa – come inside.'

The girl walked through the balcony doors and scowled at Lahnos. 'What's he doing here? I thought he was trying to kill Gunstians? Has he come for me?'

'Stay off the balcony for now,' said Leona.

'Why?' said the girl.

'Rylan wants Lyla,' Lahnos said, 'and he may come here to try to kill her.'

Lyla emerged from her room. 'What did you say, Lahnos? Is the dragon coming for me?'

'I don't know,' said Lahnos, 'but I'm not taking any chances.'

He walked to the front door and opened it. Efizel was standing outside with the three Bullan guards assigned to protect the women and girl in the apartment.

'Get every Bullan into this building,' he said, 'and I want a company of Zamatan soldiers guarding the perimeter; and scouts on the walls watching for any approaching dragon.'

The Bullan glanced at each other.

'If Lord Rylan comes,' Lahnos said, 'then we shall resist him. Is that understood?'

Efizel saluted. 'Yes, sir.'

Lahnos slipped back into the apartment and locked the door. He turned, and saw Leona, Lyla and Arrosa all staring at him.

Lahnos sat down heavily onto the couch, and Lyla joined him.

'If that beast Rylan attacks us with flames,' said Arrosa, 'then everyone inside this building will die.'

'He won't attack,' said Leona. 'If he does, he will lose all support among the Zamatans and the island's defences will collapse.'

'Maybe he doesn't care any more!' Arrosa yelled.

'He cares,' said Leona. 'The Gunstians will torture and kill him if they take this island, and he knows it.' She glanced at Lahnos. 'He may hate us, but he still needs us.'

CHAPTER 23
UNPROVOKED

Igatz, Serpent Isle – 10th Kolinch 1588

The cavernous quarters were far easier to clean with no dragon present, and Cisca was able to sweep, mop and scrub the shadowy corners of the hall that she had previously missed. Lord Givra had been surprised that morning when the Governor of the island had called for him to join the attack on the Gunstian marines, but he had accepted the summons without complaint, and had departed, giving Cisca several hours to work undisturbed. She cleared out the remainder of the soiled blankets and gutted the storeroom, removing everything with a bad odour clinging to it. It was laborious, but she threw herself into it, so that she didn't have time to think about Bauchlie, Jair, the Dominion, or any of the other things that occupied her thoughts as she lay in bed each night.

Midway through the afternoon, she was interrupted by one of the people who had been keeping her awake.

'It certainly smells a lot better in here,' Jair said, as he strode into the chamber.

Cisca came to attention and saluted, her left hand clutching the handle of a mop.

'Lord Givra will be returning soon,' he said, his eyes on the glass sparkling in the balcony doors. 'You've done a decent job here; perhaps I should get you round to clean my apartment.'

'Is that an order, sir?'

He eyed her. 'No, Captain; it was a joke. You were supposed to laugh. You know, it's a pity that you wasted so much time cleaning this place, as it will shortly be unoccupied.' He reached into a pocket and withdrew a small ceramic bottle. 'Take this.'

Cisca picked up the bottle from his extended palm. 'What is it, sir?'

'Pour the contents into Lord Givra's water trough.'

'What will the effects be? Will he realise that something is wrong?'

Jair smiled. 'Just do as I say.' He glanced around at the chamber. 'Lord Givra will be back soon, so it would be best if you pour it into his water now. I shall watch.'

Cisca stared at the small vessel in her hand, then she turned to glance at the long water trough positioned close to the balcony doors. Was it poison? Lord Givra was a grandchild of Gahad, and was presumably resistant to many different poisons; but if there was any substance that could harm or incapacitate him, even temporarily, then Lord Rylan and Jair would know. Jair's eyes narrowed a little, and she walked over to the trough. She pulled the little stopper from the end of the vessel and emptied its clear contents into Givra's water supply. Cisca stood over the trough for a few moments, but could detect no change in the smell, and the water seemed clean and pure. Had it just been another test of her obedience? Perhaps there had been nothing but water in the ceramic bottle, and Jair had been pushing her, to see how far she was willing to go.

Jair gave her a slight nod. 'There's something else I felt you should know, Cisca.'

'Yes, sir?'

'I sent scouts up to Medamuna Gatzoun.'

Cisca turned to face him.

'They discovered the bodies of those who had been poisoned,' he went on. 'Bauchlie was among them. The rebel commander is dead.'

Cisca tried to retain her composure as her blood chilled.

Jair smiled. 'I thought you would be more pleased, Cisca. The man who held you prisoner can no longer hurt you. You are free of him.'

He turned and strode away, leaving the chamber through a side door. Cisca remained where she was, her hands still clutching onto the ceramic container.

Bauchlie. Was it true? Had the rebel commander died along with the others when the ale had been poisoned? If so, then nothing remained on the island for her. She thought back to the small glimpses of kindness that she had seen within him. Perhaps, if things had been different, then the two of them might have stood a chance... She stopped herself. It was over. She quelled the tears that threatened to leak from her eyes. Lord Givra was coming, and she was still holding the vessel that she had emptied into his water trough.

She walked to the storeroom and dropped the container into a large bin, then she re-arranged some of the contents to hide it. She was reminded of the way that Lady Takri had used her in Zamata Gataza; once again, she was being blackmailed into doing the bidding of others.

She heard the sound of the tall doors opening, and turned to see Lord Givra enter his quarters. Cisca steadied her features, and then she hurried from the storeroom and bowed low. She tried to push Bauchlie from her mind. She was an officer, and she needed to hide her feelings from the dragon.

'My lord,' she said; 'welcome back.'

'What a waste of time that proved to be,' the dragon said. 'Rylan had every dragon out, but he abandoned the attack on the Gunstians as soon as the Gift of Pain was unleashed. Coward.' He raised his head a fraction. 'What is that smell?'

Cisca swallowed. 'Smell, my lord?'

'Yes. I enjoy the smell of a clean chamber. Well done, Captain; what an improvement.'

'Thank you, my lord.'

'Lady Natali and Lord Sigum have been sent away again,' the dragon went on, as he strode further into the cavernous hall; 'and Lord Rylan is out flying alone, watching his useless soldiers fail to dislodge the Gunstians from their positions. It would be amusing were it not so tragic.'

'Lady Natali and Lord Sigum have gone, my lord?'

'Yes. I assume that they will return tomorrow, after chasing a few more boats across the vastness of the ocean. If I plan to do anything to alter my situation, it will be tonight.'

'What do you intend to do, my lord?'

He glanced at her. 'I am still unsure whether to completely trust you, Captain. I want to, but Lord Rylan has many spies working for him, all under the control of that vile rodent Jair.'

Cisca flinched a little at the mention of the captain's name.

'I sense that you hold Rylan's favourite human in contempt,' said the dragon; 'or was that fear in your eyes?'

Cisca said nothing, and the dragon walked towards the balcony, and the water trough. Cisca quashed the rising panic as she watched. Did she want Rylan to kill Givra? Or would it be better if Givra deposed the Governor? Did it matter? Both dragons seemed equally ruthless and arrogant. Rylan talked about uniting the island, but his actions seemed to offer only proof of his desire for power; while Givra would likely betray the Zamatans in order to win the chance to return to Inopei. For once, Cisca thought, she should act in her own interests. With Bauchlie gone, she realised that she longed to return to the East. She stared at the dragon as he began to lower his jaws towards the trough.

'Stop!' she cried.

Givra turned his head to look at her.

'Don't drink the water,' she said. 'Jair forced me to put something in it.'

'What – poison? It smells fresh enough.'

'I don't know what it was. It might be nothing; perhaps he was testing my loyalty, to see if I would do it. Please wait here, my lord.'

She ran to the storeroom and rummaged in the bin until her fingers clasped hold of the ceramic vessel. She held it up, then hurried back to the dragon.

'This is the bottle Jair gave me; then he watched as I poured it into the trough.'

Givra stared at her, then he lowered his head a fraction and sniffed the ceramic vessel.

'I recognise the odour,' he said. 'Jair gave you this? Are you his spy?'

'He is my commanding officer. He ordered me to do it. I asked him what it was, but he wouldn't say.'

'It is a remedy extracted from poppy seeds, designed to render a dragon unconscious for a short time,' said Givra. 'Had I drunk my fill, I would have soon succumbed to its powers. Captain Cisca, I owe you my life; for it is clear to me now why the so-called Governor has sent his sister and Lord Sigum away. He means to destroy me; but I shall destroy him instead.' He raised his head, his eyes glowing with rage. 'I will rampage through this palace, killing and burning; and I shall tear out the throat of my worthless uncle.'

Cisca took a step back. 'There is another way, my lord. A more subtle way.'

'And does your way also result in the death of Rylan and his minions?'

'It does, my lord.'

'Then speak on, my faithful servant,' the dragon said; 'I am listening.'

Cisca ran through the wide marble hallways of the palace. Grief, uncertainty, fear, and no small measure of guilt coursed through her as she hurried towards the main audience chamber within the centre of the palace. For better or worse, she had chosen her side. If successful, she would be able to leave the Serpent Isle at last, and sail with Lord Givra to Inopei and her old life. She tried not to think about what would happen to the Zamatans if Givra was victorious and then made a deal with the Gunstians. If she got back to Nom Karta alive, she could put it all behind her. Perhaps the dragons would allow her to see Lord Kheran again, and she could spend the rest of her life caring for the young grandson of Gahad, instead of being trapped amid the wide ocean.

She reached the arched entrance to the audience chamber and peered inside. Lord Rylan had returned, and was speaking to Captain Jair in hushed tones. Cisca emitted a low cough, and they turned to gaze at her.

Jair strode across the marble floor towards Cisca. 'Say nothing,' he said. 'Just nod if Lord Givra has quenched his thirst this evening.'

Cisca nodded.

Jair turned back to the Governor. 'It is done, my lord.'

The grey and yellow dragon took a few steps forward, then lowered his head. 'Is his lordship asleep?'

Cisca bowed her head. 'Yes, my lord.'

'Then Major Lyla will have to wait, for it is time to deal with Lord Givra,' said Rylan. 'When Lady Natali arrives back at the palace tomorrow, she shall be told that I was the victim of another unprovoked attack. Lord Givra has never given me his full support, and was merely waiting to catch me alone in the palace.'

'That is the truth of it, my lord,' said Jair.

The two captains stood to the side as Lord Rylan began to walk from the hall.

'What should I do now, sir?' Cisca said.

'You will be coming with us,' said Jair. 'I shall need you to dispose of the evidence. Empty and scrub the trough, and refill it with fresh water. You will also need your mop again; this might get a little messy.'

They waited until Rylan had left the hall, then followed him towards Givra's quarters.

'What did the Governor mean by *Major Lyla will have to wait*, sir?' whispered Cisca.

Jair shrugged. 'That is none of your concern. Concentrate on the next few minutes.'

They passed several Bullan soldiers on guard duty, who saluted the dragon, and Cisca held her tongue. She could feel a knot of anxious tension in the pit of her stomach, but she was getting better at controlling her features. If nothing else, Lady Takri and Captain Jair had transformed her into a proficient liar. She thought over Lord Rylan's words again. Inadvertently or not, he had said *another* unprovoked attack, as though he had also engineered the death of Lord Gradham. She remembered being glad that Bauchlie had not taken Rylan's life beneath Zamata Gataza; he had seemed more reasonable than Lord Malum and Lady Macsin, though he had also been afraid of them. Had Cisca been wrong about Rylan, or had power twisted him until he was no longer recognisable?

The dragon came to a halt outside the tall doors leading to Givra's quarters.

'My friend and kin,' Rylan called out; 'my noble nephew; may I enter?'

No response came from within.

'Lord Givra,' Rylan went on, 'I must speak with you; it is urgent. Are you at home?'

Again, there was nothing but silence from the dragon's quarters. Lord Rylan extended a forelimb and pushed at the door. It swung open, revealing the dark interior. A shaft of light was coming in through the balcony doors, and the shape of a resting dragon was visible in the thick shadows in the corner of the chamber.

'Lord Givra?' said Rylan. 'Are you awake?'

The dragon within remained still and silent. Rylan turned his head to Jair.

'Get in there,' he said. 'Check that Givra is held deep within the bounds of unconsciousness.'

'Yes, my lord,' said the captain.

Jair strode forwards and entered the chamber. He approached the dragon, his boots rapping off the polished floor, and stopped a yard from the massive head. He stared at the dragon for a few moments, then reached out with a hand and pushed at his face.

'Wake up, my lord,' he said. 'Lord Givra, wake up.'

The dragon remained still, apart from the low sound of his breathing. Jair drew his sword, and poked the scales of the dragon with the tip of the blade, scoring a line just under an ear.

Nothing.

Lord Rylan walked into the lair, then he turned his neck to look at Cisca.

'Enter, and close the doors, human,' he said.

'Yes, my lord,' said Cisca, bowing. She hurried into the chamber and swung the double doors shut behind her.

'Now you, my faithful officer,' Rylan said to Jair. 'Stand by Captain Cisca, and ensure no one enters.'

Jair bowed low, then walked to the door. He sheathed his sword and stood next to Cisca.

'You did well,' he murmured to her. 'Once this is over, we shall see what other little jobs you can do for me, Captain Cisca.'

Cisca said nothing, her gaze fixed on Rylan. The grey and yellow dragon walked up to Givra, and sniffed him.

'So, Givra Mon Girvine,' Rylan said, 'you are helpless, and you are mine. Did you believe that you could defy my will with impunity? There is but one Governor of Zamata, and it is I, not you. You were ever unworthy, ever spiteful, ever narrow-minded. Had you submitted to my reign, you could have been a useful servant, but now your fate is set, and you will feed the crows of Igatz this night. They will feast upon your broken flesh, and I shall rejoice at the sight.'

Rylan raised his head and opened his great jaws. 'Die alone and friendless, son of Girvine.'

Givra launched himself upwards, the claws on both forelimbs extended, and ripped great wounds down Rylan's chest. Rylan staggered back in shock and pain, and Givra's head lunged at him. Rylan moved his neck, and Givra's jaws clamped onto his shoulder, his fangs piercing Rylan's scales as they closed. Rylan screamed in agony, then brought up his own forelimbs, his claws tearing three bloody lines down the side of Givra's face. Givra released Rylan's shoulder, and the grey and yellow dragon retreated, smashing through the double doors as Jair and Cisca dived out of the way. Givra followed Rylan, and the two dragons faced each other in the wide hallway outside his quarters.

'I could barely contain my laughter during your pathetic little speech,' Givra said. 'Did you think I would be tricked by a sleeping elixir, usurper and traitor?'

Rylan stared at him, as blood dripped down from his chest and right shoulder, splashing onto the marble floor.

'Nothing more to say?' Givra said, as he edged forward. 'That makes a welcome change.'

Givra sprang forward, and Rylan responded, the two dragons raising their forelimbs and clashing amid the hallway. Their heads darted out at each other, then Rylan sent a burst of flames into Givra's eyes, and he roared in agony. Back by the doorway, Cisca pulled herself to her feet, then she felt the blade of a sword next to her throat.

'Don't move,' said Jair, pushing her against the wall. 'You lying little bitch.'

'No!' Cisca cried. 'I did exactly what you told me to do – you saw me empty the vessel into his water.'

Jair narrowed his eyes, then he lowered the sword as several Bullan soldiers ran into the hallway. They stared from one dragon to the other, their weapons ready.

'Loose at my enemy, Bullan!' Lord Rylan cried, as he retreated from Givra again.

'Do not listen to the words of a traitor,' Givra said. 'Kill the one who has forsaken the Dominion – you know your duty, Bullan.'

The Bullan soldiers did nothing. Givra lunged at Rylan again, and scored fresh wounds across the other dragon's flank with his claws, and Rylan retreated once more.

'Come back, you coward!' Givra cried.

Rylan fled through the wide passageways of the palace, trailing blood, as Givra gave chase. Aucterian soldiers were bowled over by a sweeping tail as the two dragons reached the hall by the main entrance of the palace. Outside, the lamps of the garden had been lit, and the waxing moon was shining over Igatz. Rylan backed away, and came up against the marble frame of the entrance, and Givra pounced. The two dragons wrestled by the open doors, each using their hind limbs to gouge and slash, while their jaws went for each other's necks. They rolled in one direction, crushing a soldier trying to flee from his post by the doors, then they rolled the other way, and crashed through the entrance and down the wide marble steps, tearing the doors to pieces as fragments of masonry fell from the arched opening. The dragons reached the expanse of lawn, their limbs still entwined and their claws flashing red, while more soldiers appeared, their eyes wide as they stared. Jair grabbed Cisca by the arm and pulled her to the side of the palace entrance, where they stood next to a growing crowd of Aucterians and Bullan. Other soldiers ran out from their posts by the wall enclosing the garden to watch, and Cisca saw groups of civilians staring through the iron fence at the battling dragons.

Rylan ran his claws down Givra's face, tearing through his ears and gouging out his left eye. Givra howled in pain, and rolled back, felling half a dozen trees that lined a path. Rylan moved in, his jaws open, and Givra blasted him with flames. For a moment, Rylan's head and shoulders were invisible behind the roiling fires, then his jaws darted out and he tore a great gash down Givra's right wing. Rylan stamped a heavy forelimb onto Givra's neck, then his jaws released the wing and clamped round Givra's throat. Givra writhed and struggled, his limbs thrashing around, but Rylan's grip held.

By the entrance, the crowd had become so large that Cisca and Jair were pushed forward. Jair's foot slipped in a pool of dragon blood on the top step, and he fell, pulling Cisca with him. Cisca lashed out as she tumbled down the stairs, and her fist caught Jair's eye. He let go of her as his hand went to his face, and Cisca ran.

She heard a sickening crack of bones splintering as she sprinted down a path towards the gates, and turned her head. Rylan's jaws were still clamped around his enemy's neck, and Givra's head was hanging limp. Rylan used his forelimbs to rip the head from its shoulders, then he threw the head to the side and roared in triumph.

Cisca reached the gates surrounding the palace gardens, where every soldier was standing frozen, their eyes fixed on the sight of Rylan's victory. Cisca leapt up onto the fence, climbed, and then swung her legs over. She landed on the other side amid a crowd of terrified Aucterian civilians and kept running, oblivious to whether she was being followed. Fear powered her steps, and she raced away from the palace, until Rylan's roars had faded into silence.

It was past midnight by the time she reached her destination. She had changed her mind several times on her flight from the Dragon Palace, and was still unsure if she had chosen correctly as she approached the high battlements. She had considered returning to Medamuna Gatzoun to look for Bauchlie's body, and she had even given serious thought to hiding on board the empty dragon carrier anchored in the Cyasarta; but, in the end, she had chosen a different place to seek refuge.

Two soldiers in the uniform of the old Zamatan militia were standing by the gates, and they eyed her as she approached.

'My name is Captain Cisca of the Dragon Corps,' she said, 'and I am here to see Lahnos Laimos.'

Ten minutes later, Cisca was sitting alone in a small chamber to the rear of the monastery chapel. Soldiers were guarding the entrance, but no one had spoken to her since she had been admitted into Tsallon Anura. She wondered what was happening in the Dragon Palace. Was Jair searching for her? Would he guess where she had gone? And what was Lord Rylan doing? Givra had dealt the Governor several nasty-looking wounds, which would take time to heal.

A Bullan soldier opened the door. 'On your feet,' he said.

Cisca stood.

'Are you armed?'

'No.'

'What is the purpose of your visit?'

'To ask Lahnos to shelter me. Lord Rylan has just slain Lord Givra, to whom I was assigned, and he wants to kill me next. Please; I have nowhere else to go.'

The Bullan studied her for a few moments, his expression unreadable.

'Were you followed here?' he said.

'No. Well, I don't think so. I crossed the Cyasarta on the last ferry, and it was almost empty.'

The Bullan nodded. 'Come with me.'

She followed him out of the room, and they emerged back into the night air. The Bullan led her to a heavily-guarded building, where dozens of Zamatan soldiers were posted outside, and they passed more uniformed soldiers by the entrance. They ascended the stairs, and came to a door which had another four Bullan on duty.

'Search her,' said one of them.

Cisca lifted her arms, and a soldier patted her down.

'She's clean, sir.'

The other soldier nodded, then he opened the door. Cisca stepped inside, flanked by two Bullan. Her eyes went to the long couch, where Lahnos was sitting up, a blanket draped over him. Next to the couch, Leona was standing with a dressing gown on, her arms folded over her chest.

The Bullan soldier who had accompanied Cisca tilted his head before Lahnos and Leona.

'This Dragon Corps officer says that the Governor of Zamata has slain Lord Givra, sir, ma'am,' he said. 'She claims that she is seeking refuge, and that Lord Rylan wishes to execute her.'

'Givra's dead?' said Lahnos. 'That would explain the flames we saw in the sky over Igatz.'

Cisca narrowed her eyes. Why was Lahnos sleeping in Leona's apartment?

'She also claims that she wasn't followed,' the Bullan said.

'It makes no difference whether or not she was followed,' Leona said. 'You have chosen an odd place to hide, Cisca. We are expecting Lord Rylan to come here to attempt to arrest Major Lyla.'

'I know that,' said Cisca. 'Where else could I go? I knew that Lahnos had refused to allow Lyla to be taken away, and... and I hoped that you could protect me, too.'

'Why does Rylan want you dead?' said Lahnos.

'Because he tried to involve me in a plot to assassinate Lord Givra. I pretended to cooperate, but instead, I warned Givra, and he lay in wait for Lord Rylan. They fought all over the palace, but Rylan killed him out on the lawn. Jair had me, but I managed to escape.'

'Captain Jair was involved?' said Leona.

Cisca nodded.

'Why did you help Givra?' said Leona.

'I... I, uh...' Cisca's voice tailed away. Leona would sense any lie she uttered, and the truth would damn her. 'I need to confess something,' she said. 'It was me who told Jair about Lyla and the Demon Witch. He interrogated me, but I didn't believe your story about the Demon Witch, and so I told him.' She lowered her gaze. 'I am sorry. I didn't mean to place Lyla's life in danger.'

'Jair tried to kill her,' said Leona. 'If she had died, you would have been responsible.'

Cisca said nothing.

'And I notice that you didn't answer my question about Givra,' Leona went on. 'Instead, you offered me something else, something that Lahnos and I already suspected about you. You fled from Bauchlie, did you not, and ran straight into the arms of Jair, to whom you betrayed Lyla. Can you give us a reason not to kill you?'

Cisca shook her head. 'No.'

'Get on your knees,' said Leona.

Cisca lowered herself to the floor.

'You will give one word answers to my questions,' Leona went on. 'Are you working for Jair?'

'No.'

'Did he send you here?'

'No.'

'Does Rylan truly want you dead?'

'I… yes. I think so. I didn't wait to see if that was true, but Jair will have told him by now.'

'Told him what?'

'That I had warned Givra.'

'And why did you warn Givra?'

Cisca said nothing.

Leona turned to Lahnos. 'I am minded to send Cisca's head in a box to Lord Rylan as a present. What do you think?'

A side door opened before Lahnos could respond, and Lyla walked into the room wearing a nightdress.

'Why is everyone up in the middle of the night?' she said, then she caught sight of Cisca kneeling on the floor. Her eyes narrowed, then she gasped. 'Cisca?'

'Hello, Lyla,' Cisca said.

Lyla ran across the room, knelt by Cisca and threw her arms around her.

'You came back!' she cried, as tears fell down her cheeks. 'I missed you, Cisca. Thank you; thank you for looking after me.'

Leona frowned.

'I guess that settles it,' said Lahnos, as he got to his feet. He walked over to the two women and helped them stand.

'Lyla,' he said, 'Cisca has come here asking for our help. Lord Rylan wants to arrest her, just as he wants to arrest you. Should we let her stay?'

'Of course,' said Lyla. 'Cisca was Major Lyla's friend.'

'Major Lyla's friend?' said Cisca.

'Yes,' said Lyla, 'and I share Lyla's memories. I can remember you, you know, from before the dragon ritual; before I was placed into Lyla's body.'

Cisca stared at her. 'Then it is true? You are the Demon Witch?'

'I am Lyla,' she said, 'and I am the Demon Witch; and I have a thousand questions to ask you.'

CHAPTER 24
THE OATH BREAKER

Kaugatz, Serpent Isle – 11th Kolinch 1588

Leona lay awake on the floor of the bedroom, unable to get back to sleep after Cisca's unexpected arrival. Lyla had experienced no such problems, and Leona could hear her shallow breathing coming from the bed. Lyla may have drifted back to sleep, but in doing so she had awoken Arrosa, with whom she was sharing the bed, and the girl was fidgeting restlessly. Lahnos and Cisca were still up, their low voices seeping under the bedroom door from the living area.

'Who is Lahnos talking to?' Arrosa whispered.

Leona turned her head, but couldn't see the girl in the darkness. 'Go back to sleep.'

'I can't. Lyla's snoring. Did Reyn come back?'

'No.'

'Then who is it?'

'It's Captain Cisca.'

'The Cisca that Lyla used to talk about all the time? She's here?'

The girl moved around on the bed, then her feet touched the floor next to Leona's head.

'What are you doing?'

'I'm going to see Cisca,' said Arrosa. 'I can't sleep.'

'Wait,' said Leona. 'I'll come with you. I don't think there's much chance of me getting any more sleep tonight, either.'

She sat up, and sensed Arrosa's presence next to her. 'It will be dawn soon; we might as well get dressed. But do it quietly, so we don't wake Lyla.'

Leona pulled on some clothes in the dark, and heard Arrosa do the same. A faint glow was coming in through the shutters of their east-facing window, and Leona slowly began to make out the interior of the bedroom. She yawned and stretched her arms as Arrosa finished dressing.

'I wish there was some coffee left,' she said. 'Come on.'

They went to the door and Leona opened it. Arrosa strode through into the living area, and Leona followed. Lahnos and Cisca were still on the couch, and the Dragon Corps officer was weeping softly.

'My name is Arrosa,' the girl said. 'Why are you crying?'

Cisca looked up. She glanced at the girl, but said nothing.

'Bauchlie's dead,' said Lahnos.

Leona raised an eyebrow. 'Says who?'

'Jair told me,' said Cisca. 'He sent soldiers to Medamuna Gatzoun, and they found Bauchlie's body.'

Leona kept her eyes on Cisca, but there was no tingle in the back of her mind.

'I'm not sure I would believe anything Jair told you,' she said.

Cisca wiped her eyes. 'Do you think he might have been lying to me?'

Leona shrugged. 'Maybe. I think I would have heard the news if Bauchlie was dead.'

'Cisca believes it,' said Arrosa. 'Even if it isn't true, she believes it.'

'I know,' said Leona. She narrowed her eyes. 'Lord Givra wanted to do a deal with the Gunstians, didn't he, Cisca?' she said. 'Is that why you helped him? You thought Bauchlie was dead, and you were going to betray the island so that you could return to the East.'

'Is that true?' said Lahnos. 'I heard the same story – that Givra would have allowed the Gunstians to take the island in exchange for letting him leave on the last dragon carrier.'

Cisca said nothing.

'Fortunately for the rest of us,' said Leona, 'their plan failed. Did you think that you would be able to hide this from us, Cisca?'

'I didn't know what else to do,' the Aucterian woman said, her eyes still lowered. 'With Bauchlie gone, I couldn't face being trapped on this island forever.'

Leona strode to the front door and opened it. Outside, the on-duty Bullan guards saluted her.

'I need a messenger to fetch one of my agents. His name is Saewa and he lives in the house directly opposite my old home in Kaugatz. Have him brought here as quickly as possible.'

'Yes, ma'am,' said one of the Bullan.

'Thank you,' said Leona, then she closed the door again.

'What was that all about?' said Lahnos.

'We need to discover the truth about Bauchlie,' she said. 'If he's dead, then why hasn't Rylan announced it?' She eyed Cisca. 'As for this little traitor, my idea about the box still stands.'

'What box?' said Arrosa.

'We're not going to kill her, Leona,' said Lahnos.

'Why not? She was quite happy to allow all of us to be slaughtered by the Gunstians.'

'Do you really think you are better than me?' Cisca cried, getting to her feet. 'You're a hypocrite, Leona, and your hands are bloodier than mine! Perhaps I should tell Lahnos the truth about you; about what you did that day in Kaugatz for Lord Malum.'

Leona stared at Cisca.

'What truth?' said Lahnos.

Cisca pointed a finger at Leona. 'She helped Malum and Macsin massacre the Gunstian civilians! She told me all about it, when she was pretending to be Lady Takri.'

The room fell into silence.

Arrosa glanced up at Leona's face. 'You helped the dragons kill my family?'

'I didn't help them!' Leona cried. 'But... I was there. I saw them do it, and I didn't do anything to stop them. What could I do? They would have killed me, too.'

'You wanted the Gunstians to die,' said Cisca. 'People like you will only be happy when you've got rid of everyone on this island who isn't Zamatan.'

'That's not true!' said Leona.

'Would you have done nothing if it had been Zamatans being slaughtered?'

Leona's next words faltered on her lips. If she denied Cisca's claim, then would Arrosa's Gift of Truth discern a lie? Would it be a lie? A wave of repressed guilt swept over her, and she remembered how she had felt that day in Kaugatz – the screams, the blood, the children. She looked down at Arrosa. The girl was staring at her, her features twisted in fear and anger.

'Are you Lady Takri?' Arrosa said.

'Yes, but...'

'Don't touch me!' the girl cried. 'I hate you.'

Arrosa looked as though she wanted to run away, but there was nowhere to go. She glanced at the locked balcony doors, and at the entrance guarded by the Bullan soldiers, then she burst into tears.

'How could you, Leona?' said a voice from the other side of the chamber. Lyla had emerged from the bedroom, and she was glaring at Leona. Arrosa ran to the young woman's side, and Lyla placed a protective arm around her.

'You told me it wasn't my fault,' said Leona. 'I was plagued with guilt, and you told me that there was nothing I could have done.'

Lyla narrowed her eyes. 'I don't remember that. Is she lying, Arrosa?'

'No,' said the girl.

Lahnos got to his feet. 'Did you kill any of the Gunstians yourself?'

Leona shook her head.

'Then it is wrong to say that you helped them.'

'I helped the dragons identify the Gifted agents who had destroyed the wheat fields,' Leona said. 'I thought that, if they executed the agents, then they might let the others go free. Arrosa, I'm sorry.'

'We have all made mistakes,' Lahnos went on; 'but you, Cisca, and you, Leona – your mistakes were caused by fear, and you found yourselves having to go along with the evil plans of others. Malum and Givra – they are the ones responsible, and Rylan, too. Dragons who treat this island as their personal fiefdom, or who are prepared to sell it to the Gunstians. Was our biggest mistake allying ourselves with a Child of Gahad?'

'Are you saying Bauchlie was right?' said Cisca.

'No,' said Lahnos. 'Not all dragons are evil; but the powerful ones, the immortal ones – they act as though humans are worth nothing. I'm sick of it. Yesterday, Rylan accused us of conspiring to bring him down – maybe we should start.'

'He's wounded,' said Cisca. 'Lord Givra's claws and teeth did a lot of damage.'

'But how would we get into the palace?' said Leona. 'And how would we get close enough to kill Lord Rylan? He has two hundred Bullan surrounding him.'

Lahnos glanced at Lyla. 'The Demon Witch could have done it. She would have made us invisible.'

'I don't know how to do that any more,' Lyla said; 'and even if I could remember, then maybe my old powers don't work properly in a new body.'

'Lahnos could do it,' whispered Arrosa. 'He has the right Gifts.'

Lahnos frowned. 'I could hardly touch every single Bullan soldier in the Dragon Palace, and my head would explode from all those memories.'

'I'm not talking about those Gifts,' the girl said. 'I mean the other one.'

'This again?' said Lahnos. 'I've told you; I don't have any other Gifts.'

'Did you know you were a death-reader before it happened?' Arrosa said. 'Or a death-seer? Most Gifted people never find out about their Gifts. I sense them all the time; they walk about Kaugatz, thinking they're ordinary people; but they're not. I passed an old man last year who had the Gift of Despair, but he didn't know anything about it. He lived his whole life not knowing he was Gifted.'

'What other Gift does Lahnos have?' said Leona.

The girl scowled at Leona and said nothing.

Lahnos shook his head and sat. He reached for his boots and began to pull them on.

'Where are you going?' said Lyla.

'Back to the Chain Castle,' he said. 'I have a job to do.'

'Don't you want to know about your Gift?'

'Arrosa will tell me if she wants to,' he said. 'Remember that she believes me to be a demon; and demons don't deserve Gifts.'

'That's right,' said Arrosa.

'But this new Gift could help us,' said Leona.

Arrosa ignored her.

'Don't be mean to Leona,' said Lyla. 'She said she was sorry; it wasn't her fault that the Gunstians were killed. The dragons killed them, not her.'

'We'll try to think of a way to get to Lord Rylan when I get back,' Lahnos said, as he stood.

'I might know a way into the Dragon Palace,' said Cisca; 'a way that could get us past the Bullan soldiers.'

Sudden movement through the balcony windows distracted Leona before she could reply, and she turned. The predawn light was spreading in the east, and she could see dozens of soldiers running through the grounds of the monastery, then her gaze went to the battlements. Soldiers there were pointing and shouting, then the form of an enormous dragon rose into view. His great grey and yellow wings were extended, and the wounds across his chest and flanks were visible.

'Rylan!' Leona cried. 'He is here.'

Lahnos and the others rushed to the balcony windows, as Lord Rylan hovered over the ancient battlements of Tsallon Anura. He eased forward, then lowered himself down into the open area in the centre of the cloisters, his talons scoring the flagstones as he landed.

'Soldiers of Zamata,' the dragon's voice boomed out; 'I am here to speak to General Laimos. Where is he?'

'Stand back from the balcony,' Lahnos said to the others in the room; 'and stay out of sight.'

He took a key from a pocket and unlocked the balcony door.

'If you are going out there,' said Leona, 'then I will stand by your side. Lyla, take Cisca and Arrosa, and hide in the bedroom. Please.'

Lyla nodded, and shepherded Arrosa away from the glass doors, then Cisca followed them into the other room. Lahnos pushed the door open and then he and Leona stepped out on to the balcony. Down in the cloister, Rylan was surrounded by hundreds of Zamatan soldiers, many of whom were staring at the wounds covering his body.

'My lord,' said Lahnos; 'I am here.'

Rylan raised his head and stared at Lahnos. 'It grieves me that I have been forced to come to Tsallon Anura in person, General Laimos,' he said, 'but you have left me with no alternative. You are harbouring a wanted fugitive, a danger not only to this island, but to the entire world. If you hand Major Lyla over into my custody, then I am prepared to forgive and forget – as the unity of Zamata is more important than punishing you for disobedience.'

'And if I refuse?' said Lahnos.

'If you refuse,' said Rylan, 'then my wrath will be terrible to behold. To your feeble human eyes I may seem wounded and vulnerable, but do not be fooled. I remain more than a match for the soldiers in this monastery. I will burn and kill, and the end result will be the same; only the defence of this island will have been weakened by your intransigence. Do you care so little for Zamata, General Laimos?'

'You would murder five hundred soldiers?' said Lahnos. 'Can we not have a civilised conversation first? The Demon Witch is not who you think she is. She is not trying to destroy the Dominion.'

'I will give her a fair hearing if you hand her over; I swear it.'

'He's lying,' Leona whispered.

Lahnos nodded. 'Did you give Lord Givra a fair hearing, noble Governor?'

'That vile dragon wanted to betray Zamata to the Gunstians – he deserved to die.'

'You tried to drug him first, so that you could kill him as he slept. What happened to your honour, Lord Rylan?'

'Who has told you these foul lies?' Rylan cried. 'Is Captain Cisca here? Is this where that cowardly little traitor fled? If you have her, Laimos, you would be wise to hand her over as well.'

'Why don't we defeat the Gunstians first,' said Lahnos, 'and then we can resume this disagreement when the island is safe?'

The dragon turned his gaze towards the hundreds of soldiers within the grounds of the ancient monastery.

'Do you hear what General Laimos is saying, men of Zamata?' Rylan said. 'He swore an oath and was greatly rewarded with titles and power; and yet he is refusing to obey an order from his sovereign lord. He is harbouring dangerous rebels, traitors and fugitives; hiding them inside Tsallon Anura. Why would he do such a thing? Is it possible that he is trying to usurp power? Look at the woman standing by his side – Leona of Kaugatz, otherwise known as Lady Takri.'

Several soldiers stared, their mouths opening.

'Yes, it is true,' Rylan went on; 'Leona is Takri, the notorious terrorist and spy who assisted Lord Malum's cruel reign. Laimos and Leona are the true enemies of Zamata, conspiring with the Gunstians to divide the island between them.'

Lahnos laughed. 'You are a fool, Lord Rylan, if you think that anyone here will believe that I am working for the Gunstians. And I already knew that Leona and Takri were the same person. She was a spy – that part was correct. She infiltrated the inner circles of power to thwart Lord Malum, not to assist him. Are these insults the best you can do?' He laughed again. 'You should leave before you embarrass yourself even more.'

The dragon's eyes flashed with rage. 'I will ask you this question only once, General Laimos – are you loyal to the oath you swore to me?'

'I will fight the Gunstians,' Lahnos said, 'and anyone else who tries to destroy this island.'

'Listen to his words, men of Zamata!' the dragon cried. 'Lahnos Laimos is an oath breaker! His promises are empty, his vows meaningless!'

'Go back to your palace, dragon,' said Lahnos. 'You are wasting my time – I should be leading the attack on the Gunstian marines besieging the northern Chain Castle, not listening to this tantrum.'

'You are not worthy to lead my soldiers, Laimos,' said the dragon; 'and I hereby strip you of your rank and discharge you from my service. I will, however, spare your life if you give me Major Lyla, and anyone else you are protecting.'

The balcony door opened and Lyla stepped out next to Lahnos and Leona. The dragon stared at her, and sparks leapt across his open jaws.

'I am Lyla,' she said; 'I am the one you seek.'

'Get back inside,' Lahnos hissed.

'No,' said Lyla. 'Lord Rylan has come for me, and it is not fair that you suffer on my behalf.'

Rylan extended a forelimb, and reached up towards the balcony.

Lyla stared into his eyes. 'You shall not touch me.'

The huge forelimb halted two feet from her, the claws glistening in the dawn light. Rylan grunted, as though he was struggling with something, and his eyes tightened.

'You will leave us now,' said Lyla. 'Fly back to the Dragon Palace and forget about me. I am not important enough to be worthy of a dragon's time and consideration.'

Rylan took a single step backwards, his muscles tensed. 'Get out of my mind, witch,' he gasped. 'You shall not do to me what you did to Lenta and Macsin.'

Lyla raised a hand but she, too, seemed to be struggling. The soldiers down by the cloister backed away from the shuddering dragon as his rear claws gouged lines in the flagstones.

'You will leave us,' Lyla repeated. 'Go.'

'No,' grunted Rylan. 'I am the stronger, and you the weaker. You have lost much of your power since Lord Malum placed you into this new body, Demon Witch; no longer are you able to best a Child of Gahad.'

'Leave us,' Lyla cried, her hand shaking.

'I will not!' roared Rylan.

Lyla collapsed to the floor of the balcony. She convulsed, then her eyes closed. Leona crouched down next to her unconscious body, as Lahnos moved to block Rylan's way.

'I am victorious,' cried the dragon. 'I have defeated the Demon Witch, and now I shall carry her back to Igatz, where her head shall be mounted by the gates of the palace. It is over, Laimos; you have lost. Step aside, or your head will be displayed next to Major Lyla's.'

'No,' said Lahnos. 'I do not surrender my friends to their enemies. You asked me if I was loyal to you, and my answer is no. You have proved that your sole desire is for power. You are not my sovereign. You are nothing.'

Rylan opened his jaws and raised both forelimbs, preparing to strike. Twin shadows flashed overhead, and a silvery-green dragon dived down from the sky as Rylan readied himself. Sigum landed in front of the Governor, cracking dozens of flagstones as the buildings of the monastery shook.

'My lord!' Sigum cried. 'Stay your claws and fire!'

Rylan stared at the silvery-green dragon. 'Are you going to betray me, too, my old friend?'

'It is not my wish to do so, my lord,' said Sigum, 'but I will not allow you to hurt Lahnos.'

Another dragon landed behind Rylan. 'What is this, brother?' said Natali. 'Why are you here? Lord Sigum and I crossed the Cyasarta inlet on our way back from patrolling the ocean. The Gunstian marines are assaulting the northern Chain Castle, while the Zamatan regiments watch from a distance, leaderless.' Her gaze tightened. 'Who has wounded you?'

'Stay out of this, sister,' Rylan said. 'Return to the palace.'

Leona got back to her feet. 'Rylan murdered Givra,' she cried. 'Rylan tried to kill Givra as he slept, and then he ripped out his throat on the lawn of the Dragon Palace.'

Natali eyed Leona, then turned back to her brother. 'Does this woman speak the truth?'

'Lord Givra attacked me,' Rylan said. 'I was forced to defend myself, and I...'

'Did you take his life?' cried Natali.

'I had to,' said Rylan.

'And now you are threatening Lord Sigum?' Natali said. 'Has your mind been poisoned by insanity? With four dragons, we had a chance against the Gunstians, and you wish to reduce our numbers to two?'

'I shall reduce it to one if you defy me, sister,' said Rylan.

'That *one* shall not be you, brother. If you attack us, Lord Sigum and I will tear you to pieces.'

'Sigum is protecting Laimos, and Laimos has the Demon Witch,' said Rylan, his gaze going between Natali and Sigum as he edged away. 'The witch who murdered our father is within reach, sister. Help me punish her. Help me gain vengeance for the sake of our family.'

'You betrayed your family when you proclaimed yourself sole ruler of this island, brother,' said Natali. 'Lord Givra was also part of our family, and Lord Gradham, too. Who shall gain vengeance for their deaths? It is you who shall be returning to the palace; for if you do not, then this hour shall be your last.'

Lord Rylan stared at his sister, then he turned to glance at Lahnos, before he extended his wings and rose into the sky without another word. He banked above the monastery, then soared away towards Igatz. The soldiers in the cloisters sagged in relief, then Lord Sigum tilted his head.

'Thank you, my lady,' the silvery-green dragon said.

'My brother's thoughts are troubled,' said Natali. 'I shall go to the palace and try to reason with him. You will remain here; and you, Laimos – return to your post by the northern Chain Castle at once. Your soldiers are in need of their general.'

'Lord Rylan stripped me of my rank, my lady,' said Lahnos. 'I no longer have any authority over the regiments.'

'That is irrelevant,' said the dragon. 'The soldiers will follow you. Go.'

Natali turned, then she ascended into the air over Tsallon Anura and flew in the same direction that her brother had taken.

'I thought we were all going to die,' said Leona. 'Lord Sigum, thank you.'

'It was his noble sister that Lord Rylan listened to, not me,' said the silvery-green dragon. 'Did you speak the truth about Lord Givra – did the Governor use a shameful trick to murder him while he slept?'

'He tried,' said Leona, 'but someone warned Givra.'

'Who?' said Sigum.

'Me,' said Cisca, appearing at the balcony door.

'You did the honourable thing,' said the dragon. 'Lord Givra may have died, but at least he did not fall in such a shameful manner.'

Leona suppressed an urge to tell Sigum about the other part of Givra and Cisca's plan. 'What will Lord Rylan do now?' she said. 'Will he attack Lady Natali?'

'I saw the wounds suffered by the Governor,' Sigum said. 'Lord Rylan is not strong enough to defeat his sister in an open confrontation; he will need time to recover.'

'I have to go,' said Lahnos. 'Sigum, will you stay here to protect my friends?'

'I shall,' said the dragon. 'I will defend Tsallon Anura against all comers.'

'Thank you. We shall speak more when I return.'

Lahnos leaned over, and Leona helped him pick up the body of the unconscious Demon Witch.

'I saw what happened,' said Cisca, as they walked back into the apartment. 'Lyla isn't strong enough to beat Rylan. If the Governor attacks again, once he has healed, then how will we stop him?'

'Maybe Lyla is still getting stronger,' said Lahnos. 'Lower her onto the couch for now.'

He and Leona set Lyla down, and Cisca placed a blanket over her.

'I'd better go,' said Lahnos. 'I will see you all this evening.'

'Good luck, Lahnos,' said Leona, as she watched him hurry out of the apartment. She turned to Cisca. 'Don't think that I have forgiven you. You were going to betray this island, and then you told the others that I was Lady Takri.'

'They deserved to know the truth about you,' said Cisca. 'You are a devious little witch, and it's only a matter of time before Lahnos sees through you.'

'Devious? Cisca, by the time I'm finished with you...'

Leona's voice tailed away as someone knocked on the door.

'We shall continue this later,' she said to Cisca, then she walked to the door and opened it. The four Bullan outside were with Saewa, who was shaking.

'I got here a while ago, miss,' Saewa said, 'and walked right into the middle of those arguing dragons.'

Leona gestured for him to enter, and he squeezed past the Bullan and walked into the apartment's main living area. He noticed Cisca, but said nothing.

'I have a job for you,' Leona said. 'Someone in the Dragon Palace informed Captain Cisca that Bauchlie's body was seen dead following the poisoning of Medamuna Gatzoun. I need you to...'

'That's not true, miss,' said Saewa. 'Bauchlie survived the poisoning. I don't think he touched the ale, or so my contacts told me. They've seen him.'

'They've seen Bauchlie?' said Cisca. 'He's alive?'

'Hold on a moment, miss,' Saewa said. 'I hadn't finished. Those same contacts have also told me that Bauchlie and the surviving members of his rebel band were ambushed yesterday by Aucterian soldiers outside Fidalaimos. Several soldiers and rebels were killed, and witnesses saw Bauchlie being dragged away in chains.'

'They have him?' said Leona. 'Shit.'

'Where did they take him?' said Cisca.

'I don't know, miss. The Dragon Palace, most likely. I imagine there will be a quick trial, and an even quicker execution.'

Leona nodded. 'Thank you for the information, Saewa. If you find out any more, please let me know.'

Saewa gave a half-smile, then he left the apartment, the Bullan closing the door behind him.

Cisca lowered her eyes. 'Why would Jair lie to me?'

'Does it matter?' said Leona. 'Perhaps he knew how you felt about Bauchlie, and wanted you to feel powerless.'

'I'm going back to Igatz.'

'Feel free to leave any time you like,' said Leona, 'but you don't have a hope of saving Bauchlie if Rylan has him.'

'I have to try,' said Cisca.

'I will help her,' said a small voice from the bedroom door.

Leona turned. 'No, Arrosa; it's far too dangerous.'

'I don't care what you say any more,' said the girl. 'You watched my family be torn to pieces by dragons, and you did nothing to help them.'

'No,' said Cisca. 'Leona is right. The Dragon Palace is no place for a child, not while Lord Rylan is in charge.'

Arrosa shook her head. 'You will fail without me. You will need my Gifts.'

'My answer is no,' said Leona. 'You will be staying here, Arrosa, where it is safe.'

'Safe?' said the girl. 'Nowhere on this island is safe any more. There is nowhere to hide, and nowhere to run. And I don't feel safe with you, Lady Takri; I hate you.'

Leona kept her features still. 'Go to your room, Arrosa. Now.'

The girl shot her a look of contempt, then she walked into the bedroom and slammed the door. Leona glanced at Cisca as the Aucterian woman crouched by Lyla, then she turned for the balcony and strode outside. The sun had risen, but the light of the new day did nothing to raise Leona's spirits. She stared across the Cyasarta at Igatz, then she closed her eyes to prevent the bottled-up tears from spilling down her face. What hope was left? The Gunstians had a foothold on the island, the food stores were depleted, and the dragon Leona had decided to trust had turned out to be almost as bad as the other members of his family. Where had she gone wrong? She had tried her best to save Zamata, but the fate of the island seemed inevitable.

Leona felt despair course through her, and then she hardened her heart.

She had failed, but she would go down fighting.

CHAPTER 25
FROM THE FRONT

Kaugatz, Serpent Isle – 11th Kolinch 1588

The streets of eastern Kaugatz were teeming with people as the sun rose. Some had already been queuing for hours by the outlets that distributed the daily rations, while others were leaving their homes to begin the search for food. Tempers flared among the crowds, much of it directed at the small groups of soldiers protecting the food stores. Trying to leave the outlets was the most dangerous part of the day for many civilians, as groups would wait in the back lanes to attack and rob the meagre amount of rations that they had been given. Lahnos and Efizel tried to keep clear of trouble as they hurried along the road that led to Tzalla Pen and the northern Chain Castle, but their horns made them stand out, and they were met with a seething anger from the hungry masses of Zamatans.

'A few days ago,' Lahnos muttered, as an old man hurled abuse at him, 'these people were cheering us.'

'Humans may seem rational,' said the Bullan, 'but hunger sweeps away the veneer of civilisation that binds them together. It will get worse, my friend. When the stores of food are exhausted, Kaugatz will burn.'

'My children haven't eaten in three days,' cried a woman by the side of the road. 'Please help us, Lahnos.'

'I have to reach the Chain Castle,' Lahnos said, as the crowds thickened around him and Efizel. 'We must stop the Gunstians breaking into the Cyasarta.'

'Where are the dragons, Lahnos?' a man shouted. 'Why aren't they helping us?'

'Feed us,' cried another. 'Your men have food in Tsallon Anura; why should we starve?'

'My men are on the same rations as everyone else,' Lahnos said.

'Lies!' shouted another man. 'Leona is hoarding food for her friends.'

The anger in the crowd increased, and Efizel tensed, his hand hovering over the hilt of his sword.

'Leona is doing all that she can to provide food for every Zamatan,' Lahnos said. 'She isn't the enemy – the Gunstians are. Let me through, so I can fight them.' The crowd stared at him. 'Do you think the Gunstians will feed you if they take this island?' he went on. 'You know what they will do. The streets of Kaugatz will run with blood. This is the moment when we have to remain united; for if we fight each other, the Gunstians will trample us into the dirt. Hold on for a little longer, and let me do my job. Have I ever let you down?'

Despite their anger, the crowd slowly began to part. Lahnos and Efizel strode through the gap, and then ran towards the vineyards on the eastern edge of the town.

'I doubt that will work a second time, sir,' Efizel said, as they passed the last buildings on the street. 'You should not leave the monastery without an armed guard; had they attacked us, I would have been unable to save you on my own.'

'If the Gunstians break through the chains, then none of this will matter,' Lahnos said.

They ran for twenty minutes, taking the road that led south-east towards the Chain Castle, then they reached the start of the open fields where the previous day's battle had taken place. The Zamatan regiments were lined up in a long arc, but were not engaging the Gunstian marines, who had begun their assault on the fortifications guarding the Chain Castle. A newly-constructed siege tower was being positioned closer to the curtain walls, and a ferocious exchange of crossbow bolts was taking place between the marines and the castle garrison.

The Zamatan soldiers cheered at the sight of Lahnos, and the Aucterian officers hurried from their camp. Lahnos paused to catch his breath as the battalion commanders approached.

'What are our orders, sir?' said one.

'Why aren't you attacking the Gunstians?' said Lahnos.

'We were left without specific instructions, sir,' said a captain. 'We debated what to do at first light, but we had concerns.'

'What concerns?'

'We doubted that the Zamatans would accept our orders if you were not here, sir,' said another officer. 'Some of us wanted to attack regardless, while others felt it better to await your presence.'

'I'm here now,' said Lahnos. 'When did the Gunstians begin their assault?'

'They were working on the new siege tower all night, sir,' said the captain, 'and they moved it up to the walls as the sun was rising.'

They turned to stare at the Gunstian encampment encircling the landward side of the Chain Castle. The ditches were manned, but with fewer marines than the day before, while the rest of the Gunstians were supporting the siege tower, flanking it with raised shields as it trundled closer to the walls. Up on the battlements of the Chain Castle, the Zamatan garrison was loosing bolts down into the marines, and a few were falling.

'We have to stop the siege tower,' Lahnos said. 'If the Gunstians get inside the castle walls, they'll be impossible to dislodge, and the chains will be cut. Get the battalions ready for an immediate attack, and find me armour and a war axe.'

'Do you intend to fight today, sir?' said an officer.

'Yes. I will lead from the front.'

'But the Gunstians will see you, sir. Your horns...'

'I am happy to draw their attention,' Lahnos said. 'I will take the centre, but I want the flanks to be reinforced. They can attack by the cliffs while the Gunstians concentrate on trying to kill me.'

'And if you fall, sir?'

'You will continue the assault. There is no going back. If the regiments retreat, then it's over for Zamata. Attack, until every last Gunstian marine is dead or has surrendered – that is my order.'

The officers saluted, and Lahnos accompanied them down the gentle slope toward the lines of Zamatan soldiers. Efizel walked by Lahnos's side, his gaze lowered. The Bullan's features were giving nothing away, but Lahnos knew that he disapproved of his decision.

'Will you fight by my side?' Lahnos said.

'You know the answer to that, sir,' said Efizel. 'Tell me; do you wish to die this day? Have you given up hope?'

'Do you remember watching these soldiers fight yesterday?' said Lahnos. 'That was the moment I realised that I am not suited to being an officer. I have never felt more useless and weak than when I had to stand by the edge of the vineyard and witness my men dying. I will not do it again. If I order an attack, then I must be willing to place myself at the front, where the soldiers will see me.'

'That will help with morale, sir, but only until the moment you are struck down. After that, it will be chaos. I do not believe these soldiers will continue to assault the Gunstians if you fall. They will flee in despair.'

'They will not,' said Lahnos.

'I respectfully disagree, sir. I am not questioning their courage, but discipline comes from training, and these men have had almost none.'

An Aucterian officer approached with a handful of Zamatans, and they began to strap padding and steel armour over Lahnos's militia uniform, while Efizel was given a large shield. One soldier then handed Lahnos a war axe, and he took it. He walked out to the front of the assembled ranks of Zamatans and raised the weapon into the air.

'Men of Zamata,' he cried. 'You know me, and I know you. Everything we went through in Gunst was for one solitary purpose – to return here, to our homes upon this island. When our ships arrived in the Cyasarta, for one brief moment we knew peace and joy, but the enemy followed us, and now we must fight again. This time, we are fighting to defend our homes and those dear to us – our families, our friends, and our beloved Zamata. Are you with me?'

The soldiers roared, raising their crossbows and swords aloft. Lahnos turned to face the enemy ditches, as Efizel moved his shield up to protect them both. The Gunstian marines had seen the Zamatans line up for the attack, and had redoubled their efforts to move the siege tower forwards. Lahnos stared at them in silence for a few moments, as fear rippled through him. At his rear, he overheard a few muttered and whispered prayers to the serpent gods, and he wondered if the Gunstians were praying to Chadura. It was all a waste of breath. If any gods existed, they cared nothing for the Zamatans and Gunstians about to shed each other's blood.

Lahnos raised his axe, and charged.

The Zamatan battalions rushed forward, and Efizel kept pace with Lahnos, holding his shield high as they crossed the churned-up field. Ahead, the Gunstians in their defensive ditches aimed along the sights of their crossbows, waiting.

Mayhem descended as the Zamatans entered crossbow range. Bolts whistled out from the Gunstian lines, striking armour, shields, helmets and flesh. Lahnos's legs almost faltered, but he drove himself on as men around him started to fall. A few Gunstians pointed at him, his horns marking him out, and they began to focus their aim at him. A bolt thudded into Efizel's shield, then another ricocheted off the Bullan soldier's steel breastplate, as the distance between the two sides closed. Fifty yards, thirty, twenty, and still the charge continued. Amid the screaming and cries, Lahnos marvelled at the courage of the Gunstian marines as they lay in their ditches facing the oncoming Zamatans. None flinched or froze, and none ran.

Efizel took a bolt to his unprotected neck and was slammed backwards, his shield falling, as Lahnos leapt down into the first ditch. A Gunstian gazed up at him, and Lahnos brought the axe down, cleaving through the man's skull. All at once, the Gunstians attempted to swap their bows for swords as more Zamatans jumped down into the ditch. Terror enveloped Lahnos, but he kept moving, ramming the spiked end of the axe down into the back of a Gunstian marine too slow to get up. Lahnos took a moment to see what was going on further down the line, his eyes searching for the Gifted warrior, and he almost lost his head as a sword swung at him. It was parried by the blade of another Zamatan, and Lahnos jabbed his axe into the Gunstian's face, splitting his nose open. The marines began to retreat, and several were hit by their comrades in the second ditch. Zamatans were loosing back as they paused in the first ditch, but Lahnos knew they had to press on, so he raised his axe and charged again. He was halfway across the gap when he realised that Efizel was no longer with him, and he almost broke down as he ran. His feet slipped on the mud, and he went crashing to the ground as bolts flew past him. He turned his head and looked back to see dozens of Zamatans staring at him. Would they flee if he didn't get back up? Terror and grief for Efizel seemed to press down upon him, pushing him to the earth, and he shuddered as tears threatened to engulf him.

He remembered lying amid the heap of dead in Gunst, and how the Demon Witch had given him the courage he needed to keep going, and his right hand gripped the handle of his axe.

He would do it himself; he had to.

Lahnos pulled himself up and charged into the second ditch, screaming as he swung the axe. The blade bit into the side of a Gunstian marine, then the butt of a crossbow struck Lahnos's stomach, and he gasped. A robed man pointed a finger into his face, then the Gifted Gunstian was bowled over by the surging mass of charging Zamatans, and was hacked to pieces on the muddy ground. Lahnos fell to his knees as the Zamatans crowded round him, killing the last of the marines in the second ditch. With the Gifted warrior dead, the Zamatan flanks were also breaking through the Gunstian lines, and swarms of them overran the marines' encampment. The Gunstians by the siege tower started to flee, and were cut down by the garrison from the castle walls; and then, it was over, as the remaining Gunstians dropped their weapons and raised their hands in the air.

An Aucterian officer took control of the surrendering marines, and Lahnos was pulled to his feet by a mob of Zamatans. He staggered, and someone gripped his arm to stop him falling.

'Destroy the siege tower!' cried an Aucterian captain. 'Bring it down.'

Lahnos staggered through the crowds of cheering Zamatans, his feet stumbling on the bodies strewn by the two lines of ditches. He scanned the ground, looking for Efizel, and instead he saw the dismembered body of the Gifted warrior.

'You did it, sir,' said another Aucterian officer, a large smile on his face, but Lahnos pushed past him without a word. His eyes caught sight of the Bullan soldier by the lip of the first ditch, and he ran forwards. Blood was covering the side of Efizel's neck, and Lahnos could see that the bolt had passed through, ripping out a chunk of flesh. Lahnos knelt by his side. The Bullan's chest was still rising and falling, and Lahnos tore a strip off Efizel's sleeve and pressed it against the wound.

'Is he alive, sir?' said the Aucterian officer.

Lahnos nodded, too stunned to speak.

'We will take him and the other wounded back to the camp, sir,' the officer said. 'The orderlies there shall look after them.'

Two soldiers pulled Lahnos from Efizel, then others lifted the Bullan and carried him away. Lahnos sat on the mud by the edge of the first ditch, and gazed at the carnage. Bodies studded with crossbow bolts were lying where they had fallen, and the ditches were filled with the dead and wounded. The surviving marines were being herded away from the Chain Castle, while several Zamatans had begun looting the Gunstians' supplies, opening crates of food and filling their empty stomachs.

Lahnos closed his eyes, the victory tasting bitter in his mouth.

. . .

The next hour was spent clearing the battlefield. The gates of the Chain Castle were opened, and the men of the garrison mingled with their liberators, while the Gunstian dead were piled into heaps amid the blood and the broken earth. An Aucterian officer had brought a casualty report to Lahnos, but he hadn't listened to the man's words being read out, not wanting to learn the truth. After that, he had gone to sit on his own by the edge of the vineyard, trying to clear his thoughts.

Lahnos, can you hear me? a voice said in clear Gunstian.

He jumped.

It is me; it is Lyla; can you hear me?

Yes. How are you doing this?

I am dreaming, I think. My body is still sleeping after being awake most of the night, and I found myself rising above the island.

You are doing this in your sleep?

Yes. I looked for you – you were easy to find. You won the battle.

All I did was charge at the enemy like an idiot, he said. *It was sheer luck that I wasn't shot in the face.*

Are you able to do more?

Why?

Several Gunstian ships have broken away from the main fleet and are sailing towards the chains across the Cyasarta, unaware that their marines have been defeated. The lead vessel has a barbed iron ram and I think they are going to try to cut their way through. Stop them, Lahnos.

The voice fell silent and Lahnos got to his feet. He rubbed the sweat and dirt from his face and began walking towards the castle. An Aucterian officer saw him, and Lahnos gestured for him to approach.

'We need soldiers down by the jetty,' Lahnos said, 'and back up on the battlements of the castle.'

'Sir?'

'The Gunstian navy is coming; get the men organised. I will go into the castle and take a look.'

'Yes, sir,' said the officer, then he signalled to a couple of sergeants. 'Get the walls of the castle manned; the garrison must return to their posts immediately.'

Lahnos strode towards the main gates of the castle as the soldiers were ordered into their units. The garrison was sent back into the castle, while the officers started selecting fit soldiers from among those who had charged the Gunstian marines.

Hungry and exhausted soldiers saluted Lahnos as he entered the castle forecourt, and he gestured to a corporal.

'Where is the path down to the jetty?'

The corporal pointed at a small postern gate set into the southern curtain wall, next to where the keep stood. 'That way, sir.'

A squad of Zamatans arrived in the forecourt and formed up in front of Lahnos.

'Follow me,' said Lahnos. 'This battle isn't over.'

A soldier ran ahead and opened the postern gate as Lahnos and the squad reached it. Beyond, the clear waters of the Cyasarta were shining in the morning sunshine, and Lahnos stood for a moment to take in the view. On the opposite side of the straits, the southern Chain Castle was visible, and the twin lines of chains curved down between the two coasts, their central sections disappearing just under the waves. To the left, the Imperial Gunstian Fleet was stretched out for miles, but a small group of sleek frigates was flanking a large battle cruiser with a long jagged ram attached to its bow. The ram looked new, as though it had recently been forged, and it was slicing through the waves as the cruiser sailed towards the chains.

'Shit,' muttered the squad's sergeant.

'How do we stop it?' said Lahnos.

The sergeant pointed at the steep steps cut into the side of the cliff. 'Down there, sir. There are a couple of ballistae fixed to the end of the jetty. They're old, but usable.'

They raced down the steps with the sergeant and Lahnos leading the way. Above them, bolts started flying down from the castle battlements, aimed at the decks of the approaching frigates and cruiser, but they were doing little damage; while, below them, the soldiers stationed by the jetty had seen the looming threat and were running towards the two ballistae. Lahnos's legs were aching by the time they reached the small docks at the bottom of the cliffs. The chains were strung across the Cyasarta about twenty yards from the stone jetty, and the soldiers began shooting up at the nearest frigate, while tarpaulin sheets were removed from the ballistae. Gunstian marines by the bow of the battle cruiser were also loosing, and a Zamatan soldier was hit in the shoulder, sending him dropping into the waters of the inlet.

The iron-tipped bow of the cruiser reached the chains and sailed onwards. The links of the two chains became lodged in the barbed tip of the ram, and they began to strain. The two chains rose dripping from the water as they were pulled taut by the massive weight and momentum of the cruiser, but they held, and the cruiser ground to a halt. The ballistae on the jetty were aimed and loosed, and two yard-long bolts tore across the foredeck of the cruiser, striking a cluster of marines by the railings, impaling two.

'Keep loosing!' Lahnos yelled, as he stared at the chains. They were grinding and squealing under the pressure, but remained unbroken. More marines appeared on the deck of the cruiser, and a steady stream of bolts began to rain down onto the jetty, killing and injuring the crews operating the two ballistae. At the same time, a narrow wooden platform was being lowered off the port side of the cruiser's bow, laden with marines armed with huge bolt-cutters, saws and other tools. Four ropes were eased out, and the platform jerked and bumped its way down towards the chains, as the marines prepared to cut them manually.

'Aim for the platform!' Lahnos cried, but few soldiers were able to respond. Lahnos glanced along the jetty, and saw over a dozen dead or wounded Zamatans, their bodies riddled with bolts. Lahnos grabbed the sergeant by the arm and pulled him towards a small single-sailed vessel berthed by the jetty.

'Gather everyone who's left and get them on board,' Lahnos said.

The sergeant nodded, then urged the remaining Zamatans to run onto the deck of the small vessel. Lahnos joined them, and pulled the axe from over his shoulder as a soldier cast off the ropes. The sail was raised, and the Zamatans on board guided the vessel away from the jetty, the sergeant at the tiller. The craft bucked up and down on the waves, the bow of the cruiser towering over it, as it sailed south for twenty yards then banked. The platform came into full view. It had been lowered to a distance of just a few feet over the Cyasarta, and the marines were level with the chains where they crossed the bow-ram. They were attacking the thick links with bolt-cutters and saws, and none had seen the small vessel approaching from the south.

Lahnos waited until the small craft was almost under the port flank of the cruiser, then he raised his axe.

'Loose!' he cried, and the soldiers on board shot their bows into the marines on the platform. Most bolts missed as the craft rose on the waves, but three marines cried out and fell into the water. Lahnos climbed up onto the bow of the vessel and leapt across the gap, landing on the platform. He swung the axe at the ropes on the right side of the wooden beams, slicing through them both, and the end of the platform plunged into the Cyasarta, sending Lahnos and the marines into the water.

Lahnos let go of the axe as he floundered beneath the waves, his heavy armour weighing him down. He pulled at the straps, and his breastplate came loose. He pushed it away and kicked out with his legs, re-surfacing. He gasped for air, then saw the sailing vessel and began to swim for it. Another hail of crossbow bolts rained down from the deck of the cruiser, and the soldiers on board the small craft were cut down. The sergeant by the tiller tried to stand, but was shot in the back as he was about to dive into the water. Lahnos filled his lungs and drove himself under the surface of the Cyasarta as bolts fell around him. He swam until his chest was bursting, then re-surfaced close to the jetty, and turned. The cruiser was in the same position, unable to move forward or backward, the chains and the bow-ram tangled together.

A shadow flitted over the sun, and the form of an enormous dragon appeared above the battle cruiser. The marines on board cried out in alarm, and began to aim their bows into the air.

'Do not loose, Gunstians,' said Natali, her voice booming out over the Cyasarta; 'I am not here to fight you. Listen. If you allow me and

Lord Rylan to leave this island unmolested upon the sole remaining dragon carrier, then I will destroy the chains. Do we have a deal?'

No one on the battle cruiser responded as Natali beat her wings and hovered over them, then a woman in black robes appeared by the bow. Lahnos stared at the Gifted agent, then at the dragon, and began to swim to shore. He reached the stone jetty and pulled himself up, panting as he lay sodden on the flagstones.

'You will break the chains, dragon?' said the robed woman.

'I shall,' said Natali. 'The island is yours, but only if you swear to let me and my brother depart in peace. Do you swear it?'

'I swear it, dragon,' said the robed woman. 'You and your brother shall be allowed to leave Zamata.'

'No,' gasped Lahnos; 'Natali, no.'

The dragon reared up, then she soared over the waters of the Cyasarta. She banked and turned, then swooped down, her forelimbs extended. She grasped hold of the chains and ripped them asunder, tearing the links apart. The cruiser jolted forwards, and the marines on board raised their arms and cheered. Then the Gifted woman raised her own arm, and Natali cried out in pain. She tried to gain altitude, but the black-robed Gunstian was standing only yards from her, and the dragon bore the full brunt of the Gift of Pain. Her neck arched, her eyes wide with agony, then a ballista was loosed at close range from the port side of the cruiser. The yard-long bolt slammed into Natali's face, passing through her right eye and driving deep into her brain. The dragon seemed to hover above the Cyasarta for a moment, then she plummeted downwards, striking the surface of the water with a crash and disappearing beneath the waves.

The battle cruiser sailed on, flanked by its escort of four frigates, as Lahnos tried to get to his feet on the jetty. Marines by the cruiser's bow saw him, and began loosing their bows down at him. Lahnos leapt into the water, and sheltered by the jetty as the long ship passed. He wept bitter tears as the sudden realisation of what had happened struck him. The Gunstians had pierced the chains and, within hours, their entire fleet would be in the Cyasarta. Despair gripped him, and he almost gave up, his body exhausted as he huddled in the cold water by the stone jetty. The frigates and battle cruiser fanned out as they entered the Cyasarta, and more ships from the fleet began to make their way towards the island. One of the frigates dropped a launch into the inlet, packed with marines, and they rowed towards the jetty. As they were about to climb up from the boat, they cried out, and ducked their heads as another dragon soared overhead, twisting to avoid the bolts being loosed from the frigate. The dragon wheeled round, then swooped and plucked Lahnos from the water, the silvery-green forelimb clutching him round the chest.

Bolts sped through the air around the dragon as he rose into the sky, then Sigum turned and soared away from the ships, carrying Lahnos with him. They reached the height of the cliffs, and Sigum flew on until they were out of the range of the weapons on the Gunstian ships. He set Lahnos down onto a rocky outcrop, and landed next to him. Lahnos lay on his back on the hard ground, panting and shivering.

'Are you injured?' said the dragon, as he peered down at him.

'You saved me,' Lahnos gasped.

'Lyla told me where you were,' the dragon said. 'She was watching you. I saw what Lady Natali did as I flew here. Why, Lahnos? Why would she do such a thing?'

'I don't know. Maybe she lost all hope. The Gunstians are through; the chains...'

'Yes. What is to be done? I cannot confront the entire Imperial Gunstian Fleet on my own, Lahnos. You saw what their Gifted did to Lady Natali. If you will it, I will fly you to the Gunstian coast, some two hundred and fifty miles from here. We would be safe there, for a time, at least.'

'You would carry me?'

'If it is the only way to save you, then yes, my friend; I will carry you.'

'Then take me to Tsallon Anura,' Lahnos said. 'Thank you, but I cannot leave. If this island falls, then I shall fall with it.'

Sigum lowered his head and nuzzled Lahnos. 'So be it. We shall fight together, and we shall fall together. I will not desert you, Lahnos.'

'We still have Lyla, Sigum,' Lahnos said. 'She might know a way.'

'Then let us go to her.'

The dragon extended his great wings, then he clutched Lahnos in a forelimb and picked him up from the outcrop. Lahnos felt the wind in his face, then the dragon soared away, leaving the ruined chains of the Cyasarta behind them.

CHAPTER 26
A FINAL CONSOLATION

Kaugatz, Serpent Isle – 11th Kolinch 1588

Loud cries awoke Cisca. She opened her eyes and, for a moment, could not recall where she was. Then, she remembered. She was lying on the couch in Leona's apartment in Tsallon Anura. She sat up, the thin blanket tangling round her legs.

'Hello,' said Arrosa.

Cisca jumped at the sight of the girl sitting on the end of the couch by her feet.

The girl stared at her. 'You said you knew a secret way into the Dragon Palace.'

'What?'

'You talked about it before Rylan got here,' Arrosa said. 'Is it true? Do you know how to get inside the palace?

Cisca glanced around the room, but only she and the Gunstian girl were present.

'The Gunstians have broken through the chains,' Arrosa went on, 'Sigum has flown away to rescue Lahnos, and Leona is down in the cloister, organising the soldiers. If we leave now, we might be able to get out of Tsallon Anura without anyone noticing.'

'Slow down,' said Cisca. 'The Gunstians have broken through the chains?'

'Yes. It was Natali – she did it. She broke the chains because she thought the Gunstians would let her leave the island, but they killed her because she was an evil demon. Lyla has fallen asleep again; she only woke up for a few minutes to tell us what she had seen in her dreams, and to ask Sigum to find Lahnos.'

'I don't understand,' said Cisca. 'How did Lyla know what was happening?'

'I told you,' said the girl; 'she saw it all in her dreams. Then said she was tired out and went back to bed, so it's only the two of us awake in the apartment. Should we go?'

Cisca frowned. 'Why would Leona leave us alone if Lyla was sleeping?'

The girl sighed in frustration. 'Lyla was still awake when Leona left. Do you want to go or not?'

'I want to find Bauchlie,' said Cisca, 'but why would you want to go?'

'I hate Leona. She thinks I'm a stupid child, but I know all about Lady Takri and what she did that day. She helped the dragons kill my family. I can't stay here any more, not with *her*. I refuse to stay here.'

'But the Gunstians will soon be in Igatz.'

'The Gunstians won't kill me.'

'Yes, but they will kill me.' Cisca frowned. 'Do you want the Gunstians to win?'

The girl said nothing for a moment, then she shook her head. 'No.'

'Why not? You are Gunstian.'

'I was born on Zamata, and this island is my home,' Arrosa said. 'The *other* Gunstians are... different. They want to kill every Zamatan, and they will burn Igatz and Kaugatz; I don't want that to happen. I am going to Igatz. There is something I have to do.'

Cisca said nothing.

Arrosa shrugged, then she picked up a bag and slung it over her shoulder. 'Stay here, if you like. It's up to you; but don't try to stop me leaving.'

The girl stood and began to walk to the balcony. Cisca stared at her. If the girl was determined to go to Igatz, then someone should go with her, to keep her safe. And she might be useful.

'Wait,' said Cisca. 'If I come with you, will you use your Gifts to help me?'

'Bauchlie is probably dead, Cisca.'

'I know, but I have to try.'

'All right. I will help you. Can you climb?'

'Why?'

Arrosa looked at her as though she was stupid. 'How else are we going to get out of here? The demon-Bullan are guarding the front door.'

Cisca swung her legs off the couch and pulled her boots on. Her stomach rumbled from hunger, but she ignored it, and walked with Arrosa to the balcony door. The girl stepped outside, and Cisca followed her.

'Stay close to the left,' Arrosa said. 'That way, no one will see us from the ground.'

Cisca glanced over the network of narrow alleyways and red-tiled roofs, and saw Leona and a few Bullan standing in the middle of the cloister. Leona was addressing a crowd of terrified-looking Zamatan soldiers, and had her back to the building where Lahnos's apartment was located. Cisca turned, but Arrosa had already gone. She frowned, and peered over the left-hand side of the wide balcony. The girl was clambering down the wall, using the grooves between the building blocks for toe and finger-holds as she went. Cisca took a breath, then hauled herself over the railings and began to climb down after her. They reached the next balcony down and kept going, then, with a few feet to go, Arrosa dropped to the ground. Cisca did the same, and landed in the alleyway next to her. She glanced in all directions, but the soldiers who had been guarding that flank of the building were all in the cloister, listening to Leona.

Arrosa took off, running down a narrow lane between two other buildings, and Cisca ran after her. They reached a side gate leading out of Tsallon Anura, and found it unguarded.

'Where are the soldiers?' said Cisca.

'Leona summoned them all,' Arrosa said. 'They will be back in a few minutes.'

They walked through the gate, then Arrosa turned and spat upon the walls of the monastery.

'Filthy demon-worshippers,' she muttered. 'I don't mind if the Gunstians kill all of the monks. Come on; let's get across the Cyasarta before the fleet blocks the ferries.'

Tsallon Anura lay half a mile from the nearest ferry terminal, and it took Cisca and Arrosa less than an hour to board a vessel bound for Igatz. The news about the chains being breached had yet to spread beyond the monastery, and the Zamatans and Aucterians filling the open deck were grumbling about the latest cut in rationing, with no idea that the island was about to be overwhelmed.

Cisca remained at a quiet spot by the stern with Arrosa, trying to remain calm, but her gaze kept turning to the east, as though she expected the Gunstian fleet to arrive at any moment.

'Don't be silly,' whispered Arrosa. 'The fleet will take hours to get here.'

Cisca frowned at her. 'Why are you so calm?'

'I told you; if the Gunstians land in Igatz, then they won't kill me, especially once they find out I'm Gifted.'

'But you don't care that they will kill all of the Aucterian settlers?'

'Did the Aucterians care when the dragons slaughtered the Gunstians who lived on the island?'

'Yes, many of them probably did. Even Lord Rylan seemed to care at the time. I thought you said this island was your home? Do you not care about everyone who lives here?'

Arrosa raised an eyebrow. 'The demon dragons started this war. They invaded Gunst. That's why the Gunstians are attacking Zamata.'

'For revenge?'

'No, to stop the dragons invading Gunst ever again.'

'If you hate Aucterians, then why are you helping me?'

Arrosa frowned and looked away. 'I didn't say I hated Aucterians. You don't like Leona; that's why I'm helping you. That's right, isn't it? You hate Leona?'

Cisca narrowed her eyes. 'I don't hate her.'

'Ow!' Arrosa cried, rubbing her head as several passengers turned to see what had happened.

'What's wrong?' said Cisca.

'Lies hurt my head. Every time you tell a lie, it's like someone hits my head with a stick.'

'Sorry. I guess I do hate her. She... well, she treated me badly when we were in Zamata Gataza; but I suppose she was just doing her job. She also stole Lyla from me, but...'

'But what?'

'I can't deny that Lyla has improved a lot since she was brought to Kaugatz. Maybe Leona had a point.'

She glanced back across the sparkling waters of the Cyasarta, but the girl had been right – there was no sign yet of any Gunstian warships.

'Tell me more about Lyla seeing things in her dreams,' she said.

'All right. I was in the bedroom with her, but I wasn't sleeping; then Lyla woke up and called for Leona. She said she had been inside Lahnos's head, and had seen what he had seen. Then she told us about Natali and the chains, and she ran to the balcony and asked Sigum to fly away. Leona told Lyla to stay in the apartment to watch over me, and then she left and Lyla went back to bed. It only took a few minutes.'

'And everyone believed Lyla?'

Arrosa shrugged. 'Yes. The Demon Witch could do that sort of thing. Maybe more of her powers are coming back.'

'Perhaps we should have brought Lyla with us.'

'Why? She falls asleep after using her powers. I don't do that. Also, she might have said no and then told Leona. I knew you wouldn't tell Leona.'

Cisca chewed her lip for a minute, feeling a wave of guilt roll through her. 'When we get to Igatz, I want you to stay on the ferry and go back to Tsallon Anura.'

'What?' cried the girl. 'No. I'm not going back there. Ever.'

'But this is too dangerous for a girl your age. Leona and Lyla will look after you; and Sigum and Lahnos, too.'

'You can't make me go back.'

'I can.'

'If you try, I will scream and tell everyone that you were trying to kidnap me. The Bullan will arrest you and put you in prison.'

'You little...'

'What? I'm a little what?'

Cisca turned away, saying nothing. She tried to think ahead. Getting to Igatz would be the easy part, but was she prepared to take a small girl into the Dragon Palace? It occurred to her that Arrosa was probably one of the few people on the island who might survive a full scale Gunstian invasion, but that wouldn't protect her from Lord Rylan, or Captain Jair.

The ferry neared the pier on the shores of Igatz, and the sailors got to work, tying ropes to secure the vessel, and setting a gangway in place to allow the passengers to disembark. A handful of wagons trundled up a wide ramp, and Cisca got to her feet. Arrosa stared at her, and then stood.

'You can come with me for part of the way,' Cisca said, 'but you have to stay out of danger. I want you to run at the first sign of trouble. Deal?'

'No,' said Arrosa.

They walked up to the gangway and crossed over on to the long pier, squeezing past the line of people waiting to board the ferry for its return journey. The streets of Igatz were quiet, but everyone Cisca saw had a look of hunger about them. A few children were begging on the street corners, but the adults were walking past as though they hadn't noticed them.

'What now?' said Arrosa.

'It's half a mile to the palace,' said Cisca.

'I know that,' said the girl. 'I meant, how are we getting inside the Dragon Palace?'

Cisca kept her mouth closed.

'You used to live there, didn't you?' Arrosa went on. 'You worked for the demons, as their servant; or slave. Did you have to clean up their poop?'

'I was an officer in the Dragon Corps.'

'Yes, that's what I said. My mama told me that the Dragon Corps had the worst jobs in the world – having to look after demons.'

'It wasn't so bad,' Cisca said. 'Without the Dragon Corps, dragons would live in caves like wild animals. They aren't able to build castles or palaces, so they need humans to do all that for them. And we build dragon carriers for them, too – if it wasn't for humans, the dragons wouldn't be able to cross the ocean.'

Arrosa eyed her. 'And do you think allowing dragons to cross the ocean was a good idea? If they had stayed in the East, then they wouldn't have invaded Gunst three times. Why do they keep invading Gunst?'

'Have you heard of a god called Nathaniel?'

'I've heard of him, but he's not a god. Anyway, Lyla told us that he was dead.'

Cisca raised an eyebrow. 'It was Nathaniel who brought Gahad, the other dragons, and the Aucterians to this world.'

'I know that, but why do they think the whole world belongs to them?'

'They, uh... they believe that it is their right to rule Athumia.'

'Do you believe that, Cisca?'

'I used to. It's what I was taught in school. The Gunstians were evil and the dragons were good, and therefore the dragons should conquer Gunst. It took me a long time to realise that I was wrong.'

'Why, are you stupid?'

Cisca smiled. 'You know, Arrosa, you were also taught things that, when you are older, you might realise were wrong.'

'Such as?'

'I'm saying nothing more on that subject. Just try to keep an open mind.'

They slowed as the high fence surrounding the palace gardens came into sight. Cisca ushered Arrosa to the side of the street and into the shadows of a shallow alcove, where an old shop front had been boarded up.

'Stay here for a moment,' she said to the girl, 'while I scout ahead.'

Arrosa opened her mouth to object, then she glanced at the Bullan soldiers guarding the perimeter of the Dragon Palace.

'I still think you should go back to Tsallon Anura,' Cisca went on. 'I know that you don't like Leona, but she cares about you; and so do Lyla and Lahnos. Give Leona another chance.'

Arrosa frowned. 'But you hate her.'

'Not any more. There – did your head hurt?'

'No.'

'Stay hidden and out of sight,' said Cisca. 'If there's trouble, run.'

'Will you come back for me?'

Cisca hesitated, knowing that any lie would trigger Arrosa's Gift. 'I will check if it is safe. Stay here.'

She turned and hurried down the street, leaving Arrosa in the shadows of the alcove. Cisca skirted the Palace District, using the streets that ran parallel to the wall that enclosed the Dragon Palace, until she had entered the Temple District. She turned left, and took a narrow lane behind the grand buildings that lined the square where the Temple of the Undying Serpent sat. Cisca followed the lane, and then emerged by the shore of the Cyasarta a hundred yards south of the palace. She glanced out over the inlet, and caught her first glimpse of the Gunstians. Two miles away, five enemy warships had halted in the narrowest part of the straits, waiting for the rest of the fleet to move into position behind them before beginning their assault. The ships were tiny at that distance, with only their sails visible, but it was enough to convince Cisca that Lyla had been telling the truth – the chains had been breached, and Zamata was lying open and almost undefended.

How long did they have before the fleet moved between Igatz and Kaugatz? An hour? Two? Then Cisca remembered that Lady Natali had been slain by the Gunstians after her ill-judged attempt to strike a deal with them. With Lord Rylan still wounded, that left Lord Sigum as the only fit dragon on the island – a feeble mortal compared to the mighty scions of Gahad.

Cisca turned away from the sight, but decided to press on with her plan. If Bauchlie was still alive, then at least she would have one last chance to see him before the population of the island was annihilated. She walked along the coastline until she came to an outflow pipe that emptied into the waters of the Cyasarta. It was designed to carry excess rainwater from Igatz into the inlet, and extended under the palace itself. The officers stationed there had often joked that it was used to expel dragon waste; but none of them had known that the pipe was large enough for a small dragon to hide inside. When Lord Kheran had hidden there during a game, it had taken Cisca several hours to find him, and he had delighted in showing her the secret network that lay under the palace.

She clambered over the low fence and climbed down the rocky shore until her feet were submerged in the Cyasarta, then she dived into the water and began swimming. She reached the end of the pipe, turned, and began to crawl inside. The pipe was sloped, and she left the water behind as she was enclosed by darkness. She got to her feet and counted her steps until she was sure she was under the palace, then she began to look up for a drain. She found one after another few paces – a metal grille set into the floor of a wide drainage channel. She reached up and heaved with all her strength, and the grille moved. She pushed it to the side and climbed up and out of the pipe, emerging into a basement cellar deep under the palace. The chamber reeked of damp, and water from the recent rains was dripping down from the walls. She refitted the grille into place, and set off.

She came to a passageway, and then a set of stairs, which took her up into the level that she guessed contained the prison cells. She halted at the top of the steps, listening, but heard nothing. If she had been able to see the ships of the Gunstian fleet anchored in the Cyasarta, then the same applied to the soldiers in the palace. Had they been summoned by the Governor? Perhaps Jair was briefing them at that moment, or perhaps they had fled in panic. The thought almost made her laugh – where could they go? She carried on, passing storerooms and more corridors, until she came to the chamber where Major Lyla had handed herself over after Lord Malum had accused her of treason.

Two Bullan soldiers were standing by the wall, guarding the doors that led off from the chamber. They saw Cisca approach and saluted. Cisca blinked, then remembered that she had run from the palace the previous evening. Had the soldiers been informed about her part in the death of Lord Givra? She kept her features steady as she walked into the room.

'I am here to interrogate the prisoner,' she said.

The two soldiers frowned, and one glanced at her sodden uniform.

Cisca held out her hand. 'Give me the keys to Bauchlie's cell.'

Her heart began to pound as the soldiers said nothing. Was Bauchlie in the cells? Had he already been executed? Her only hope was to remain calm and assured. She was a captain, and out-ranked the pair of Bullan.

'Captain Jair did not inform us that the prisoner was to be interrogated, ma'am,' said one.

'You are being informed now,' said Cisca. 'Are you aware of the current situation? The Gunstians are approaching, and I would ask you not to waste any more of my time. The keys.'

'Yes, ma'am,' said one, placing his hand to his belt; 'though we shall have to report this to Captain Jair.'

'Then report it,' said Cisca, 'but do not obstruct me while I am carrying out my duties.'

The soldier unhooked a set of keys from his belt and handed them to her.

'Which door?' she said.

He gestured to the entrance on the left.

'Thank you,' she said. 'I won't be long.'

She went through the door and came into a passageway that was lined on both sides by cells. Each had a thick wooden entrance with a small barred section at eye level, and she closed the door behind her and approached the first cell. She knew that at least one of the soldiers would be hurrying upstairs to ask Captain Jair for confirmation that she had been ordered to carry out an interrogation, but that was a problem for the future. She peered through the bars of the first door – empty.

'Bauchlie?' she whispered. 'Are you in here?'

A sound came from further down the passageway, and Cisca ran to another cell door. She squinted into the gloom, and saw a man getting to his feet.

'Cisca?' he said. 'Is this where you came when you ran from Medamuna Gatzoun? You betrayed me?'

'Shut up,' she said, as she fumbled with the keys. 'I'm trying to get you out of here.'

Bauchlie stared at her through the barred opening. She found the correct key and slid it into the lock. She turned it, swung the door open, and found herself standing a yard in front of Bauchlie. Part of her wanted to throw her arms around him, but he had a suspicious glint in his dark eyes, as though he wasn't sure if he should trust her.

'We don't have long,' she said. 'I think the Bullan guards suspected me, and the Gunstians are on their way. Lady Natali broke the chains and let the Gunstians into the Cyasarta, Bauchlie. They're coming.'

'Why did you leave me, Cisca?'

'Did you not hear me? The Gunstians...'

'I searched for you; I looked into every cavern under the monastery, thinking that you were lying dead somewhere, poisoned. My mother told me that you had fled, but I didn't believe her; and you came here? Why?'

'Your mother was holding me captive, Bauchlie. I wasn't allowed to leave my room, and I had guards outside to make sure I did what I was told.'

'I told my mother to protect you, not imprison you. I was trying to keep you safe. And now... now I have lost everything.'

'You haven't lost me, Bauchlie. I am standing right here.'

He raised a hand, and his fingers touched her face, then he leaned down and they kissed, his hand pulling her face towards him. She closed her eyes, and the world outside seemed to retreat for a brief moment.

'Bauchlie,' she said, 'we have to leave.'

'It's a little late for that,' murmured a voice from the passageway.

Cisca turned her head and saw Jair standing in the shadows to her right, flanked by several crossbow-wielding Bullan soldiers.

'Welcome back to the palace, Captain Cisca,' he said. 'I see you've met our prisoner. That was a touching moment, poignant even, considering that you are both about to be executed.'

Bauchlie clenched his fists and lunged at Jair, but the Bullan soldiers raised their weapons, some aiming at him, others at Cisca; and Bauchlie halted.

Jair laughed, but it sounded bitter. 'It is over,' he said; 'not only for you two, but for everyone else on this accursed island. Lady Natali is dead, and her brother the noble Governor is in a rage, railing against all those who have betrayed him. You, Bauchlie, were one of the few not to do so – your opposition to him never faltered, and that at least makes you consistent. As for Cisca and the others who swore oaths to Lord Rylan... let's just say that the noble Governor dearly wishes to rip them all to pieces with his own jaws before the Gunstians have the chance to kill them.' He nodded to the Bullan. 'Bind their wrists and take them upstairs.'

The soldiers moved forwards, and Bauchlie lashed out, striking one in the face with his right fist. The others used their bows to club him, and Cisca was pulled to the side as Bauchlie was beaten to the ground. Two soldiers knelt on his back as his arms were pulled behind him, while another bound his wrists with cord. Cisca's hands were also bound, then Bauchlie was hauled to his feet and they were dragged along the passageway. A dozen more soldiers were waiting for them in the large chamber, and they flanked the group as they ascended the stairs to the ground level of the palace.

A low roar was rumbling through the wide marble corridors, and Cisca could feel the floor vibrate through her boots. The sound grew louder as they neared the central audience hall, which was lined with Bullan soldiers. Jair strode into the hall, as Cisca and Bauchlie were dragged along behind him. Lord Rylan was standing in the middle of the huge chamber, his claws extended and his jaws open. His eyes were burning with a savage intensity, and he did not seem to notice Jair as he growled and clawed at the floor.

Jair bowed. 'My lord,' he said, 'we have a visitor. Captain Cisca has decided to return to our warm embrace.'

Rylan ignored him.

Bauchlie lifted his bleeding and bruised head. 'I would curse you, lizard, but the Gunstians will soon make you suffer more than any curse would. This is the last day of dragon rule over this island, this land that you thought to enslave. Did you order your sister to break the chains, or did she do it to spite you?'

The low growling roar ceased, and Rylan lowered his head, as sparks and forks of lightning flashed over his open jaws.

A Bullan soldier raced through one of the arched openings. 'My lord,' he cried, 'the Gunstian fleet is advancing through the straits. What are our orders?'

The dragon kept his stare on Bauchlie. 'Let them land. Let them burn this faithless island and slaughter its treacherous inhabitants. Let the Zamatans die screaming. All I ask is that you defend this palace to the last man, so that I am spared long enough to watch the island suffer.'

The Bullan soldiers glanced at each other, and at Jair, who said nothing.

'Bring these two prisoners to the viewing gallery,' the dragon went on. 'I want them to witness the destruction of their homeland.'

The dragon turned, then Jair nodded to the soldiers surrounding Cisca and Bauchlie, and they were dragged along in Lord Rylan's wake. They left the huge audience hall, and made their way to a raised gallery, with a view that encompassed much of the Cyasarta, including a long stretch of the Kaugatz coastline. To the south-east, the lead ships of the Imperial Gunstian Fleet were inching their way past the straits, and sailing towards Igatz.

'I will likely die this day,' Rylan said, as he gazed out over the crystalline waters of the Cyasarta; 'but I will take pleasure from watching this island burn; it shall be my final consolation.'

Cisca and Bauchlie were pushed forwards to the edge of the gallery by the soldiers.

Bauchlie caught her glance and held it. 'There is something I should have told you a long time ago, Cisca,' he whispered; 'and now it is too late.'

'It is never too late,' she said.

'If this island falls,' Bauchlie said, 'then I shall be proud to die by your side. That will be my final consolation.'

CHAPTER 27
DEMON SLAYER

Kaugatz, Serpent Isle – 11th Kolinch 1588

Leona turned her gaze upwards to scan the skies as the assembled soldiers began to disperse. She had ordered the men to return to their posts and to leave the gates open to allow fleeing civilians to enter the monastery, before sealing them as soon as the Gunstians landed. It was a futile gesture, but Leona refused to allow despair to consume her. She narrowed her eyes, staring towards the east, searching for a glimpse of the silvery-green dragon. She had told the soldiers that Lahnos was on his way back, and she hoped it was true. It was strange, she thought, how, within the space of a few days, Lahnos had moved from being an acquaintance and ally to becoming someone important to her. She wanted Lahnos to live, and not only because he was essential to the defence of the island.

The slow minutes dragged on, and she wondered if she should check on Arrosa and the others in the apartment, but she wanted to be down in the cloister when the dragon returned. She had been calm and rational while addressing the soldiers, but it had been for show. Over the course of a single year, she had experienced two invasions of Zamata – one by the Gunstians and another by Dominion forces, but from the sheer scale of the fleet sailing through the Cyasarta, she knew this one was intended to obliterate all opposition on the island. The Gunstians would not stop until they had killed all who resisted; perhaps they would be faithful to their promise to slaughter the entire population. Would death by the sword be preferable to a slow lingering end through starvation?

Someone shouted from the battlements, and she stared into the sky. There – she saw it. A small dark speck soaring above the rooftops of eastern Kaugatz. As the dragon got closer, Leona could see that he was carrying something in one of his forelimbs, and she felt the tension in her chest increase a fraction. Lord Sigum was flying at speed, hurtling over the town towards the monastery. He wasted no time in circling, and descended into the cloister, opening his grasp and allowing Lahnos to spill out onto the ground. Leona ran towards him, then she slowed to a halt as Lahnos was surrounded by cheering soldiers. They helped the part-Bullan to his feet as the dragon landed a few yards away.

'Thank you, Lord Sigum,' Leona said. 'Thank you for bringing him back.'

The dragon tilted his head. 'He was exactly where Lyla said he would be. He is wet, but uninjured. However, Lyla also spoke the truth about the chains – they have been broken, and the Gunstian fleet is advancing into the Cyasarta.'

Lahnos walked over. 'If it weren't for the Gunstians,' he said, 'I might have enjoyed that flight.'

'I have briefed the garrison inside the monastery,' said Leona. 'I ordered them to allow in as many civilians as we can fit. Tsallon Anura will be as good a place as any for a last stand.'

'I don't want a last stand,' said Lahnos. 'I want to win. How is Lyla – can she use any more of her powers?'

'Let's ask her,' said Leona. 'I left her looking after Arrosa. Cisca will also be there, though she told me that she wants to leave.'

'And go where?'

'Igatz,' she said. 'Bauchlie is alive, it turns out, but he has been arrested; and Cisca wants to leave so that she can rescue him.'

Lahnos turned to the dragon. 'Give us a few moments to speak to Lyla.'

The dragon tilted his head again. 'I shall be waiting here for you.'

Lahnos and Leona walked towards the apartment block, then Lahnos diverted to speak to the Bullan soldiers standing outside the entrance. They spoke in hushed tones for a while as Leona stood back, then Lahnos returned to her side and they entered the building.

'I was telling them about... my Bullan sergeant,' Lahnos said. 'He was wounded in the battle for the Chain Castle, and he will still be there, along with the rest of the two regiments.' He eyed Leona as they ascended the stairs. 'We defeated the Gunstian marines, but it was for nothing. Natali... she...'

'I know, Lahnos,' Leona said. 'Lyla told us everything.'

They reached the landing at the top of the stairs, and the three Bullan soldiers on duty saluted Lahnos.

'Is Cisca still inside?' said Leona.

'No one has left the apartment, ma'am,' said one of the Bullan.

Leona nodded, then she opened the door to silence. She and Lahnos walked into the apartment, and Leona frowned at the blanket lying on the couch.

'Arrosa,' she called out; 'are you awake?'

There was no reply, and Leona walked to the bedroom door and opened it. The chamber was wreathed in shadows, and it took a moment for her eyes to adjust. She saw a sleeping figure on the bed, but no one else. She went over to the bed and shook Lyla's shoulder.

The young woman groaned and opened her eyes.

'Where is Arrosa?' said Leona.

Lyla looked around the room, her eyes groggy as though she was confused.

'I asked you to look after Arrosa,' Leona said.

'I was so tired,' Lyla said, her voice low. She saw Lahnos standing by the doorway, and half-smiled. 'Lord Sigum found you?'

'He did,' said Lahnos. 'Thank you for sending him to fetch me.'

'Is Arrosa in the bathroom?' said Leona.

Lahnos shrugged. 'I'll knock on the door and check.'

He turned and strode away, then Leona sat on the bed, her anxiety rising. 'Did anything happen while I was away?' she said.

'No,' said Lyla. 'I told Arrosa to stay away from the balcony, and then I had to lie down.'

'How are you feeling now?'

'A little better. Using my powers in my sleep makes me need even more sleep. I was able to see the entire island while I dreamt.'

Lahnos appeared back at the door. 'Arrosa isn't here; neither is Cisca. I've looked everywhere.'

Leona's fists clutched the thin blanket as she suppressed a scream.

'I thought she would be safe here while I slept,' said Lyla. 'How could she get out?'

'She must have climbed down the balcony,' said Lahnos. 'Either that, or there's a Gift of Invisibility that I've never heard of. Is there one?'

'No,' said Leona. She got to her feet and then she and Lahnos went out onto the balcony. Lahnos leaned over the railings, his eyes scanning the exterior wall of the building.

'It's climbable,' he said; 'but where would she go, and why would she leave?'

Leona rubbed her face.

Lyla walked out to join them. 'I'm sorry,' she said. 'I was so exhausted that I had to sleep, but I should have asked the Bullan to come inside to watch them. Has Cisca taken her?'

'Cisca will have gone to Igatz,' said Leona. 'She wants to find Bauchlie; and Arrosa... she hates me, I guess. What I did as Lady Takri... she...'

'It wasn't your fault,' said Lahnos.

'No, Lahnos; it is my fault. I should never have let her out of my sight – and now Cisca is marching her into danger. I have to go; I have to look for her in Igatz before the soldiers catch them.'

'I will come with you,' said Lyla. 'It was my fault, too. I will help you find her, Leona.'

'Wait a moment,' said Lahnos. 'I agree that we need to look for them, but don't forget that the Gunstians will be here soon. Sigum is ready to fight, but he will be alone. Is there anything you can do to help him, Lyla?'

Lyla frowned. 'I don't know what you mean.'

'You protected Leona from the dragon's truth spell – can you protect Sigum from the Gifts?'

'No, Lahnos, I can't. The Gifts of Theodora are... impenetrable to me. Even before I was placed into this body, I couldn't see who had Gifts, or how anyone could be protected from them. I could sense them being used, but nothing more than that. I will not be able to defeat the Gifted.'

'What about your seeing powers? Can you use them to keep track of the position of the Gunstian warships?'

Lyla shook her head.

Lahnos narrowed his eyes. 'But you could see me at the Chain Castle.'

'I know, but I was sleeping when I did that – dreaming. I don't know if I can do it again, because I don't know how I managed it last time; and I can't do it while I am awake.' She glanced down. 'I am useless. Weak and useless.'

'You are not useless,' said Leona. 'You just saved Lahnos's life and, despite his... tone, I am sure that he is very grateful.'

'I am,' he said. 'Sorry about getting angry, but I can't give up. I won't. If there is a way to beat the Gunstians, then I have to find it.'

'What about your other Gift?' said Lyla. 'Arrosa has mentioned it several times.'

'But how am I supposed to know what it is? I have no idea what I'm looking for. Is it a sensation, a feeling? Should I raise my hand and close my eyes and hope for the best?'

'If anyone can work it out, it's you,' said Leona.

Lahnos snorted. 'You have more faith in me than I do.' He gazed out towards Igatz. 'If you are going to look for Arrosa, then you should leave. They will have crossed the Cyasarta by now. There is a boat tied up by the monastery's jetty – take it, and take the eleven Bullan with you. I will stay here and defend Tsallon Anura.'

'We'll come back as soon as we find her,' said Leona.

'Why?' said Lahnos. 'Tsallon Anura will not be safe; not for Arrosa, and not for you and Lyla. It's the only fortification in Kaugatz – it's a certainty that the Gunstians will be coming here.'

'I can't leave you to fight alone.'

'I won't be alone – I'll be with Sigum.'

'But you'll be on the ground, while he is flying through the air.'

'I had a strange dream a few nights ago,' said Lyla. 'In the Major Lyla part, I was watching someone speaking to a dragon in Aucteran. I think it was Aucteran. In the Demon Witch part, I was also watching someone talking to a dragon – a huge black dragon; only this person was sitting on the dragon's shoulders, with some kind of saddle that had straps to stop her from falling off.'

'She was riding the dragon like a horse?' said Leona.

'Not exactly, but yes; I suppose so.'

Leona and Lahnos glanced at each other, then they both laughed.

'Was that funny?' said Lyla, her brows furrowed.

'Can you imagine asking a dragon to let you ride on its back?' said Lahnos. 'They would rip your head off and eat it.'

'It was only a suggestion,' said Lyla. 'That way, you and Sigum could fight together.'

'How would I kill Gunstians from the back of a dragon?' said Lahnos. 'You don't need to answer that – you should go. Get Arrosa, and then hide somewhere where the Gunstians won't find you.'

'Will we ever see you again?' said Lyla.

'Probably not.'

Leona nodded, then she attempted to embrace Lahnos, but changed her mind before her arms reached him.

He eyed her, then he pulled her towards him and they hugged.

'Take care,' he said.

'You, too.'

She released him, then Lyla also reached out, and Lahnos embraced her, too. The two women walked from the balcony and left the apartment. The three Bullan soldiers standing outside the front door saluted her.

'Come with me,' she said; 'all of you.'

'One of us should remain here, ma'am,' said a soldier; 'the Gunstian girl requires our protection.'

Leona gave him a wry smile. 'I will explain later. Follow me.'

Leona and Lyla descended the stairs, the Bullan coming after them.

'Shit,' Leona muttered. 'I shouldn't have done that.'

'Done what?' said Lyla.

'Embraced Lahnos.'

'Why not? He is our friend, and we might not see him again.' She glanced at Leona. 'Did it mean more to you?'

'No,' Leona said. 'Of course not, but he might think... He's still in love with Reyn.'

'I don't know about that,' said Lyla. 'He was hurt when she left, but I think they had been drifting apart for a while. Do you like him?'

'I don't want to talk about it. We have a boat to catch.'

They reached the front door of the building, and Leona assembled the eleven Bullan soldiers who had remained in Tsallon Anura while Lahnos had taken his sergeant to the Chain Castle.

'Arrosa and Cisca escaped the apartment,' she said to them.

Their faces fell.

'But we were on duty outside the door at all times, ma'am,' said a corporal.

'They climbed down the balcony,' Leona said. 'The blame is partly mine, because I summoned the soldiers together, including the ones who were watching the outside of the apartment block. Hence, I do not hold you responsible; but I do now require your assistance in retrieving Arrosa. I care nothing about Cisca – she is free to do as she pleases, but Arrosa is eight years old, and we need to find her. Most likely, they will have taken a ferry to Igatz, as Cisca wishes to look for Commander Bauchlie. Therefore, Lahnos has granted me permission to take you all with me, and Lyla will also be coming. We shall cross the Cyasarta, and begin our search there.'

'Very well, ma'am,' said the corporal, 'but I shall first have to check with Lahnos that this is the case. I will...'

'There's no need to look for me,' said Lahnos, as he emerged from the building. 'Go with Leona and obey her orders. Protect her and Lyla, and help them find Arrosa. When you do so, protect her, too.'

The Bullan saluted. 'Yes, sir.'

Lahnos approached Leona, a half-smile on his face. 'Don't you hate it when you bump into people after you've already said goodbye to them?'

'I will find you when this is over, Lahnos,' she said.

He looked down at her. 'All right. Goodbye, again.'

'Goodbye.'

She turned and walked away, Lyla by her side, and the eleven Bullan following.

'I don't like this,' Leona muttered, as they strode towards the postern gate leading to the small jetty. 'Of all the damn times to start...'

'Start what?' said Lyla.

'Nothing. Forget it.'

A Zamatan soldier opened the gate for them, and they filed through. A small sailing vessel was berthed by the side of the jetty, and the Bullan corporal ordered the other soldiers to board, then Leona and Lyla stepped down onto the wooden deck.

'If you two would sit close to the bow, ma'am,' the corporal said, 'that will give us space to work.'

Leona nodded, and then she and Lyla took their places by the front of the vessel as the Bullan raised the sail and loosed the ropes attaching them to the jetty. The craft began to move off, the breeze filling the sail as the Bullan guided the bow towards Igatz. Leona glanced to the east, but no Gunstian vessels were yet visible in the Cyasarta between Kaugatz and Igatz.

'Where in Igatz shall we berth, ma'am?' said the corporal.

'Take us to the nearest ferry terminal,' said Leona. She turned to

Lyla. 'You said something to Lahnos earlier – that you could sense when Gifts are being used.'

'Yes,' said Lyla. 'That was how I first found Lahnos, when he read his grandmother's memories.'

'So, if Lahnos used his Gifts again, would you be able to sense them?'

'I think so.'

'Can you sense my Gift?'

Lyla frowned.

'I have the Gift of Truth,' Leona went on, 'and it doesn't work like most of the other Gifts. Instead of being used now and again, my Gift is always working, always alert for lies being uttered. The Gift of Kenning is the same, I think; therefore, in theory, shouldn't you be able to sense either Truth or Kenning being used? In other words, if you can sense my Gift, then maybe you can use that ability to track down Arrosa – she has Truth and Kenning.'

'I think I understand,' said Lyla, switching to Gunstian. 'I am not aware of having ever sensed your Gift of Truth, but we have spent so much time in each other's company since... since I became aware of things, that maybe I have been missing it.'

'Tell me a lie,' Leona said, 'and see if you can feel my Gift.'

Lyla nodded. 'I am not scared of the Gunstians.'

Leona felt a tingle in the back of her head, and Lyla smiled.

'Did you feel it?' said Leona.

'Yes. It was as though part of you was amplified for a brief moment, and now I can sense the underlying Gift that courses through you.'

Leona raised an eyebrow. 'When do you think you will be able to speak that fluently in the Divine Tongue? Your Gunstian is better than mine.'

'I'm still waiting to dream about that,' said Lyla. 'If I don't then I will have to learn it the hard way.'

The corporal turned to them. 'We'll be landing soon, ma'am.'

They turned, and saw the built-up coastline of Igatz get closer. Berthed by a pier fifty yards away was a ferry preparing to make the short journey across the Cyasarta to Kaugatz, and a huge crowd had gathered, pushing and jostling as hundreds tried to leap onto the deck from the pier at the same time.

'They are fleeing,' said the corporal; 'fleeing Igatz.'

'Take us east for another hundred yards,' said Leona; 'otherwise they might try to swamp this boat.'

'Yes, ma'am,' said the corporal. He shouted out a few orders, and the vessel began to turn before it reached the ferry terminal's short breakwater. The crowd on the pier saw them, and many started to cry out, pleading with them to enter the harbour.

'Why are they fleeing?' said Lyla. 'Kaugatz is in as much danger as Igatz.'

'Most of them are Aucterians,' said Leona, as she watched the frightened, desperate crowds overrunning the ferry terminal. 'Maybe they think the Gunstians will be less ruthless towards the Zamatans.'

'And will they?'

'I don't know,' said Leona. 'I hope so. They might show mercy to those who bow before Chadura. Have you searched for Arrosa?'

'No. I will do it now,' said Lyla.

The young woman closed her eyes and fell into silence, as the vessel sailed east along the coast of Igatz. A mile away, the white marble façade of the Dragon Palace was gleaming in the sunshine, its domes and towers rising high above the skyline.

'This is as far as we can go, ma'am,' said the corporal. 'Any further, and we will reach the heavily-guarded area surrounding the palace.'

Leona glanced at the coast. There were no harbours or jetties along that stretch of Igatz, but the sea wall was only a few feet high, and looked easy to climb. She nodded at the corporal, and the boat eased towards the shore. The sail was taken down, and the craft rose up and down on the waves and then bumped against the wall. Two Bullan soldiers clambered up onto the street that ran along the shore, and others threw them ropes. The two Bullan caught them, and they pulled the vessel closer to the wall. The corporal extended a hand towards Leona, but Lyla was still in a trance.

'Should we carry her up, ma'am?' said the corporal.

'Yes,' said Leona. 'Be careful – I don't want to interrupt what she is doing.'

More soldiers climbed up onto the street, then they leaned down as Lyla was lifted and passed up to them. They set her down onto the ground, then they reached down again, and pulled Leona up. The corporal was the last to climb the wall, and he looked at Leona for instructions.

'Tie the boat to that lamppost,' she said, pointing. 'Someone will likely steal it, but I don't want to let it drift away.'

The soldiers did as she ordered, then they gathered round the still form of Lyla.

'Is she sleeping, ma'am?' said the corporal.

'No. She is trying to use her powers to sense the location of Arrosa.'

'She is the Demon Witch, then, ma'am? There is no doubt about it?'

'She is, or she was. Before you say anything else, you should know that she killed King Gahad in self-defence. Gahad was threatening her children. She didn't set out to turn this world upside down.'

'But she did, all the same, ma'am.'

'Yes, she did. And now she's trying to help us find a little girl.'

'We have no desire to hurt her, ma'am. We are loyal to Lahnos, not Lord Rylan.'

One of the Bullan muttered something in their own language.

'What did he say?' said Leona.

The corporal eyed her. 'He said that he agrees, ma'am. He also said that our oath – the oath our people swore to the Dominion – died with King Gahad.'

'Do you share that view?'

The corporal glanced away. 'I am not certain, ma'am.'

Lyla gasped and opened her eyes. 'I have found her.'

Leona crouched down by her side and helped her sit up.

'She is within the grounds of the palace,' Lyla went on. 'In the gardens.'

'But the gardens will be swarming with soldiers. Has she been arrested?'

'I couldn't see any of that. I could only sense her location, not what was happening to her.'

The Bullan pulled them both to their feet, and Leona pointed towards the palace.

'We are going after her,' she said. 'We lost her, and now we have to find her.'

The Bullan nodded, and they set off at a run, bounding along the coastal road with the waters of the Cyasarta on their left.

'We need to stay close to the shore,' said Lyla, as they ran. 'That's where Arrosa is.'

'Can you still sense her?' said Leona.

'Yes. Now that I know what I am looking for, she is like a tiny light amid the darkness.'

The wall surrounding the palace gardens came to an abrupt end where it met the Cyasarta, and they hurried towards it. The stonework of the wall rose a few feet, and was topped by a tall iron fence, through which the northern end of the garden was visible. That section of the grounds had been spared most of the fighting during the previous invasion, and several tall palm trees were standing amid the flowerbeds, perfect lawns, and flowering shrubs of rosemary and sage. A few Bullan soldiers were on duty, guarding a gate close to where the wall met the Cyasarta, and several more were rooting around a line of thick bushes, as though they were searching for something.

'That's where she is,' whispered Lyla, pointing at the place where the soldiers were gathered. 'I think she's hiding in there.'

They slowed and came to a halt by the fence, fifty yards from where it terminated by the water's edge. Leona gazed through the bars, her eyes on the soldiers. A shriek came from the bushes, and a Bullan dragged Arrosa out from her hiding place, pulling her by a shoulder.

'Get off me, demons!' the girl shouted.

'She's with us!' cried Leona. 'Over here! Please – the girl got lost. She's with us.'

The soldiers glanced over, as Arrosa writhed and struggled in their grasp, and one of them, an officer, approached the fence.

'Do you claim this girl, ma'am?' said the Bullan.

'Yes,' said Leona. 'Thank you for finding her, sir. She's my daughter.'

'Ow!' cried Arrosa, her free hand rubbing her head.

'Take her to the coastal gate,' said the officer.

The soldiers led Arrosa towards the gate by the Cyasarta, and Leona and the others followed on the opposite side of the wall. Several of the Bullan in the gardens were staring at their kinsfolk walking with Leona and Lyla, and few muttered something to the officer.

'I think they suspect us, ma'am,' whispered the corporal.

'Remain calm,' said Leona, 'but get ready to fight.'

The two parties reached the gates at the same time, and the officer peered through the bars. His eyes went over the eleven Bullan, then they settled on Lyla for a moment.

'Open the gates,' he said.

The Bullan next to him obeyed, unfastening the heavy chains draped over the latch and then swinging the gates open.

The officer turned to Leona. 'Now, ma'am; I just need your names before we hand over the girl.'

'But I don't want to go with her!' cried Arrosa. 'Let me go!'

'Seize the women!' cried the officer, and the Bullan surged forward through the gate. One reached out to grab hold of Lyla, and a Bullan by her side rammed his fist into his kinsman's stomach, doubling him over. The two groups of Bullan glared at each other. One of them shouted something in their own language, then both sides drew their swords and charged. A Bullan fell dead as they clashed, but Leona didn't know whether he had been a friend or an enemy. She tried to run forward to reach Arrosa, but too many Bullan were in the way. Another soldier fell, a sword cleaving through half of his neck, then Lyla raised her arms.

'Stop!' she cried. 'We surrender. Don't kill each other over us.'

The Bullan lowered their weapons, and separated back into their two sides.

'Are you Major Lyla of the Dragon Corps?' shouted the officer.

'I am,' she said, 'and I willingly hand myself over, as long as you let these other Bullan go free.'

'We swore to protect you, ma'am,' cried the corporal, his sword raised.

'I know you did,' said Lyla, 'and I thank you for it, but go; save your strength for the Gunstians.'

The corporal eyed Leona. 'Ma'am?'

Leona glanced into the gardens. The skirmish by the gates had attracted attention, and more soldiers, both Bullan and Aucterian were hurrying over; while Arrosa remained out of reach in the grip of two soldiers.

'Do as she says,' said Leona. 'We surrender.'

The ten remaining loyal Bullan edged back from the gate, then turned and ran. The officer gestured to his men, and they rushed forward, surrounding Leona and Lyla and dragging them into the gardens. The gates were closed and locked, and then the soldiers began to lead the three prisoners towards the Dragon Palace.

Leona glanced down at Arrosa as they crossed the wide lawn. 'Why? Why did you run away?'

'You know why, Lady Takri,' Arrosa spat. 'You should have stayed in Tsallon Anura; I was doing fine until you arrived.'

'Leona risked everything to come here to find you,' said Lyla. 'She cares about you.'

Arrosa snorted. 'Now you sound just like Cisca.'

Leona frowned. 'Cisca said that?'

'And why did you say you were my mother? You will never be my mother.'

'She's too young to be your mother,' said Lyla. 'She should have told them that I was your mother; that might have been more believable.'

The officer eyed them and laughed. 'Drawings of your likenesses have been seen by every Bullan in the palace. We knew who you were as soon as we saw you.'

'The Bullan's oath to the Dominion is no longer valid,' said Leona, 'and Lord Rylan has illegally usurped authority over this island. Why are you obeying his orders?'

The officer's smile fell away. 'No more talking.'

They entered the wide, cool corridors of the palace, and made their way to the vast audience chamber. They passed under a high arch, but no dragons were present inside the hall.

'Where is Lord Rylan?' the officer asked a group of Bullan soldiers on duty.

'He went to the viewing gallery, sir, to watch the approach of the Gunstian Fleet.'

The officer nodded, then gestured to his men and they carried on, leaving the hall by another arched entrance. They traversed a long passageway, then turned and came out on to the wide gallery, where more Bullan soldiers were gathered. Lord Rylan was also there, his gaze focussed on the vast numbers of Gunstian warships sailing past the headland of Igatz. By the railings, three humans were also standing, two with their wrists bound, and Leona recognised them even though they were facing the opposite direction.

'My lord,' said the officer, bowing. 'We have apprehended Major Lyla and Leona of Kaugatz.'

The dragon's neck turned, and his eyes flashed as he saw the three prisoners.

'What is this?' said the dragon. 'How was this feat accomplished? I ordered all Bullan to defend the palace.'

'That's where we found them, my lord,' said the officer. 'They were at one of the palace gates.'

'They came to me?' cried the dragon. 'What fortune amid such despair! And Lord Sigum and the horned boy Laimos?'

'There was no sign of them, my lord. The two women were looking for this girl.'

Rylan glanced down at Arrosa, as though noticing her for the first time.

'Don't stare at me, you demonic reptile,' said Arrosa. 'The Gunstians are going to hack your scaly head off and dance around your corpse.'

The dragon said nothing for a moment, then he smiled. 'Yes. They probably are. Before that, however, I shall have the privilege of slaying not only the commander of the rebels, but also the treacherous Lady Takri and the murderous Demon Witch. Bullan, place our fresh captives next to Bauchlie and Cisca; let them be reacquainted as we watch Zamata fall.'

The Bullan pushed them forward until they were pressed against the railings.

Bauchlie nodded down at Leona, and she noticed the bruises and cuts marking his face.

'I told you to wait outside the palace grounds,' Cisca said to Arrosa.

The girl shrugged.

'If you hadn't fled, Cisca,' said Leona, 'we would all be in Tsallon Anura right now.'

'I wouldn't,' said Bauchlie. 'I would still be in my cell.' He turned his dark eyes towards Leona. 'Do you acknowledge that I was right about Lord Rylan?'

'I do not regret my choices,' she said.

Jair looked over at them. 'Shut up, all of you. The Gunstians will begin landing soldiers in less than an hour.'

'Was it all worth it, Captain Jair?' Leona said. 'All your schemes and plans, and look at where they got us.'

Jair slapped Leona across the face. 'How dare you?' he cried. 'We swore oaths to Lord Rylan, and you betrayed him – you and that horned bastard in Tsallon Anura. We could have held out indefinitely, were it not for your treachery.'

'My treachery?' said Leona, her cheek stinging. 'It was Natali who broke the chains, not I.'

Jair raised his fists.

Lyla stared at him. 'Do not touch her again,' she said.

Jair flinched, his fists lowering, then Lord Rylan emitted a low, mocking laugh.

'This again, Demon Witch?' the dragon said. 'Your powers may work on Captain Jair, but they have no effect on me.' He stared down at her. 'I can feel you, even now, as you try to enter my mind. Perhaps there is no need for you to watch the destruction of Zamata; perhaps it is time for you to bid farewell to your new body, as it seems to have so weakened you.'

Lyla lifted her hand higher. 'No,' she cried. 'You will not kill me; you cannot kill me.'

'Oh, but I can and I will, Demon Witch. This is for my father, and for all the pain and suffering upon this world that you have caused.'

The dragon opened his jaws and lowered them towards Lyla's head, as Jair shoved Leona out of the way. Arrosa slipped under the captain's arms and dived forward, her hand stretching out until her fingertips brushed against one of the dragon's forelimbs.

'Die, lizard!' the girl screamed.

The dragon seemed to hesitate for a split second, his eyes amused by the sight of the girl touching him, then his movements slowed. His mouth remained open, just a foot above Lyla's head. Sparks and little forks of lightning flashed across his great fangs, then they ceased and the dragon let out a roar that knocked Lyla off her feet. The Bullan stared, but did nothing, not understanding what was happening to Lord Rylan, then Jair tried to drag Arrosa away. The girl let out a scream and touched the officer's leg with her free hand, then her eyes closed and she slumped to the floor of the gallery. Jair froze, his arms still reaching out for Arrosa, but no longer moving, then both he and the dragon were transformed into glass, the light from the sun shining through the hard, green, translucent substance.

Leona edged away, staring, her mouth open. Rylan and Jair's glass forms looked like statues, every detail perfect and in place, from the dragon's scales, claws and fangs, to Jair's outstretched arms. Leona crouched by Arrosa and Lyla. Both were unconscious but breathing.

'The dragon is dead,' said Bauchlie, his eyes on the Bullan soldiers. 'You are no longer bound by any oath you swore to him. Captain Cisca is now your commanding officer. Release her from her bonds.'

The Bullan remained where they were for a moment, then the

officer pulled a knife from his belt and cut through the cords binding Cisca's wrists.

'What are our orders, ma'am?' he said.

'Defend Igatz from the Gunstians,' Cisca said. 'Rally all forces and repel the enemy as they land. We shall not be surrendering; we will fight to the end.'

The Bullan saluted, then they scattered, running back along the passageways towards the front of the palace. Cisca untied the cords around Bauchlie's wrists, and they stared at each other. Leona glanced up from where she was crouching next to Arrosa and Lyla, then she lowered her gaze as Cisca and Bauchlie kissed.

Arrosa spluttered and opened her eyes.

'You did it,' Leona said. 'You killed Rylan.'

The girl stared up at the huge sculpture of green glass towering above her.

'I am a demon slayer,' she whispered.

Leona smiled. 'You are. You are also someone I am very fond of, Arrosa. I wish we could have had the chance to get to know each other a little better.'

'We still might.'

Leona said nothing, then her eyes went to the dozens of Gunstian warships sailing past the viewing gallery, and a tear spilled down her cheek.

'Don't cry,' said Arrosa, taking Leona's hand. 'Lahnos will save us.'

CHAPTER 28
FIRE AND PAIN

K**augatz, Serpent Isle – 11th Kolinch 1588**

Lahnos watched Leona walk away. Was there something different about her? She had been looking at him in a strange way, and he wanted to know why. It reminded him of... no. That was just about the most stupid notion that had ever crossed his mind. They were friends, nothing more. He strode away from the apartment building and found Sigum waiting for him in the cloisters.

'I saw Leona and Lyla leave with the Bullan,' said the dragon. 'Where are they going?'

'Arrosa has run away,' Lahnos said. 'They're going to Igatz to look for her.'

Sigum tilted his head. 'And why would she flee from the monastery? I know she considers the serpent faith to be abhorrent, but Tsallon Anura remains the safest place in Kaugatz.'

'She was angry with Leona.'

'That does not seem like a rational foundation upon which to base such a drastic decision.'

'She's eight years old, Sigum. She's not rational. She thinks you and I are demons.'

'Even if they are successful,' the dragon went on, 'the Gunstians will have landed before they will be able to return to Kaugatz. That is a pity, for I had grown to respect Leona of Kaugatz. She may be ruthless, but she is also compassionate.'

Lahnos rubbed his face.

'Do you have no opinion on the subject?' said Sigum. 'You and she are close, are you not?'

'What is that supposed to mean?'

'Nothing other than the words I uttered, Lahnos. You are friends, and now you are parted, perhaps forever. I would understand if this knowledge upsets you.'

'I'm fine.'

The dragon peered at him. 'You do not seem fine, my friend. You have an air of regret about you. Should I fetch Leona back here? Do you wish to speak to her?'

'No. Let her go. She has her job and we have ours.'

'Ah yes, our meeting with death. I am ready, my friend. We shall fight to the end, and die with honour. I only wish we could fight together.'

Lahnos glanced up at the dragon. 'Uh... Lyla said something...'

'Yes?'

'She recovered another one of her memories.'

'Go on.'

'In this memory,' Lahnos said, 'she saw someone riding on the shoulders of a dragon. There was a saddle of some kind.' He looked away, feeling foolish. 'It was just an idea.'

'You wish to ride on my back?'

'Thank you for not laughing,' he said. 'I know how stupid that suggestion sounded.'

The dragon smiled and tilted his head. 'Do you consider me a horse?'

'All right; you can laugh now. I will stay here, up on the battlements, and watch you fly. If you stay close to Tsallon Anura, then you can shield us when the Gunstians attack. We still have five hundred soldiers in the monastery, and we...'

'Hush,' said the dragon. He turned his head, and spied a group of Zamatan soldiers. 'Are there any artificers among you? I require the construction of something. Fetch me the best artisans in the monastery; any who work with leather would be preferable.'

The soldiers saluted, then hurried away.

'What are you doing?' said Lahnos.

'My dear friend,' said Sigum; 'the chances of us living through this day are remote, and if I must die, then it would be an honour to die by your side. Let us fly together, for the first and final time.'

'You would do this?'

'I feel... connected to you. Do you feel the same?'

'I do.'

A few soldiers emerged from a building, leading several brown-robed monks. The monks bowed low before Lord Sigum, while ignoring the presence of Lahnos.

'My lord,' said one of the monks; 'I am told that you require some leather-work? I have brought the best craftsmen in Tsallon Anura. Please allow us to help you. What do you need?'

'Time is short,' said the dragon, 'and I will require the work to be carried out as quickly as possible, before the Gunstians assault the monastery. I need you to fashion a large saddle, with harnesses and straps. You could perhaps rework an existing saddle, but it will need to be able to keep its rider secure.'

'Very good, my lord,' said the monk, 'but there are no horses left in Kaugatz; they were slaughtered some time ago.'

The dragon kept his eyes on the monk. 'The saddle is for me. I intend to carry Lahnos Laimos into battle.'

The monks blinked, and several looked aghast.

'No, my lord,' said the lead monk; 'such talk is blasphemy; a sacrilege. You are a serpent god, and Lahnos is... um, well, he...'

'Say it,' said Lahnos. 'You think I am a soulless demon.'

'We promised that we would not utter such words during your stay here,' said the monk. 'Leona of Kaugatz made us swear it.'

'You will carry out this work for me,' said Sigum. 'Feel free to take my measurements. Begin now, that is my command to you, faithful brothers of the serpent gods.'

The monks bowed again, then started to return to the building.

'You have one hour, brothers,' said Sigum. 'Do not disappoint me.'

Lahnos spent the next hour on Leona's balcony, gazing out at the Cyasarta as the Gunstian fleet rounded the headland of Igatz. He had intended to go upstairs to his own apartment, but the memories of Reyn's presence were raw, and some of her things were still lying around. He had been meaning to tidy them away, but every time he had gone to do it, he had made an excuse not to.

She might come back. She might come to the conclusion that she had made a mistake, and return to Tsallon Anura. Lahnos frowned. Did he want her to? If he had been asked that question in the days following her departure, his answer would have been an instant *yes*, but did he still feel that way?

No. Whatever fire had bound him and Reyn together had flashed briefly, and was now extinguished. She had her own life, and her own friends, and they had grown to desire different things from life. He still cared about her, but his love had dissipated; and he was sure that she felt the same. It was sad, but the world moved on, caring nothing for the fate of two part-Bullan inhabitants of Zamata.

He tried to adjust his thoughts on to the approaching storm; thinking about Reyn was a waste of time when the end of Zamata was coming. He didn't want to die, but the thought of going down fighting while upon Sigum's shoulders gave him no small amount of pride; and then he wished that he had accepted the dragon's suggestion, and had allowed him to fetch Leona back, so that he could have spoken to her before she had left for Igatz. Why? What did he want to say to Leona of Kaugatz? That she had become someone important to him, and that he didn't want her to die without her knowing that? He knew that what he was feeling might be a passing phase, brought about by close proximity and the daily threat of danger; and perhaps it could be explained by simply not wanting to be alone when the end of Zamata came; but the thought of Leona gave him hope – that if, somehow, they could survive, then something durable and vital might develop between them. It was a small hope, and he felt ridiculous for even considering it while the Gunstian fleet made its way along the Cyasarta, but when had he ever cared about how things might look to others?

He heard the door open behind him, and turned to see a Zamatan soldier trying to get his attention.

'Lord Sigum is ready, sir,' he said.

'Thank you,' said Lahnos. 'I will be down in a moment.'

He gazed back at the view, trying to get his thoughts in order. The lead ships of the Gunstian fleet were passing the ferry terminal a quarter of a mile to the east of the monastery – huge battle cruisers, sleek frigates, and ungainly troopships that sat low in the water. There was no sign of any dragon flying above the white palace, but that did not surprise Lahnos. The Governor had sent his sister to strike a deal with the Gunstians, and the enemy had taken what was on offer and then killed her anyway. The Gunstians would give no quarter and show no mercy; but at least that provided clarity to the situation – fight or die, there was no middle ground.

Lahnos strode from the apartment and descended the stairs to the ground level. The interior of the monastery was packed with people – soldiers who had gathered there to defend the battlements, and civilians praying that the ancient sandstone walls would save them. A murmur of nervous anticipation arose from the massed crowds as Lahnos appeared at the entrance to the apartment block, and he tried not to show any fear or despair as he passed through them. They expected something from him – the horned boy who had brought the men of Zamata home; and now they needed another miracle.

Soldiers escorted him to the western end of the cloister, and Lahnos saw Sigum speaking to the same group of monks from before. Soldiers had formed a cordon around the dragon, and hundreds were watching as Lahnos was allowed through.

Sigum raised his head. 'Lahnos, the brothers have completed their work – what do you think?'

Lahnos walked up to the dragon, as the monks averted their gaze from him. Perched atop the dragon's broad shoulders was a saddle taken from the empty stables, complete with stirrups and a bar grip at the front. The saddle had been secured to the dragon by means of long leather straps that criss-crossed their way down Sigum's flanks, reaching around his chest where the buckles met. Lahnos extended a hand and pulled on the straps, but they remained in place.

'It looks good,' Lahnos said. 'It's not too tight, is it?'

'No. I can barely feel it,' said the dragon. 'Climb up.'

A soldier handed Lahnos his war axe, and he slung it over his shoulder. The same soldier then gripped his hands together to create a foothold. Lahnos placed his left boot into it, grabbed the straps, and clambered up the dragon's flank. The noise from the crowd began to increase as those watching realised what was happening. A few monks groaned in dismay, and Lahnos laughed at them, a sense of joyous exhilaration sweeping through his body. He reached the saddle and placed his feet into the stirrups, then he gripped the bar at the front. He glanced down at the silvery-green scales covering the dragon's shoulders, flanks and neck, then he turned to gaze at Sigum's wings as they began to extend.

The dragon turned his head to look at Lahnos. 'Your thoughts, my friend?'

'This is better than I could have possibly imagined,' Lahnos said. 'Are you sure that you are fine with this?'

'I am certain of it,' said Sigum. 'Perhaps you should say something to the people who have come to see us. Your words would mean much to them.'

Lahnos glanced around at the staring crowds, then he pulled the war axe from his shoulder and raised it high above his head.

'People of Zamata,' he cried out, 'the time has come to fight for everything we hold dear – this island, our friends, our brothers and sisters, our children. We cannot promise you victory, for the forces aligned against us are powerful, but I shall promise you this – we will fight to the end to defend you, not for glory, or for riches, but out of love. I have not always loved this island, for it has not always loved me; but this day, Lord Sigum and I will be proud to fight for its people; our people. Watch us as we fly, but do not pity us if we fall; just remember us.'

Sigum beat his wings and ascended into the skies over Tsallon Anura, as the crowds packing the monastery stared upwards. The dragon circled once, and Lahnos gazed around at the view of Kaugatz, the Cyasarta and Igatz, almost overwhelmed by the sight. He glanced west, and saw the twin mountains of Medamuna and Hodzulat, then the dragon rose higher, and he could see the entire island spread out below them.

'It's so small,' he said. 'Beautiful, but small.'

'A tiny speck in the vastness of the ocean,' said the dragon. 'Do you feel safe up there?'

'Yes,' said Lahnos. He slung the axe back over his shoulder and started to laugh. 'But don't fly upside down.'

'I will try to remember that,' said Sigum. 'You are extremely light; I can hardly feel you on my shoulders.'

'And it's cold up here,' Lahnos said; 'colder than I'd imagined.'

'Listen to me for a moment, my friend. My offer from this morning still stands. If you wish, I will turn towards the west and fly to the shores of Gunst. It would take perhaps six hours to reach a deserted part of the Gunstian coast where we would be safe to rest and take shelter. After that, we could fly north to the remoter parts of that continent where few dwell. We could live unmolested in the mountains, far from the cities of Gunst. We could hunt for food, and find caves in which to sleep. It would be a primitive life, but we would survive this terrible day.'

Lahnos turned his head to stare out at the ocean to the west of the island. The landmass of Gunst was far over the horizon, lost amid the rolling waves.

'We would survive,' he said, 'but both of us would know why. The shame would divide us, and the guilt would never stop eating at our souls.'

'I heard the speech you made, Lahnos – was every word of it true? Do you no longer hate the island? You have often mentioned how you were scorned by your own people; loathed and feared because of your horns, and despised because you refused to conform to the ideals of others.'

'All of that is true,' said Lahnos, 'but even so, Zamata is my home. I am frightened, Sigum; I admit that freely, but I would rather die than live with the knowledge that we had deserted the same people we brought out of Gunst.'

'So be it, my friend. I had hoped you would deliver this answer, but it was incumbent upon me to make the offer. You are still young, while I have lived for many centuries, and the fear of death holds no sway over me. How shall we do this – how should we attack?'

Lahnos glanced down. Even at that altitude, the warships of the Imperial Gunstian Fleet were visible, their wakes carving little white lines through the Cyasarta.

'We should travel south a little,' he said, 'and then come in low, just above the surface of the water around Handshore, so that the Gunstians don't see us until the very last second. And then...'

'Then I shall release my flames, and burn all that I can before I am struck down.'

Lahnos said nothing.

'Hold on tight, my friend,' said the dragon, then he banked towards the south and soared over the island, his speed sending the cold wind whistling across Lahnos's face. They crossed over the landmass south of Kaugatz, and then reached the Hansarta, before Sigum aimed his head downwards, and dived. Lahnos gripped the bar at the front of the saddle as his stomach lurched. The waters of the Hansarta rushed towards them, then the dragon banked again in a long arc, until they reached the Cyasarta just south of the Fortress of Atzoun. At the last moment, Sigum pulled up, his underside brushing over the peak of a wave, then he began to race north, following the line of the Cyasarta.

Soldiers on the battlements of Atzoun saw them, and then so too did the crowds gathered by the coasts – Aucterians to the right and Zamatans to the left, as the dragon flew faster and faster. Sigum eased to the north-east, passing Handshore in a blur. The sole surviving dragon carrier was anchored close to the naval base, and Sigum was flying so low that the flight deck passed high above them on their left; and then the first ships of the Gunstian fleet came into view – the ram-tipped battle cruiser that had tried to pierce the chains, and its escort of four frigates. Tsallon Anura flashed by on their left, and still the dragon remained fast and low. The distance between Sigum and the battle cruiser shrank until Lahnos could see the Gunstian sailors by the bow staring and pointing at them; and then the dragon opened his jaws. Sparks ignited, followed by a great burst of flames aimed at the front of the battle cruiser. Sigum started to ascend, the unceasing flames sweeping over the masts and deck of the huge ship until it was burning from bow to aft, then he turned to the two frigates off the cruiser's starboard flank. The sailors on board could see what was coming, but there was nothing they could do to save themselves, as the flames washed over the two ships. Sigum banked, low and tight. He flew past the stern of the cruiser and attacked the two frigates off its port side, coming at them from behind while never once letting the flames stop for even a moment. The two frigates erupted into flames, their sailors and marines caught in the conflagration. Lahnos glanced over his shoulder at the rest of the fleet. The dragon had destroyed five ships in less than a minute, but all surprise had been lost, and the Gunstians would be prepared for the next attack.

Sigum banked low, and sped along the Cyasarta towards the bulk of the fleet. A hailstorm of ballistae bolts pelted through the air before he had a chance to open his jaws, and the dragon ascended, twisting to avoid the yard-long shafts of steel as he rose through the sky. Lahnos glanced down, and saw the dozens of ballistae dotted over the decks of the Gunstian warships. They ceased loosing as Sigum rose out of range, then they began again as the dragon dived. Sigum turned, dodging the missiles as he ascended above them for a second time.

'There is no way through,' said the dragon. 'I cannot get close enough to burn any more of the ships.'

Lahnos frowned. 'There weren't as many bolts that time,' he said. 'Do you think they might be running low on munitions? Do you remember the four supply ships you sunk with Lady Natali?'

'I do,' said the dragon. 'Let us try once more.'

Sigum circled over the lead vessels of the fleet, then he descended at speed again. Ballista bolts spat up at them, but far fewer than before, and the dragon was able to dodge them with ease. Sigum opened his jaws as he executed a tight turn, then Lahnos sensed something odd but strangely familiar coming from the blazing battle cruiser. It was weak at first, then Lahnos looked down and saw a woman in black robes emerging onto the burning deck. She raised her hand.

A wave of pain struck Lahnos, a pain so all-consuming that it occupied every corner of his mind; and yet, somehow, it seemed as though he understood its nature, as though the Gift flaying his nerves also belonged to him. Sigum cried out in torment as he tried to ascend away from the Gifted woman, then he began to spiral and tumble. He crossed the northern coast of the Cyasarta, still moving at great speed as he hurtled like a stone across the sky. They crossed Kaugatz, losing altitude with every moment that passed, then they crashed into the terraces of a vast olive grove, ploughing through the ancient trees and gouging great furrows in the earth. Lahnos was flung to the side, his hands ripped from the saddle bar, and he landed on the ground, rolling and coming to a halt by the roots of an olive tree, his axe landing several feet from him. The agony from the Gift was fading, but he groaned in the dirt as a hundred new pains emerged.

Still conscious, he raised his head from the ground. Sigum was lying twenty yards away, his eyes also open. The dragon turned his head, and their glances met.

'You are alive,' said Sigum.

'So are you,' said Lahnos. 'You flew us out of danger.'

'And then I crashed. How badly injured are you?'

'I'm winded and dazed, but nothing's broken,' said Lahnos, as he pulled himself into a sitting position. 'We forgot about that Gifted woman on the cruiser. Can you still fly?'

The dragon hauled himself up from the ground, then collapsed back down. He grunted, tried again, and managed to stand. He turned his head to inspect his dust-covered wings.

'We were very fortunate,' the dragon said. 'I remember being attacked by the Gift of Pain over Gunst. That time, the force of the assault almost killed me. Perhaps the Gifted Gunstian on the battle cruiser had been weakened by the flames and smoke when she attacked us.'

'She was weakened?' said Lahnos. 'I have never felt pain like it.' He frowned. 'Although, it... This will sound stupid, but it felt familiar.'

Sigum eyed him. 'Did you bump your head in the fall, Lahnos?'

'I don't think so.' He stared at his hands. 'I can still feel it,' he said; 'as though my body recognised it; almost welcomed it. What does it mean? Is this what Arrosa was talking about? Did she know?'

The dragon stared at him, but said nothing.

Lahnos got to his feet. 'Can you fly?'

'Yes. Shall we try once more? We may have regained the element of surprise if the Gunstians think we fell to our deaths, and they will be vulnerable if they are running out of ballista bolts. Perhaps we should attack from the rear this time. We may be able to sink a few more ships before the other Gifted aboard the fleet are able to reach us.'

'No. Let's attack the battle cruiser again.'

'But the Gifted woman will still be there, Lahnos. Our attack would not last for long.'

'Do you trust me?' Lahnos said, as he began to climb back up into the saddle.

'Of course,' said the dragon.

'Then we should go straight for the cruiser. Let the Gunstians see us before we attack. I want them to see us.'

Sigum said nothing. Instead, he rose back into the sky, as though resigned to his fate. Lahnos gripped the saddle bar with his left hand and stared at his right, trying to recreate the sensation he had felt when he had sensed the Gifted woman. If his plan failed, then at least the end would be swift; but if it worked...

The dragon flew back over Kaugatz, and reached the Cyasarta. Three of the four frigates had sunk, while the fourth was still ablaze. The cruiser was also afloat, though flames were eating through its deck. By the bow, several marines were lowering a small vessel over the side, and the black-robed Gifted woman was standing next to them, ready to flee to another ship. Sigum circled high over the Gunstian fleet, making sure that he was seen, then he dived at the cruiser.

A marine turned to the Gifted woman, his finger pointing at the sky, and the robed Gunstian glanced up.

She began to raise her arm, but Lahnos's right hand was already pointing at her. He felt the power of her Gift start to increase, and it triggered something within him; and then he unleashed a blast of Pain at the bow of the ship so strong that he almost fell off the saddle. The Gifted woman screamed as the marines fell and writhed next to her, and then Sigum sent down a brief burst of flames, incinerating them.

Lahnos laughed. 'I have the Gift of Pain, Sigum; did you see that?'

'I saw it, my friend, and now the only question I have is this – can you do it again?'

'I could do it for hours.' His eyes tightened, and he swept aside all feelings of remorse and pity from his mind. 'Take us down, Sigum. This is our day; this is our time. No mercy. Kill them all.'

The dragon banked over the burning battle cruiser, and then turned for the fleet.

'With pain and fire we shall deliver death, my friend; pain and fire.'

With thousands watching from the shores of Igatz and Kaugatz, the dragon and horned part-Bullan filled the Cyasarta with flames and agony, striking down the Gifted with Pain and incinerating them, until the sky hung heavy and thick with smoke and screams. A few ballista bolts were loosed at them, but not enough to threaten the dragon as he burned and burned. Troopships broke apart under the weight of the blistering inferno, and frigates on fire slipped beneath the waves. True to his word, Sigum showed no mercy, and he swept over the waters burning all who had jumped into the Cyasarta. The mighty battle cruisers held out the longest, until they, too, succumbed to the flames of the dragon, their Gifted warriors rendered useless by Lahnos's own Gift. When the last warship was aflame, Sigum closed his jaws and rose high into the sky, and Lahnos looked down at the slaughter he and the dragon had wrought upon the Gunstians. From Handshore to the straits, three miles of unceasing destruction lay below them. Lahnos felt drained and empty, and he sensed that the dragon was also tiring; but he knew that they had one final job to do.

'Take us to the Dragon Palace, my friend,' he said to Sigum.

'Have we not done enough?' said the dragon.

'Lord Rylan will trample over this island if we allow him to recover from the wounds Givra gave him. We have to stop him.'

'Perhaps we could reason with him.'

'Do you believe that he will ever allow the people of this island to be free?'

'No. I do not. We shall do this, my friend, but it feels like a bitter ending to our day's work.'

Sigum soared over Igatz, descending as he flew, and Lahnos could see the gardens of the palace below, where hundreds of Bullan and Aucterian soldiers were gathered, each staring upwards. Sigum passed over the palace, then banked low over the Cyasarta, turning to face the huge building's eastern side.

'I see him,' cried Sigum. 'I see Lord Rylan...'

The dragon's voice faded away, and Lahnos stared ahead. The figure of Lord Rylan was standing in the centre of an open viewing gallery cut out of the palace's eastern flank, his jaws open but facing downwards. Lahnos frowned. The colouring of the dragon seemed wrong, his grey and yellow scales transformed into a green that was reflecting the flames from the vessels burning in the Cyasarta.

Sigum descended again, and hovered a few yards over the gallery, but Rylan did not move. To Lahnos's eyes, it was as though he was looking at a beautiful statue of a dragon, carved from a solid block of green glass.

'Lord Rylan is no more,' said the dragon.

'Lahnos!' someone cried.

Lahnos narrowed his eyes, searching for the source of the voice. There were other people in the viewing gallery, each of them staring up at Sigum. Lahnos pulled his feet from the stirrups and clambered down the dragon's flank, dropping the last few feet to the ground. He climbed up the side of the gallery, then hauled himself over the railings.

Arrosa grinned at him. 'I told you. Didn't I tell you?'

Lahnos smiled at the girl, then he saw Cisca and Bauchlie, and Lyla, who was lying unconscious on the floor of the gallery. Leona ran towards him. She paused a foot from where he stood, and he gazed down at her.

'You...' she said, her eyes wide. 'I...'

Bauchlie approached with tears running down his cheeks and slapped Lahnos across his back. 'You have saved the island, Lahnos; you have saved us all.'

'It was Sigum who saved us,' said Lahnos.

'Do not be overly modest,' said the dragon, as he landed next to the gallery. 'Lahnos has the Gift of Pain; we did what we did together.'

'I never thought I would say this,' said Bauchlie, 'but, dragon, you have my thanks.'

'Yes, thank you, Lord Sigum,' said Cisca. 'You are now the only dragon on the island.'

'That grieves me,' said Sigum. 'I had not wished it so.'

Lyla stirred, and Cisca helped the young woman get to her feet. Lyla stared at the green glass of Rylan and Jair, then she reached out and touched them with her fingers.

'That was me,' said Arrosa. 'You aren't the only one here with weird powers.'

Lyla turned and looked out at the devastation in the Cyasarta.

'And that was the work of the two demons,' Arrosa went on; 'Lahnos and Sigum. They burnt everything.'

Lyla started to weep as she stared at the destruction. 'Thousands of Gunstians have died, Arrosa,' she said. 'Are you not saddened by this?'

'They were going to kill my friends,' said the girl. '*That* would have made me sad.' She glanced at Sigum and Lahnos. 'I suppose that makes you my friends, even though you are demons.'

'We should get to work,' said Bauchlie. 'The food supplies are almost gone, and we need to send boats to Irlan to buy up whatever we can before the people begin to starve. We also need to think about how we are going to govern this island. There is much to do.'

Leona glanced at the faces of those who had spoken, but remained silent. She retreated a step, her gaze lowering.

'Can I speak to you alone for a minute?' said Lahnos.

She nodded, a frown on her face.

They walked out of the gallery, and into a hallway where the others couldn't see them.

Leona looked at him. 'What is it, Lahnos?'

Lahnos stared at her, but the words he had been planning to speak caught in his throat.

'Do you have something to say to me?' Leona went on.

'When you left Tsallon Anura,' he said, 'I thought I would never see you again, and that made me feel worse than knowing the Gunstians were coming. I don't care if you think I'm foolish for saying this, but I think I might be falling for you.'

Leona's frown dissolved, and she laughed. 'Just kiss me, Lahnos.'

AUTHOR'S NOTES

AUGUST 2023

Thank you for reading Death Seer – the last book of the Serpent Isle Trilogy, and book three of the Dominion series. After the easy joy of drafting Demon Witch, Death Seer was more of a struggle. Early in the planning stages of this book, I was tempted to change the plot of Death Seer to make it all about the Demon Witch. As readers of my earlier series will know, the Demon Witch has a long history in the Magelands; and I reasoned that if she was in the story, then perhaps she should *be* the story. In the end, I decided to keep to my original vision – the Serpent Isle Trilogy would remain true to the trio of Lahnos, Leona and Cisca. After all, it is their island.

RECEIVE A FREE MAGELANDS DOMINION SHORT STORY

Building a relationship with my readers is very important to me.

Join my newsletter for information on new books and deals and you will also receive a Magelands Dominion short story that is currently EXCLUSIVE to my Readers' Group for FREE.

www.ChristopherMitchellBooks.com/dominion

ABOUT THE AUTHOR

Christopher Mitchell is the author of the Magelands epic fantasy series.

For more information:

www.christophermitchellbooks.com

info@christophermitchellbooks.com

Printed in Great Britain
by Amazon

35785032R00243